WALLS, BORDERS, BOUNDARIES

I0091246

SPEKTRUM: Publications of the German Studies Association

Series editor: David M. Luebke, University of Oregon

Published under the auspices of the German Studies Association, *Spektrum* offers current perspectives on culture, society, and political life in the German-speaking lands of central Europe—Austria, Switzerland, and the Federal Republic—from the late Middle Ages to the present day. Its titles and themes reflect the composition of the GSA and the work of its members within and across the disciplines to which they belong—literary criticism, history, cultural studies, political science, and anthropology.

Walls, Borders, Boundaries

Spatial and Cultural Practices in Europe

~:~

Edited by

MARC SILBERMAN, KAREN E. TILL & JANET WARD

berghahn
NEW YORK · OXFORD
www.berghahnbooks.com

First published in 2012 by

Berghahn Books

www.berghahnbooks.com

©2012, 2015 Marc Silberman, Karen E. Till, and Janet Ward
First paperback edition published in 2015

All rights reserved. Except for the quotation of short passages
for the purposes of criticism and review, no part of this book
may be reproduced in any form or by any means, electronic or
mechanical, including photocopying, recording, or any information
storage and retrieval system now known or to be invented,
without written permission of the publisher.

Library of Congress Cataloging-in-Publication Data

Silberman, Marc
 Walls, borders, boundaries: spatial and cultural practices in Europe / edited by Marc
Silberman, Karen E. Till, and Janet Ward.
     p. cm. -- (Spektrum: publications of the German Studies Association; v. 4)
  ISBN 978-0-85745-504-8 (hardback: alk. paper) -- ISBN 978-1-78238-686-5
(paperback: alk. paper) -- ISBN 978-0-85745-505-5 (ebook)
  1. Europe--Boundaries--History. 2. Europe--Historical geography. 3. Geopolitics--Eu-
rope--History. 4. Territory, National--Europe. 5. Ethnicity--Europe--History. 6. Europe-
-Civilization. I. Silberman, Marc, 1948- II. Till, Karen E. III. Title.
  D104.W35 2012
  320.1'2094--dc23

                                                                    2011051785

British Library Cataloguing in Publication Data

A catalogue record for this book is available from the British Library

Printed on acid-free paper.

ISBN: 978-0-85745-504-8 hardback
ISBN: 978-1-78238-686-5 paperback
ISBN: 978-0-85745-505-5 ebook

~: CONTENTS :~

III. Migrating Boundaries

~: ILLUSTRATIONS :~

❧ ACKNOWLEDGMENTS ❧

The essays in this project on walls, borders, and boundaries form a dynamic contribution to the ongoing "spatial turn" in humanities- and social science-based research. Brought together in this volume's ensemble are a dozen scholars in anthropology, cultural and religious studies, geography, history, literature, performance art, political science, and sociology; even as coeditors we reflect a blending of the ways, working as we do in departments of German (Marc Silberman), geography (Karen E. Till), and history (Janet Ward). Interdisciplinarity at its best does not retreat from but rather embraces broadly encompassing and comparative enquiries. Topics such as ours that regroup both audiences and debates may impact the research questions we ask, the topics we teach, and the communities we influence. Far from being a feared distillation of any "essential" identity of a discipline (especially those in the liberal arts), the transformational component contained within interdisciplinarity is proving to be key to any knowledge field's adaptability and its degree of social relevance.

It is to the German Studies Association's ability to host and creatively foster interdisciplinary events that we three editors owe our first debt; and specifically to the recent formation of the GSA standing committee on Interdisciplinary Initiatives, which encouraged our initiative to coordinate a series of topical panel sessions at an annual conference. The series itself, organized to mark the twentieth anniversary of the fall of the Berlin Wall, engaged participants from multiple countries and disciplines and forged interrelated debates. This inspired us to develop and structure the wide range of essays for this volume, as a combination both of selected and expanded papers from the panel series and of invited original essays. We are pleased that our volume's focus reflects the interdisciplinary focus of the GSA's Spektrum series with Berghahn Books. We would especially like to thank the readers of the manuscript for the press for their helpful commentaries. Our thanks are due to Allison Heck (Virginia Tech University), who compiled the preliminary bibliography for the volume; to Daniel C. Villenueva (University of Nevada, Las Vegas), who translated Olaf Briese's essay; and to Claire Davis (University of Wisconsin, Madison), who compiled the volume index. Finally, we wish to thank our respective universities for their support: the Center for German and European Studies and Department of German, University of Wisconsin, Madison; the School of Public and International Affairs, Virginia Tech University and the Department of Geography at the National University of Ireland, Maynooth; and the Departments of History at both the University of Nevada, Las Vegas and the University of Oklahoma.

Contributors

~:~

David E. Barclay is Executive Director of the German Studies Association and Margaret and Roger Scholten Professor of International Studies in the History Department at Kalamazoo College. He received his PhD at Stanford University. He has published extensively on topics of eighteenth- and nineteenth-century Prussian history, on twentieth-century social democracy, and more recently on postwar Berlin. Among his books is *Schaut auf diese Stadt: Der unbekannte Ernst Reuter* (Berlin, 2000). A 2007 Fellow at the American Academy of Berlin, he is currently working on a history of West Berlin from 1948 to 1994.

Muriel Blaive is a historian and project leader at the Ludwig Boltzmann Institute for European History and Public Spheres in Vienna. She works on the communist and post-communist period in Central Europe, especially on Czechoslovakia and the Czech Republic. She coauthored with Berthold Molden *Grenzfälle. Österreichische und tschechische Erfahrungen am Eisernen Vorhang* (Weitra, 2009) and authored the monograph *Une déstalinisation manquée. Tchécoslovaquie 1956* (Brussels, 2005). She also coedited with Christian Gerbel and Thomas Lindenberger *Clashes in European Memory: The Case of the Communist Repression and the Holocaust* (New York, 2010) and coedited with Georges Mink *Benešovy dekrety. Budoucnost Evropy a vyrovnávání se s minulostí* (The Beneš Decrees: The Future of Europe and Dealing with the Past, Prague, 2003).

Isa Blumi is Associate Professor of History and Middle East Studies at Georgia State University; he is author of *Rethinking the Late Ottoman Empire* (2003), *Chaos in Yemen* (2010), *Reinstating the Ottomans* (2011), *Foundations of Modernity: Human Agency and the Imperial State* (2011), *Ottoman Refugees, 1878-1939: Migration in a Post-Imperial World* (2013), and co-editor of *War and*

Nationalism: The Balkan Wars, 1912-1913 (2013). He is currently exploring the intersection of Southeast Asian Muslim Emirates in the mid nineteenth century and the expansion of European commercial interests in the South China Sea as well as the effect of Habsburg and Ottoman imperial fragmentation on the constitution of "transitional" political orders in a variety of communities within the Balkans and in the Balkan diaspora throughout the world.

Olaf Briese received a Gerda Henkel Foundation fellowship for his book project on the different aesthetics of the Berlin Wall. He has held positions as Assistant Professor of Religious Studies at the Freie Universität Berlin and Visiting Professor at several universities in Germany. He is the author of a wide range of interdisciplinary books on modern German cultural history, including *Steinzeit. Mauern in Berlin* (2011), the four-volume *Angst in den Zeiten der Cholera* (2003), *Konkurrenzen. Zur philosophischen Kultur in Deutschland 1830–1850* (1998), *Die Macht der Metaphern. Blitz, Erdbeben und Kometen im Gefüge der Aufklärung* (1998), and *Der Anspruch des Subjekts. Zum Unsterblichkeitsdenken im Jungen Deutschland* (1995). He is also the editor of two essay collections.

Patricia Ehrkamp is Associate Professor of Geography at the University of Kentucky. She researches immigrant identities, migrant transnationalism, and citizenship, as well as social relations between migrants and nonmigrants in immigrant receiving societies. Her research examines expectations for immigrant assimilation in the context of exclusionary discourses about migrant transnationalism and Islam in Western Europe, attending to the relationship between religion, gender, secularism, and democracy. Most recently, she has begun work on a US National Science Foundation funded research project entitled "Places of Worship and the Politics of Citizenship: Immigrants and Communities of Faith in the U.S. South." She is coeditor of the special issue "Rethinking Immigration and Citizenship: New Spaces of Migrant Transnationalism and Belonging" (*Environment and Planning A*). Her work has been published in *Journal of Ethnic and Migration Studies, Space and Polity, Urban Geography, Transactions of the Institute of British Geographers, Social and Cultural Geography,* and *Gender, Place and Culture.*

Eric Jarosinski, formerly at the University of Pennsylvania, is a columnist for the German weekly *Die Zeit,* regular contributor to the *Frankfurter Allgemeine Zeitung,* and author and editor of *Nein. Quarterly,* a "Compendium of Utopian Negation" found on Twitter. His first book, *Nein. A Manifesto.,* is forthcoming from S. Fischer Verlag.

Jeffrey Jurgens is a cultural anthropologist at Bard College, where he is Academic Co-Director of the Consortium for the Liberal Arts in Prison as well as Fellow for Anthropology and Social Theory at the Bard Prison Initiative. His research focuses on migration, public memory, and civic engagement among people of Turkish backgrounds in the Federal Republic, and he is currently at work on a book, *Postmigrant Pasts and Futures: Pluralism, Memory, and Citizenship in Germany.* He also has secondary interests in public representations of the Berlin Wall, Islamic activism, and the cultural politics of incarceration. He has recently published in *American Ethnologist, Journal of Middle East Women's Studies, Policy and Society,* and *Transit.*

Gülgün Kayim is cofounder of Skewed Visions, a Minneapolis-based, site-specific performance collective; Affiliate Faculty at the University of Minnesota Department of Theatre Arts and Dance; and Director of Art, Culture, and Creative Economy for the City of Minneapolis. Her artistic work uses performance, movement, installation, and sound to investigate the cultural resonances of violence and conflict through location, biography, and memory. Her large-scale performances in Cyprus and the US have been recognized through awards and fellowships from the Shannon Institute, Creative Capital Foundation, Archibald Bush Foundation, Jerome Foundation, Minnesota State Arts Board, and Walker Art Center. Her work has received critical acclaim in the US, Russia, and London. Kayim has administered programs at the Weisman Art Museum, Intermedia Arts, Archibald Bush Foundation, and Minnesota Visible Fringe Festival. Her curent work investigates large-scale terror training scenarios in the town of Playas, New Mexico.

Thomas Lindenberger is a historian of twentieth-century Germany and Europe, focusing mainly on the history of communism, physical violence, everyday life and film. He is Director of the department Communism and Society at the Center for Contemporary History in Potsdam, Germany, and teaches at Potsdam University. From 2009 to 2013 he was director of the Ludwig Boltzmann Institute for European History and Public Spheres. Selected publications include *Straßenpolitik. Zur Sozialgeschichte der öffentlichen Ordnung in Berlin, 1900–1914* (Bonn, 1995); *Volkspolizei. Herrschaftspraxis und öffentliche Ordnung im SED-Staat, 1952–1968* (Cologne, 2003), as coeditor *Conflicted Memories: Europeanizing Contemporary Histories* (New York/Oxford, 2007); *Cold War Cultures. Perspectives on Eastern and Western European Societies* (New York/Oxford 2012); and *Underground Publishing and the Public Sphere. Transnational Perspectives* (Vienna, forthcoming).

Steffi Marung (née Franke) is Senior Researcher at the Center for Area Studies of the University of Leipzig, where she is working on a project investigating the history of African studies in the Soviet Union and teaches in the Global and European Studies Institute. Having received her Ph.D. in Global Studies, her research includes border regimes and territoriality, European integration history, and the history of area studies. Publications include *Die wandernde*

Grenze. Die EU, Polen und der Wandel politischer Räume, 1990-2010 (Vandenhoeck & Ruprecht, 2013), a volume coedited with Katja Naumann, *Vergessene Vielfalt. Territorialität und Internationalisierung in Ostmitteleuropa seit der Mitte des 19. Jahrhunderts* (2014), a special issue "Border Research in a Global Perspective" coedited with James Scott for *Comparativ: Zeitschrift für Globalgeschichte und Gesellschaftsforschung,* and articles on territorialization, border regimes, and European integration. As a member since 2005 of the board of the European Network in Universal and Global History (ENIUGH) she co-organizes the European Congress on World and Global History.

Yair Mintzker is Assistant Professor of History and Class of 1942 University Preceptor at Princeton University. He is the author of *The Defortification of the German City, 1689–1866* (New York: Cambridge University Press, 2009) as well as essays on the discursive shift in mid-eighteenth-century French enlightened thought (*History of European Ideas,* 2008), urban fortifications (*Weimar-Polis: Multi-disciplinary Journal for Urban Theory and Practice,* 2009), and the conceptual history of space (*Historical Reflections/Reflexions Historiques,* 2009). He is the recipient, among others, of the Fritz Stern Dissertation Prize (2010), the Urban History Association Best Book Award (2011-2012), and fellowships from the Institute for Advanced Study in Princeton (2011/12) and the Wissenschaftskolleg zu Berlin (2013/14).

Marc Silberman is Professor of German and Affiliate Professor in Theatre and Drama as well as Film Studies at the University of Wisconsin, Madison. He has also directed the Center for German and European Studies and chaired the Department of German. Previously he taught at the University of Texas in San Antonio, and he has held guest professorships at UCLA, Freie Universität Berlin, and Universität Freiburg. He has published monographs on GDR literature (1975), the dramatist Heiner Müller (1980), and the history of German cinema (1995); edited over twenty volumes and journal special issues, including six volumes of the *Brecht Yearbook* (1990–95) as its managing editor; and translated texts by Bertolt Brecht, Heiner Müller, and Herbert Achternbusch, among others.

Karen E. Till is Senior Lecturer of Geography at National University of Ireland, Maynooth, and has held positions previously at Royal Holloway (University of London), University of Minnesota, and Virginia Tech. Her geo-ethnographic research and curatorial practice explore the interrelationships between place-making, personal and social memory, public art, and cultural politics in contemporary cities. Her publications include *The New Berlin: Memory, Politics, Place* (2005), the coedited *Textures of Place: Rethinking Humanist Geographies* (2001), the exhibition catalogue *Mapping Spectral Traces* (2010), and essays in *Memory Studies, History Workshop Journal, Social and Cultural*

Geography, German Historical Institute Newsletter, and *cultural geographies.* Till was Visiting Professor at the University of Calgary's Faculty of Environmental Design; is co-convener of "Mapping Spectral Traces," an international artists-scholar-practitioner network; and directs the Space&Place Research Collaborative. She is currently working on two book-length projects, "Interim Spaces" and "Wounded Cities."

Daniela Vicherat Mattar is Assistant Professor in the Global Challenges Program at Leiden University College in The Hague. Previously she was a Marie Curie postdoctoral fellow in economic and social history at the University of Edinburgh, where she worked on the prevalence of walls in shaping contemporary European cities. One of the results of that research project was an Irmgard Coninx and Social Science Research Center (WZB) Research Prize for her essay "Urban Development Flanked by Religion and Politics: Reflections from the Belfast History" (2009). She is currently revising for publication that essay as well as her PhD thesis, which was completed at the European University Institute, on public spaces and the experience of democracy.

Janet Ward is Professor of History and Faculty Fellow for Research in the Humanities and Social Sciences at the University of Oklahoma. She is the author of *Post-Wall Berlin: Borders, Space and Identity* (2011) and *Weimar Surfaces: Urban Visual Culture in 1920s Germany* (2001), as well as co-editor of *Transnationalism in the German City* (2014), *German Studies in the Post-Holocaust Age* (2000), and *Agonistics: Arenas of Creative Contest* (1997). She has published a wide range of interdisciplinary essays and articles on visual culture and urban studies. Her current projects include a book, "Sites of Holocaust Memory," and a new project on Nazi spatial and racial planning across central and Eastern Europe.

INTRODUCTION

Walls, Borders, Boundaries

MARC SILBERMAN, KAREN E. TILL, AND JANET WARD

Walls are built and then fall, borders are fortified and then shift, bound-aries are demarcated and then transgressed. And then they are con-structed all over again. As (post)moderns living in an age of globalization, we weary of our seemingly old-fashioned political and market-oriented boundar-ies: walls and fences are a nuisance to build and maintain, they invite vandalism and intrusion (rather than guarantee privacy or protection), and public surveys often reveal disapproval of national boundaries for moral, aesthetic, and eco-nomic reasons.[1] Indeed, recently erected walls and borders intended to sever communities or fortify political and economic boundaries between neighbor-ing countries rarely solve the underlying political problems; more often they result in increased criminal activity, violence, and alienation.[2]

The contradictory yet simultaneous functions of walls, borders, and bound-aries—to divide and connect, to exclude and include, to shield and constrain—are fundamental to all cultures. Expressed in primitive man's first utterance, "this is mine" (*ceci est à moi*) is, as Jean-Jacques Rousseau perceived, an innately territorial and tragic instinct.[3] While mutable borders are a sign of life, closed borders signify ethnic or political division and often literally cause death. Dur-ing World War I, for example, the trenches of the Allied Western Front be-came a fixed and deadly no man's land for years, an absurd "system in depth" of paralyzed offense, defense, and supply.[4] Even in peacetime, borders have often been perceived as dead zones, as peripheral regions separated from the nation's "core"—its wealth, its power, and the independence of its capital city. When the wall, border, or boundary is closed or remote, these zones usually function as conquered, relatively empty second-class areas.[5] This was certainly true of the western edge of the Iron Curtain: where capitalism ran right up against communism, it was more difficult to make either work. Hardened lines of de-marcation also undercut border peoples' ability to coexist. Our territorializing tendencies offer a sense of stability by marking off a space through which to establish relational systems of identity, yet even as territoriality differentiates

Self from Other, it paradoxically provokes us to look across, through, or even over those very boundaries. As G. W. F. Hegel made clear in his *Elements of the Philosophy of Right* (1821), our identities are founded on boundary-based differentiation and co-constitutive social relations, a metaphor he extended from individuals to nations, which are, he states, at times necessarily engaged against one another. Spaces and social structures thus are constantly forged, just as they are negotiated and challenged.[6]

Walls, borders, and boundaries—their function as a crucial asset in individual and nation-based identity formation notwithstanding—also are traced far beyond and deeply within the obvious edges of nation-states. We have increasingly seen over the last century that internal borders dividing countries against themselves, no matter how artificial, only cement social differences on each side the longer they remain in place. When walls, borders, and boundaries become completely sealed off, they cause hardened social "edges" to emerge: groups essentially split in two and different communities develop on each side.[7] Two Germanys evolved during the Cold War, when the world itself became defined by reified borders between the superpowers of communism and capitalism, Eastern Bloc and Western Bloc. This can also be witnessed in the dangerous, half-century-old division on the thirty-eighth parallel between North and South Korea, a line more closed than the Iron Curtain ever was. Only in the late 1980s did the geopolitical map of Soviet-controlled Eastern Europe become increasingly destabilized, its substance changing in tandem with the evolving (and, as it turned out, imploding) pressures of the Cold War. That map's most famous edge, the Berlin Wall, finally gave way, and the East Germans' "Peaceful Revolution" ended on 9 November 1989 without bloodshed.

In the globalized final decade of the twentieth century, many were optimistic that the Internet and other innovative communications technologies would offer opportunities to create new forms of democratic and transnational public spaces—in short, that we might start to move beyond the physical restrictions of borders and bodies to enjoy global, universal access to events, networks, social groups, and other resources. But instead of heralding a new boundary-free era, more than twenty years after the demise of Berlin's Wall we confront the harsh realities of the Israeli-Palestinian and US-Mexico barriers that divide worlds and generate conflict and violence, walls that some scholars interpret as symbolic responses to our post-Westphalian age of waning sovereignty.[8] Moreover, if 1989 reminded us that walls fall and iron curtains open, then earthquakes, acid rain, ozone holes, radioactive emissions, water wars, marine oil spills, tsunamis, and global warming have already demonstrated the futility of modernist techno-rational attempts to contain "our environment" within abstract, linear political boundaries.

New strategies of surveillance and intelligence data collection, including artificial drones, geographic information systems (GIS), geospatial positioning systems (GPS), biodata-based border security checks, and proposed virtual fences (networks of cameras, sensors, and radar) run through and alongside more traditional forms of monitoring, such as barbed wire, fences, walls, military and police obstacles, filters, depth barriers, extraterritorial legal spaces, and zoning, as well as the increasing use of paramilitary privatized troops.[9] Far from ushering in a new age of connections without walls, borders, and boundaries, these promising technological developments seem only to intensify differences and hostilities between states and peoples through spatially reductive imaginaries. As the refortification of border technologies and policing in the wake of 11 September 2001 have made only too clear, "the extraordinary power and performative force of colonial modernity" remain very much part of our present-day experience.[10]

Nonetheless, geopolitical and geo-economic state strategies are far from coherent or unidirectional in intent, execution, or effects and should be considered "a field or network of policy designs whose exercise over space is far from orderly."[11] Meanwhile, local groups use the borderless technologies of the Internet to advance their own tactics of survival and protest, including virtual sit-ins inspired by the Zapatista movement, mass protests such as those in the Middle East catalyzed by micro-blogging with SMS-texting and tweets, Internet resource libraries, and YouTube video postings documenting state repression. Ricardo Dominguez, with colleagues Brett Stabaum, Micha Cárdenas, and Amy Sara Carroll of the Electronic Disturbance Theater/b.a.n.g. lab (an artist-based research group located at the University of California, San Diego and the University of Michigan), for example, recently developed the Transborder Immigrant Tool (TBT), a humanitarian safety-net device housed in GPS-enabled cellphones and intended to help individuals navigate to water caches on the US side of the border.[12] The artists hope to reduce the death toll of immigrants crossing from Mexico into the US, which they describe as a "humanitarian crisis," by distributing the TBT to churches and nongovernment organizations. The project received a great deal of media attention in December 2009 and was both praised by the international community and accused of criminal activity within the US.

Even the very materiality of walls and barriers can be refashioned to achieve unexpected cultural and political practices. In the Irish Nationalist area of West Belfast, peace line barriers, which have grown in size and number in recent years to separate Protestant and Catholic areas of the city, were used to physically frame a local festival. In direct response to the local media's designation of the area as a "terrorist community," residents, feeling this portrayal was far more restrictive than the physical walls that cordoned them off, organized to celebrate their community's creativity, energy, and passion for the arts. Beginning in 1998, Féile an Phobail, known locally as "the people's festival," has now become one of the largest community festivals in Europe, providing a new form of political expression and community-driven postwar reconciliation.[13]

Creative uses of new globalizing technologies, then, cannot overcome walls, borders, and boundaries, but they can certainly subvert and rechannel their materialities and functions. Despite humankind's perennial attempts to barricade, separate, and define, the work of activists and artists shows that barrier lines are neither merely passive stages upon which tales of human greed unfold through history, nor simply abstract containers that those in power mark off, map out, or fill with meaning.

Spatial and Cultural Practices

Michel de Certeau's concepts of *strategy* and *tactic* offer a useful way to understand how such spatial and cultural practices and productions of power accompany the making and remaking of walls, borders, and boundaries. He defines a strategy as the creation of an "exterior" space, defined by threats and enemies, to delineate one's "own" territory and locus of power vis-à-vis the "Other." De Certeau describes three effects of strategies made commonplace since René Descartes first mapped the cogito in bodily and perspectival terms: marking the triumph of space over time, mastering places through vision and a system of surveillance, and transforming the "uncertainties of history into readable spaces." Spatial strategies are inherently relational, even as those strategies produce spaces that appear to be concrete, readable, and absolute: "A Cartesian attitude, if you wish: it is an effort to delimit one's own place in a world bewitched by the invisible powers of the Other. It is also the typical attitude of modern science, politics, and military strategy."[14] The "attitude" de Certeau refers to here is associated with modern scopic regimes, whereby the godlike, disembodied, and disciplining bird's-eye "view from nowhere"—be it of the scientist, surveyor, explorer, planner, or political authority—seemingly renders space (and the peoples, relations, and networks coursing through and constitutive of those spaces) transparent.[15] The spatial strategy of drawing lines therefore is not only a political process that delineates internal/external spaces of Self/Other: strategies also *naturalize* territorial practices, the disciplining of subjects, and the separation of space-times. As de Certeau concludes, once a locus of power is established, strategies expand and build upon theoretical and representational sites, including "systems and totalizing discourses" that articulate "an ensemble of physical places in which forces are distributed."[16]

Just as the authors in our volume acknowledge the ways that territorial border thinking and strategies of surveillance remain structured by traditional political and Cartesian imaginaries, they also pay attention to spatial and cultural practices that navigate architectures of division and exclusion beyond apparent intransigencies. We refer to de Certeau's discussion of *tactics* as an alternative to hegemonic Western forms of territorial space, even though it is but an "art of the weak":

> The space of a tactic is the space of the other. Thus it must play on and with a terrain imposed on it and organized by the law of a foreign power. It does not have the means to *keep to itself*, at a distance, in a position of withdrawal, foresight, and self-collection: it is a maneuver "within the enemy's field of vision," as von Bülow put it, and within enemy territory.... It must vigilantly make use of the cracks that particular conjunctions open in the surveillance of the proprietary powers. It poaches in them. It creates surprises in them. It can be where it is least expected. It is a guileful ruse.[17]

Following this "guileful ruse," then, the following chapters reveal that walls, borders, and boundaries are far from fixed, static entities; barrier sites and barrier processes do not solely offer tales of domination and separation. They are much more than just histories of *surveiller et punir* (control and punish); rather, they offer narratives of Foucauldian "anti-discipline" as well as possibilities of identity formation.[18] Walls, borders, and boundaries are dynamic spaces of inhabitation that exceed those of the nation-state; they offer possibilities of survival and adaptation and the hope of self-transformation. They may be also understood as activist markers that encourage people to assume "political responsibility for pursuit of a decent life" extending "beyond the borders" of individual countries.[19]

The work of Henri Lefebvre, a defining influence on de Certeau, is also helpful in establishing how walls, borders, and boundaries inform spatial and cultural practices.[20] In *The Production of Space*, Lefebvre analyzed how modern spaces are conceived, enacted, and made. He introduced a historical analysis of modern space according to three interrelated concepts: *representations of space*, *spaces of representation*, and *spatial practice*.[21] This intersecting "trialectical" approach (to borrow a term from Edward W. Soja) means that there is always a tension between these three components of space, whereby each affects and is shaped by the other two.[22] While space must be always understood according to all of these aspects simultaneously, distinguishing between them is nonetheless a crucial analytical device for examining complex intersections of space-time.

Representations of space are those dominant knowledge systems in a society produced by modern professionals who conceptualize, depict, and implicitly evaluate space. These strategic representations are produced (in a Marxian sense) by managers and professionals who work in bureaucratic institutions and have a distanced, "expert," but often non-experiential understanding of space as absolute, bounded, and measurable; they also often promote the interests of capital. Planners, engineers, architects, surveyors, policy makers, and state officials not only have the power to conceive of and represent space through maps, flow charts, or information systems, but they also use those representations to legitimate their understanding of the world (sometimes projecting these spatial concepts onto the "reality" of others). Gerard Toal uses the term "geo-power" to discuss the representational practices and discourses used by these power elites to assert claims to "truth" about how political space is ordered and administered.[23] Furthermore, these dominant representations of space have other material effects; standing for reality, they are used to make and remake built and natural environments.

Consider the Berlin Wall.[24] Once it was erected in 1961, it was not just a real physical object but a metaphor for the Cold War's division of the world's two major geopolitical systems, generating symbolic confrontations and grand narratives of systemic struggle on both sides. Yet it was a system that demanded ideological mirroring. For someone unfamiliar with the topography or history of the city, it was not immediately clear from a bird's-eye view which side was fortified against the other, in which direction the wall was actually "facing," and against whom it was aligned. In an abstract sense, the Other (whether the West's Cold War Other or the East's, depending on one's situational perspective) became a necessary condition for the common line of separation. Without the Other there is no sense of identity and no concept of home (*Heimat*).

One reason, then, for the sheer power and continued aura of walls, borders, and boundaries has much to do with their ability to signify and symbolize on a scale far greater than their literal ability to separate, defend, or guard. The human need to draw lines has a more benign import and functions as a cultural practice in its own right, for example, in designing and constructing the physical walls of a house. Lefebvre was particularly interested in distinctions between and overlays of dominant representations of space and their lived counterparts. For this reason he introduced the concept of spaces of representation to refer to the intimate knowledge that individuals have of the spaces they move through, inhabit, and make. Spaces of representation "tend towards more or less coherent systems of non-verbal symbols and signs" and include psychological attachments and memories, as well as the physical qualities of a social space. For Lefebvre the space of representation is "directly *lived* through its associated images and symbols, and hence [it is] the space of 'inhabitants' and 'users'.… This is the dominated—and hence passively experienced—space which the imagination seeks to change and appropriate."[25]

Lefebvre's category of everyday spatial practice is associated with a given area or locale. Spatial practice is evaluated according to place, individual performance, and individual and collective relationships to that social space—all of which interact in complex ways. Thus any number of identities imploded along with the Wall when it "fell" in November 1989. Sociologically the loss of the Wall resulted in multiple instances of German-German alienation. As German author Peter Schneider predicted, when the physical Wall fell, a "wall in the head" would replace it. Remember the joke in the mid 1990s? "So this East German says to a West German: We are one people! And the West German answers: So are we!" ("Sagt ein Ossi zu einem Wessi: wir sind ein Volk! Antwortet der Wessi: wir auch!") Despite this potential for disequilibrium and change, spatial practice ensures for Lefebvre at least some degree of social cohesion and continuity, a cohesion that "implies a guaranteed level of *competence* and a specific level of *performance*."[26] Useful in this regard are Paul Ricoeur's reflections on the significance of how we interact with the "constructed space" of cities.[27] As urban dwellers we bring together the subjective spatial experiences of our bodies and the detached configurations of geometric space. Our ability to localize our environment grants us the gift of creating a recognizable sense of place out of space.[28] Individuals growing up in various social settings learn how to "read" a landscape (which includes bodies and social cues) and intuitively know what activities are appropriate and expected in a locale. Such mutations in cultural practice are both diachronic and synchronic: even if one is the same person, being an East German during the German Democratic Republic is not the same as being an Eastern German in today's reunified Germany, just as being Jewish in New York is not the same as being Jewish in Berlin, and being Mexican in El Paso is not the same as being Mexican in Ciudad Juárez.

De Certeau's tactics thus are similar to Lefebvrean spatial practice insofar as both include transgressions that challenge dominant norms about appropriate ways to act, dress, or move in a social and political space, and thus may create new spatial imaginaries for the future. As Lefebvre makes clear, "[t]he body, at the very heart of space and of the discourse of Power, is irreducible and subversive."[29] Such spatial practices are even at work against what is often referred to as today's iconographic Berlin Wall: namely, the Israeli security barrier. On 9 November 2009, a group of Palestinian activists in Qalandiya staged a symbolic felling of a section of the West Bank wall that encircles them in direct reference to the liberation of the East Germans that night twenty years earlier. First charted out in 2000 along the former boundary of the Green Line to protect Israelis against Palestinian terrorist attacks, the barrier is becoming a fortification of spatial segregation and apartheid. It encompasses Palestinian communities in an insanely complex, circuitous route in the West Bank. Eventually it will wrap itself around all Palestinian areas in the occupied territories, surrounding them "lest they expand" and making the Palestinians into demoted outsiders who live in "landlocked" archipelagos within the state—as walled in and controlled, ironically, as the first ghettoized Jews of Renaissance Venice once were.[30]

Although Palestinians avoid using the term white intifada, nonviolent, multilateral protest actions against Israel have not received the same mainstream media attention as Palestinian suicide bombers, Israeli military incursions, or Hamas's stealth bombings, yet they offer alternative strategies of survival. Activist Ayed Morrar, together with local residents, Hamas and Fatah members, Israeli activists, and other international activists, prevented the path of the Israeli security fence from running through the center of his home village Budrus, sparing 95 percent of the village's olive trees and arable farmland and preventing the village's local cemetery from being defaced. Stories such as these—of nonviolent protest actions by Israelis and Palestinians working together and told through documentary films shown in international circuits and through an Internet network and resource library—are an important part of the work pursued by the activist nonprofit organization Just Vision.[31]

Sometimes a border-crossing act of transgression can counteract the negative imagery of, say, the fence/wall being built along the US-Mexico border. A Tijuana house in which a drug-smuggling border tunnel had been uncovered became the site of a poetry event in 2007 where Mexican and American poets literally read their work across the border with the help of bullhorns. As the mayor of Tijuana insisted: "We're connected, border or no border."[32] Further, the performance collective Border Art Workshop/Taller de Arte Fronterizo, based in San Diego, California, conducted a month-long journey in 1990 along the border in a zigzag fashion during which artists, residents, migrant workers, border patrol officers, the Pacific Ocean, deserts, and the border itself formed a variety of "staples" as crossing points "to heal the wound of the border," a terrain considered to be both a "great tragedy and a place where social upheaval also produces the possibility of constructive transformation of both Mexican and American cultures."[33] Such spatial practices as cultural practices can be thought of as mappings that, to borrow from Derek Gregory, are "not of replication, reflection, or reproduction—the usual codings—but of *interference*, in which boundaries [whether in the personal body or in the body politic] take provisional, never fixed, never finished shape and in which all sorts of fusions become possible."[34]

Despite debates resulting from Arizona's Senate Bill 1070 (a controversial, stringent anti-immigration law), the ability of the US-Mexican borderlands to counteract the US border fence aligns this barrier with the fate of the Iron Curtain and also points to a possible future end to the Israeli security infrastructure of barriers, roads, and settlement occupation. We know that during the last fifteen years, over 5,000 border crossers have died at *la linea* (what Lefebvre would call a representation of space). Nonetheless, people are forging cultural and infrastructural connections in *la frontera* (what Lefebvre would term a lived space of representation that includes creative spatial practice).[35] *La frontera* refers to "on-the-ground" micro-geographies of the ten million inhabitants whose daily cultural and economic interactions confirm productive border fusions and frictions in the two thousand-mile zone. A borderland should ideally demonstrate interaction between both sides of the permeable line, which in the case of Mexico and the US makes social and economic sense. Fortress

America may not like it, but transboundary, collective identities emerging from what would otherwise remain harsh asymmetries have changed the hegemonic identity of American urban life.[36]

Recognizing this, historian Oscar J. Martínez has advocated the "border integration" of a regionally cohesive, ethnically mixed society on each side of the line, one in which models of "coexistent," "interdependent," and ultimately "integrated" borderlands would replace the earlier closed, "alienated" stage of national boundaries.[37] Significantly, this permeability should be understood as functioning through time as well as through space, an indication that this border in particular is now reaching an end phase and moving beyond the historical weight of colonialism that it has traditionally borne, including that of the American frontier.[38] In other words, when walls, borders, and boundaries are understood as spaces of representation and spatial practices *as well as* dominant representations of space, we are asked to pay scholarly attention to the polysemous possibilities of multicultural zones and to consider how our own analyses may have contributed to border thinking according to the historically inevitable, politically closed, or culturally immutable.[39]

European Case Studies

The contributors to this volume—engaging the spatial and cultural practices of walls, borders, and boundaries that we have outlined above—present case studies from the social sciences and humanities that draw upon a range of places, states, and regions in Europe. They employ multiple disciplinary, theoretical, and scalar approaches to (re)reading walls, borders, and boundaries according to their spatial strategies, physical presences, racial impacts, symbolic functions, or geopolitical effects. Moreover, the range of concepts and topics raised within and across the volume's three overlapping sections—City Walls, Border Zones, and Migrating Boundaries—will challenge those interested in border studies from various perspectives. At least one essay in each section focuses on the city of Berlin as an enduring touchstone for considering European social borders or for addressing topics of ongoing relevance, such as memory and commemoration (chapters 2, 3, 6, and 10). At the same time, each section offers fresh perspectives beyond Berlin on the fortification of European cities in France, Ireland, Italy, Spain, and Cyprus (chapters 1, 4, and 11), as well as on the porosity of Europe's boundaries at the shifting borderlands of what we used to consider Eastern Europe (chapters 5 and 7). Significantly, our authors also examine transnational and translocal processes, including migration, citizenship and human rights, and ethnic conflict, all-too-human issues that call for alternative understandings of national borders (chapters 4, 8, and 9).

Part I (City Walls) considers how throughout history city walls have served not only to protect from without but also to separate from within. Renaissance Venice was the first city to segregate Jews into two ghettos, closed-in communities considered inner islands in the city. In the US the twentieth century's trend toward spatial residential segregation, suburbanization, and ex-urbanization reflects a similar drive that now is spreading globally: Cape Town, the Côte d'Azur, São Paolo. Particularly in these purified, exclusive communities (now often gated, master-planned, and securitized), the physical markers of social segregation, including gates, walls, highways, blocks of buildings or natural features, and land use zoning restrictions, communicate widening income and social gaps. While our urban condition, then as now, has remained consistently dependent on multiple acts of inner walling, medieval perimeter walls have, of course, long since disappeared from the maps. In chapter 1, "The Dialectics of Urban Form in Absolutist France," Yair Mintzker offers a new reading of a key moment in modern urban history: the defortification of European cities. He demonstrates that the Crown consciously aligned the loss of urban walls in seventeenth-century France with a renewed focus on exterior state borders. Thus a closing (refortification) of the French state was the dialectical companion piece of the opening (defortification) of the French city; urban walls were transformed to—and in the emphasis on the *glacis* (embankment) had to some degree a transformative impact upon—the level of the nation-state. This change had an impact on selfhood as well as statehood: henceforth, one's rights and identity came increasingly from the territorially defined state rather than the locality into which one was born. Yet as Benjamin K. Barber has noted, the newly refortified modern nation-state gained new "vulnerabilities" and became "surrounded by frontiers that serve[d] the same purposes as the fallen walls of medieval towns."[40]

Like Mintzker's reading of the epistemic shift in urban fortifications in the seventeenth century, Olaf Briese argues that Berlin's walled history is in fact far more extensive than the infamous Cold War Wall that divided the city. In chapter 2, "The Camp in the City, the City as Camp: Berlin's Other Guarded Walls," he proposes a contextualized urban historical take on Giorgio Agamben's linkage of the camp and modernity. Drawing on Primo Levi, Agamben sees the camp everywhere. As Levi wrote, we are all in a sense walled in: "[W]e are all in the ghetto … the ghetto is walled in … outside the ghetto reign the lords of death, and … close by the train is waiting."[41] Briese's focus here is threefold. First, he points to Berlin's role as the capital city Germania and as capital of the camp cosmos, directing the Third Reich's concentration camp universe both across Germany and in Central and Eastern Europe. Second, he reveals the city's own concomitant de-formation as a leading "barracks" city of forced labor, participating fully in the Nazis' production system of slave labor and death; containment walls were at the core of this universe's design. His third focus is on the often shameful, less well recognized continuities in location, design, and surveillance techniques between Berlin as a city of Nazi camp walls and its subsequent postwar re-formation as a center for refugee and prison camps both in the immediate postwar period and beyond into the Cold War.

Not all of Berlin's walls have been imprisoning ones, preventing access to or obscuring attempts at knowledge about the other side. Some have been designed with an opposite message, inviting public engagement and even provoking reflection on the nature of government and state legitimacy. In chapter 3, "'Threshold Resistance': Dani Karavan's Berlin Installation *Grundgesetz 49*," Eric Jarosinski proposes a critical interpretation of a glass wall designed by Israeli artist Dani Karavan for the renewed German capital city. Celebrated in official and popular discourse as a symbol of postwar (West) Germany's strong foundation as a liberal, democratic society, this wall elicits other, more ambiguous readings of transparency. Similar to Mintzker's analysis of the dialectics of defortification at the beginning of the modern era, Jarosinski highlights how Karavan's installation and its surroundings tend to undermine the officially encouraged democratic transparency motif and point instead to methods of viewing more aligned with the consumerist "threshold" gaze of window shopping. Placed symbolically near the Reichstag in the government quarter at Spree River Bend (Spreebogen)—a new area marked by a growing number of nation-based statements and memorials—the installation on nineteen glass slabs offers a contemporary interpretation of and interaction with Germany's Basic Law (the 1949 text inscribed upon the wall's sections). Karavan has delivered here an ironically apt recrafting of a much earlier set of (stone) tablet inscriptions, namely the law for the Jewish people received by Moses in Exodus 34. Because of these deviations from its intended representational function, Karavan's wall is neither a block nor a hindrance to German memory and identity but a space of representation that invites critical reflection. Insisting on how material walls are haunted by the past, Jarosinki shows that they can be highly imaginative representational tools in the practice of urban memory.

Other urban walls that both suture and mirror, bridge and separate, are presented in chapter 4 by Daniela Vicherat Mattar, "Did the Walls Really Come Down? Contemporary B/ordering Walls in Europe." She reconsiders the impact of the fall of the Berlin Wall in the context of recent European national strategies of containment toward unwanted urban pockets of religious strife or ethnic difference. The democratic project itself is put into question in today's Europe, where certain groups of people are expected to disappear from the inner as well as outer urban map behind newly constructed barriers. Vicherat Mattar explores three examples of post-Wall European urban walls: a recent wall built to block off a housing project of overcrowded immigrants in Padua, the encircling walls of the Spanish autonomous city of Ceuta that serve as part of the Schengenized EU's anti-immigration external border with Morocco, and the "Peace Lines" in Belfast that separate residential areas for Catholics and Protestants. Drawing upon Henk van Houtum, Olivier Kramsch, and Wolfgang Zierhofer's concept of b/ordered spaces, she describes how these walls function as borders and political orders, while acknowledging how they may work against themselves as borderlands that sustain urban cohesion over fragmentation and occasionally even democratic and minority rights.[42]

Part II (Border Zones) addresses sociocultural transformations in three distinct border communities separated for decades as a result of the political divisions of the Cold War. Mapping these communities today reveals palimpsests, multiple historical layers (both Cold War and post-Cold War) that obscure and erase geopolitical experiences but also reveal traces of past habits in the present. Muriel Blaive and Thomas Lindenberger's coauthored chapter 5 on "Border Guarding as Social Practice: A Case Study of Czech Communist Governance and Hidden Transcripts" narrows in on the Cold War frontier between the former Czechoslovakia and Austria, where a Soviet-inspired, fortified border was constructed to stop hostile interventions from the other side. Designed as an impenetrable space in a permanent state of emergency, this section of the Iron Curtain between East and West was typified in the town of České Velenice. Based on oral interviews conducted there in 2008, the authors reconstruct the impact of communist practices of border regimentation such as territorial administration, the militarization of everyday life, and the homogenization of the population. Their micro-historical approach yields insights that go beyond the conventional wisdom of fear and repression as the driving forces behind the inhabitants' participation in border guarding and denunciation, revealing material advantage and patriotic convictions as equally powerful motivations. Moreover, the interviewees provide evidence for the layering effect of historical experience, concealing shame but also disclosing motivations. Blaive and Lindenberger demonstrate how the instrumentalization of history also creates spaces of representation, specifically in the appeal to anti-German feelings among the Czech residents in the border town that can be traced from the Beneš decrees of 1945 that led to the expulsion of the German residents, adapted by the communist regime through 1989, and still functional today in the Czech Republic.

David E. Barclay brings us back to Cold War Berlin as a space of representation, asking in chapter 6, "A 'Complicated Contrivance': West Berlin behind the Wall, 1971–1989," why the separated, "outpost" life caused by the Wall had come to seem "normal" to West Berliners by the time it was ready to fall. Like Vicherat Mattar's image of enclosed urban communities creating a sense of urban cohesion, Barclay provides a case study of insularity behind a protective wall. With twenty years' hindsight and access to previously unavailable archive sources, he shows how the Four Power Agreement of 1971 and the accompanying inter-German agreements that recognized the sovereignty of two German states marked a major caesura between the generational experience of those who experienced the "heroic" years of the Cold War stand-off along the inner-German border and those who became accustomed to West Berlin's insularity in the wake of détente and *Ostpolitik*. As Barclay suggests, not only West Berliners but also the Western Allies themselves began to take for granted the Allied presence in the walled-in city of the 1970s and 1980s. Its increasingly hollowed-out demographic of young people and retirees with their diverse alternative cultures and subsidized provincialism mirrored, in an odd way, the growth of what has been called a niche culture (*Nischengesellschaft*) in East Germany, referring to the emergence of private spaces as protection from state surveillance and supervision. Barclay's characterization of West Berlin's artificial normalcy suggests a more general paradigm for assessing the last two decades of Cold War division and its legacy in the post-communist era.

Steffi Marung's essay shifts attention to the eastern border of post-communist Europe as a historically inflected representational space. In chapter 7, "Moving Borders and Competing Civilizing Missions: Germany, Poland, and Ukraine in the Context of the EU's Eastern Enlargement," she takes as the point of departure Poland's pivotal position between Germany and Ukraine. Poland's historical and often traumatic experience with shifting borders, as well as its long-standing tradition as both subject and object of "civilizational" discourse, helped to shape the new border regimes on the EU's eastern fringe. In particular Marung considers two key moments: Poland's exclusion from the EU following the collapse of the communist states, and the development of an "Eastern Policy" toward Ukraine on Poland's part after its accession to the EU in 2004. Recognizing the unusual pace and unpredictability of changes in the continent's political and symbolic order, she attends to the spatial hierarchies of social self-description in Poland's public discourse and foreign policy initiatives, showing how the telos of the nation and normative coherence gave way to new patterns of affiliation and membership. Just as Blaive and Lindenberger's conclusions about personal identification and motivation vis-à-vis a repressive regime relate micro- to macro-historical issues, Marung too confirms how local, regional, national, and transnational practices come into play as strategic and constantly renegotiable modes of self-definition.

Part III (Migrating Boundaries) moves from the spatial and cultural practices located on the East-West divide to examine how communities negotiate the boundaries of established Western European democracies in the wake of transborder processes such as racism, migration, and diaspora. Each contributor explores larger questions of belonging and citizenship, negotiated Otherness, and tactics of surviving exclusion and violence. Whereas new theories of multiculturalism and citizenship have facilitated a better understanding of these realities of globalization and boundary crossings, governments and residents of receiving countries have responded to their migrants with heightened surveillance and differentiated expectations of citizenship in an age of "the war on terrorism." The chapters in this section offer historical comparisons to recent anti-immigrant declarations by European leaders, showing continuity with the ways that populist, xenophobic anxiety adapts metaphors of violence during a period of economic uncertainty.

In chapter 8, "Migrants, Mosques, and Minarets: Reworking the Boundaries of Liberal Democracy in Switzerland and Germany," Patricia Ehrkamp examines expressions of Islamophobia in recent debates about immigration, citizenship, and democratic participation in Western Europe. Echoing the "civilizational" discourse Marung identifies as underpinning the policy formulations on the EU's eastern fringe, Ehrkamp points to examples of Othering (Muslims) in Switzerland and Germany—voter support of bans on minarets, debates about German *Leitkultur* ("guiding" culture), anti-Islamic citizens' initiatives, and resistance to the construction of prestigious mosques—that provide insights into the real-world problems with assimilationist expectations for migrants. In so doing, she raises key questions about the construction of democratic political subjectivities in immigrant-receiving societies. In contrast to the traditional assumption that immigrants should integrate into the host culture and belief systems, most migrants today maintain transnational ties across political borders. For Ehrkamp, when secularism becomes a means to govern difference or when democratic values such as tolerance and equality are used to justify exclusion, prejudices about the "acceptability" of newcomers also affect longer-term residents. Rereading claims to secularism and democratic values in the context of debates about immigration thus interrogates the very meaning of belonging to a polity: citizens' basic rights, freedoms, and responsibilities. Assimilationist demands and expectations of secularism in the name of democracy reveal assumptions about community homogeneity underlying the self-understanding of democratic participation. The author calls for a rethinking of liberal democracy from a representation of space that naturalizes state borders to a space of representation that both is "emergent and emerging" and includes symbolic and lived boundary crossings of transnational immigration and cultural difference.

While Blaive and Lindenberger reference anti-German sentiment as a crucial component of the spatial imaginary of the Czech-Austrian border since 1945, in chapter 9 Isa Blumi focuses on the invisibility that West German policy makers assigned to Kosovar Albanian men from the 1960s to the present as a paradigm of managing migrant labor for the postwar economic recovery. Their blanket (mis)classification as "Turks," "Greeks," or "Yugoslavs" had negative effects for migrant families, their children, and the larger society. In "Not Our Kind: Generational Barriers Dividing Postwar Albanian Migrant Communities," Blumi examines how a bureaucratic migrant classification system created a "secondary boundary" of Cold War division, a process of marginalization that is still producing social and spatial distances between Self and Other, West and East. By imposing a singular label, such as "Yugoslav," onto a range of migrants as diverse as the Albanians, Alevis, and Kurds who were fleeing state and social persecution within their own supposed home countries, individuals were defined as an ethnically and culturally homogenous group upon their arrival and were hence never legally recognized in their difference. Migrants who arrived in Europe from a transit country, such as Turkey, were labeled "Turks" because the country of last departure was assumed to be the "country of origin."

Not only did the classification system conceal the domestic agendas of some sending countries, including ethno-national strategies of homogenization within their own political boundaries, but upon arrival in the host society this rather arbitrary label also sustained hierarchies of exclusion, empowering some migrants while marginalizing and victimizing others. Based on informal interviews, Blumi examines some of the distancing effects this secondary boundary had on multiple generations of immigrants and host-society citizens living in German cities, including problems with illegitimate "ethnic community" spokespersons, unintended consequences of zoning restrictions for heterogeneous and sometimes adversarial ethnic enclaves, and the social pathologies resulting from forced ethnic mis-identities. Many of his interview partners blamed their "host" neighbors, coworkers, policemen, and classmates for their individual and collective traumas. Blumi insists that future migration studies must take into account these defining boundaries among and between immigrant groups.

Chapter 10 adds a different dimension of migrant invisibility and voicelessness to Blumi's example of faulty classification in the preceding chapter. Jeffrey Jurgens's "Invisible Migrants: Memory and German Nationhood in the Shadow of the Berlin Wall" focuses on Turkish immigrants whose presence has remained largely hidden in narratives about Berlin's division and subsequent reunification. Turkish migrants—the object of West Germany's most extensive labor recruitment efforts—lived in disproportionate numbers in the traditional working-class districts that abutted the western face of the Berlin Wall, and thus in contrast to many non-immigrant West Berliners who tended to forget about the Wall in their insularity, as Barclay describes in chapter 6, these residents were confronted on a daily basis with its reality. In a case study of a five-year-old Turkish boy who in 1975 drowned in the canal separating East and West in Berlin's Kreuzberg district, Jurgens considers the public reactions to the event at the time, which quickly elevated the local tragedy to the level of a Cold War ideological struggle defining border sovereignty. Symptomatic of the discourse of Wall victims and related commemorative practices since unification, the invisible victim without a voice in Jurgens's ethnographic presentation speaks more generally of the marginalized minority voices in the dominant culture's postwar practice of constructing national memories, suggesting that a fuller retrieval of these stories is a process that has yet to be realized.

One such minority voice makes itself heard in chapter 11, "Crossing Boundaries in Cyprus: Landscapes of Memory in the Demilitarized Zone," in which artist and migrant-refugee Gülgün Kayim exposes the cultural practice of repressing experiences of violence, war, and migration that she inherited as a second-generation Turkish Cypriot growing up in London. She thus personalizes the b/ordered space concept discussed by Vicherat Mattar in chapter 4. Asking what happens to the subjectivity of someone dislocated by migration and having connections only to an officially maintained no-man's-land, Kayim formulates a rather different kind of response than the memories of Blaive and Lindenberger's interviewees about the Czech fortified border. Our volume closes with her deeply personal journey, which reflects upon the use of performance art as a strategy of survival. Since art is the artist's home, she shares her transgressing of those "secondary boundaries" of Cold War division, including her search for belonging. Kayim describes the difficulties of inheriting divided national histories of violence, learning about one's family through others' stories and photographs (or post-memories), and struggling with nostalgic yearnings for a lost ancestral home. She layers and juxtaposes stories, sounds, objects, and scenes from others' plays to create a performance vocabulary that communicates the challenge of narrating family trauma a generation and country removed. Indeed, her plays are also installations: located in abandoned industrial buildings at historic sites in foreign countries, these places as theater sets become symbolic spaces of representation that invite the viewer to consider the legacy of trauma related to the complicity of war and violence. Returning home, moving across the lines of the demilitarized zone as she prepares her current work in progress, Kayim ends on an optimistic note that resonates with all the contributions in this volume: ruptures and breaks can lead to new and different ways of thinking about boundaries in the future.

Writing across the Lines

The myriad topographical, material, and conceptual contexts of walls, borders, and boundaries that the essays here elaborate suggest the rich fusions and frictions of the now-burgeoning field of border studies.[43] Border studies first emerged in the 1970s and 1980s through postmodern and postcolonial interrogations in historical and cultural studies and artistic practice, resulting in groundbreaking work since then at and beyond the US-Mexican-Native American borderlands.[44] The "spatial turn" in the social sciences and humanities ushered in similar interventions and new models of scholarly inquiry in which border theory played a formative role.[45] With the radical, post-Iron Curtain shifts in European national boundaries in the 1990s, the closed territory of the nation-state is increasingly being put into question.[46] Newly opened archives have resulted in historical and historiographical studies of borders and boundaries, and ethnographic micro-histories have undone myths about Cold War border communities.[47] Influenced by the epistemic break of the fall of the Berlin Wall, border topics have also emerged as a dominant trope in contemporary German literature and film.[48] Border research in European cultural studies increasingly focuses on the shifts in European identity.[49] A major focus of border studies is advocacy of new opportunities for migrant communities.[50]

Yet inevitably—and intriguingly—even in a volume such as ours, we sense how disciplinary training still holds firm and helps shape arguments. The essays presented here bear these traces of the authors' disciplinary biases and habits, even as we strove in this introduction to write "across the lines" that separate us, seeking words and concepts that help frame the volume, ground productive communication, and preserve intellectual rigor. Our editing enterprise confirmed that a shift in focus to peripheral zones certainly has implications for our knowledge culture, because they mark spaces of vulnerability and interdependence that generate contact and encounters. Indeed, the risk at the project's outset was the chain of unpredictable access to the unfamiliar; the gain was to discover unexpected connections, breaking down precisely those barriers that motivated our critical engagement from the outset. The scholars in this volume may use different approaches, yet they encounter overlapping issues, terminology, and perspectives in their research. Readers will notice that while we and our contributors employ our respective but different vocabularies and expectations as defined by our disciplines, we have also sought to identify key patterns of design and behavior across the disciplines and in response to bordered spaces that extend through different historical and geographical contexts.

Taken together, therefore, we hope that the essays of this volume will cross existing (disciplinary) lines to chart the new territory of transdisciplinary border studies. At the same time we aim to engage a twofold dialogue, among the essays and with our readers, whom we challenge to become active participants. We invite our readers to reconsider, with the help of these essays, how borders are invested with meaning and by whom; the political inevitability, psychological necessity, and creative challenges of such spaces and places; and alternative mappings of the frailties of the human de- and re-territorializing imagination.

Notes

1. John Brinckerhoff Jackson, *Discovering the Vernacular Landscape* (New Haven, 1984), 16.
2. Joseph Nevins, *Operation Gatekeeper: The Rise of the 'Illegal Alien' and the Remaking of the U.S.-Mexico Boundary* (New York, 2002); Michael Sorkin, ed., *Against the Wall: Israel's Barrier to Peace* (New York, 2005).
3. Jean-Jacques Rousseau, *Discours sur les sciences et les arts; discours sur l'origine et le fondement de l'inégalité parmi les hommes* [1754], ed. Jacques Roger (Paris, 1971), 205.
4. George L. Mosse, *Fallen Soldiers: Reshaping the Memory of the World Wars* (Oxford, UK, 1990), 4.
5. Stein Rokkan and Derek W. Urwin, *Economy, Territory, Identity: Politics of West European Peripheries* (London, 1983); Richard Muir, *Political Geography: A New Introduction* (New York, 1997), 121–23.
6. G. W. F. Hegel, *Philosophy of Right*, trans. S. W. Dyde (Kitchener, ON, 2001), §360; Chris Brown, "Borders and Identity in International Political Theory," in *Identities, Borders, Orders: Rethinking International Relations Theory*, ed. Mathias Albert, David Jacobson, and Yosef Lapid (Minneapolis, 2001), 129.
7. David Newman, "Boundaries," in John A. Agnew, Katharyne Mitchell, and Gearóid Ó Tuathail (aka Gerard Toal), eds., *A Companion to Political Geography* (Malden, MA, 2003), 127 and 130.
8. Wendy Brown, *Walled States, Waning Sovereignty* (New York, 2010).
9. Matthew Sparke, "A Neoliberal Nexus: Economy, Security, and the Biopolitics of Citizenship of the Border," *Political Geography* 25, no. 2 (2006): 151–80; Eyal Weizman, *Hollow Land: Israel's Architecture of Occupation* (London and New York, 2007).
10. Derek Gregory, *The Colonial Present: Afghanistan, Palestine, Iraq* (Cambridge, MA, 2004), 4.
11. Matthew Coleman, "U.S. Statecraft and the U.S.-Mexico Border as Security/Economic Nexus," *Political Geography* 24, no. 2 (2005): 189.
12. Micha Cárdenas, Amy Sara Carroll, Ricardo Dominguez, and Brett Stalbaum, "Commentary: Academics Make Statement with Project," *San Diego Union Tribune*, 7 March 2010, http://www.signonsandiego.com/news/2010/mar/07/tooling-around-the-border/ (accessed 24 June 2010); Ricardo Dominguez and Brett Stalbaum (Principal Investigators), "Transborder Immigrants Tool: A Mexico/U.S. Border Disturbance Art Project," Funded by Arts and Humanities as Transborder Grant 2007–8, University of California, San Diego: http://humctr.ucsd.edu/awards/awards.shtml#Transborder; see also http://post.thing.net/node/1642 (both accessed 24 June 2010).
13. Lorraine Dowler, "In the Shadow of the Berlin Wall: The Peace-Lines of Belfast, Northern Ireland," *Political Geography* 31 (forthcoming 2012).
14. Michel de Certeau, *The Practice of Everyday Life* [1980], trans. Stephen Rendall (Berkeley, 1984), 36. Rendall's translation uses "place" in referring to specific spatial concepts, including location, site, territory, and space. To avoid confusion with Anglophone theoretical discussions about these spatial concepts, we indicate our understanding of de Certeau accordingly. See Derek Gregory, "Geography and the Cartographic Anxiety," in *Geographical Imaginations* (Cambridge, MA, 1994), 70–205. See also the critique of Cartesian perspectivalism by Gearóid Ó Tuathail (aka Gerard Toal) in *Critical Geopolitics: The Politics of Writing Global Space* (New York, 1996), 23–24. On Descartes's

theory of corporeally filled space-extension, see Edward S. Casey, *The Fate of Place: A Philosophical History* (Berkeley and Los Angeles, 1997), chap. 7.

15. Michel Foucault, *Discipline and Punish: The Birth of the Prison* [1975], trans. Alan Sheridan (New York, 1977); Donna Haraway, "Situated Knowledges: The Science Question in Feminism and the Privilege of Partial Perspective," *Feminist Studies* 14, no. 3 (1988): 575–99; and Thomas Nagel, *The View from Nowhere* (New York, 1989).

16. De Certeau, *The Practice of Everyday Life*, 38.

17. Ibid., 37. Emphasis in the original.

18. Foucault, *Discipline and Punish*.

19. John A. Agnew, "Borders on the Mind: Re-Framing Border Thinking," *Ethics and Global Politics* 1, no. 4 (2008): 176; Agnew's use of the phrase "decent life" is from Jonathan Seglow, "The Ethics of Immigration," *Political Studies Review* 3, no. 3 (2005): 329.

20. On the direct influence of Lefebvre on de Certeau, see Michel Trebitsch, "Preface: The Moment of Radical Critique," trans. Gregory Elliott, in Lefebvre, *Critique of Everyday Life*, vol. 2, *Foundations for a Sociology of the Everyday* [1961], trans. John Moore (New York, 2002), xxiv–xxv; and Stuart Elden, *Understanding Henri Lefebvre: Theory and the Possible* (London, 2004), 120.

21. Henri Lefebvre, *The Production of Space* [1974], trans. Donald Nicolson-Smith (Cambridge, MA, 1991). Here we follow Rob Shields's translation of Lefebvre's concept "espaces de la représentation" as "spaces of representation" rather than Nicolson-Smith's "representational spaces." See Shields, *Lefebvre, Love and Struggle: Spatial Dialectics* (New York, 1999).

22. Edward W. Soja, *Thirdspace: Journeys to Los Angeles and Other Real-and-Imagined Places* (New York, 1996).

23. Ó Tuathail (aka Toal), "Introduction," *Critical Geopolitics*, 1–20.

24 24. On Berlin's relationship to its former Wall, see Marc Silberman, ed., *The German Wall: Fallout in Europe* (New York, 2011); and Janet Ward, *Post-Wall Berlin: Borders, Space, and Identity* (New York and Basingstoke, UK, 2011). On the history and culture of the Wall and German-German division, see e.g., Philip Broadbent and Sabine Hake, eds., *Berlin, Divided City 1945–1989* (New York, 2010) and Patrick Major, *Behind the Berlin Wall: East Germany and the Frontiers of Power* (New York, 2010).

25. Lefebvre, *Production of Space*, 39. Emphasis in the original.

26. Ibid., 33.

27. Paul Ricoeur, *Memory, History, Forgetting*, trans. Kathleen Blamey and David Pellauer (Chicago, 2004), 150.

28. Yi-Fu Tuan, *Space and Place: The Perspective of Experience*, 2nd ed. (Minneapolis, 2007).

29. Henri Lefebvre, *The Survival of Capitalism: Reproduction of the Relations of Production*, trans. Frank Bryant (New York, 1976), 89; cited in Gregory, *Geographical Imaginations*, 159.

30. Eyal Weizman, "Strategic Points, Flexible Lines, Tense Surfaces, and Political Volumes: Ariel Sharon and the Geometry of Occupation," in *Cities, War, and Terrorism: Towards an Urban Geopolitics*, ed. Stephen Graham (Malden, MA, 2004), 187 and 188. See also idem, *Hollow Land*; and Michael Sorkin, ed., *The Next Jerusalem: Sharing the Divided City* (New York, 2002).

31. Just Vision won honorable mention at Documenta Madrid 10 for the film *Budrus* (Julia Bacha, 2010), which tells the story of activist Ayed Morrar. See http://www.justvision.org/budrus (accessed 30 June 2010).

32. Marc Lacey, "Cities Mesh Across Blurry Border, Despite Physical Barrier," *New York Times*, 5 March 2007, A4.

33. Border Art Workshop/Taller de Arte Fronterizo webpage: http://www.borderart-workshop.com/index.html (accessed 1 July 2010); Susan Leibovitz Steinman, "Border Sutures 1990," in *Mapping the Terrain: New Genre Public Art*, ed. Suzanne Lacy (Seattle, 1995), 206–7.

34. Gregory, *Geographical Imaginations*, 163. Gregory refers here to Donna Haraway's use of the concept "inappropriate/d" from Trin T. Minh-Ha, *Woman, Native, Other: Writing Postcoloniality and Feminism* (Bloomington, IN, 1989). See Haraway, *Simians, Cyborgs and Women: The Reinvention of Nature* (New York, 1991).

35. We borrow the distinction between *la linea* and *la frontera* from Mike Davis, *Magical Urbanism: Latinos Reinvent the U.S. City* (New York, 2000). On the militarization of the border, see Peter Andreas, "Introduction: The Wall after the Wall," in *The Wall around the West: State Borders and Immigration Controls in North America and Europe*, ed. Peter Andreas and Timothy Snyder (Lanham, MD, 2000), 4; and Joseph Nevins, *Operation Gatekeeper*.

36. Alan K. Henrikson, "Facing Across Borders: The Diplomacy of Bon Voisinage," *International Political Science Review* 21, no. 2 (2000): 121–47.

37. Oscar J. Martínez, "The Dynamics of Border Integration: New Approaches to Border Analysis," in *Global Boundaries*, ed. C.H. Schofield (London, 1994), 1–15; idem, *Border People: Life and Society in U.S.-Mexico Borderlands* (Tucson, 1994), 6.

38. Jeremy Adelman and Stephen Aron, "From Borderlands to Borders: Empires, Nation-States, and the Peoples in Between in North American History," *American Historical Review* 104, no. 3 (June 1999), 815–16. Sankaran Krishna also argues for postcolonial (not postmodern) reimagining of boundaries, sensitive to "critical aspects of a Third-World reality that often escapes the metropolitan eye"; see Krishna, "Boundaries in Question," in *A Companion to Political Geography*, ed. Agnew, Mitchell, and Ó Tuathail, 310.

39. David Sibley, *Geographies of Exclusion: Society and Difference in the West* (New York, 1995), 50–51 and 116.

40. Benjamin K. Barber, "Epilogue. An Architecture of Liberty? The City as Democracy's Forge," in *Out of Ground Zero: Case Studies in Urban Reinvention*, ed. Joan Ockman (New York, 2002), 189.

41. Primo Levi, *The Drowned and the Saved*, trans. Raymond Rosenthal (New York, 1988), 69.

42. Henk van Houtum, Olivier Kramsch, and Wolfgang Zierhofer, eds., *B/ordering Space* (Aldershot, UK, 2005).

43. For a historiographical essay charting the trajectories of border studies, see Vladimir Kolossov, "Theorizing Borders: Border Studies: Changing Perspectives and Theoretical Approaches," *Geopolitics* 10 (2005): 606–32. Useful recent reflections on the field can be found in Corey Johnson, Reece Jones, Anssi Paasi, Louise Amoore, Alison Mountz, Mark Salter, and Chris Rumford, "Interventions on Rethinking 'the Border' in Border Studies," *Political Geography* 30 (2011): 61–69.

44. Gloria Anzaldúa, *Borderlands: The New Mestiza = La Frontera* (San Francisco, 1987); and Nancy A. Naples, "Borderlands Studies and Border Theory: Linking Activism and Scholarship for Social Justice," *Sociology Compass* 4, no. 7 (July 2010): 505–18. See also works by artist Guillermo Gómez-Peña, such as *The New World Border: Prophecies, Poems and Loqueras for the End of the Century* (San Francisco, 1996), *Dangerous*

Border Crossers (New York, 2000), *Homo Fronterizus* (a collection of collaborations with cinematographer Gustavo Vazquez, 2008), as well as the Hemisphere Institute of Performance and Politics, established by performance studies theorist Diana Taylor, http://hemisphericinstitute.org/hemi/ (accessed 16 July 2010).

45. The seminal text for the shift in the humanities is Fredric Jameson, *Postmodernism, or, The Cultural Logic of Late Capitalism* (Durham, NC, 1991). On the spatial turn, see Edward W. Soja, *Postmodern Geographies: The Reassertion of Space in Critical Social Theory* (London, 1989). On the intersections of border theory with postmodernity and the endurance of borders in a globalized word, see, e.g., David Newman, "The Lines that Continue to Separate Us: Borders in Our 'Borderless' World," *Progress in Human Geography* 30, no. 2 (2006): 143–61; idem, "Boundaries, Territory and Postmodernity: Towards Shared or Separate Spaces?" in *Borderlands under Stress*, ed. Martin Pratt and Janet Allison Brown (London, 2000), 17–34. Newman's political geographical approach can be compared with that of sociologist Zygmunt Bauman, *Liquid Times: Living in an Age of Uncertainty* (Cambridge, UK, 2007).

46. On the impact of transborder interactions on the nation-state, see, e.g., Brown, *Walled States*; Alexander C. Diener and Joshua Hagen, eds., *Borderlines and Borderlands: Political Oddities at the Edge of the Nation-State* (Lanham, MD, 2010); Sterling Evans, ed., *The Borderlands of the American and Canadian Wests: Essays on Regional History of the Forty-Ninth Parallel* (Lincoln, NE, 2006); Vera Pavlakovich-Kochi, Barbara J. Morehouse, and Doris Wastl-Walter, eds., *Challenged Borderlands: Transcending Political and Cultural Boundaries* (Aldershot, UK, 2004); Anssi Paasi, "Europe as a Social Process of Discourse: Considerations of Place, Boundaries and Identity," *European Urban and Regional Studies* 8, no. 1 (2001): 7–28; and Annemarie H. Sammartino, *The Impossible Border: Germany and the East, 1914–1922* (Ithaca, 2010).

47. Daphne Berdahl, *Where the World Ended: Re-Unification and Identity in the German Borderland* (Berkeley, 1999); Astrid M. Eckert, "Greetings from the Zonal Border": Tourism to the Iron Curtain in West Germany," *Zeithistorische Forschungen* 1 (2011): 9-36; and Edith Sheffer, *Burned Bridge: How East and West Germans Made the Iron Curtain*, foreword by Peter Schneider (New York, 2011).

48. Elke Brüns, *Nach dem Mauerfall. Eine Literaturgeschichte der Entgrenzung* (Munich, 2006); Katharina Gerstenberger, *Writing the New Berlin: The German Capital in Post-Wall Literature* (Rochester, NY, 2008); Helmut Schmitz, ed., *Von der nationalen zur internationalen Literatur: Transkulturelle deutschsprachige Literatur und Kultur im Zeitalter globaler Migration* (Amsterdam, 2009); and Jaimey Fisher and Barbara Mennel, eds., *Spatial Turns: Space, Place, and Mobility in German Literary and Visual Culture* (Amsterdam, 2010).

49. Cosmopolitan cultural studies form the focus of Pheng Cheah and Bruce Robbins, eds., *Cosmopolitics: Thinking and Feeling beyond the Nation* (Minneapolis, 1998). On New European identities, see Ruben Zaiotti, *Cultures of Border Control: Schengen and the Evolution of European Frontiers* (Chicago, 2011); Noel Parker, ed., *The Geopolitics of Europe's Identity: Centers, Boundaries and Margins* (Basingstoke, UK, 2008); Michael Heffernan, *The European Geographical Imagination* (Stuttgart, 2007); Ulrike Hanna Meinhof and Anna Triandafyllidou, eds., *Transcultural Europe: Cultural Policy in a Changing Europe* (Basingstoke, UK, 2006); Ulrich Beck, *The Cosmopolitan Vision*, trans. Ciaran Cronin (Cambridge, UK, 2006); and Etienne Balibar, *We, the People of Europe? Reflections on Transnational Citizenship*, trans. James Swenson (Princeton, 2004).

50. On European migration, see Ray Taras, *Europe Old and New: Transnationalism, Belonging, Xenophobia* (Lanham, MD, 2009); Ruth Mandel, *Cosmopolitan Anxieties: Turkish Challenges to Citizenship and Belonging in Germany* (Durham, NC, 2008); Deniz Göktürk, David Gramling, and Anton Kaes, eds., *Germany in Transit: Nation and Migration, 1955–2005* (Berkeley, 2007); Riva Kastoryano, *Negotiating Identities: States and Immigrants in France and Germany*, trans. Barbara Harshav (Princeton, 2002); and Yasemin Nuhoğlu Soysal, *Limits of Citizenship: Migrants and Postnational Membership in Europe* (Chicago, 1995).

I

City Walls

CHAPTER 1

~:~

The Dialectics of Urban Form in Absolutist France

YAIR MINTZKER

At the beginning of the seventeenth century, there were thousands of cities in continental Europe. Old or recent, populated or half-deserted, politically independent or not, practically all continental cities were separated from their surroundings by physical barriers: city walls. By the beginning of the nineteenth century, however, the majority of European cities had lost their fortifications. With scarce exceptions, city walls were nowhere to be found. They had been destroyed—sometimes by literally undermining them and blowing them up—and removed. This process is known as "defortification"—the turning of a city from a walled to an open place.[1] The first coherent defortification policy on the continent took shape in seventeenth-century France. It began under Richelieu in the 1620s and reached its climax during the War of the League of Augsburg (1688–97). The French Crown's defortification policies were motivated by the political philosophy of absolutism, which looked with suspicion—and sometimes with outright hostility—upon the old urban privilege to protect the city through fortifications. But the French Crown was not entirely hostile to the idea of urban fortifications: even while defortifying many French towns, it refortified others and even built new fortresses along the country's borders. Ultimately, the Crown's defortification policies in the seventeenth century strove to turn France itself into a "fortified city" of sorts—commercially active, populated, and demilitarized internally; defended by fortification lines along its borders; and surrounded on its exposed side by a moat (the Rhine River) and a glacis (its right bank). In brief, Crown policies toward urban fortification were dialectical in nature, encompassing both destruction and construction: an attack on the city's traditional, fortified form but also a transformation of this very form onto the level of the state.[2]

An analysis of defortification policies in seventeenth-century France provides one way to understand the complex relationships between state, city, and walls. Two opposing arguments characterize historiographical debates about the nature of the relationship between the French Crown and its cities during the seventeenth century. Some historians, following de Tocqueville, have claimed that the Crown's relationship with its cities was based on subjugation.[3] More recent studies have emphasized the occasional cooperative relationship in early modern France between the Crown and urban elites.[4] An exploration of the Crown's defortification policies demonstrates that these two seemingly irreconcilable interpretative traditions are not necessarily mutually exclusive. At the same time the Crown was subjugating many of France's *bonnes villes* through the demolition of their walls, it was also constructing new fortifications and refashioning the many qualities or the form of the fortified city to serve in the overall defense of the state. What, then, was the nature of the dialectics of urban form in seventeenth-century France? What was its political significance? Who stood behind it? For what reasons and with what results? To answer these questions, this chapter looks back to the seventeenth century, first providing a short description of the physical form and various roles of city walls in the early modern period, and then continuing with an assessment of three related stages in defortification policies in absolutist France: (1) the demolition of chateaux and urban fortifications under Richelieu, (2) the creation of the *ceinture de fer* ("iron belt") by Louvois and Vauban, and (3) the "annihilation policies" of Louis XIV on the right bank of the Rhine during the War of the League of Augsburg. It concludes by examining the significance of defortification as a physical expression of the complex relationship between Crown and city in seventeenth-century France.

The City and Its Walls

Lexical definitions of the city in the seventeenth and eighteenth centuries almost always underscored that a place was entitled to be called a town or a city only if it was surrounded by physical walls. "A city," we find in the first edition of the *Dictionnaire de l'Académie française* (1694), "is a collection of many buildings and houses spread along streets and enclosed by a communal physical barrier, which is usually made out of walls and a moat."[5] This exact definition would be used in all the editions of the Académie's dictionary during the eighteenth century.[6] Even in Diderot's *Encyclopédie* this definition is repeated, with a short addition. "[I]n order to define the city more precisely," Jaucourt, the entry's author, writes, "it is [first of all] a walled settlement, which contains several quarters, streets, public places and other buildings."[7] A city, Jaucourt makes clear, is, to be precise, a walled settlement; the settlement's quarters, streets, public places, and other buildings are secondary to its definition. The centrality of protection to the city's lexical definition can be found in Germany at this time, too. Across the Rhine men of letters used very similar terms to define the city in the seventeenth, eighteenth, and sometimes even the nineteenth centuries. An unfortified place is simply not a city, argued the prominent jurist Johann Heinrich Gottlob von Justi (1717–71), for instance. A settlement can be big, beautiful, or densely populated, but if it is not surrounded by a wall, von Justi writes, "it lacks the most important sign [*Wahrzeichen*] of a city and should therefore not be called by that name."[8]

The idea of the city as a protected, walled settlement was not just a lexical phenomenon but also reflected the actual usage of the term "city" in the seventeenth and eighteenth centuries. Thus, in the prolific correspondence of the leading figures in France's military establishment in the late seventeenth century, the word "demolition" and the expression "to raze a city to the ground" (Fr. *raser*) are used in a restricted sense. They signal only the destruction of the city's fortifications, *not* the destruction of the city's footprint. These acts were equivalent to demolishing a city's defenses, because by doing so one turned the city "back" into a village. We should therefore not be surprised to find that in Louvois's correspondence a city he just "demolished" or "razed" reappears in his missives within a month or even a week with its buildings and streets intact and its inhabitants unharmed. Its walls demolished, the settlement's status as a city was taken away; the city, as such, was gone.[9] Such deployment of the term "city" and the verb "to raze" could be found in contemporary German as well. Indeed, as late as the first decade of the nineteenth century Goethe would still claim, via Charlotte, one of the characters in *Elective Affinities*, that newly defortified cities were not cities at all.[10] The fact that the market, the streets, the churches, and all other buildings were left intact did not matter. With the destruction of their walls, these settlements ceased to be cities and turned back into unbounded, rural communities (*große Flecken*).

Urban fortifications had military, police, economic, and legal functions. They allowed inspection of the movement in and out of the city, they facilitated taxation of locals and foreigners alike, and they usually marked the borders of the city's legal jurisdiction. At this convergence of boundaries it was also most appropriate to present the city's symbols and coat of arms. When princes, bishops, or ambassadors visited a city, it greeted the visitors at its gates according to strict ceremonial protocol (the famous *entrée*, or royal entry). To demolish the walls, then, constituted an assault on the city's symbolic form: the way the urban community defined or imagined itself, the way the community made a distinction between (literal) insiders and outsiders.

Generally speaking, seventeenth-century European cities had three interrelated parts: the built environment, the fortifications, and the glacis. The built environment—the streets and the public and private buildings—went unfortified, an expression of the burghers' liberties within the walls. Around the city's interior lay the city's fortifications, constructed (in well-fortified cities) according to star-shaped geometrical patterns—the famous *trace italienne*—and surrounded by moats. Finally, beyond the walls and the moats lay the glacis, a downward slope stretching from the city's walls toward the fields around it, providing the city's gunners with a clear field of fire in case of a siege. The glacis was either completely devoid of tall vegetation and buildings or contained only structures that could, if necessary, be quickly demolished.

The many defortifications of French cities during the seventeenth century consequently entailed a simultaneous attack on the city's ability to protect itself militarily, to police itself, and to tax its population; an attack on the old lexical definition of cities and their legal definition; and an attack on the urban community's tradition and even honor. But at the same time that the Crown resorted to such policies, it also used metaphors drawn from the practice of fortifying cities to construe itself, even using the three-part form of the fortified city—built environment, fortification, and glacis—as a model for the state as a whole. It was by no means the *only* model for the state, but it was certainly an important one. By the end of the seventeenth century France too shared three key characteristics with the old city: it would be internally defortified, it would have lines of fortifications along its borders, and it would even strive to create a moat and a glacis beyond these lines. This dialectical process, encompassing both large-scale destruction and enormous projects of construction, progressed chronologically, starting in the state's hinterland, continuing near the borders, and finally reaching beyond the state's boundaries into Germany with the creation of a glacis of enormous size beyond the Rhine.

Defortifying the Hinterland

Already in the *Estates General* of 1588 (Blois) we hear of a plan to dismantle France's internal fortifications.[11] In the context of the political turmoil of the civil wars, the Third Estate demanded that the newly built citadels of the nobility be demolished.[12] But only three decades later one finds the beginning of a systematic royal policy of defortification under Cardinal Richelieu. As in 1588, the defortification suggested in the 1620s took place in the context of the Wars of Religion. Now targets included not only the chateaux, but also cities used by the Huguenots as military bases. In 1626 Richelieu ordered the defortification of as many Huguenot bases as possible, and three years later, after Louis XIII's army finally managed to take the Huguenot stronghold of La Rochelle (which the king immediately defortified as a symbolic act to signal the reduction of the city to the status of a village), the order was reiterated: "Now that La Rochelle is taken," Richelieu wrote, "if the King wants to become the most powerful monarch in the world ... he has to consider carefully and secretly ... the situation of both his person and his state."[13] In terms of the French state, Richelieu claimed, the situation had two separate but related aspects: one concerning the state's interior, the other relating to foreign affairs. In terms of internal policy the most important task facing the monarch was the "destruction of the rebellion of heresy, and the taking of Castres, Nismes, Montauban and all other fortified positions in Languedoc, Rouergue, and Guyenne." Defortification, it now became clear, was the order of the day: "[o]ne needs to defortify [*raser*]," Richelieu continued, "all the places that are not close to the country's frontiers, do not protect river passages, or do not allow the state to control important, mutinous cities."[14]

The scope of defortification during this period is not known with certainty because the edict's execution was often left to individual communities. That defortification took place in many cities, however, is unquestionable. The peace of Alais (28 June 1629) contains a stipulation that close to forty Huguenot *places de sûreté* should be defortified, and the subsequent defortification wave affected cities as different—and as distant—as Angers, Buis les Baronnies, Chantelle, La Rochelle, Loudon, Mévouillons, Montauban, Mortemart, Namur, and Nyons.[15] In the Dauphiné alone, where the local assembly of notables adapted Richelieu's order after 1626, and then again after the siege of La Rochelle, dozens of cities and chateaux were affected. These included Livron, Vienne, Valence, Die, Embrun, Nyons, and Puymore. Other cities, such as Briançon, Crest, Grenoble, Montélimar, and Valence, did not physically demolish their walls in the seventeenth century but neglected their fortifications to such an extent that by the end of the century they had lost all military value.[16] All of this is not only important as an indication of the scope of the defortification waves of the early-seventeenth century, for as the case of the Dauphiné demonstrates, and as historian Michael Wolfe reminds us, not all defortifications were imposed on particular cities. In many cases local assemblies agreed to and even assisted in the defortification of cities and towns.[17]

The early defortification cases in France were politically motivated. By defortifying such towns and chateaux, the French Crown rendered them defenseless, unable to fight each other or militarily oppose the king's sovereign will. Only along the borders and at strategically important points in France's interior did the Crown strive to keep some fortified cities. In this respect the Crown's policies amounted to a direct attack both on specific cities and on the old definition of the city as a fortified place. But Richelieu's thoughts in the wake of the siege of La Rochelle already indicate the Janus face of such attacks. As the Crown demolished fortified places so that the king, in Richelieu's words, might be "obeyed by great and small" alike, it also slowly assimilated qualities of the fortified city, repurposing them for the overall defense of the state.[18] In the very same document in which he urged his king to demolish fortified towns in

France's hinterland, Richelieu deployed metaphors stemming from the fortified city to conceptualize a defense strategy for the state:

> In terms of foreign policy, one needs to have a general plan for stopping the progress of Spain ... France, consequently, has to think about *how to fortify itself* and how to build gates and open others [*batir, et s'ouvrir des portes*] in order to enter into all of its neighboring countries.... One must fortify very strongly border towns ... and consider fortifying Metz and an advance on Strasbourg in order to have a possible entrance into Germany.... And one should turn Versoy into a great fortress ... to have, as it were, an open gate into Switzerland.[19]

For the first time, perhaps, we see here the full scope of the dialectics of absolutist urban form in seventeenth-century France. Richelieu urges his king to demolish *and* construct, to attack the fortifications of specific cities *and* to fortify France, to raze fortifications to the ground while at the same time "batir, et s'ouvrir des portes" for the state.

There was nothing "natural" or inevitable about the defortifications of the 1620s and 1630s. They were not the result of the "uselessness" of urban fortification at the time or of urban expansion. Rather, defortification was the result of human choice and political will, of edicts and communal decisions, and sometimes (though not always) of military action. Most important, defortification was the result of a novel political philosophy and political culture— absolutism—that denied recognition to boundaries within the state while emphasizing the boundaries between states. Thus, even in those places where physical barriers between city and countryside continued to exist in the seventeenth century, their symbolic roles were nonetheless thoroughly undermined. In Marseilles the Sun King deliberately avoided entering the city through the *porte réale* (the traditional site of the king's *entrée* into the city) in 1660, preferring to make a new break in the walls to avoid tacitly acknowledging the city's republican past.[20] Indeed, beginning in the 1660s no Bourbon monarch would have any elaborate *entrée* ceremony into a French city for over a century.[21] Such a ceremonial practice would have meant the recognition of France's internal boundaries, and the absolutist monarchy's very nature worked against such recognition.

The inherently political nature of the early defortifications in France becomes even clearer by comparing the situation in absolutist France with neighboring Germany, where no local prince began to defortify his cities until well into the eighteenth century.[22] The solution to the political upheaval in France, as it slowly evolved from Richelieu's time onward, was rooted in the idea of the king's undivided sovereignty—hence the attempt to demilitarize any corporation or individual who threatened the king's power. Seventeenth-century Germans faced a similar problem of civil wars and religious strife but reached an exact opposite political conclusion. In Germany the eventual solution to religious conflicts, as it emerged in the peace treaties of Westphalia (1648), was to ensure that none of the Reich's princes, including the emperor himself, could attain the means to threaten the independence of the empire's members. The Reich, it was therefore agreed, should have neither a standing army nor any fortress towns under its direct control. If the Reichstag declared a general war, the emperor was entitled to raise an imperial army and use existing fortified cities in the empire to support his campaigns. But it had been the general consensus ever since the mid-seventeenth century that the emperor and the Reichstag should have no say in the construction of new fortifications in the cities and no right to interfere with the decisions of particular territorial states to fortify or defortify their cities and towns. Such provisions were recognized as constitutional liberties accorded to members of the Reich. The construction of modern fortifications in seventeenth- and eighteenth-century Germany was never, and could never have become, a general matter for the empire, as in France. That practically all urban fortifications in Germany survived the seventeenth century (with the important exception of the western provinces, as will be discussed below) while such a massive demolition surge swept neighboring France was the physical manifestation of the two different political cultures east and west of the Rhine, not of anything "natural" or inescapable in terms of demography or developments in military technology.

Fortifying the State Boundaries

While the first stage in turning France into a kind of a fortified city writ large concerned the defortification of the hinterland, the second stage concerned the borders. The dialectics of urban form with respect to state borders is stated in one of the most important documents of French military history: Vauban's letter to Louvois from January 1673, in which the idea of the *pré carré* (the "square field") is first explicitly stated. Note that even in this letter, famous for Vauban's suggestion that many new fortresses needed to be built, the construction of urban fortifications and the demolition of city walls go hand in hand: they are not opposing practices but part of a larger plan. "But seriously, *Monseigneur*," Vauban wrote to the war minister only two years after Paris had been defortified in 1671:

> [T]he King must think a little about making his *pré carré*. I do not like this confusion of friendly and hostile places *pêle-mêles. You should keep one of every three of your fortified places*; your people, as it stands, are tormented, your expenditures too high, and your forces overstretched; and it is almost impossible to keep all your fortresses in a good state and arm them properly. Moreover, if, in the conflicts we so often have with our neighbors, we shall, God forbid, find ourselves one day in a minority, the majority of our fortified places will go as they came.

This is why, either through a treaty or through military actions, *Monseigneur*, preach always the straight lines, not the circle, but the *pré*.[23]

Vauban's plan to defend France's borders in a novel way had major consequences for many French cities and indeed for all of France. Vauban not only proposed that internal fortifications be demolished (as Richelieu had ordered four decades earlier in the wake of the siege of La Rochelle), but he also suggested that two of every three fortress towns on France's borders be defortified, citing strategic and financial considerations. Otherwise, he claimed, the king might run into political and financial problems: residents of fortress towns would become frustrated with the presence of state troops, and military expenses would empty the state treasury. And indeed, though Vauban helped create the greatest chain of fortresses ever built on European soil, as he is usually portrayed in history books or museum exhibitions to have done, he was not just a great builder: he also engaged in the demolition of many fortresses considered too weak or insufficiently advantageous for the defense of the state geopolitically, especially during the 1690s.[24]

The symbolism of French fortifications was as important as their practical benefits. The king's sovereignty extended throughout his lands, stopping only at their frontiers. In much the same way that the city walls symbolized the strength of the urban community (and were therefore demolished or ignored by the absolutist monarchy), the boundaries of the kingdom were an excellent place in which to demonstrate the king's sovereign power.[25] Crucial military fortress towns were consequently also important symbolic elements in the construction of the state's boundaries. One eighteenth-century writer, observing Vauban's *ceinture de fer*, put this idea as follows:"the quantity of artillery pieces placed on the ramparts [of a border-fortress], the well-supplied, orderly arsenals; all these *announce* the monarch's might."[26] From a practical perspective the defortification of France's hinterland and the construction of a cordon of fortress towns along the kingdom's perimeter were very closely related. Once France's internal fortifications were gone, strengthening its borders was crucial to preventing an invasion of the country's vulnerable interior, and once the country's external borders were refortified, it became easier to persist in defortifying the hinterland. The two processes relied on one another. But one should not conclude from the demolition of city walls in France's hinterland—and especially the Parisian ramparts after 1671—that the king no longer wanted symbols of his military power in those cities, as historian Colin Jones has suggested.[27] The city walls had both immense physical presence and great symbolic power; they were an indispensable part of every urban community and an essential element in almost every lexical definition of the city in the seventeenth and eighteenth centuries. This is why it was the absence of the Parisian ramparts, for instance, that contemporaries found so conspicuous, why they felt that the lack of military defenses had to be explained.[28]

Along the country's borders the king "announced" his power through the physical presence of the fortresses, visible signs of the king's sovereignty. By demolishing the ramparts in Paris and other French cities, the king put this same might on display by way of an absence. He proclaimed that inside the state's territory his sovereignty was literally indivisible. Demolishing his capital's ramparts also demonstrated that he no longer needed what practically every other prince in seventeenth-century continental Europe so eagerly sought, a fortified residence for a rainy day. The Sun King projected a different image: he was a stronger, more powerful monarch than any of his peers or predecessors. Their fortified residences showed their inherent weakness; his open residence demonstrated his power. The demolition of the Parisian ramparts and of French city walls more generally did not, therefore, undo the ostentatious display of military power in cities. On the contrary, it created an ostentatious display of a novel form of political power, perhaps physically invisible but conspicuous and awe-inspiring nonetheless.

The Glacis

Fifteen years after Vauban's letter to Louvois, when the work on France's fortifications in the northwest was already well under way, Louis XIV decided to wage war on the Holy Roman Empire. This had very little to do with his stated rationale, a desire to protect the rightful succession to the archbishop of Cologne. Indeed, the disastrous consequences of the Sun King's decision to invade the western parts of the empire caused great distress to Elisabeth-Charlotte, the second wife of Monsieur (Louis XIII's second surviving son, Philippe I, Duke of Orléans) and the woman on whose behalf the Sun King supposedly invaded the empire. In the wake of the siege of Philippsburg in 1688, she noted to the Dauphin (who was involved in the siege) that "if you take my advice, you will remain at home, for I own to you that I feel grieved, not pleased, at the thought that my name will be used to ruin my own poor country."[29] A short time thereafter, after hearing about the preparations for the siege and destruction of Mannheim, she noted in her diary how "[i]t makes my heart bleed, yet they [the king and his generals] are angry at my grief."[30] Louis XIV, in other words, was not concerned with Elisabeth Charlotte's claims to parts of the Palatinate. Instead, he used her name as an excuse to wage war on both sides of the Rhine and to execute what French historian Camille Rousset would later call the "Glacis Theory."[31]

The campaign in the Palatinate, Baden, Swabia, and even parts of Franconia progressed rapidly from the autumn of 1688 onward. The French attacked Philipsburg in the fall of 1688 and after the city's surrender in October continued to attack other cities in the region: Mannheim, Frankenthal, Oppenheim, Kaiser-slauten, Heidelberg, Speyer, and Mainz, among others. After the troops settled into their winter quarters and the circles of the empire prepared their counter-offensive, French forces defortified an occupied zone about fifty miles wide and over two hundred miles long. By March 1689 they had begun to physically de-molish entire cities in addition to defortifying them. Heidelberg was set ablaze and Mannheim completely destroyed; Speyer, Oppenheim, Bingen, and many dozens of smaller fortresses, towns, and villages were either defortified or set to the torch. The campaigns reached as far inland as the city of Pforzheim in the Black Forest, a city whose fortifications the French had partially undermined in 1689, though not completely destroyed, because of the approaching imperial forces.[32]

The plan to defortify the Palatinate had little to do with the progression of the war. It had been conceived before the war began, it was executed during the war regardless of the position of the German troops, and it continued to serve as a desirable political and military aim long after the war. And so we find Lou-vois at the beginning of the campaign writing to one of his generals concerning Mannheim:

> I see the King disposed to completely demolish [*raser*] the city and the citadel, and in such a case to entirely demolish the buildings so that *no stone would be left on the other*, and in the future, after a peace treaty, no Elector will be able to rebuild it. His Majesty also wishes that this project will be kept highly secret for the time being. You can communicate it [to your generals] with the order that [they] should not utter a single word about it to anyone.[33]

In the following year, when the French left the cities they had occupied, the defortification order was reiterated. Louvois wrote at the time to Montclar that "His Majesty orders you to destroy all the places you have been occupying from the upper to the lower river Neckar, so that the enemy would not find there any subsistence, nor would be even able to approach this area."[34] And in those places they had to leave in a hurry, such as Heidelberg, it was noted that although they were unable to complete the defortification of the entire zone over the Rhine at that point, in the future "we shall certainly do a better job."[35]

Both contemporaries and later historians spilled much ink on this bru-tal policy, trying to come to terms with its reasoning. The Comte de Mélac (1630–1704) himself—the chief executioner of the scorched earth policy in the Palatinate—is reputed to have said upon receiving the order to destroy Pforzheim that "it must be the devil himself who presides over the *conseil de guerre* in Paris."[36] Vauban, too, was alarmed by the brutality and the logic of such an endeavor. He argued that defortification on such a scale was senseless and suggested to Louvois that one must resort to political negotiations rather than brutal force in determining the fate of the Palatinate.[37] Modern historians raised similar questions about the French campaign's overall logic in the Palatinate. On the one hand we find especially German historians of the 1930s, who saw Louis XIV's actions during the war as nothing but a sign of the French's "spirit of annihilation" (*Zerstörungsgeist*), condemning the lack of any moral— or for that matter military—justification.[38] On the other hand French historians, foremost among them Louvois's biographer Camille Rousset, claimed that the decisions of 1688–89 had been the result of a "glacis theory": an attempt to create an empty belt, devoid of fortification but not necessarily inhabitants, beyond France's new fortification lines.[39] With Vauban's fortresses on the Rhine's left bank, with the Rhine itself as a kind of a moat (and in that respect, as a natural border), and with the destruction of a wide belt beyond the river, Rousset and others saw a flawed but nevertheless explainable policy. It is important to note the political context of this *Historikerstreit*: while Rousset's work had been written in the 1860s, German historians' responses arrived only in the 1930s, at a time of heated debate about the demilitarization of Germany's western provinces in the wake of the Treaty of Versailles. In short, there was more to these debates than a disinterested scholarly dispute about what happened in and to the Palatinate in the late seventeenth century.

In more recent years, historian John A. Lynn set out to battle the "glacis theory"—in an otherwise fascinating essay about the events in the Palatinate—by claiming that the term "glacis" is "a poor" and "strange metaphor" for what the French were doing in the Palatinate.[40] He makes this claim even though he also demonstrates how Louis XIV's policies during the War of the League of Augsburg were intended "to create an artificial desert that would preclude the enemy from undertaking offensive operations"—a seventeenth-century "glacis," after all, was exactly this kind of "artificial desert" or "no-man's-land" stretching outward from the fortress walls.[41] This specific argument in Lynn's essay is based upon his important observation that the building of a fortress and the construction of the defense of a whole state are not identical and therefore ought not to be conflated. In this he is undoubtedly right. But one needs to be careful here and distinguish between "is" and "ought": the fact that the French, for both military and moral reasons, ought not to have constructed a glacis of immense dimensions in the Palatinate does not mean they had not done so in practice. As we saw, Richelieu used metaphors borrowed from military history, in particular regarding the defense of the city, when he spoke about the defense of the state. In the seventeenth and eighteenth centuries he was by no means the only European to do so. In the early modern period it was common practice to compare certain cordons of fortresses along the state's boundaries with the "outer-works" of a single fortress, to call rivers along the state's boundaries "moats," or to compare certain fortresses, as Richelieu did in the 1620s, with "gates."[42] Furthermore, considering the overall evolution of French fortification and defortification policies in the seventeenth century, the plausibility of

Rousset's glacis theory is strengthened. The attempt to create a huge "demili-tarized zone" beyond the Rhine seems to have been the logical consequence of the policies pursued by the French Crown beginning in the 1620s. France was internally defortified and had fortification lines along its borders and even a moat in the Rhine River. The only thing it lacked was a glacis.

If any further proof is needed for the fact that French engineers and generals often conflated the form of the fortified city and the form of the fortified state, then Louis de Cormontaigne (1695–1752), Vauban's most important student, provides it. Two decades after the destruction of the Palatinate, Cormontaigne set out to analyze and summarize the events of the preceding few decades in terms of what he called the "space of the state" and its defense.[43] To his theo-retical treaty he also added a series of maps, by which he explained how a state could be best protected by the creation of an empty, demilitarized territory within its borders and lines of fortifications along its frontiers. When Cormon-taigne's maps and drawings are compared to a typical drawing of a well-fortified early modern city, the close resemblance is striking.[44] For Cormontaigne, the main difference between the defense of the city and the defense of the state was the scale. Otherwise they were almost identical. The fortified city provided Cormontaigne with a fundamental model for the defense and, indeed, the over-all "space" of a kingdom. One should keep this in mind—as well as the many other instances when a state's fortifications were compared to city walls in the seventeenth and eighteenth centuries—when dismissing out of hand the very real possibility that the creation of an enormous glacis in the Palatinate was exactly what Louis XIV had intended.

Why did the city's defense system serve as a source of metaphors for—and perhaps even of actual practices in—the defense of the state? Why did absolut-ist France, which did so much to undermine the idea of the fortified city, end up resembling a fortified urban system at the scale of the state? I am not sug-gesting here that the dialectics of urban form in the seventeenth and eighteenth centuries was an uncomplicated, literal transposition of the form of the city onto the form of the state. The state itself was not, obviously, a fortress, nor did anyone in the early seventeenth century (Richelieu included) set up a plan to transform the state into one. My claim about the inherent dialectics of urban form in seventeenth-century France relies on a different and more nuanced ar-gument. First, defortification and fortification were two sides of the same coin. They were not opposing practices but complementary ones: an understanding on the one hand that individual cities needed to be defortified as a response to the revolts of the nobility and the religious wars, but also the realization on the other hand that the state now more than ever had a need to assure the overall security of its vulnerable interior by establishing strong, fortified cities along the borders. The two processes relied on each other; viewed together, they do not constitute a contradiction but a synthesis.

The long-standing dual process of defortification and fortification also makes clear that the form France's defenses took in the seventeenth century was not simply the result of a "chain reaction" of tactical considerations. Rather, terms and modes of thought stemming from urban fortifications served as metaphors for the defense of a state that did its best to demolish most of its cities' walls. Cormontaigne's thoughts and drawings on the subject of the "space of the state" demonstrate this better than any other document. This can be best explained in terms of the structure of military theory at the time. Only from the mid eighteenth century on do we find in military theory the modern, clear division, so self-evident today, between tactics and strategy. For us, strategy concentrates on the abstract or higher conduct of warfare *for the state*. On the other hand, tactics focuses today on the lower and mechanical level of war in that physical encounter we call a battle. Seventeenth-century French generals lived at a time when this now clear division still lay in the future. Richelieu, Louvois, Louis XIV, Cormontaigne, and to a lesser extent even Vauban thought that these two levels of military practice were in fact analogous: specifically, defense of a country was comparable (though not completely identical) to the defense of a fortified city. For this reason they took the existing repertoire of terms (and even, as Cormontaigne's case demonstrate, the very geometry) from the defense of the city—back then the most advanced and sophisticated of all military matters—and raised it to a common metaphor for the defense of the state in general. This too is why with hindsight one can criticize their actions but also why one cannot claim with Lynn that they could not have done it. In the seventeenth century it was not yet clear that there might be a fundamental difference between these two realms of military theory.

It is true, however, that it did not take long for contemporaries to realize that something was askew with the elevation of terms stemming from the defense of a single place to the level of the defense of the entire state. Vauban was probably one of the first to draw attention to the fact that the different dimensions (in the plural) that distinguished the state's defense from the city's defense turned strategy into a realm of knowledge of a different dimension (now in the singular) from tactics, and that to think about the state's defense in terms of the defense of a fortified city could be a fundamental error, based on a false epistemological conflation between two realms of knowledge that should be kept analytically apart. It is one thing, for instance, to create a glacis of a few hundred meters around a city; it is quite a different issue (politically and practically) to strive to create a glacis of a few dozen miles beyond the country's fortification lines. For better or worse (mostly, it seems, for worse), the conflation of tactical with strategic matters remained characteristic of French military operations throughout the eighteenth, nineteenth, and even parts of the twentieth century, up through the most extreme logical expression of the dialectics of urban form in the French case: the construction of the Maginot Line in the 1930s. From the seventeenth century on, the idea of the state as a kind of a city writ large was part of the French geostrategic imagination, a hegemonic spatial concept that seemed to lose its power only after the debacle of the summer of 1940.

Conclusion

The dialectics of urban form in the seventeenth century—the dual process of defortification and fortification and the lifting-up (*Aufhebung*) of terms from the defense of a single city to that of the state as a whole—should not be of interest to military historians alone. It should also interest historians of absolutism as a political culture and, for that matter, all historians who write about borders. For historians of absolutism, the dialectics of urban form in seventeenth-century France provides a possible model with which to tackle larger questions about the relationship between Crown and city. Current historiographical debates about French absolutism concentrate, as mentioned earlier, on the question of whether the Crown imposed its will on cities or politically negotiated an absolutist relationship with them. However, this important, indeed crucial discussion has evolved in such a manner that historians appear to be trapped in a binary opposition that can lead to a methodological impasse. After all, for every example of the imposition of the Crown's will on a city one finds a counterexample of negotiation and vice versa. For every La Rochelle, if you will, there is a Marseille; for every Loudon a Dijon, and so forth.[45] As long as historians remain trapped in this logic, a fundamental historical development remains understudied: under absolutism the city was much more than a site of imposition or negotiation. At the same time that the ancient physical form and lexical definition of the city as a fortified place were under attack, the city also served as an important source of metaphors for the form or "space" of the absolutist state itself. This is true in military terms (now the state, too, had fortifications, gates, and perhaps even a glacis) as well as in other realms. Most important, consider the market—both as a real, physical entity in the city and as an abstract concept for the state's economy. The relationship between Crown and city was consequently not a question of either-or (imposition versus negotiation) but rather a dialectical one: a relationship that included an attack on the old form of the city *and* a synthesis of this form from a physical and particular one onto the level of the state. In an important sense, then, the absolutist state not only undermined the old form of the city, but also preserved it through imitation, adaptation, and synthesis, extending it into a broader realm.

What is true for the history of absolutist practices in France is also true for historians of any field who are interested in questions about boundaries and "space." Boundaries by definition create an opposition between two entities: between states, regions, people, and diverse social groups. But this very fact should not lead one to tell and analyze the *stories* of boundaries in a binary fashion as well.[46] The construction and demolition of boundaries sometimes have quite unexpected, even paradoxical, consequences. In the case of the demolition of the centuries-old physical boundaries of French cities in the seventeenth and eighteenth centuries, one such unexpected consequence was that, while the absolutist monarchy strove to demolish so many of its cities' walls, it also adopted the many qualities of the fortified city onto the general level of the state. Another unexpected consequence was that the very monuments the state now took over from its burghers would later serve against it. Is it not worth mentioning that the French Revolution's most important symbolic event was the storming of the Bastille, a monument originally built as part of the old fortifications of Paris? Is it not paradoxical that Louis XVI's flight to Varennes (June 1791) was stopped near one of those fortresses Vauban built to defend the very existence of the absolutist French monarchy?

Notes

1. For a full discussion of defortification and its historical significance see Yair Mintzker, *The Defortification of the German City, 1689–1866* (New York, forthcoming 2012).
2. Compare with Joan E. DeJean, *Literary Fortifications: Rousseau, Laclos, Sade* (Princeton, 1984), who claims that seventeenth-century France became a kind of a fortress but overlooks the dialectics inherent in the transformation of France into a fortified city. On urban fortification in early seventeenth-century France see Michael Wolfe, *Walled Towns and the Shaping of France: From the Medieval to the Early modern Period* (New York, 2009).
3. Nora Temple, "The Control and Exploitation of French Towns during the Ancien Regime," *History* 51 (1967): 16–34.
4. Hilary J. Bernstein, *Between Crown and Community: Politics and Civic Culture in Sixteenth-Century Poitiers* (Ithaca, 2004).
5. "Ville," *Dictionnaire de L'Académie Française* (1694), 644. ARTFL Dictionnaires d'autrefois (Winter 2009 edition, accessed October 2009), ed. Robert Morrissey, http://artfl-project.uchicago.edu/.
6. Only in the sixth edition (1832–35) do we find the first qualification of this definition: "A city is a collection of buildings ... *usually* enclosed by a communal barrier" (my italics). "Ville," *Dictionnaire de l'Académie française* (1832–35), 2: 937. ARTFL, ibid.
7. Louis de Jaucourt, "Ville," in *Encyclopédie, ou dictionnaire raisonné des sciences, des arts et des métiers*, ed. Denis Diderot and Jean le Rond D'Alembert. ARTFL, ibid., 17: 277.
8. Johann Heinrich Gottlob von Justi, *Staatswirtschaft*, vol. 1 (Leipzig, 1758), 491.
9. Camille Rousset, *Histoire de Louvois et de son administration politique et militaire*, 3rd ed., vol. 4 (Paris, 1863), 160.
10. Johann Wolfgang von Goethe, *Elective Affinities*, trans. R. J. Hollingdale (Harmondsworth, 1971), 217–18.

11. George-Marie-René Picot, *Histoire des États généraux considérés au point de vue de leur influence sur le gouvernment de la France de 1355 à 1614*, 4 vols. (Paris, 1872), 3: 214–15, 321, 441–42.

12. Ibid., 3: 214–15.

13. Armand Jean du Plessis, duc de Richelieu, *Letres d'vn solitaire av Roy, princes, et seigneurs faisans la guerre aux Rebelles* (Poitiers, 1628); and Pierre Grillon, *Les Papiers de Richelieu: Section Politique Intérieure, Correspondance et Papiers d'État* [1629], vol. 4 (Paris, 1980), 24.

14. Grillon, *Les Papiers de Richelieu*, 4: 25.

15. *Articles de la grâce accordée par le Roy au duc de Rohan, et autres ses subjects rebelles, de la Religion prétendue réformée, envoyés par S.M. à M. d'Halincourt* (Lyon, 1629).

16. For the case of the Dauphiné see René Favier, *Les Villes du Dauphiné aux XVIIe et XVIIIe Siècles: La Pierre et l'Ecrit* (Grenoble, 1993), 140–45.

17. Wolfe, *Walled Towns*.

18. Grillon, *Les Papiers de Richelieu*, 4: 25.

19. Ibid., 4: 25–26 (my italics).

20. André Zysberg, *Marseille au Temps du Roi-Soleil: La Ville, les Galères, l'Arsenal, 1660 à 1715* (Marseille, 2007), 55ff.

21. Simon Schama, *Citizens: A Chronicle of the French Revolution* (New York, 1990), 57.

22. For a full account of the German case see Mintzker, *The Defortification of the German City*.

23. Albert de Rochas d'Aiglun, *Vauban, sa Famille et ses Écrits, ses Oisivetés et sa Correspondance: Analyse et Extraits*, vol. 2 (Geneva, 1972), 89 (my italics).

24. See Daniel Halévy, *Vauban* (Paris, 1923); Isabelle Warmoes and Victoria Sanger, eds., *Vauban, bâtisseur du Roi-Soleil* (Paris, 2007); Geoffrey Parker, *The Military Revolution: Military Innovation and the Rise of the West, 1500–1800* (New York, 1988), 41–43.

25. On the question of state-building, national identity, and borderlands see Peter Sahlins, *Boundaries: The Making of France and Spain in the Pyrenees* (Berkeley, 1989).

26. Joseph de Fallois, *L'École de la Fortification ou les éléments de la fortification permanente, régulière et irrégulière* (Dresden, 1768), 45 (my italics).

27. Colin Jones, *Paris: Biography of a City* (London, 2004), 161.

28. On Paris's changing boundaries in the seventeenth century see Pierre Lavedan, *Histoire de l'Urbanisme á Paris, Nouvelle Histoire de Paris* (Paris, 1993), 185–99. About the demolition of the ramparts see Nicolas de La Mare, *Traité de la Police* (Amsterdam, 1729).

29. Charlotte-Elizabeth d'Orléans, *Life and Letters of Charlotte Elizabeth* (London, 1889), 31.

30. Ibid., 32.

31. Rousset, *Histoire de Louvois*, 4: 226.

32. Johann Georg Friedrich Pflüger, *Geschichte der Stadt Pforzheim* (Pforzheim, 1862), 508–37.

33. Roland Vetter, *"Kein Stein soll auf dem andern bleiben." Mannheims Untergang während des Pfälzischen Erbfolgekriegs im Spiegel französischer Kriegsberichte* (Heidelberg, 2002), source 71.

34. Ibid., source 78.

35. Ibid., source 118.

36. Quoted in Antoine Béthouart, *Le Prince Eugène de Savoie: Soldat, Diplomate et Mécène* (Paris, 1975), 96.

37. Vetter, "*Kein Stein*," source 41.
38. Kurt Raumer, *Die Zerstörung der Pfalz* (Munich, 1930).
39. Rousset, *Histoire de Louvois*, 98ff.
40. John A. Lynn, "A Brutal Necessity? The Devastation of the Palatinate, 1688–1689," in *Civilians in the Path of War*, ed. Mark Grimsley and Clifford J. Rogers (Lincoln, NE, 2002), 93, n. 57.
41. Ibid., 92–93.
42. Thus, Outer Austria was compared to the "outer works" of the Habsburg monarchy, or the Palatinate to the fortifications of the Holy Roman Empire. See Generallandesarchiv Karlsruhe, Abt. 65, Nr. 1443, *Die neue europäische Fama* (Leipzig, 1735), 1: 612. On moats in the late-eighteenth-century Rhine see Johann Wolfgang von Goethe, *Hermann and Dorothea*, trans. Daniel Coogan (New York, 1966), 17–19. On gates, see Calais in Famianus Strada, *Histoire de la guerre de Flandre* (Brussels, 1712), 29, or Dinant (modern-day Belgium) in Eustache le Noble, *La Pierre de touché politique* (London, 1691), 3.
43. Service Historique de la Défense, Vincennes, France, Archive Collection *Mémoires Historiques*, Item Nr. 1752.
44. Allain Manesson Mallet, *Kriegsarbeit oder Neuer Festungsbau*, trans. Filip van Zesen (Amsterdam, 1672).
45. For the case of Marseille see Junko Takeda, *Between Crown and Commerce: Marseille and the Early Modern Mediterranean* (Baltimore, 2011), 1-77. The case of Loudon is the topic of much scholarly and artistic debate: it served as a model for Aldous Huxley's *The Devils of Loudun*, as well as for an opera, a play, and a movie by (respectively) Krzysztof Penderecki, John Whiting, and Ken Russell. In his recent book on Dijon, Michael Breen argues for a middle way between imposition and cooperation: *Law, City, and King: Legal Culture, Municipal Politics, and State Formation in Early-Modern Dijon* (Rochester, NY, 2007).
46. For recent scholarship on border studies see Vladimir Kolossov, "Theorizing Borders: Border Studies: Changing Perspectives and Theoretical Approaches," *Geopolitics* 10 (2005): 606–32.

CHAPTER 2

~:~

The Camp in the City, the City as Camp
Berlin's Other Guarded Walls

OLAF BRIESE

"The camp" and modernity belong together, like twins. Mass society, mass mobility, and mass bureaucratic domination constitute an organic whole, and "the camp" seems to present a corresponding organizational and architectural model for urban modernity. A longitudinal cross section of Berlin offers a case study of this symbiosis, in particular of the developmental arc that camps have undergone since the early twentieth century. Such a chronology, moreover, demonstrates both how enclosed mass camps fuse with "closed" totalitarian societies on the one hand, and how camps may transform, multiply, and diversify in "open" societies on the other. In spite of historical and political differences in function, all camps exhibit at least one essential similarity: a fortified boundary. This boundary is the decisive hinge between the camp and society. It divides and joins, it includes and excludes in both a real, tangible sense and a symbolic, imaginary one. Using the example of Berlin, this chapter focuses on physical boundaries to explore different types of material-symbolic borders in cities, including walls, barbed wire, fences, and segregated urban residential structures such as ghettos and housing blocks, both of which preceded modern detention, labor, concentration, and extermination camps.[1]

Ghettos in Berlin?

The term "ghetto" is of Italian origin, but its exact etymology has not been clearly traced. In 1516 a law was enacted in Venice requiring the city's Jews to live in the *geto novo*, a plot of land accessible only via a single bridge. Gates were installed, outer walls were bricked up, an evening curfew was enacted, and guards were hired at the expense of the Jews themselves. Yet such ghettos, forced ghettos, existed in Europe before the advent of the word *geto novo*. The driving force behind this legal and physical district was the Roman Catholic Church. One of the first decisive laws decreed by the Third Lateran Council in 1197 stated: "the Jews should not live intermingled with Christians. Rather, they should have their houses in a segregated part of the city or village such that the Jewish district is to be separated from the common living areas of the Christians by a wall, fence, or trench."[2] Forced ghettos like the one in sixteenth-century Venice were subsequently established, including in Trier (1235), Valencia (1390), Frankfurt (1462), and Kraków (1495). Jews faced discrimination against their will, although ghettos offered a semblance of protection in the context of the anti-Jewish phobia created and promoted by the Church and the feudal state in the late Middle Ages. Before these enclaves were recognized as legal minority settlement districts, Jews had created spatial concentrations in European towns and cities, including Berlin. For example, the so-called *Judengassen* (Jewish alleys) or *Judenhöfe* (Jewish housing blocks) provided the positive features typical of dense communal life: short travel times and quick communication routes, territorial solidarity and protection, economic benefits, and a mental cocoon. Dieter Hoffmann-Axthelm describes this self-chosen spatial clustering in Berlin's medieval *Jüdenhof*.[3]

After the National Socialists came to power in 1933, plans for direct, forced ghettoization in Berlin were implemented. However, "creeping" ghettoization through discrimination had already begun. The Jews lost one legal right after another; one discriminatory ruling followed the next. The local population either actively contributed to this exclusionary process or simply ignored their Jewish neighbors. By April 1935 the Berlin rabbi Joachim Prinz noted in the weekly newspaper *Jüdische Rundschau*: "The ghetto for us is the outdoors. At markets, on the roads, in restaurants. The ghetto is everywhere. It has a sign. It is called neighborless."[4] Forbidden areas, that is to say, *negative* ghettoization, strengthened this isolation and spatial segregation. For example, on 6 December 1938 Jews were banned from entering movie theaters, museums, stadiums, and other public venues. The first urban *Tabuzone* (forbidden zone) was declared on the same day; it included the government district as well as the main boulevard, Unter den Linden; in the course of time other zones were added. As of May 1939, official policy forbade Jews from relocating to popular and "fashionable" districts in the western part of Berlin. And on 24 March 1942 Jews were prohibited from using public transportation in the city. The first deportation of Berlin Jews, on 18 October 1941, was destined for the ghetto in Litzmannstadt, today the Polish city of Łódź. Berlin's Jews were literally ghettoized, but it occurred outside the country. Berlin—the city that was to become *judenfrei* (free of Jews)—remained *ghettofrei* (free of ghettos).

On the other hand, there were also plans for direct, forced ghettoization in Berlin. In late summer and fall of 1938, in conjunction with demolition plans for the construction of the world capital "Germania," Hitler's chief architect Albert Speer argued that tenants who became homeless owing to these demolitions should be moved into Jews' homes. Those Jews who in turn became homeless would be either forced to emigrate or moved to a planned *Judensiedlung* (Jewish housing estate) to be located in the northeast Berlin suburb of Buch.[5] This plan was not implemented. Instead, on 30 April 1939 the national Gesetz über Mietverhältnisse mit Juden (Law Concerning Rental Arrangements for Jews) took effect. This law forced Jews to take other Jews into their homes (except in the more affluent neighborhoods). Such a living arrangement came to be called a *Judenhaus* (Jewish house).[6] Additional measures included forced segregation in Jewish hospitals and senior housing, which were gradually transformed into *Sammellager* (detention camps). As of February 1943, four such central detention camps existed. Berlin's Jews were deported mainly from these camps to external ghettos, concentration camps, or extermination camps. Berlin-Germania was to be *judenrein* by 20 April 1943, the Führer's birthday.[7] That goal was not met, for, as an irritated Goebbels remarked in his diary in January of that year, around 4,000 people had already disappeared underground.

The Cosmos of Camps after 1933

Gudrun Schwarz identifies a total of seventeen camp types in her 1990 study of the National Socialist terror regime, including work-education camps, child welfare camps, camps for foreign civilian workers, forced labor camps, police detention camps, "irregular" concentration camps administered by the SA, "regular" concentration camps organized by the SS, ghetto camps, and extermination camps.[8] Except for the last two categories, all of the above camps existed in and around Berlin. *Zwangsarbeiterlager* (forced labor camps) permeated the city. In a memoir of his time as a forced laborer in Berlin, François Cavanna reported that the entire city seemed to be a wooden barracks.[9] In even the smallest corners of the metropolis, islands of tar paper-covered wooden blockhouses popped up, squeezed in among residences, monuments, train stations, and factory buildings. Berlin had mutated into a city of camps. It was a European Babylon, populated by civilians who first came to the city freely but later were taken there under increasing force from nearly all European countries. All told, there were 4,901 such camps within the Autobahn ring around Berlin, concentrated in locations near the armaments industry, such as the districts of Spandau, Köpenick, Treptow, Steglitz, and Charlottenburg, although it is no longer possible today to distinguish real camps from other types of lodging in terms of physical structure.[10] Confinement solutions to the task of corralling forced la-

borers came in many varieties: barbed wire alone, barbed wire shamefully cam-
ouflaged with reeds, wooden walls, factory walls, and dwelling walls. Wherever
one went, a camp was almost always in sight. Whether "unseen" (because of
their location in bars, dance halls, movie theaters, gyms, schools, and factory
halls) or more obviously "visible" (barracks squeezed into the wastelands of the
already overflowing municipal organism), these camps were often overlooked.

Who were the forced laborers? Under various auspices, many different
groups of people were enticed or taken to Berlin from 1939 to 1945.[11] Their
labor proved to be as economically necessary as their social groups were considered to be politically and ideologically undesirable and suspicious. The first
group of forced laborers included foreign civilian workers, so-called *Fremdar-
beiter*. These were male and female workers who came from "allied" countries
(Bulgaria, Italy until 1943, Romania, Hungary, Croatia, and Slovakia) and
were contracted to work for a specific period. At the end of their contract they
could depart the country; thus they were not *Zwangsarbeiter* in a strict sense.
Second, there were forced laborers from European countries who were either
directly deported to Germany and Berlin or arrived there based on a system of
extorted quotas. Members of this group enjoyed a relatively acceptable standard of living and a certain freedom of movement compared to the third group,
forced laborers from Poland and the Soviet Union. This third group from the
east was pitted against a fourth group: prisoners of war, concentration camp
inmates, and Jewish prisoners who were forced to work under camp-like conditions in Berlin, especially during the last years of the war.

The various recruitment goals for attracting forced laborers to Berlin also
underwent visible change as the war progressed. If in the beginning the purpose had been to support the folly of building "Germania, the world's capital
city," once war broke out, deployment for a "bunker-building program" took
precedence. As the regime became increasingly desperate in the war's final years,
deployment in private companies and corporations dominated the armaments
industry. By mid 1944, therefore, Berlin's population was supplemented by a
coerced one of some 400,000 forced laborers. The various categories of workers more or less corresponded to specific types of lodging. Initially there were
private quarters, as well as Albert Speer's plan for a workers' city of "foreign
laborers" in the barracks city known as "Great Hall" in Spandau. But as forced
recruitment increased with the war's progression, there was more pressure to
place everyone together. Simply put, there was a four-class housing hierarchy
that those in power attempted to regulate by law. First, there were private quarters; second, open camps in the style of collective housing; third, relatively open
camps; and fourth, closed camps with varying degrees of confinement.

The fascist state, highly modern in this sense, adhered to a unified, bureaucratic organization for these labor camps. For example, with the offensive
against the Soviet Union, large numbers of forcibly seized *Ostarbeiter* (East-

ern workers), as they were called, streamed into Berlin, and the camp regime intensified. A phobic, barbed-wire fence policy was implemented, draconian observation methods were introduced, and defensive scenarios to deal with possible revolts were gamed out.[12] However, as Soviet forced laborers in particular became known as surprisingly willing workers (having gone from one dictatorship to the other), the restrictions were reduced. To stimulate their productivity, interned persons were granted "leaves"; the use of barbed wire was forbidden for all new forced-labor camps (but was retained where it had already been installed); and only an "enclosure to prevent flight" was prescribed.[13] A law decreed throughout the German Reich on 14 July 1943 mandated that the spatial arrangement of forced labor camps should serve to "preserve the joy of work" and that barriers should merely prevent entry of unauthorized persons *into* the camps.[14] This was a surprising National Socialist charm offensive. On the one hand forced laborers were supposed to be motivated to higher production levels, but on the other the alarming decrease in resources forced savings in how "captivity" was organized. As the end of the war neared, improvisation and on-the-spot modification became the norm in the camps. Officials responsible for respective levels of state decision-making relaxed certain camp restrictions—even for Soviet prisoners of war, who increasingly lived and worked in the city in small groups that were relatively unsupervised. The camp cosmos in its various iterations drifted apart, with each of the various confining structures developing in its own way (fig. 2.1).

Figure 2.1. Forced labor camp Berlin-Schöneweide (now a memorial). Photograph © Olaf Briese.

Not only labor camps but also a tangled web of concentration camps—the translation of horizontal power into a hegemonically occupied vertical space— had begun to proliferate throughout Berlin after 1933. Camp practices had always affected those Jews and other Berliners who were incarcerated and de- ported, but this boom of camps took place directly in Berlin, thereby chang- ing the spatial structure of the city. Immediately after the Reichstag fire at the end of February 1933, numerous so-called *wilde* (irregular) concentration camps were established. Here the SA rabble let off steam, either tolerated or encouraged by police and judicial authorities. They ran riot on opponents who seemingly fell into their hands at random: communists, social democrats, Jews, members of Parliament, intellectuals, pacifists, Christians, those haphazardly denounced, or simply neighbors with whom one had unfinished business. As in other cities, any place that seemed isolated enough to carry out covert, sa- distic torture and to prevent escape was feasible for such a spontaneous con- centration camp: monastery buildings (Breitenau), castles (Dornburg), ships (Bremen), airport terminals (Nohra), aquatic stadiums (Kassel), gymnasiums (Senftenberg), youth hostels (Coburg), sports fields (Radeberg), orphanages (Kyritz). We must also not forget the many *Sturmlokale*—bars where the SA units that frequented them could torture on their home turf, in a manner of speaking. In addition to the SA *Sturmlokale*, many similar spaces of tor- ture were well hidden by walls in Berlin, including the community center in Rosinenstraße, the jail of the district court in Köpenick, the water tower in Prenzlauer Berg (the so-called *Maschinenhaus*), the home for single men in Greifswalder Straße, and the "Universum" state fairgrounds in the district of Moabit, to name a few—around 150 sites in all.[15] Finally, extended periods of torture took place in such facilities as the Gestapo protective custody camp in the "Columbia-Haus" and the concentration camp in the former railway bar- racks in General-Pape-Straße.

Terror from the Architectural Drawing Board

National Socialist camp policies underwent considerable change over time. The "irregular" concentration camp Oranienburg, located near Berlin and used espe- cially for political opponents forcibly brought there from the capital, makes this abundantly clear. At first it was a spontaneous SA camp; then it retroactively became a concentration camp administered and financed by the state govern- ment in Potsdam. Located in a brewery that had been shut down years before, this provisional camp, expanded for nearly 3,000 prisoners, was created on 21 March 1933 and existed for a mere sixteen months. It consisted of an industrial building with a street side that exhibited the usual imposing industrial walls (with guards at the gate), and in back, toward the open fields, it was protected with barbed-wire barriers (anti-tank obstacles). The violent expulsion of the SA, who had previously been tolerated by SS units, occurred on 2 July 1934 in conjunction with the Night of the Long Knives (Röhm Putsch). The SS transported numerous prisoners to other camp facilities and dissolved the Oranienburg camp only a few days thereafter.[16] Here too the spontaneous, "popular," anarchic terror ceased, to become nationalized and systematized "from above." After 1936 it was replaced by the new concentration camp Sachsenhausen, built not too far away in the "open fields" near Oranienburg—the first model for a genuine National Socialist camp. The SS, which had forcibly assumed all responsibility for the concentration camps, sought other solutions—grand solutions—including new modernist architectural designs for camps. These did not merely consist of reworking old spaces. New spaces, *ideal* spaces, had to be procured. Gigantic concentration camps appeared as master-planned cities of terror, the first of which was realized in 1936 with Sachsenhausen.

The Dachau concentration camp in Bavaria also assumed a pioneering role in this development. Installed after 22 March 1933 in a mothballed explosives and munitions factory that was already surrounded by high walls, Himmler (then Munich's police chief) conceived it from its inception as a model camp and training center for SS guard details. The commander of this government-run camp, Theodor Eicke, took over in June 1933; Eicke also played a prominent role in the murder of the SA leader Ernst Röhm, the subsequent demobilization of the SA, and the closure of the SA concentration camps. A few days after Röhm's murder, Eicke was named "Inspector of the Concentration Camps" and "Commander of the SS Guard Details." Using this position of power, he realized his ideal geometric architecture of control and social-geometric oppression throughout Germany. As first implemented in Sachsenhausen, this panoptic spatial structure also shaped the new camp buildings in Dachau beginning in 1937, which thereafter featured the following barrier elements:

> The new camp measured 583 x 278 meters. It was surrounded by a high wall which had four rows of taut and electrically charged barbed wire on top. On the inside of the wall was also an electrically charged barbed wire fence and in front of that a wide tangle of coiled barbed wire. A trench 2.5 meters wide and two meters deep created a further barrier, in front of which lay the three meter wide strip of the "neutral" zone.[17]

Yet Dachau had a decisive flaw: in the end the camp could not cast off its (modest) origins. Its prior history as a former factory complex was part of its historical and structurally embarrassing design.

In contrast, Sachsenhausen was an absolutely new creation. It manifested all the spatial and political criteria for a National Socialist utopian camp: a total camp, a *total institution*, embodying total terror on "virgin land." The one decisive difference was that this utopia became a topos: the ideal, "genuine" camp took on a physical, material form. Sachsenhausen became the model for at least five reasons. First, it was located near the Reich's most populous city, Berlin, where one practically breathed down the necks of one's political opponents. Second, because it was located near the capital, the road to the powerful decision-makers was a short one. Third, Sachsenhausen was segregated enough to avoid unnecessarily confronting the public with everyday terror and to enable quick apprehension of escapees in the hinterland. Fourth, Sachsenhausen was both near enough to—and far enough from—Berlin to cluster certain leadership committees and housing developments for a secret SS central office and to bring in enough SS *Totenkopf* (Death's Head) guard details in case of internal power struggles. And fifth, the camp was sui generis, a completely new creation without need for architectural attention to prior environment or potential precursor edifices. It was an authentic National Socialist site without traces of an earlier architectural civilization.

A bold leap from mere meadows and forests led to total National Socialism in its most genuine form—the ideal type of differentiation between rulers and the ruled. Many vectors of utopian, ideal urban architecture of the early modern period, of the Enlightenment's panoptic control architecture, and of the twentieth century's architecture of *Neues Bauen* (the New Building style of the 1920s) overlapped in Sachsenhausen. The camp also inherited the utopian ring-city designs of the Renaissance and Baroque. The triangular external form, which carried out the Enlightenment ideal of enforcement architecture, enabled optical and panoptic control over the camp. Seriality, striation, and zoning (as in prisoner camps, special zones, troop camps, commanders' areas, SS housing, and production facilities) realized the demands of *Neues Bauen*. Walls were central to these urban designs.

In 1938 and 1939 the Sachsenhausen camp complex surrounded its barbed-wire fence with a wall made of limestone and concrete blocks, similar to the wall at Dachau. A lethal death strip came into existence. The women's concentration camp at Ravensbrück in Fürstenberg, located near Berlin and established in 1938 as a satellite of the Sachsenhausen camp, also was enclosed by a wall. Here it seemed to attain a symbolic meaning as well:

> The camp wall was at once both the architecturally most unassuming and functionally most meaningful structure. Concentration camp expansions always began with the extension of the camp wall.... The wall itself was around four meters high and on the inner side at approximately three meters high there were eight electrically-charged cables, strung parallel and mounted on cantilevered supports with insulators.... For structural reasons the outer camp wall had the characteristic columnar reinforcements.... On the interior in front of the wall was an approximately two-meter-wide no man's land secured with barbed wire.[18]

The wall was a "must." Changes in protective barricade techniques, however, did occur during the period of the Nazi regime. The concentration camps' protective installations again experienced a metamorphosis. The first "irregular" concentration camps in Berlin had been interior spaces, preferably surrounded by courtyard and barrack walls, but these were closed by 1934 at the latest. A few years later the newly established concentration camps Sachsenhausen and Ravensbrück, with their complex barricade systems (death strips, barbed wire, walls), were added to Berlin's hinterland.

At least two more developments in spatial architecture emerged during the war. First, beginning in 1944 a variety of sub-concentration camps and external sites migrated back to Berlin (where the arms industry was located) from Sachsenhausen and Ravensbrück.[19] In other words, the largest camps were broken up, and Berlin had concentration camps once more. As capital city of the entire German camp empire, Berlin had become a camp empire itself. Second, most of the some thirty smaller concentration camps in Berlin, each with a few hundred inmates, were surrounded by barbed wire draped with temporary imitation walls (using grass and reeds as noise and visual barriers). Sometimes these camps had existing embankments or walls upon which barbed wire was placed, but from 1944 on, the dominant form of mobile camp architecture was barbed wire and barracks.[20]

The New Era Begins with Us

With the end of the war in May 1945 came an upsurge of mobile camp architecture in Berlin. As a rule, these were not prison camps per se but administrative camps used to organize the flow of people streaming in. They included transit camps, stopover camps, reception camps, transfer camps, detention camps, main camps, and distribution camps. In the immediate postwar era humankind brought forth a new type of being, the *homo barackensis*.[21] Ten to twelve million people were in transit throughout all of Germany. Nomadic beings in permanent flux meandered through the country and more or less willingly passed through the relentless distribution catapult of Berlin. These included refugees and expelled Germans from Southern and Eastern Europe; prisoners of war (POWs) of all nationalities waiting to be repatriated from the giant *Stalags* in and around Berlin; German soldiers who had been released from Western captivity and immediately found themselves in Soviet POW camps; forced laborers, both men and women, on the way back to their native countries; concentration camp inmates streaming back to their home countries from Berlin and its suburbs; and Jews who had become homeless, wandering as "displaced persons" (DPs) from DP camp to DP camp. Berlin's municipal administration estimated that in 1945 alone more than 1.5 million people were registered and accommodated in the city's existing camps.[22]

Morever, new prison camps created by Soviet occupiers added to the total. There were filtration camps for POWs, forced laborers, and concentration camp inmates from the Soviet Union (who were constantly suspected of having collaborated with the Germans); and there were *Speziallager* (special camps) for Russian emigrants, members of the Vlasov Army (units of Russian POWs, forced laborers, and immigrants who had fought on the German side as volunteers), Nazi functionaries, and those Germans whom the Russians considered suspicious. Germany consisted again of a camp cosmos, especially in the Soviet occupation zone. The "new era," despite its different political economies, shamelessly continued the old spatial order, and former concentration camps such as Sachsenhausen and Buchenwald were now used for different classes of inmates.[23]

Three types of postwar camps could be distinguished in four-power occupied Berlin: DP camps for Jews, special camps run by the Soviet Interior Ministry/Secret Police, and refugee camps in the western occupation sectors. Displaced Jews presented specific problems. On the one hand, many did not want to return home, specifically to their native countries in Eastern and Southern Europe. On the other, some wanted to go to a particular place: Palestine. The British, who held power there under a governing mandate, wished to prevent this movement. Three Jewish DP categories existed in the Berlin camps: Jews of German origin (who nominally did not have displaced person status); Jews who had been forcibly transported to Germany; and Jews who had illegally entered Germany in the months following the war, especially from Poland. Distinctive spatial accommodations for Jewish DPs reflected the respective political preferences of the occupation administrators. In the first few months after the war, Jews were housed in the former central institutions of Jewish life in Berlin (senior homes, hospitals, and community centers), located primarily in the Soviet sector. Yet each of the four occupying powers processed Jewish DPs in very different ways based on the priorities of their international political agendas. The Americans practiced liberal and generous policies, waiting to see how the others would react while pressuring the British to open up Palestine. The British strictly rejected this and tried not to set up a single DP camp in their Berlin sector. The Soviets also refused to grant Jews any special status and wanted to repatriate them to their native countries. The French, the occupiers with the smallest power base, simply waited it out.

On 1 December 1945, a regular displaced persons camp was opened in the French sector (Eichborndamm). On 5 December the British decided not to allow any more Jews to emigrate from Berlin to their occupation zone in western Germany, and the Americans joined in this policy. This created a severe "refugee bottleneck" throughout Berlin, and as the situation took on dramatic proportions, on 23 December the all-Berlin municipal government considered opening camps outside the city. In the end the only explicit decision taken was to "set up closed camps" in the city itself that would no longer be under Jewish self-administration but under municipal control.[24] In January 1946 the Soviets, who like the British wished to severely curb the stream of refugees, proposed constructing a Jewish camp in Prenzlau, north of Berlin. The Americans reacted to this situation by erecting camps solely for Jewish DPs during the months that followed in Berlin-Düppel and Berlin-Mariendorf. The Mariendorf camp received a barbed-wire ring fence (for the protection of inmates, not their repression), and autonomous Jewish camp police regulated the camp regime for the most part without conflict until it closed during the Berlin Airlift. Unlike other camps, there were no curfews that lasted for days, ensuing storming of camp gates, or violent conflicts with guards deployed by the British (as happened, for example, in mid 1946 in the DP camp at Bergen-Belsen).[25]

In addition to the Jewish DP camps, a second kind of postwar camp was the "special camp" (*Speziallager*), run by the Soviet Interior Ministry/Secret Police. These camps had a history tied to the Soviet Union: Lenin and Trotsky had recommended setting up concentration camps for political opponents as early as 1918, and in 1923 at the latest a whole system of camps had taken shape (*gulags*, the Russian acronym for Главное Управление Исправительно-Трудовых Лагерей и колоний, headquarters for corrective labor camps and colonies). This system of repression or gradual elimination of (supposed) domestic political enemies gained ever more ground in the following decades and was exported to Germany immediately following the war. There were ten special camps that sometimes changed location; four were located directly in or near Berlin, including Sachsenhausen.[26] These camps took on very different forms, but according to memoirs and eyewitness accounts a relatively unified regime of barrier technology prevailed.

Under this regime a new, supplemental barrier element was added to the existing National Socialist camp system: the wooden fence. In its ideal form, the fascist concentration camp should have been fully enclosed within walls, but this goal was only partially realized, even in Berlin. As the war continued and the number of external concentration camps grew, barbed-wire walls became the rule. The Soviets, however—masters of camp mobility and effective barrier creation—favored flexible walls made of wood, based upon their growing body of empirical experience. In addition, the Soviet Union had an inexpensive surplus of wood. Both temporally and logistically, when compared to the other occupying forces, the Soviets therefore had a decisive experiential advantage when it came to the creation of "camps." Against this backdrop, the Provisional Regulation of the NKVD, Special Camps on the Occupied Territory of Germany, issued on 27 July 1945, ordered that all camps had to be located "behind a secure boundary fence or tangled barbed wire at least three meters high."[27] This minimum requirement led to complex solutions on the ground. As a rule, "a secure boundary fence" was combined with "barbed wire." In the case of Jamlitz (Special Camp 6), we read:

> The upgrading of the boundary fence, which at first consisted only of a simple barbed-wire fence, took place in the fall of 1945. Now an eight-meter-wide no-man's-land was installed around the camp, which was delimited with barbed-wire fences on both sides and in the middle of which were placed two rolls of coiled barbed-wire obstructions. A thirty-meter-wide killing field was added facing outward, which was also demarcated by a barbed-wire fence. A wooden fence surrounded the camp as an internal boundary measure.[28]

After a short courtesy pause and an appraisal of the new sobering reality, the old National Socialist concentration camps were put to use again, and new types of walling-in came into use. Buchenwald and Sachsenhausen were re-opened in August 1945. The short-term timidity regarding war victims had evaporated, and the next dictatorship made itself at home in the remains of the one that had been chased away. This also meant the redesign of camp walls. In the nearly five years of its postwar existence, 60,000 people were cooped up behind walls in Sachsenhausen, the largest *Speziallager* in the Soviet occupation zone (it contained a camp for men and for women). The previous camp's grounds were taken over, and a zonal system with interior dividing walls was established:

> The entire camp was surrounded by a 2.5-meter wall with barbed wire. In addition, there was a high-voltage fence. A restricted area with barbed-wire rolls and guard dogs was added. The outer sentry gates and watchtowers were mounted with spotlights and corresponding weapons. In front of the camp walls was another four-meter-wide, cleanly raked sand strip (the so-called death strip) with signs reading "Danger! Trespassers will be shot on sight."[29]

The third and last type of camp was the refugee camp. These camps were set up in Berlin's western sectors, including the *Notaufnahmelager* (emergency camp) in Marienfelde. Berlin was ahead of its time. By September 1944 the city was already divided into three (future) occupied sectors; France, the fourth occupying power, joined later. Four pie pieces and four different occupiers—the divided city's residents were poised for ample encounters with their new masters. The communists, who had not developed enough charm on account of the nature of their regime, were the least favored in occupier rankings. A Berliner rarely fled from the West to the East, while Easterners fled westward in droves.[30] But to where? To the refugee camps and to *the* refugee camp in particular: Berlin-Marienfelde. With the sealing of the GDR's border to West Germany in 1952, the only remaining way for East Germans to get to the West was through Berlin, until the building of the Wall in 1961 blocked this loophole too. To gain control of the refugee stream, newly built barracks in the Marienfelde transit camp opened on 14 April 1953. This had significant symbolic meaning, as the refugees were not arriving at a relic of National Socialist imprisonment, but instead obtaining a completely new short-term "home." The previous, decentralized intake locations, numbering around fifty, were no longer sufficient.

After a long search for a location—the new camp could not be too close to the Soviet sector, but still had to be adequately secluded—Marienfelde was chosen. This camp was different from others in that it was not an incarceration camp. No one was brought to Marienfelde against his or her will. And yet, it had at least two characteristics in common with traditional camps: hopeless overcrowding and the tall boundary fence. The Berlin Senator for Social Affairs Otto Bach insisted that a closed camp was essential: "There should be control over who enters or leaves the camp."[31] In plain language this meant barbed wire, camp rules, and identification cards. In political terms it meant that while certain intelligence services were prevented from gaining access to the hotly contested refugee commodity, access to the same commodity was to be secured for other intelligence services. State security spies from the East had to be filtered out because they stirred things up among the refugees. Western Allied intelligence service agents, who interrogated the applicants with great interest and listened for useful information, were given access. The Western Allies prudently secured this right of access in the Occupation Statute of 10 April 1949, which placed almost all administrative powers in the hands of the Berlin *Magistrat* (municipal government supervised by the occupying powers).

This resulted in more than a few complications in and around Marienfelde—after all, the intelligence services of the new West Germany wanted to have a word with the refugees as well. However, the Western occupying powers wisely barred the door, obviously to safeguard their own strategic needs. On the one hand they wanted information about East Germany and the Soviet Union, that is, about the Eastern Bloc generally, from persons they labeled as "interesting." On the other they wanted useful information about their new German friends in the West, including their possible Nazi pasts. This understandable mistrust was reciprocated in kind. A commission from the West German Federal Ministry for All-German Questions (later the Federal Ministry for Inner German Relations) went on a fact-finding trip to Marienfelde during the winter of 1955–56 and unanimously agreed that Allied interrogations of refugees "are to be objected to and do not serve our interests."[32] As a consequence, "persons of interest" to the FRG were apprehended directly at the camp gates and flown immediately to West Germany whenever possible. The Allies struck back. They demonstratively set up their administration in Marienfelde starting in January 1956. They energetically practiced their intelligence service's "right of first interrogation" on those who in fact had fled from the communist dictatorship of the secret service, a theme dispassionately discussed in Julia Franck's 2003 novel *Lagerfeuer* (Campfire).[33] After further battles behind the scenes, in 1958 the Allies secured the right to be completely and solely responsible for the processing of new refugees, a legal dictate that lasted until 1990. Nonetheless, this fenced-in camp was the outlet through which its inmates made it to a more open society (fig. 2.2).

Figure 2.2. Refugee processing center Berlin-Marienfelde (now a memorial). Photograph © Olaf Briese.

The Camp as "Nomos" of the Modern?

The camp and modernity—to return to the claim at the outset of this essay—necessarily belong together. What is the situation in Berlin today? At present, a camp inversion is taking place, a reversal of the former camp regimes. Threats to united Germany and its symbolic center, the capital city of Berlin, appear to be coming from abroad, not emerging domestically. This security threat materializes as a gruesome zombie named *refugee*. While it only appears to threaten domestic "social" security, in fact it threatens an entire world order resting on crumbling postcolonial arrangements.[34] In 1992, for example, former West German Chancellor Helmut Schmidt brashly stated in an interview with the *Frankfurter Rundschau* newspaper: "Whoever comes to Germany from Bosnia or Romania needs to know that he is going to a camp."[35] Meanwhile, refugee streams have long been coming from other regions, and the camps too are located elsewhere. Migrants are storming "Fortress Europe" from beyond its borders. Camps, primarily in Spain and Italy, await them, should they make it there. But camps can also be found even beyond the EU's eastern and southern borders, although the Arab Spring of 2011 has upset and undermined the EU's sanctioning and financing of money-hungry dictators in North Africa who eagerly detained and warehoused Europe-bound refugees and migrants before they reached the Mediterranean.

For Italian philosopher Giorgio Agamben, this evidence of migrant incarceration is used to support his claim that camps are the "the 'nomos' of the modern," the result of a benevolent security despotism named "democracy." In fact, for Agamben a state of emergency and camps are not, as represented by politicians or in the media, "states of emergency" at all. Rather, they can be said to be constitutive of democracy.[36] Yet it is possible that Agamben's theories, which enjoy a certain fashionable popularity, especially in Germany, overestimate the genuine political and biopolitical function of camps, for camps are, to put it bluntly, primarily administrative, technical artifacts of the state. People govern people, and at some point administrations will administer people. From this perspective, camps would be nothing more than banal and monstrous automatic control mechanisms of modern mass societies, themselves not controllable as mechanisms.

Translated by Daniel C. Villanueva

Notes

1. See Olaf Briese, *Steinzeit. Mauern in Berlin* (Berlin, 2011).
2. As cited in Ernst Ludwig Ehrlich, "Ghetto," in *Lexikon für Theologie und Kirche* (Freiburg, 1960), 4: 881.
3. See Dieter Hoffmann-Axthelm, *Der Große Jüdenhof. Ein Berliner Ort und das Verhältnis von Juden und Christen in der deutschen Stadt des Mittelalters* (Berlin, 2005).
4. Joachim Prinz, "Jüdische Situation – Heute (1935)," in *Die Verfolgung und Ermordung der europäischen Juden durch das nationalsozialistische Deutschland 1933–1945*, ed. Wolf Gruner, vol. 1, *Deutsches Reich 1933–1937* (Munich, 2008), 427.
5. Susanne Willems, *Der entsiedelte Jude. Albert Speers Wohnungsmarktpolitik für den Berliner Hauptstadtbau* (Berlin, 2002).
6. Ibid., 205.
7. Wolf Gruner, *Judenverfolgung in Berlin 1933–1945. Eine Chronologie der Behördenmaßnahmen in der Reichshauptstadt* (Berlin, 1996), 88.

8. Gudrun Schwarz, *Die nationalsozialistischen Lager* (Frankfurt am Main, 1990).

9. See François Cavanna, *Das Lied der Baba* (Berlin, 1988), 228ff., 278f.

10. Cord Pagenstecher, Bernhard Bremberger, and Gisela Wenzel, *Zwangsarbeit in Berlin. Archivrecherchen, Nachweissuche und Entschädigung* (Berlin, 2008), 62.

11. Laurenz Demps, *Zwangsarbeit und Zwangsarbeiterlager in der faschistischen Reichshauptstadt Berlin 1939–1945* (Berlin, 1986); Leonore Scholze-Irrlitz and Karoline Noack, eds., *Arbeit für den Feind. Zwangsarbeiter-Alltag in Berlin und Brandenburg 1939–1945* (Berlin, 1998); Berliner Geschichtswerkstatt, *Zwangsarbeit in Berlin 1940–1945* (Erfurt, 2000); Winfried Meyer and Klaus Neitmann, eds., *Zwangsarbeit während der NS-Zeit in Berlin und Brandenburg. Formen, Funktionen und Rezeption* (Potsdam, 2001).

12. Helmut Bräutigam, "Zwangsarbeit in Berlin 1938–1945," in *Zwangsarbeit in Berlin 1938–1945*, ed. Helmut Bräutigam, Doris Fürstenberg, and Bernt Roder (Berlin, 2003), 46.

13. Helmut Bräutigam, "Nationalsozialistische Zwangslager in Berlin IV. Fremdarbeiterlager 1939 bis 1945," in *Berlin-Forschungen*, ed. Wolfgang Ribbe (Berlin, 1989), 4: 261.

14. "Verordnung über die lagermäßige Unterbringung von Arbeitskräften während der Dauer des Krieges (Lagerverordnung, 14. Juli 1943)," *Reichsgesetzblatt, Teil I* (1943): 389.

15. See a provisional list in Helmut Bräutigam and Oliver C. Gliech, "Nationalsozialistische Zwangslager in Berlin I. Die 'wilden' Konzentrationslager und Folterkeller 1933/34," in *Berlin-Forschungen*, ed. Wolfgang Ribbe (Berlin, 1987), 2: 155–72; see also Wolfgang Benz and Barbara Distel, eds., *Der Ort des Terrors. Geschichte der nationalsozialistischen Konzentrationslager*, 9 vols. (Munich, 2005–09), 2: 39ff.

16. Günter Morsch, ed., *Konzentrationslager Oranienburg* (Berlin, 1994); Bernward Dörner, "Ein KZ in der Mitte der Stadt: Oranienburg," in *Terror ohne System. Die ersten Konzentrationslager im Nationalsozialismus*, ed. Wolfgang Benz and Barbara Distel (Berlin, 2001), 123–38; Günter Morsch, "Oranienburg – Sachsenhausen, Sachsenhausen – Oranienburg," in *Die nationalsozialistischen Konzentrationslager*, ed. Ulrich Herbert, Karin Orth, and Christoph Dieckmann (Frankfurt am Main, 2002), 1: 111–34.

17. Stanislav Zámečník, "Dachau-Stammlager," in Benz and Distel, eds., *Der Ort des Terrors*, 2: 246; on Dachau generally see Harold Marcuse, *Legacies of Dachau: The Uses and Abuses of a Concentration Camp, 1933–2001* (Cambridge, UK, 2001); Wolfgang Benz and Angelika Königseder, eds., *Das Konzentrationslager Dachau. Geschichte und Wirkung nationalsozialistischer Repression* (Berlin, 2008).

18. Reinhard Plewe and Jan Thomas Köhler, *Baugeschichte Frauen-Konzentrationslager Ravensbrück* (Berlin, 2001), 52. Concerning the walls in Sachsenhausen see Manuela R. Hrdlicka, *Alltag im KZ. Das Lager Sachsenhausen bei Berlin* (Opladen, 1991), 53.

19. Stefanie Endlich and Wolf Kaiser, "KZ-Häftlinge in der Reichshauptstadt. Außenlager in Berlin," *Dachauer Hefte* 12 (1996): 230–54. For a detailed description of the "external camps" of the Sachsenhausen concentration camp in Berlin see Benz and Distel, eds., *Der Ort des Terrors*, 3: 98–224.

20. Concerning the careers of barbed wire and barracks as architectural elements see Henry D. McCallum and Frances T. McCallum, *The Wire that Fenced the West* (Norman, OK, 1965); Olivier Razac, *Politische Geschichte des Stacheldrahts. Prärie, Schützengraben, Lager* (Zurich, 2003); Axel Doßmann, Jan Wenzel, and Kai Wenzel, *Architektur auf Zeit. Baracken, Pavillons, Container* (Berlin 2006); Axel Doßmann, "Barackenlager. Zur Nutzung einer Architektur der Moderne," in *Auszug aus dem Lager. Zur Überwindung*

des modernen Raumparadigmas in der politischen Philosophie, ed. Ludger Schwarte (Berlin, 2007), 220–45.

21. Volker Ackermann, "Homo Barackensis – Westdeutsche Flüchtlingslager in den 1950er Jahren," in *Anknüpfungen. Kulturgeschichte – Landesgeschichte – Zeitgeschichte*, ed. Volker Ackermann, Bernd-A. Rusinek, and Falk Wiesemann (Essen, 1995), 330–46.

22. Rajan Autze, *Treibgut des Krieges. Flüchtlinge und Vertriebene in Berlin 1945* (Munich, 2001), 13.

23. Peter Reif-Spirek and Bodo Ritscher, eds., *Speziallager in der SBZ. Gedenkstätten mit "doppelter Vergangenheit"* (Berlin, 1999).

24. "Magistratsbeschluß 23. Dezember 1945," in *Die Sitzungsprotokolle des Magistrats der Stadt Berlin 1945/46*, ed. Dieter Hanauske (Berlin, 1995), 1: 742.

25. See Angelika Königseder, *Flucht nach Berlin. Jüdische Displaced Persons 1945–1948* (Berlin, 1998); idem, "Das Lager für 'Displaced Persons' in Mariendorf," in *Tempelhofer Ansichten*, ed. Matthias Heisig and Sylvia Walleczek (Berlin, 2002), 39–57; Angelika Königseder and Juliane Wetzel, eds., *Lebensmut im Wartesaal. Die jüdischen DPs (Displaced Persons) im Nachkriegsdeutschland* (Frankfurt am Main, 1994); Fritz Bauer Institut, *Überlebt und unterwegs. Jüdische Displaced Persons im Nachkriegsdeutschland* (Frankfurt am Main, 1997).

26. Sergej Mironenko, Lutz Niethammer, and Alexander von Plato, *Sowjetische Speziallager in Deutschland 1945 bis 1950*, 2 vols. (Berlin, 1998); Reif-Spirek and Ritscher, eds., *Speziallager in der SBZ*; Eva Ochs, *"Heute kann ich das ja sagen". Lagererfahrungen von Insassen sowjetischer Speziallager in der SBZ/DDR* (Cologne, 2006).

27. NKVD is the English abbreviation for the People's Commissariat for Internal Affairs. See "Vorläufige Anordnung über die Speziallager des NKWD auf dem besetzten Territorium Deutschlands (27 Juli 1945)," in Peter Erler and Thomas Friedrich, *Das sowjetische Speziallager Nr. 3 Berlin-Höhenschönhausen (Mai 1945 bis Oktober 1946)* (Berlin, 1995), 51.

28. Andreas Weigelt, "Jamlitz – Speziallager Nr. 6 (September 1945–April 1947)," in Jörg Morré, ed., *Speziallager des NKWD. Sowjetische Internierungslager in Brandenburg 1945–1950* (Potsdam, 1997), 36.

29. Lutz Prieß, "Sachsenhausen – Speziallager Nr. 7 (August 1945–März 1950)," in Morré, ed., *Speziallager des NKWD*, 66.

30. Volker Ackermann, *Der "echte Flüchtling". Deutsche Vertriebene und Flüchtlinge aus der DDR 1945–1961* (Osnabrück, 1995).

31. Quoted in Bettina Effner, "'Eines der größten Wohnungsbauprojekte in Berlin'. Zur Gründungsgeschichte des Notaufnahmelagers Marienfelde," in *Mitteilungen des Vereins für die Geschichte Berlins* 102, no. 1 (2006): 294f.

32. *Bundesausschuss für gesamtdeutsche Fragen. Bericht (1956)*, quoted in Elke Kimmel, "Das Notaufnahmeverfahren," in *Flucht im geteilten Deutschland. Erinnerungsstätte Notaufnahmelager Marienfelde*, ed. Bettina Effner and Helge Heidemeyer (Berlin, 2005), 128.

33. Julia Franck, *Lagerfeuer* (Cologne, 2003).

34. Tobias Pieper, *Die Gegenwart der Lager. Zur Mikrophysik der Herrschaft in der deutschen Flüchtlingspolitik* (Münster, 2008).

35. Helmut Schmidt, Interview, *Frankfurter Rundschau*, 12 September 1992, 8.

36. See Giorgio Agamben, *Homo sacer. Die souveräne Macht und das nackte Leben* (Frankfurt am Main, 2002); *Ausnahmezustand (Homo sacer II.I)* (Frankfurt am Main, 2004).

CHAPTER 3

~:~

"Threshold Resistance"
Dani Karavan's Berlin Installation Grundgesetz 49

ERIC JAROSINSKI

The year 2009 marked the twentieth anniversary of the fall of the Berlin Wall—as well as the tenth anniversary of a second wall built to secure its remnants. An airy grate ("luftiges Gitter") shielding the erstwhile "Anti-Fascist Protective Rampart" (the Wall's official designation in East Germany), this decidedly anti-tourist fortification protects one of the last stretches of the Wall along Niederkirchnerstraße, adjacent to the Martin-Gropius-Bau and the Topography of Terror.[1] During the Cold War it was joked that the first thing Germany would do after the fall of the Wall was build a new one: here, at least, it has. As but one of many post-Wall ironies marking the last two decades, its construction is telling—not only of the dramatic changes in Berlin's landscape, both topographical and political, but also of the new tensions that unification has generated. In this particular case, the desire to publicly preserve the last traces of what for decades had been the most visible marker of Berlin's Cold War division (and one of the city's leading tourist attractions) is pitted against the urge to privately possess a concrete piece of that history, to literally chisel away at it.

In the following I explore another instance of a simultaneous removal and reinscription of city walls in Berlin. My focus, however, is neither on the remains of the Wall nor on the motivation of the would-be souvenir-hunter, but on the dematerialized, "airy" quality of the latticework obstacle keeping the two apart, namely its transparency. As various scholars have outlined in recent years, (West) German political culture has made much of equating architectural transparency with accessibility, accountability, and democracy since the immediate postwar era.[2] In my own analysis of the rhetorical construction of the "New Berlin" in post-1989 political discourse, I have proposed elsewhere that the ritual invocation of transparency can be read as a powerful, self-naturalizing synthesis of aesthetics and politics, yet also as the rhetorical mobilization of a metaphor that over the past century has proved difficult to control.[3] Seen in this light, the transparent—often positioned as a clear break from the dark side of German history or as a ritual cleansing of the specters of Berlin's past—reveals itself to be haunted by many of its own ghosts, not least its overlooked role in the rhetoric of National Socialism and as the preferred architectural idiom of Italian fascism. While the valorization of democratic transparency typically trades in simplistic notions of truth, access, and understanding, the concept becomes more revealing when seen less as a highly instrumentalized and easily dismissed staging of insight than as a potentially illuminating reflection of multiple overlapping desires, agendas, and tensions. In other words, while a highly contrived display of transparency is easily recognized, the more compelling question is to ask what its deployment might in fact reveal—apart, that is, from its putative object.

Such will be the task of my discussion of yet another Berlin wall to rise in the wake of 1989: the installation *Grundgesetz 49* (Basic Law 49) by the noted Israeli artist Dani Karavan. Unveiled in 2002, the work is situated just outside the Jakob-Kaiser-Haus, a parliamentary office building adjacent to the Reichstag. It consists of a small sculpture garden enclosed by a glass wall engraved with the constitutional *Grundrechte* or Basic Rights established in 1949. In keeping with the preferred aesthetic of political self-representation within the "Berlin Republic," *Grundgesetz 49* has been positioned in official parliamentary publications—with such programmatic titles as *Einblicke* (Insights), *Blickpunkt* (Focal Point), and *Glasklar* (Crystal Clear)—as a window onto democracy and a locus of public access, participation, reflection, and debate. All metaphors aside, however, Karavan's installation also clearly serves as a wall, a protective border monitored by security cameras policing the perimeter of a secured government building (fig. 3.1).

Unsettling this binary of window versus wall, much as the Bauhaus itself did in the 1920s with the advent of the glass "curtain wall," we might best consider Karavan's installation as fulfilling both functions in its role as a medium or interface. Simultaneously active and inert, the installation employs transparent glass to visually reveal an interior, while also serving to generate, frame, and foreground that which it exhibits to the outside. In this sense an often overlooked affinity of the installation's design comes to mind: its kinship with the shop display windows that for much of the past century have functioned as a key feature of the modern city, perhaps most visible in Berlin today on nearby Friedrichstraße and Potsdamer Platz. If, as Janet Ward has suggested, such sites of retail transparency signify "the most interesting underbelly of post-Wall Berlin's reconstruction craze" both for what they say about the (potentially hopeful) state of postmodern urbanism and a more problematic nostalgia for the imagined Berlin of the Weimar Republic, they might also reveal the dynamics of transparency in the political aesthetics, and aestheticized politics, of Berlin today.[4] Criticism of the "shopping mall architecture" of the many see-through facades of new government offices, party headquarters, and embassies in Berlin is often dismissed as so much stodgy architectural conservatism. My contention here, however, is that the political mobilization of transparent glass is related to its dual function in retail, in which boundaries are both transgressed and reinforced in the complex transactions of consumer fantasy and economic exchange.

Figure 3.1. A viewer's reflection upon the glass wall of *Grundgesetz 49.* Photograph © Matthew Stratton.

Window Shopping

Perennially debated by psychologists, marketing professionals, consumer an-
thropologists, and other expert analysts, the exact nature of the economy of
window display remains a subject of debate.[5] The two main poles are divided
along varying notions of passive versus active insertion of oneself into the fe-
tishized consumer fantasy the window creates. In examining the dynamic between interior and exterior, obstacle and entry, I borrow the term "threshold
resistance" to describe the staging of the political, a concept that originates in
the use of glass in shop display windows and, later, the disappearance of the
door altogether in the advent of shopping malls. The term, if not the original idea, stems from Alfred Taubman, a "visionary" commercial real estate de-
veloper and for many years one of the largest builders of malls in the United
States. He defines it as "the physical and psychological barriers that stand between your shoppers and your merchandise. It's the force that keeps your customer from opening your door and coming in over the threshold."[6] To reduce
these barriers, thereby limiting the space between customer and merchandise,
he brought the store as close to the sidewalk as possible through the use of
large, shallow display windows and an overall design that sought to "turn the
store itself—with its merchandise, human activity, and light in full view—into
the display."[7] In Taubman's 2007 autobiography, the concept expands to serve
as a guiding metaphor for a successful career that has shaped the look and function of retail spaces internationally (and culminated in time spent behind bars
for price-fixing).

According to this "open" model of retail sale, at the same time that potential
shoppers are invited in, they are also immersed in a carefully controlled space,
finding themselves no longer simply visiting a store but absorbed into a "retail
environment." As various critics of consumer culture have written as early as
Walter Benjamin's analysis of nineteenth-century Parisian shopping arcades,
this environment sets a paradoxical dynamic into motion for the subject turned
consumer, turned consuming object of consumption. Kevin Hetherington's recent analysis of "cultural spaces of the commodity," beginning with the grand
international exhibition in 1850 in London's Crystal Palace, has emphasized
the dialectic of fetishism at work here, arguing: "One took possession of this
space while at the same time being possessed by it…. In effect, subjects within
the consumer culture of modern capitalism might be said to inhabit a peculiar
world of paradox and bewilderment. They consume what they see but are also
themselves made as consuming subjects in the process."[8] Such analyses point to
close ties between the increasingly complex and absorbing architecture of consumption and the thresholds, both crossed and untested, that mark processes
of individual and social identity formation. At the same time, the evolving mechanics of commercial display have also made larger structural transformations

legible, as in Peter Sloterdijk's sweeping analysis of the development of an "integrated, experience-oriented, popular capitalism." Taking the Crystal Palace's conflation of the wall and the window as a metaphor and prototype, he detects the emergence of an "all-encompassing absorption of the outer world into a completely rationalized interior."[9] Though much has happened in the evolution of product display, branding, and marketing throughout the past century, the emphasis on immersion in the experience of consumption remains. To take a ready example, a recent industry trade journal urges retailers not to forget "the magic that comes from the overall experience." Shoppers should "walk into another world rather than just another store": "If a candy store is just a store, they may only buy something if they're hungry. But if they're in an enchanted forest where the sweets are stored in tree knotholes and in the windows of a giant ginger bread house, who can resist continuing the fun by buying some sweets to take home with them?"[10]

While retail and entertainment developments such as those that have arisen on Berlin's Potsdamer Platz since the fall of the Wall might seem far removed from such saccharine visions, their fundamental mechanics are similar. Just as a candy store should not just be a candy store, Berlin's Sony Center, for instance, presents itself as being a "landmark of Berlin," impressing the public "with transparent design, implemented through glass facades, sophisticated light reflections and light refractions."[11] Yet the "airiness and transparency," positioned as welcoming visitors, have come under increasing scrutiny as mechanisms of social exclusion in the production of semi-public private space. If the shopping mall removed the "threshold resistance" posed by the individual shop door, such a retail "forum" seeks both conceptually and physically to further erase boundaries standing between living in a city and shopping in it. It is telling in this regard that in the Sony Center's most recent update to its online introduction, an earlier rhetoric of movement, dynamism, and diversity has been replaced by tropes of organic domesticity and rootedness in the figuration of a *kreative Heimat* (creative homeland) in the "heart of Berlin," where "unity and exchange between the business world, residential areas, tourism, and entertainment are now part of one's everyday experience."[12]

Such depictions of utopian incorporation are notable for the way they draw attention to spatial strategies that, if as effective as portrayed, could also serve as dystopian mechanisms of colonization and confinement. Richard Sennett, among others, has developed a synthetic sociological and aesthetic analysis of urban space becoming both more visible and less permeable when, for example, street-level doors yield to "great sheaths of plate-glass."[13] Likewise, in reading the readily changing "palimpsest" of Berlin's own landscape, Andreas Huyssen observes the rise of large-scale retail and entertainment centers with foreboding, fearing that "the tight corporate structures, despite their gesturing toward public spaces and piazzas, will encage and confine their visitors."[14] Returning to Karavan's installation, can *Grundgesetz 49* itself be considered as situated within similarly paradoxical, if not dialectical, relations of openness and confinement? Might not the work also resist easily instrumentalized notions of democratic openness and accessibility by offering a potentially illuminating, though less conspicuous, staging of these very tensions?

Speculation and Immersion

Grundgesetz 49 is one of several site-specific artworks created for the Reichstag and surrounding parliamentary buildings as part of "Kunst am Bau" (site-specific art), a large-scale public art project administered by the Bundesministerium für Verkehr, Bau und Stadtentwicklung (Federal Ministry of Transport, Building, and Urban Development). Under the administration of Chancellor Helmut Kohl, the project drew on a budget of DM 70 million from the mid to late 1990s—an unprecedented sum—yet failed to generate much public interest in the various arts councils' decisions on competitions and commissions (apart from a heated discussion of the supposed return of "blood-and-soil" ideology in Hans Haacke's Reichstag installation *Der Bevölkerung* [To the Population]).[15] The works ultimately chosen represent a cross-section of the most notable postwar German artists (including Gerhard Richter, Sigmar Polke, and Georg Baselitz) as well as paintings and sculptures by several young German artists, representatives of the four former occupying powers, and Karavan himself. As stated in the project's guiding principles, the goal was "to increase acceptance and identification with the building, both among its users and the public, to create interest, and to add to the profile of the sites."[16] In facing this task, the project sought to avoid both explicitly affirmative "state art" as well as the empty abstraction of "highly stylized foyers in banks and corporate headquarters," favoring artists who specifically engaged with the respective building's architecture and functions.[17] Guided by the desire to choose works that reflected the political while also keeping their distance, the most unifying element among a wide range of works was, as one critic observed, their function of "representing the image of a cosmopolitan democracy that relinquishes direct manipulation of art."[18]

In its combination of elements both sculptural and architectural, abstract and historical, *Grundgesetz 49* seems ideally suited to the contradictory task of site-specific political cosmopolitanism. The wall itself consists of nineteen glass panels, each three meters tall, which are illuminated from below at night, making the nearly thirty-meter expanse appear to hover in a green glow. Using a new technique of internal laser engraving, the text of the Basic Rights is written not upon but within the glass. The sculpture garden inside the glass wall is blanketed by a green lawn, its surface ruled and divided into layers of varying depths by a series of sharp cuts running almost perpendicular to the wall. A massive metal strip underscores the design's strict linearity, its rusting expanse topped by six corroding columns, behind which a staircase descends toward but not into the building itself. The garden's geometry is repeated outside the wall by a pattern built into the pedestrian walkway and mirrored in the alignment of a row of trees alongside the bank of the adjacent Spree River. Notably absent from the rhythm of this arrangement would appear to be the tree located behind the glass wall in the sculpture garden itself. It stands alone atop a circular island of green grass, its curves accentuated by the rigid, linear arrangement of the rest of the garden. As striking as these visual elements may be, the garden's interior often tends to disappear behind the nearly singular focus on the glass in the foreground, which has come to bear the load of meanings ascribed to the work when packaged as an instance of democratic transparency on the order of Norman Foster's glass cupola for the reconstructed Reichstag.[19]

Parliamentary publications were quick to focus on the visual accessibility granted by the glass wall. Yet the wall is also central to a technology of exclusion, fortification, and security; architectural commentary both before and after the work's completion emphasizes how it served as a fortified "outer boundary."[20] Likewise, as another more technical reading states, the installation "underscores the special security aspect" of the building by shielding "precisely those meeting rooms in which extremely contentious political decisions are made."[21] In such formulations the "art" of Karavan's installation is figured as utilitarian "architecture," serving not to comment on the political, but simply to complete, embellish, or secure the building.

Within the register of national self-portraiture, however, Karavan's work is clearly figured as an entrance in well-established discourses of democratic transparency and openness. Not surprisingly, the words "Mauer" (wall), "Zaun" (fence), and "Wand" (interior wall) rarely, if ever, appear in the descriptions of the installation in speeches by government officials or parliamentary informational materials. A glass wall's connotations of confinement or exclusion (with semantic resonances uncomfortably close to those of a glass ceiling) are elided through references to "glass panels," which together form an "installation." Often positioned metaphorically not only as a window but also as a door or bridge, the work—as a figure of transparent immateriality—veils its function as a barrier. Reminders of its less transcendent qualities are never far removed, however, as witnessed by how its manufacturers have used the installation as a visible display window for their own handiwork. The firm responsible for the laser engraving, for example, described its efforts in terms far more monumental than democratic: "Classical elegance is staged anew, to be marveled at for eternity."[22] While not given to the same pathos, a Berlin glass company that repaired one of the glass panels (after it was unceremoniously shattered by a rock kicked up by a lawn mower) boasts not of what the glass makes visible, but of the invisible seams joining the three sections that make up each panel.[23] Such tensions in register between the figural and the material have not gone unnoticed, leading one recent commentator to offer a sardonic footnote to how the installation "connects" the interior and exterior: "Jargon among artists and architects: walls made of glass do not 'divide'—they 'connect.'"[24] Commentators have often remarked with Schadenfreude on such discrepancies between the material and metaphorical, especially since the glass used in many new government buildings, including the Jakob-Kaiser-Haus, has proven prone to leakage and fracture, requiring extensive repair less than ten years after the buildings were opened.[25]

Semantic residue aside, the connections made by *Grundgesetz 49* are depicted as operating on at least three levels, the first historical. As the parliament's art curator commented at the work's unveiling: "These 19 Basic Rights standing directly on the Spree, which once divided East and West Berlin, are meant to commemorate the difficult years of the founding of the fledgling democracy in Bonn."[26] Further, Karavan's installation is figured as a conciliatory or redemptive post-Holocaust link to the Jewish world, with the artist himself cast as a "builder of bridges between Germany and Israel," as he was described at the opening of the first major retrospective of his work in Berlin in the summer of 2009.[27] Born in 1930 in Tel Aviv and now based primarily in Paris and Florence, Karavan had long shunned working in Germany, but it has since become home to several of his installations, including a memorial now being built in Berlin to commemorate the Roma and Sinti murdered in the Holocaust.

Finally, depictions of the connections made by the installation repeatedly position the work as linking transparency to democracy and the viewer to the work itself. The subject's encounter with the installation is marked not only by entry but by an active experience of immersion, absorption, and incorporation, not unlike that of the retail environments Taubman pioneered. One parliamentary publication described the public's interaction with the installation as a "modern-day agora of the capital city": "The production clearly convinces and fascinates citizens.... The Basic Law has been 'brought to life' in a way it never before could have been experienced."[28] As any visitor to *Grundgesetz 49* will note, the observer in question is oftentimes a tourist, yet in such figurations the subject is commonly cast as a "citizen." Similar figures of incorporation and immersion have appeared in formulations such as the following: "The viewer becomes part of the work in that he is reflected in the glass panels with the text of the Basic Law."[29] Or, to cite one further example: "Depending on the angle of the light, the citizen himself is reflected in the Basic Rights."[30]

Such rhetorical constructions are accompanied by a corresponding visual grammar of authentic, organic access and connection. Photographs of the installation found in parliamentary publications rarely depict the work without people standing before it. Frequently depicting parents with children—common signifiers of domesticity, belonging, and generational harmony—and rather homogeneous "observers," these images are most notable for what they lack. Never do they appear with cameras, mobile phones, backpacks, maps, or other explicit reminders of the mechanics of spectacle or the transience of international flows of populations, capital, data, or images (not surprisingly, the quite visible security cameras monitoring the work also never make their way into the frame). While *Grundgesetz 49* is at once rhetorically figured as a utopian space of openness, in these official photographs it becomes a realm insulated from complexities and divisions, closed off from the potentially disruptive or anxiety-inducing transgressions of the permeable borders of the present.

The way such contradictions have been glossed over in positioning Karavan's installation within the carefully cultivated image of democratic openness and accessibility points to ongoing processes of commodification at work in the branding of post-Wall German democracy. In attempting to frame them here in terms of the mechanics of window display, it would be equally reductive not to take account of this approach's own limitations. For example, while the analysis of the encounter between shopper and window display is informed by a Marxist critique of reification and fetishization, these powerful analytical tools encounter their own formidable interpretive thresholds in contemporary stagings of the transparent. To recount the famous lines from *The Communist Manifesto* in which Marx and Engels chart the bourgeoisie's dynamic rise as it constantly revolutionizes the means and relations of production:

> All fixed, fast-frozen relations, with their train of ancient and venerable prejudices and opinions, are swept away, all new-formed ones become antiquated before they can ossify. All that is solid melts into air, all that is holy is profaned, and man is at last compelled to face with sober senses his real conditions of life, and his relations with his kind.[31]

This passage, like much of Marx's later rhetoric throughout *Das Kapital*, suggests that the transgression of boundaries leads to radical reversals, as delusion subsequently gives way to the lifting of a veil and reveals the harsh clarity of insight. Yet the question posed by a critical examination of transparency is whether the state of being "at last compelled to face with sober senses" is not the result of demystification, but an indication of the very experience and mechanics of mystification itself in the staging of what is purported to be the sober and the real.

In other words, does all that has "melted into air" again become solid in the formation of a new, though less visible, barrier to potentially transgressive insights? Indeed, as Lutz Koepnick argues, mediation is not hidden, but highlighted in stagings of the transparent: "their ambiguous materiality cannot but foreground the very process of mediation and remediation and hence the very thrill of seeing the world converted into a still or moving image."[32] As suggested here, a focus limited to the truth or falsity of the transparent might in fact blind us to more revealing dynamics of fascination, affect, and performance. At the same time, however, such an approach must not overlook the stakes involved in the production and reproduction not only of images but also of ways of seeing, of the ideological structures that underlie larger "scopic regimes." Numerous critics of various stripes—Michel Foucault, Guy Debord, Peter Sloterdijk, Jacques Ranciere, and others—have outlined over the past decades how power frequently stages a visible removal of boundaries only to reinscribe them in less apparent yet even more pernicious ways.[33]

I suggest then, that the liminal status of Karavan's work as both art and architecture, wall and window, interior and exterior, calls critical attention to the very contradictions and potential coercion embodied in the transparent. While the work invites the immersion central to the spectacular mechanics of modern retail, if we think of it as a display window, then it is one that also points to the dynamics of display itself. In the political realm, the metaphor of architectural transparency typically operates as a self-portrait of power, though it is presented as the result of the viewer's own power of sight and insight. Karavan's installation, however, lends itself to a more multivalent reading if we see its threshold as permeable enough to allow for the literal "carrying over" of such meanings in metaphor, yet also resistant to a reductive equation of transparency with democracy. Seen in this light, the installation stages something more akin to a complex allegory of the tensions in representation, perception, and participation that a more challenging sense of the term democracy would entail.

Before the Law

To read the transparency of *Grundgesetz 49* as threshold resistance is to view it as both a conduit and an obstacle to meaning, asking what else it might refer to, or it is to recall the origin of the term allegory, questioning what "other speaking" it might portend. This requires a critical stance not unlike that suggested by Roland Barthes in *Mythologies* (1957): the example of looking at scenery through a car window illustrates the economy of the mythical signifier in which meaning and form work in tandem but are never at the same place at the same time:

> At one moment I grasp the presence of the glass and the distance of the landscape; at another, on the contrary, the transparency of the glass and the depth of the landscape; but the result of this alternation is constant: the glass is at once present and empty to me, and the landscape unreal and full. The same thing occurs within the mythical signifier: its form is empty but present, its meaning absent but full.[34]

The mode of double vision and shifting perspectives that Barthes suggests here provides a useful starting point for a more multidimensional consideration of the tensions between the open and closed that are inscribed within the transparency of Karavan's installation. *Grundgesetz 49* could itself be said to comment on a double motion in the production of meaning, staging the simultaneity of that which is recognizable yet unfamiliar, material yet immaterial, revealing yet concealing.

To take one example of the careful reading the work necessitates, the Basic Rights it displays are not what they would seem at first glance. While they would come to form the Basic Law, their wording is not identical to what is in Germany's present constitution, for which they are commonly mistaken. In the intervening years, important amendments have been made to a number of articles. Notable in the context of openness and access, some of these changes have significantly altered the rights of asylum (tightening Germany's borders) and privacy (making the borders of one's home more permeable by allowing for electronic eavesdropping). As one parliamentary publication explained, "in the clear formulation of 1949, free of all additions and amendments, the essence of the Basic Law and the Basic Rights of all Germans is emphasized."[35] Such a description points to a particular notion of democratic transparency that valorizes the clear and immediate communication of readily comprehensible messages. At the same time, however, the installation presents a version of constitutional rights that is temporally bound. Citing 1949 in the work's title foregrounds the text's place in the past and calls attention to changes made in the intervening years. It thereby invites comparison of the law as displayed with that of the present, though no assistance in doing so is provided, leaving the viewer's comparison to be mediated by memory alone.

The simultaneous revelation and erasure that inform this outdated, overly basic version of "Basic Rights" is perhaps most revealing of the general erasure of explicit revelation in the installation's staging of transparency. To invoke Raoul Eshelman's concept of artistic and architectural "performatism," works such as Karavan's installation can no longer be seen according to well-worn paradigms of modernist revelation or playful postmodernist irony. It is obvious to the viewer that the transparency of such spectacles is staged, yet this is beside the point, as transparency shifts from serving as a structure of knowledge to one of belief and experience: "Performative transparency … is demonstrative and tautological. It reifies, albeit imperfectly, the possibility of transcending materiality per se rather than revealing anything particular about a structure's inner workings or essence."[36] Karavan himself has said little about the installation, but in characterizing his work, he has suggested that whatever insight it attempts to offer is directed as much at the mode as at the object of perception. The main gesture of his "site-specific" art, as he explained in a recent interview, is to "invite people to walk through it, to climb on it, to use their senses, to feel the site and to discover themselves in relation to the environment. To evoke memories and become part of it."[37] While this understanding of art relies on immersion, Karavan also positions it as the vehicle for a mode of critical self-reflection. In some ways, looking through the glass to the sculpture garden is, in fact, not unlike viewing it as if it were under water. The layered cuts into the soil, for instance, are visible, yet their depth is difficult to discern. Their apparently submerged geometry also gives rise to a performative critique: running at an angle to the glass wall, then continuing straight out into the sidewalk, they create an effect of visual refraction, the staging of a materially inflected, distorting transparency that undermines politically instrumentalized notions of pure, unmediated access (fig. 3.2).

Figure 3.2. *Grundgesetz 49* blocked off during repairs in summer 2009. Photograph © Matthew Stratton.

To experience *Grundgesetz 49* is to stand both before a display window and "Before the Law," in a moment with surely unintentional yet thought-provoking parallels to Franz Kafka's famous parable: the "man from the country" is refused admittance into "the Law" by the gatekeeper; entry is "possible," he is told, "but not at this moment."[38] Discouraged by his warning of a series of other gatekeepers, each more imposing than the next, the man from the country waits his entire lifetime before learning at the hour of his death that this entrance into "the Law" had been meant for him alone but was now being closed. While in its political instrumentalization *Grundgesetz 49* would seem to promise ready entry, perhaps extending an invitation like the one that must have beckoned "the man from the country" to "the Law," the composition of the sculpture garden behind the glass bespeaks, if not the impossibility of passage, then its utility.

What does one find behind, or within, the law itself? Few commentaries go beyond the glass, and rarely have published photographs of the sculpture garden failed to frame it within the glass wall. When seen on its own terms, however, removed from its crystalline frame, the interior is not unlike the austere, existential setting of a Beckett play, an unsettling space filled by absence, corrosion, and the passage of time. Likewise, the observer's view, should one look beyond the glass panels, is dominated by another transparent facade that reveals a series of internal elevated walkways closed off not only from the spectator, but also from the interior of the sculpture garden. The supposed inside is revealed as yet another outside. Taken as a whole, it is this staging of the failure to ever entirely negate boundaries—to fully eliminate "threshold resistance"—that represents the greatest potential of Karavan's installation to generate more transgressive insights. One such realization is that while the spectator's reflection upon the glass marks a connection with the work, it also establishes a material border between interior and exterior. Significantly, it does so within the work itself, which extends out though the walkway and to the Spree River. This draws attention not only to a multiplicity of barriers, but also to the fact that, in contemplating this transparent threshold, one has already crossed another, even less visible border to become immersed in a larger urban frame. Further, it points to the fact that spectatorship belongs to—in fact, precedes—the spectacle itself. The glass wall that invites us to look in is also watching us and anticipating our actions, as made clear both by the highly visible security cameras and our position within the work as a whole.

Not unlike Kafka's "man from the country," spectators might be tempted to approach Karavan's staging of the *Grundgesetz* seeking entrance into an affirmative vision of their own identity as members of democratic communities. The work can be thought most liberating, however, not if it simply grants entry but rather, like the gatekeeper, makes us pause long enough to pay attention to our own position already within a larger whole. As the representation of a structure of governance, the installation reminds us of its own function as a structure that governs relations of space as much as vision. Like the shop display window, the installation might promise immediate gratification at first glance, yet the staging of its transparency is also marked by a less conspicuous but pervasive sense of deferral: if the realization of a vision of democratic openness, accessibility, and participation is ever to be "possible," then "not at the moment." In the meantime the most insightful vision *Grundgesetz 49* offers is that of a threshold, a meeting between the multilayered, ambivalent experience of transparency and its one-dimensional entry into contemporary political discourse.

Notes

1. "Zaun schützt vor Mauerfall," *Berliner Zeitung*, 1 November 1999, Lokales, 1. www.berlinonline.de/berliner-zeitung/archiv/.bin/dump.fcgi/1999/1101/lokales/0190/index.html (accessed 27 June 2010).

2. Deborah Ascher Barnstone, *The Transparent State: Architecture and Politics in Postwar Germany* (New York, 2005); Lutz Koepnick, *Framing Attention: Windows on Modern German Culture* (Baltimore, 2007); Heinrich Wefing, *Kulisse der Macht* (Stuttgart, 2001); Michael Z. Wise, *Capital Dilemma: Germany's Search for a New Architecture of Democracy* (New York, 1998). For an analysis of the meanings of architectural transparency in contemporary French politics, see Annette Fierro, *The Glass State: The Technology of the Spectacle, Paris 1981–1998* (Cambridge, MA, 2003).

3. Eric Jarosinski, "Building on a Metaphor: Democracy, Transparency, and the Berlin Reichstag," in *Berlin: The Symphony Continues: Orchestrating Architectural, Social, and Artistic Change in Germany's New Capital*, ed. Carol Anne Costabile-Heming, Rachel J. Halverson, and Kristie A. Foell (Berlin, 2004), 59–76.

4. Janet Ward, *Weimar Surfaces: Urban Visual Culture in 1920s Germany* (Berkeley, 2001), 240.

5. Sankar Sen, Lauren G. Block, and Sucharita Chandran, "Window Displays and Consumer Shopping Decisions," *Journal of Retailing and Consumer Services* 9 (2002): 277–90; Anne Friedberg, *Window Shopping: Cinema and the Postmodern* (Berkeley, 1994).

6. Alfred Taubman, *Threshold Resistance* (New York, 2007), 114.

7. Ibid., 109.

8. Kevin Hetherington, *Capitalism's Eye: Cultural Spaces of the Commodity* (New York, 2007), 23–24.

9. Peter Sloterdijk, *Im Weltinnenraum des Kapitals* (Frankfurt am Main, 2005), 275.

10. Janice Davis, "5 Reasons Theatricality Will Boost Retail Sales," *Display & Design Ideas* 21, no. 11 (2009): 17.

11. Sony Center, http://www.sonycenter.de/en/center/architektur (accessed 15 June 2010).

12. Sony Germany, www.sony.de/hub/unternehmen/5 (accessed 5 March 2010).

13. Richard Sennett, *The Conscience of the Eye: The Design and Social Life of Cities* (New York, 1990), 110.

14. Andreas Huyssen, *Present Pasts: Urban Palimpsests and the Politics of Memory* (Stanford, 2003), 60.

15 See: www.spatiul-public.ro/eng/Hans Haacke/Hans_Haacke.html (accessed 4 June 2010).

16. Bundesministerium für Verkehr, Bau und Stadtentwicklung, *Leitfaden: Kunst am Bau*, http://www.bmvbs.de/Bauwesen/Baukultur-,1516/Kunst-am-Bau.htm (accessed 20 May 2010).

17. Armin Zweite, "Kunst am Bau," in *Kunst am Bau: Die Projekte des Bundes in Berlin*, ed. Bundesministerium für Verkehr, Bau- und Wohnungswesen (Berlin, 2002), 9.

18. Astrid Wege, "Who Decides What Is 'Hauptstadtkultur,' and What Is Not?" *October* 89 (1999): 127–38.

19. For a view of the installation from inside the Jakob-Kaiser-Haus, see the online "virtual tour" at www.bundestag.de/kulturundgeschichte/architektur/virtuelle_rundgaenge/hotspot32.html (accessed 20 May 2010).

20. Hans-Jürgen Heß, *Unter der Kuppel* (Berlin, 1999), 107.
21. Volker Wagner, *Regierungsbauten in Berlin: Geschichte, Politik, Architektur* (Berlin, 2001), 25.
22. Vitro Laser, www.vitro.de (accessed 4 October 2009).
23. Plickert Glaserei, www.plickert.de/neuigkeiten/newsletter-archiv-2008 (accessed 2 October 2009).
24. Josef Hüwe, "Sechzig Jahre Grundgesetz – und unerledigte Aufträge," *Humane Wirtschaft* (April 2009): 39.
25. See, for example, "Pfusch am Bau: Der Kanzleramt ist nicht ganz dicht," http://www.spiegel.de/politik/deutschland/0,1518,565445,00.html (accessed 10 April 2010).
26. Joe F. Bodenstein, "Ein Glaspalast für Volksvertreter mit viel Kunst," *die tageszeitung*, 21 January 2002.
27. http://www.bundesregierung.de/nn_23686/Content/DE/Artikel/2008/03/2008-03-14-dani-karavan-retrospektive.html (accessed 30 September 2009).
28. Andreas Kaernbach, "Vom Grundgesetz an der Spree zur planetarischen Utopie," *Die Politische Meinung* 416 (July 2004): 85.
29. http://www.bundesregierung.de/Content/DE/Archiv16/Rede/2008/03/2008-03-13-rede-neumann-dani-karavan.html (accessed 29 September 2009).
30. Deutscher Bundestag, ed., *Blickpunkt Bundestag. Sonderthema: Kunst im Bundestag* (2007): 10. https://www.btg-bestellservice.de/pdf/40128800.pdf (accessed 20 May 2010).
31. Karl Marx and Friedrich Engels, *The Communist Manifesto*, in *Karl Marx: Selected Writings*, ed. David McLellan (Oxford, 2000), 248.
32. Koepnick, *Framing Attention*, 5.
33. See Michel Foucault, *Discipline and Punish: The Birth of the Prison* [1975], trans. Alan Sheridan (New York, 1995); Jacques Ranciere, *The Politics of Aesthetics* (New York, 2004); Guy Debord, *The Society of the Spectacle*, trans. Donald Nicholson-Smith (New York, 1995); Peter Sloterdijk, "Atmospheric Politics," in *Making Things Public: Atmospheres of Democracy*, ed. Bruno Latour and Peter Weibel (Cambridge, MA, 2005), 944–51.
34. Roland Barthes, *Mythologies*, trans. Annette Lavers (New York, 1998), 123–24.
35. Andreas Kaernbach, "Dani Karavan: Grundgesetz 49," in *Kunst am Bau. Die Projekte des Bundes in Berlin*, ed. Bundesministerium für Verkehr, Bau- und Wohnungswesen (Berlin, 2002), 34.
36. Raoul Eshelman, *Performatism, or the End of Postmodernism* (Aurora, CO, 2008), 123.
37. Dani Karavan, "Where Is Dani Karavan?" Artnet Questionnaire (8 May 2008) www.artnet.de/magazine/dani-karavan-artnet-questionnaire-de/ (accessed 15 February 2010).
38. Franz Kafka, *The Trial*, trans. Willa and Edwin Muir (New York, 1968), 213.

CHAPTER 4

~:~

Did Walls Really Come Down?
Contemporary B/ordering Walls in Europe

DANIELA VICHERAT MATTAR

> Abbiamo bisogno di un muro, ma non per tenere fuori ciò che
> abbiamo paura: si tratta di darli un nome.
> —Alessandro Baricco[1]

Long-lasting: that is how walls are characterized. Yet history has proved that despite their recurrence as a device, they are not unchanging features of the built environment. Scholars have identified specific forms of dividing and bordering that affect not only a city's structure and functioning but also the nature of urban experiences and, for that matter, the *urban condition* itself. In contemporary cities, gentrified and suburban areas, luxury housing enclaves, stigmatized social housing zones, shanty towns, and abandoned areas all correlate with sociopolitical and economic divisions that, together in their disunity, structure the city as a whole. Liberalization policies of the last few decades have reshaped the urban landscape through a proliferation of divisive interventions—highways, gated communities, shopping malls, and walls—and have resituated urban residents within a network of hierarchies that establish degrees of normality, certainty, formality, and informality.

"The Wall was torn down over twenty years ago." Without further clarification we all know this refers to the fall of the Berlin Wall, the one that not only divided Berlin and Germany for twenty-eight years but also became the physical embodiment of the Iron Curtain, an expression of the Cold War period in which the world was organized by and divided between two antagonistic ideologies separated by the Wall. Acting with the agreement of the Soviet leadership, the GDR government constructed the Berlin Wall in August 1961. Its primary objective was to prevent East Germans from escaping to the West. While the concern with the loss of "human capital" was indeed a pressing economic and political issue, the East German government chose to justify and legitimate the Wall as a bulwark against "fascist infiltration" from the West.[2] At the same time it enabled the Western Allies to maintain the status quo of West Germany's tutelage. Thus, the Berlin Wall was not only a concrete division marking the postwar division of power but also the symbolic representation of an explicit ideology of antagonistic coexistence between two societal projects.

The fall of *the* Wall, however, did not eradicate *all* walls from the European landscape. Rather the event paved the way for a paradigm that continues to mold Europe. In this third decade since the demise of the Wall, it is time to ask: what are walls in contemporary Europe still aiming to separate? Since the initiation of the Schengen Agreement borders among the EU member states— which now include twenty-seven of the approximately forty countries on the European continent—have become more porous, and barriers to the flow of goods, capital, and information have been increasingly lifted.[3] Yet Schengeniza-tion has not necessarily corresponded to the lifting of barriers for all people's movement and circulation.[4] The counterpart to the softening of borders among EU member states has been the progressive hardening of the external front-lines toward nonmember states, leading to what has been called "Fortress Europe."[5] These external borders reflect not a monolith but a mosaic of spatial practices. This double policy of soft/hard borders is consistent with the main objectives of the Amsterdam treaty: Schengen provides an institutional and transnational platform for member states to cooperate in their "fight against terrorism, international crime and drug trafficking, ecological problems and threats to public health" while adapting the needs of their formal labor markets to the fluctuations of economic globalization.[6] Schengen is also a platform for enhancing Western values among the member states and correspondingly ad-justing citizens to these patterns.

The aim of this chapter is to show how in Schengenized Europe, social an-tagonisms continue to order populations according to a dualistic logic, catego-rizing difference in terms of Carl Schmitt's political paradigm of "friend versus enemy."[7] I borrow the concept of b/ordered spaces from Henk van Houtum, Olivier Kramsch, and Wolfgang Zierhofer, who introduce the term to discuss the practices of identity formation in a global—and apparently borderless— world.[8] Such practices aim to create meaningful societal orders and structures that not only serve as instruments for contingent conflict resolution, but also classify people and their interactions. Hence, a model of *the* good (or desired) society is still embedded in the act of erecting a wall; justified by various ra-tionales, wall-building delineates and demarcates space and controls peoples, things, and activities that are labeled as either belonging to or excluded from that space.

As an urban form, walls continue to be used as mechanisms to trace the norms and criteria of belonging within urban societies. Materially, walls make visible the distinction between legitimate and illegitimate types of member-ship in the polity, whereas conceptually they exemplify how freedom can only be exercised through defined patterns of association, patronage, and defense embedded in the act of walling.[9] Historically, walls have been justified to protect and to regulate conflicts. The nature of conflicts may vary, but there is a point at which the societies involved in a conflict conclude that erecting a wall may provide not just a short-term fix but an inherent solution: a wall restrains mobility, interactions, and exchange; yet it also establishes order by keeping people secured, protected, and separated. A wall can give two opposing sides time to seek an alternative solution to their conflict, but experience has shown that even when walls are built as only a temporary measure, their eradication always takes longer than expected. This is no surprise if we understand physical walls to be the expression of the mental and imaginary walls already existing between rival populations. The barriers of prejudice are always harder to dismantle than concrete ones, and ideally the dismantling of the former should precede that of the latter.

The prevalence of walls in the urban landscape of contemporary Europe is investigated in this chapter along an inductive path. First, I examine three existing walls in Europe: a neighborhood wall in Padua, Italy; the transnational frontier/urban wall in Ceuta, Spain; and the "Peace Lines" in Belfast, Northern Ireland. Built in differing contexts and with various justifications, each illustrates how the ancient device of the city wall continues to play a crucial role in defining and ordering urban life in contemporary Europe. The chapter subsequently proposes that walls can function as devices that go beyond their material roles to help build (trans)national identity and assist in forging membership dynamics and urban bonding. Walls in cities such as Padua, Ceuta, and Belfast act as b/orders that can be addressed in a pluralized way: as markers of urban fragmentation in relation to people's entitlements to attain city/zenship rights depending on which side of the wall-line they inhabit, and also as signs of urban unification. I conclude by reflecting on the counterintuitive possibility that sometimes walls even work toward their apparent opposite function, namely, enhancing urban rights by means of binding the city together rather than only fragmenting it into a multiplicity of atomized and isolated experiences.

Padua's "Wall of Fear"

Padua is an example of a traditional walled Italian city. The medieval wall surrounding the city was built to protect the "commune" of Padua, which was independent from Venice and Vincenza during the eleventh century. A thousand years later, and obviously responding to a problem entirely different in scale, even if probably not in nature, one neighborhood within the city was sectioned off from the rest of the city to protect the majority of city residents from an unwanted minority. A steel wall was built in 2006 around the northeast neighborhood of Serenissima, which not only caused public controversy at the city level but also put into question national and EU policies toward emergent ghettoized immigrant clusters. The Serenissima area in particular has become known as "the ghetto of Via Anelli." Eighty-four meters long and three meters high, the wall encircled a complex of six apartment blocks housing 287 units, each a mere twenty-eight square meters in size. At the time the wall was built, approximately 1,500 people, most of whom were of African immigrant origin, lived in the complex.[10]

The Serenissima apartments were first built as an initiative in the late 1970s to provide student housing for the nearby University of Padua. Subsequently bought by private individuals, the complex became one of the first speculative real-estate operations in economically depressed parts of the city. According to an urban planner for Padua, the small, low-cost prefab units were originally built to house students coming from other parts of the country but ended up offering their families the possibility of future rental income—and specula-tion.[11] During the second half of the 1990s the neighborhood became known for its high levels of crime, prostitution, and illegal migrant residents. By then the students had moved out, and the apartments were rented at exorbitant prices, forcing the immigrant population to become overcrowded in order to afford them.[12] Health, hygiene, and safety conditions in the complex rapidly deteriorated as a result of this overpopulation. Exacerbating the problem were turf wars related to prostitution, drug dealing, and gang activity, which turned the complex into a battleground. Serenissima's decline became an embarrass-ment for the rest of the "normal" city. After clashes between hostile immigrant gangs of Nigerian and Maghrebi origin in July 2006, a municipal order quickly resolved the situation: within a week the police had built a wall to divide and isolate the six apartment complexes from the rest of the city. According to one journalist, the wall was built to separate Nigerian and Maghrebi drug deal-ers from local consumers.[13] However, Padua's steel wall did not appear out of nowhere but rather replaced a pre-existing barbed-wire fence that for over ten years had been the scene of various drug-dealing and prostitution transac-tions.[14] That fence had already marked the border zone between the "normal" and the "abnormal" city. With the "new" wall encircling the rear of the com-plex and a police checkpoint at the front, access to Serenissima became more tightly controlled. The wall visibly demarcated the frontier between wanted and unwanted city residents, between formal and informal urban economies— between "friends and enemies," in the words of Carl Schmitt. Indeed, for the Serenissima residents the wall produced a space of judicial and existential ex-traterritoriality (fig. 4.1).[15]

Figure 4.1. Frame from the movie *Via Anelli. La chiusura del ghetto*, directed by Marco Segato (2008). © Jolefilm, Padua, Italy.

The erection of the Padua Wall was the city council's response to residents' demands for security against an otherwise uncontainable situation of crime and drug trafficking. Fear sustained the wall—fear certainly of criminal gangs but also fear of outsiders, of foreigners, of the unemployed, impoverished, non-white residents of the Serenissima complex. Built on behalf of the Padua citizenry, the wall signified an attempt by those who regarded themselves as the city's "legitimate" members to free themselves from the burden of unregulated contact with these other residents and to safeguard the well-being of the city's preexisting community. The rationale used for building the wall was the need to impose law and order. This was achieved at a high economic and symbolic cost: the steel wall enclosing the ghetto of Via Anelli cost the municipality €80,000 and also was condemned by Italian and European public opinion as an anti-immigrant wall.[16] As such, the construction of the wall gave rise to conflicting ideological debates between representatives on the political left and right alike. According to Flavio Zenonato (the left-wing mayor of Padua), for example, the wall was built as a temporary requirement to impose the rule of law and order on all citizens. While Zenonato's representatives defended the wall as a control mechanism, observers on the right accused them of "arrogant behavior" in aiming to separate "good from evil" with this physical barrier.[17] Few commentators, though, were willing to distinguish between two terms that, more often than not, were used interchangeably: criminality and immigration.

Ironically, the wall was built in Via Anelli after a housing reallocation operation for legal migrants living in the complex had started. Between 2005 and 2007, the municipal authorities reallocated housing for the legal residents and shut down each of the six buildings. In total the municipality reallocated 300 homes and more than 600 individuals; the rest, presumably illegal migrants, relocated elsewhere in the city.[18] The six-building complex today remains locked, its doors and windows blocked to prevent further occupation by new migrants. Meanwhile, the local government is seeking an agreement with the individual apartment owners to reuse this land. Such an agreement is far from being reached, however, because many owners reside in other European cities. The council is now discussing the contentious alternative of expropriation.[19]

The wall in Via Anelli was temporary, not because it was destroyed—for it still stands and blocks access to the complex—but because those residents whose housing demands could be regularized were gradually moved out of the complex to other public housing facilities throughout the city. Legal immigrants were thus able to claim their right to decent public housing; the rest used the crisis to make their situation known and demand citizenship rights or legal recognition of their status and rights as refugees.[20] The partial success story here is that the wall, in spite of the criticism it provoked, accelerated the process of redistributing legal immigrants in public housing throughout the city.[21] Yet the reallocation process has not been free of controversy. The new housing facilities were guaranteed for only two years for single individuals and for four years for families; afterward rental terms were to be renegotiated. Moreover, the most negative part of the story is that, in spite of the rhetoric that justified building the steel wall, a ghetto was in fact created, and walling was used as a contingent short-term method of institutional response to deeper social problems. By that time, Minister of Social Affairs Paolo Ferrero claimed the Via Anelli's wall was a "necessity" rather than an "end" and could be considered a model for similar situations in other Italian cities. Indeed, in practice this wall-making policy has led to others: a wall was built in 2007 to separate Roma population from other residents at Via Tribionato in Milan, and another in Padua, built in 2008, separates the Diego Valeri School from a temporary residential complex.[22]

Ceuta's "Anti-Immigration Fence"

Mirroring on a larger scale the example of Padua, the external borders of the city of Ceuta have been walled against illegal immigration, a mechanism to protect the (EU)ropean border zone of this Spanish enclave within Northern Africa. Located in northern Morocco, the city of Ceuta has been under

European jurisdiction since the *Reconquista*. This refers to a historical period of over 800 years in which the Portuguese and Spanish kingdoms recovered the Iberian Peninsula from Arab domination. Ceuta came under Portuguese domination from 1415 to 1668, after which it became an extension of Spanish territory within Northern Africa together with Melilla and Gibraltar, the latter of which joined the United Kingdom in the eighteenth century.[23] During its original affiliation with Spain, Ceuta became a military garrison due to its strategic geopolitical position within the Mediterranean. In 1863 Ceuta and Melilla acquired the status of free ports, which allowed trade to complement the military function of these urban enclaves. Ceuta was closed to the African Muslim population historically; until 1868 Spanish legislation forbade Moroccans to live in the city, and only from the mid 1980s on could Ceuties of Muslim origin claim Spanish nationality.[24] During the years of colonial intervention (1912–1956), both Ceuta and Melilla became Spanish protectorates, clearly distinguished from the Moroccan landscape.[25] Today Ceuta is part of Andalusia, hence part of Spanish territory and part of the EU area of interest, a membership that was extended with the Schengen Agreement of 1991. Since Schengen, Moroccans have needed a visa to enter Ceuta, and "in the everyday talk of the borderlanders 'Muslim' and 'Moroccan' often work as interchangeable categories. The same occurs with 'Christian' and 'Spanish.'"[26] As we shall see with Belfast, religious affiliation has, in both past and present, defined where a population lives within the city, even if in the case of Ceuta almost half of its total population was defined as being of Muslim origin by the end of 2009.[27]

Since 1998 an eight-kilometer "protective" fence has encircled the city along its land border with Morocco. This borderline delineates not only Ceuta's perimeter but also the international border between Spain and Morocco and the frontier between Europe and Africa: in short, it comes between those belonging within the EU community and those excluded from it. Ceuta's fence constitutes a multi-scalar border structure that in practice operates differently, with more or less rigor, depending on the issue at stake. Not surprisingly, it is more permeable to the circulation of goods and capital than to the movement of people. The fence also functions as a filter, depending on the "type" and "purpose" of the population on the move. The circulation of traders and workers from adjacent localities, for example, is crucial to the survival of the city. The filter also operates in reverse: Ceuties cross the border in search of lower prices on "the other side" or to acquire a second or vacation house on the Moroccan seashore.[28] Operating as it does at different scales, Ceuta's fence not only controls illegal immigration; it also displays a continuum of different affiliations to a political community as defined by urban perimeters (Ceuta), mediated by national sovereignties (Spain), and enacted in favor of a larger postnational institutional arrangement (the EU).

Civilizational and religious struggles underlie the terms by which the recognition of difference and the right to gain entry and citizenship are legitimized, or not. From the Spanish and EU perspective, Ceuta's fence was built to control illegal immigration. It serves as a control mechanism that during the last decade has become ever stricter in response to rising EU fears of terrorist attacks by Islamist fundamentalists. After numerous African migrants crossed the barriers of Melilla and Ceuta in September 2005, the authorities' response was to fortify the border by building a double fence three meters high with regular guard posts, adjacent to a no-man's-land with a road for patrols and emergency services (see fig. 4.2). Several EU agencies and divisions are responsible for the Ceuta fence security, but it is centralized at the European Agency for the Management of Operational Cooperation at the External Borders (FRONTEX, based in Warsaw since 2005). A maritime Integrated System of External Surveillance (SIVE) was implemented in 2004, which, in conjunction with Morocco's collaboration on the border, reduced by 37 percent the number of would-be migrants reaching the Spanish coast between 2004 and 2005. As a consequence, the pressure on the borders of Ceuta and Melilla has increased.[29]

Figure 4.2. Fence near a mansion in Ceuta, Benzú (2007). Photograph © Alexandra Novosseloff.

The borderline is hard, when observed from the Ceuta/Spanish/EU side, yet it becomes elastic and porous when addressed from the African perspective. Even though Moroccan authorities have consistently claimed the need to restore the territorial unity of the country and refused to recognize the long-standing Spanish sovereignty of the enclaves—disregarding the borderline signaled by the wall—they nonetheless exchange this confrontational relationship for a cooperative one when implementing border patrol security along the fence. Moroccan patrols collaborate to strengthen the Spanish border and to prevent the circulation of undocumented migrants and traders. At the same time, cooperation in the form of coexistence and sociability exists along the border among the Ceuta population and residents of adjacent localities, who work together in countless irregular commercial practices for the sake of socioeconomic survival. In short, we find here the cross-border labor dynamics and social interaction typical of people in a border zone.[30] Ceuta's fence thus exemplifies the multifaceted dynamics embedded in the act of walling: it operates as a fortified barrier against the mobility and circulation of undocumented people, while at the same time responding to national—and in this case also transnational—territorial claims. Meanwhile it also functions as a social, economic, and security bridge for those living in the border zone.

Belfast's "Peace Lines"

Since 1969, the social boundaries underlying the years of intercommunity violence in Belfast known as The Troubles have assumed a material form in the built environment and defined how residents appropriate city spaces. A number of walls in Belfast, ironically referred to as "Peace Lines," address this conflict. They are a three-dimensional articulation of a history of power, identity, and belonging as experienced by the communities of the two ethno-political and religious groups in Northern Ireland: Nationalist/Republicans (largely identified as Catholic) and Unionist/Loyalist (largely identified as Protestant).[31] Officially the Belfast Agreement of 1998 ended the large-scale violence between these groups, although sporadic and focused violent episodes still occur. Over eighty-one Peace Lines have been built since the early 1970s as temporary fences with the aim of preventing religious, ethnic, and nationalist violence between the two groups. Indeed, more than half of them were built after the 1998 Belfast (Good Friday) Agreement: according to the Interface and Security Barrier Mapping Project, forty-four out of the eighty-one security and segregation barriers listed were built after 1998, and only five have been removed.[32] They do not form a continuous wall but consist of various sets of blocks at strategic points between neighborhoods and along roads. These brick or metal walls, which divide residential areas mostly along the city's northwestern districts, are located at the interfaces between these communities. Along the longest existing Peace Lines, gates are normally open during the day, to facilitate mobility and the circulation of emergency services, and closed at night and during national celebrations, when each community honors its identity claims over the urban space.

Despite the political success of the IRA ceasefire in 1994, the 1998 Belfast Agreement, and the apparent freedom enjoyed by both sides, the temporary lines remain in place, and social segregation and intolerance seem to have increased in the last decade (see fig. 4.3). Indeed, according to the Northern Ireland Housing Survey, in 2006 almost 95 percent of public ("council") housing estates were segregated on ethno-religious and ethno-nationalist grounds.[33] However, the gentrification of the city center, especially at the waterfront, has also been an attempt to deactivate existing territorial antagonisms. The renewed downtown area remains a sign of the political neutralization of urban public space rather than the integration of different *publics* coexisting in the city. The commercialized city center is cordoned off from the conflicted northwest districts by Westlinks, a highway with only six crossing points that is easily controlled by security forces. Together with the entertainment and recreational character of the river bank areas, the highway makes explicit the city's belated modernization, that is, its transition from an industrial city to one organized by a financial and service economy. To break the traditional association with sectarian nationalist conflict and socioeconomic inequality, and to advance a more sophisticated and leisure-oriented urban environment, city marketers have promoted the regeneration of the city center as a symbol of Belfast's modern, "cosmopolitan" standing. At the same time, ethno-religious

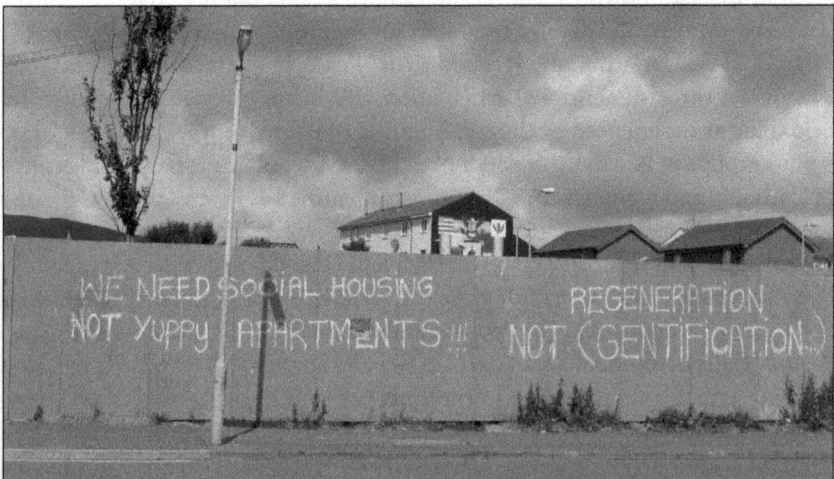

Figure 4.3. Along Cepar Way. A buffer zone between Peace Lines looking toward the Loyalist district of Shankill, with a wall and the Republican district of Falls behind it (Belfast, 2009). Photograph © Daniela Vicherat Mattar.

and ethno-nationalist conflicts are being domesticated through popular customized "political tourism" packages, rather than being addressed as a deeper problem of class and socioeconomic differentiation.[34]

By retaining the walls, policy makers have used the urban fabric to send a clear message of opposition and control, identifying which parts of the city belong(ed) to whom (and when), and who belongs where. As a result, residents are reassured of their affinities and claims of belonging, maintaining their differences vis-à-vis the other side and retaining their "own" spaces within the city. Urban segregation, then, has been the cost of peace. The walls separating the communities today are more numerous than they were during The Troubles. The problem, though, is much more complex than the explicit evidence of the number of walls hindering and segmenting the city might suggest. After all, different kinds of walls fragment—with fewer political arguments—a number of cities across the world. The Peace Lines and the related progressive gentrification (and neutralization) of the city center have severely reduced the random points of contact and common experiences usually offered by urban life. Certainly a number of efforts and initiatives for intercommunity dialogue and exchange are operating, yet the divisive walls of the Peace Lines still function as the glue that holds together the city's rival national imaginaries. Indeed, it even seems that one of the more solid visions of Belfast as a unified city has been created to satisfy the demands of a flourishing conflict-based economy of political tourism, one that oddly enough unifies the city-space under the gaze of its real others: tourists and visitors.

Transcending the Uses of Walling

Two decades after the fall of the Berlin Wall, it seems that walls are still in vogue. In Europe today there are peace lines, fear walls, anti-immigration walls, and a number of more liminal and invisible devices that aim to b/order our daily forms of exchange and coexistence. In various forms and sizes, and in response to different discursive justifications, Europe continues to build its walls to control populations as well as their expression, circulation, and mobility. Walls are built as shelters and as mechanisms that exclude those stigmatized as a threat. Walls signify a politics of separation, of control operating by means of constraining the possibilities people have to interact and eventually identify with Others—those described as different, be it in religious, ethnic, political, national, socioeconomic, or cultural terms. Walls in Schengenized Europe operate largely in a twofold sense, either as devices to pacify intra-urban conflicts or as mechanisms for mediating international relations, but in both situations they provide a "concrete" accommodation of difference through integration and segregation patterns that are embedded in the public rationale for building a wall in the first place.

It is intriguing how, in spite of being such an ancient device, walls continue to be used not only as material security instruments but also as symbolic mechanisms that demarcate membership and situate individuals within a social hierarchy at urban, national, and/or regional levels.[35] Following Peter Marcuse, we see a number of overlapping functions in the walling process: walls are used to fortify and protect the city or parts of its quarters; to trace the limitations between the private and public domains within the city fabric; to express the existence of conflicts of various kinds and the impossibility of solving them through discursive consensus; to divide, categorize, and control urban populations, defining both the scope of citizens' daily activities and of explicit segregation patterns.[36] The three examples examined above betray a certain vision of membership in the desired society, a project circumscribed either by an urban frontier (which is also national and transnational), as in the case of Ceuta, or by the struggle of a legitimate/illegitimate (pre)established political-urban community, as in the cases of Padua and Belfast. Etienne Balibar has identified cities as receptacles of identification processes, sites that define who is recognized as a member of the polity—that is, as a citizen—and who is explicitly excluded and signified as a threat or enemy. As he stresses, the case of the New Europe is in fact dependent on such processes, and the so-called "European citizen" exists "between two such poles or extremities": the *violent process of exclusion* on the one hand and the "'civil' process of elaboration of differences" in culture and education on the other.[37] In the case studies described here, the justifications employed to build and retain the walls were mainly based on the need to categorize, order, and control populations that had been vilified on grounds of identity: Muslims, Catholics, Protestants, Irish, British, Africans, nonwhites, and the impoverished.

In the case of Belfast, the Peace Lines maintain the city's definition as a place of sectarian struggles, whereas in Padua and Ceuta walls play a role in stating who belongs to the polities these cities encompass and who is excluded from them. Even though today's politicians claim to enhance multiplicity and plurality as an added value of city life, walls continue to be built as methods to control and secure a particular type of *urban experience* and to define that material space described as *urban*. Identity and difference are thus contained either inside or outside the wall line, which means that walls signify security and regularity, freedom and protection for some, whereas for others they represent exclusion, marginalization, and stigma. In other words, walls embody the hierarchy and distribution of social roles. Indeed, the places people occupy within the city-space, as in the cases of Belfast and Padua, or the cities they are not entitled to enter, as in the case of Ceuta, reflect these hierarchies and their underlying inequalities. The walls in Belfast, Padua, and Ceuta thus exemplify a threefold effect on how the urban is experienced: (1) they demarcate different territorialities in the city fabric, grading them in terms of preestablished hierarchies that assist in the city's functioning; (2) they trace and represent different clusters of identification, membership, and belonging within this network of hierarchies; and (3) they provide a sense of freedom and security according to who is situated where, who is being walled in, and who is walled out. The walls in Belfast, Padua, and Ceuta chart peoples' mobility and defend the hierarchical arrangements within these cities.

While the patterns of differentiation among the city quarters often respond to racial, class, or religious distinctions, as the cases of Belfast and Padua show, these hierarchical quarters cannot be hermetically closed without seriously compromising their reproduction and functioning. The same is true of cities more generally: they cannot be fully cut off from the surrounding landscape, as the case of Ceuta and its special relation with its neighboring localities demonstrates. The boundary lines between city and hinterland are dynamic and porous, as are the processes of identity formation and criteria of belonging to the citizenry. While walls reflect the hierarchical patterns of urban organization, their solidity cannot be taken for granted, since the lines they trace must be continually reestablished and renegotiated among the different parts. We have seen, then, that for Belfast, Padua, and Ceuta, walls have become conspicuous features of their urban and social fabric, shaping these cities' landscapes not only in terms of physical segmentation but also according to the symbolic representations of the past, present, and future expectations of their residents.

These examples show how in contemporary Europe, the juxtaposition of globalization, neoliberalism, religion, and (trans)nationalism generates a constant tension, in spite of the European expansion and turn toward cosmopolitanism that followed the fall of the Berlin Wall. National, ethnic, religious, and socioeconomic patterns of identification and distinction continue to mediate these cities' socio-spatial organization. In these case studies, the materiality of the decision and action of "walling" denotes the extent to which b/orders serve preestablished ideological and societal projects with a strong socioeconomic base. Walls function as shelters for group identities or as anti-terror instruments; as a means to control immigration or to avoid conflict and circulation internally; or, again, as anti-traffic mechanisms to control drug smuggling or prostitution. In each instance walls reflect either the state's failure to provide alternative mechanisms of social exchange and integration or its will to set specific patterns and conditions for that integration.

It used to be the case that urban walls served as markers of the connections between cities and the agriculture, dependent villages, trading networks, and sacred sites in their hinterlands. Exchange beyond the city gates supported not only commerce but also the city's political action and cultural development. The existence of walls helped the process by which protocols of urbanity developed; they indicated the presence of behavioral codes of interaction, whether tacit or explicit. While urban walls always served to demarcate, this demarcation was also necessarily a connecter, marking difference in a relational way that mediated between a city's inhabitants and foreign Others. A key question today is whether it is possible to transform the sectarian character of existing walls in cities such as Ceuta, Padua, and Belfast so that they become means of mediation that, instead of fragmenting a society, might connect differences among social groups and thereby transcend the fear they inspire.

There is hope for this because, inasmuch as they divide, walls also bind. The mere existence of the wall embeds the idea—the awareness—of the existing "other side" of the wall line. As either illusion or risk, the presence of a wall creates the possibility of connection between the divided parts. Establishing this possibility to bind and simultaneously divide reflects the nature of both our cities and our societies, for (in Georg Simmel's words) "the human being is a connecting creature who must always separate and cannot connect without separating."[38] This dual and apparently contradictory character is embedded in the walls of Padua, Ceuta, and Belfast: they have been built to divide existing communities, and yet the unity of each city prevails above and beyond the divisive effect of each wall. The three examined cases differ in scale and context; however, the walls reflect the unavoidable tensions of current political communities, nurtured by populations voicing multiple identity claims and claiming various degrees of affiliation.

Tracing borders and distinctions not only helps in forming identity but also reflects the social divisions and differences inherent in the human and urban condition. It is indeed a way of making sense of the world, of stating one's own identity and establishing a dynamic of (mis)recognition between one another.[39] For instance, the wall built in Via Anelli, although it created a de facto ghetto, did accelerate the formal processing of immigrant residence permits in Padua, recognizing the residents' identity and claim to city rights. The Ceuta fence reminds the Ceuties about the precarious, artificial, and historical nature of their border as well as telling Spaniards and Europeans more generally that the Other is not only *ad portas* but also a constitutive part of their own societies. The Peace Lines provide a sense of identity and belonging to residents in both the Unionist and Republican enclaves of Belfast, but at the same time they remind them, as well as the city's outsiders, that they are all part of Belfast. Walls, then, are not a problem per se, but rather became a problem when the borders and distinctions they trace dehumanize and vilify one of the sides, and when barriers built to create a common identity instead divide, marginalize, concretize, and rigidify what should remain elastic in the city, specifically the negotiation of patterns of identification and recognition.

We need, then, cities where the potentialities opened by difference and multiplicity are protected rather than concealed by walls, and where walls become part of the spaces that activate the opportunities for plural coexistence—not just for the elite but as part of the urban experience available to all. As Peter Marcuse has famously suggested, "we need walls that welcome and shelter, not walls that exclude and oppress."[40] Walls reflect common expectations of what is good and desirable for society's development: they provide a stage from which to project and on which to act in either inclusive or exclusionary terms. Thus, it is in observing the normative terms and rationale under which walls have been built, justified, and validated in Europe that we can challenge the terms under which liberal democracy and its corresponding neoliberal economic agenda are defended. The lines created by walls open the battleground, which compels us to imagine a kind of coexistence other than one based upon prevailing antagonisms.

Notes

1. "We need a wall, not to keep out what we fear but to give it a name." Translation by the author.
2. Anna Funder, *Stasiland* (London, 2003); Frederick Taylor, *The Berlin Wall: A World Divided, 1961–1989* (London, 2006).
3. The issue of where Europe's borders end is still contested; see Malcolm Anderson and Eberhard Bort, eds., *The Frontiers of Europe* (London, 1999); Gerard Delanty, "Borders in a Changing Europe: Dynamics of Openness and Closure," *Comparative European Politics* 4, no. 2–3 (2006): 183–202.
4. The original Agreement was signed in 1985, becoming part of EU law through the Amsterdam Treaty of 1997. Today the Schengen Area includes twenty-two of the twenty-seven EU member states and Norway, Iceland, and Switzerland, as well as cooperation with the UK. See http://europa.eu/ (accessed 25 February 2010).
5. See Peter Andreas and Timothy Snyder, eds., *The Wall Around the West: State Borders and Immigration Controls in North America and Europe* (Oxford, 2000); Etienne Balibar, "Europe as Borderland" *Environment and Planning D: Society and Space* 27, no. 2 (2009): 190–215; Bryan S. Turner, "Enclave Society: Towards a Sociology of Immobility," *European Journal of Social Theory* 10, no. 2 (2007): 287–304.
6. See http://europa.eu/legislation_summaries/institutional_affairs/treaties/amsterdam_treaty (accessed 25 February 2010).
7. Carl Schmitt, "The Concept of the Political" [1927], in *The Weimar Republic Sourcebook*, ed. Anton Kaes, Martin Jay, and Ed Dimendberg (Berkeley, 1995), 342–45.
8. Henk van Houtum, Olivier Kramsch, and Wolfgang Zierhofer, *B/ordering Space* (Aldershot, UK, 2005).
9. Nezar Alsayyad and Ananya Roy, "Medieval Modernity: On Citizenship and Urbanism in a Global Era," *Space and Polity* 10, no. 1 (2006): 1–20.
10. Marco Segato, *Via Anelli, la Chiusura del Ghetto*, DVD documentary (2008).
11. Daniela Ruffini cited in Michela Morello and Rosj Camarda, "Il muro di Padova: un muro di solida paura," *Sociología Urbana e Rurale* 86 (2008): 93.

12. According to Marco Carrai, adviser to the Padua municipal police, the 28 m2 flats were rented for up to €2000 per month; interviewed by Morello and Camarda, ibid., 95.
13. Paolo Beltramin, "Immigranti e violenze. Padova alza un muro," *Corriere della Sera*, 10 August 2006; see also Mario Porqueddu, "Ferrero: 'Padova esempio per le alter citta,'" *Corriere della Sera*, 17 July 2007.
14. Beltramin, "Immigranti e violenze"; Morello and Camarda, "Il muro di Padova," 97.
15. Giorgio Agamben, *State of Exception*, trans. Kevin Attell (Chicago, 2005).
16. Beltramin, "Immigranti e violenze"; Segato, *Via Anelli*.
17. Cited in Morello and Camarda, "Il muro di Padova," 97; Alessandro Trocino, "'Ponti, Non Barriere': Cgil e Pdci contro il muro," *Corriere della Sera*, 11 August 2006.
18. Morello and Camarda, "Il muro di Padova," 102–3; Porqueddu, "Ferrero"; Francesca Musiani, "Padua Wall: Immigration, Conflict, and Integration," *Peace and Conflict Monitor*, 25 October 2007, http://www.monitor.upeace.org/innerpg.cfm?id_article=448 (accessed 16 June 2010).
19. See Segato, *Via Anelli*; Morello and Camarda, "Il muro di Padova," 103–4.
20. Musiani, "Padua Wall."
21. Presumably the lack of stable jobs for these populations creates the risk of recurrence of overcrowded housing in the near future. See Musiani, ibid.
22. Morello and Camarda, "Il muro di Padova," 97; Musiani, "Padua Wall."
23. Henk Driessen, *On the Spanish-Moroccan Frontier: A Study in Ritual, Power and Ethnicity* (New York, 1992); Peter Gold, *Europe or Africa? A Contemporary Study of the Spanish North African Enclaves of Ceuta and Melilla* (Liverpool, 2000).
24. Ana Planet, *Melilla y Ceuta: Espacios Frontera Hispano-Marroquies*. Melilla, 1998.
25. Gold, *Europe or Africa?*
26. Xavier Ferrer-Gallardo, "Territorial (Dis)continuity Dynamics between Ceuta and Morocco: Conflictual Fortification vis-à-vis Cooperative Interaction at the EU Border in Africa," *Tijdschrift voor Economische en Sociale Geografie* 102, no. 1 (2011): 28.
27. The city's total population was estimated at over 78,674 at the end of 2009, of which 30,043 were of Muslim background. See Juanjo Oliva, "La UCIDE estima que en torno al 42% de los Ceuties es Musulman," *El Faro Digital*, 11 April 2010. http://www.elfarodigital.es/ceuta/sociedad/3320-la-ucide-estima-que-en-torno-al-42-de-los-ceuties-es-musulman.html (accessed 30 June, 2010).
28. "Moroccan citizens registered in the province of Tetouan or in the Prefecture Mdiq-Finideq are allowed to access Ceuta without a visa requirement for up to 24 hours," according to Ferrer-Gallardo, "Territorial (Dis)continuity Dynamics between Ceuta and Morocco," 8.
29. EU Commission, Mission Report, "Technical Mission to Morocco. Visit to Ceuta and Melilla. On Illegal Immigration," 7–11 October 2005.
30. Xavier Ferrer-Gallardo, "The Spanish-Moroccan Border Complex: Processes of Geopolitical, Functional and Symbolic Rebordering," *Political Geography* 27, no. 3 (2008): 301–21; Gold, *Europe or Africa?*; Sonia Cardenas, "The Contested Territories of Ceuta and Melilla," *Mediterranean Quarterly* 7, no. 1 (1996): 118–31.
31. Dominic Bryan states: "In practice the terms 'Protestant,' 'unionist' and 'loyalist' are used in some discourses almost interchangeably, as are 'Catholic' and 'nationalist'. But, that is not to say the common use of these terms is without strategy." Bryan, *Orange Parades: The Politics of Ritual, Tradition and Control* (London, 2000), 15. For Catholics in Belfast it is reported that the national identity choice as "Irish" decreased from 76

to 62 percent between 1968 and 1994, whereas Protestants who chose their national identity as "British" rose from 39 to 71 percent in the same period. See Trew (1996) cited in Mairead Nic Craith, *Plural Identities, Singular Narrative: The Case of Northern Ireland* (New York, 2002), 15.

32. Cited in Neil Jarman, "Diversity, Economy and Policy: New Patterns of Migration to Northern Ireland," *Shared Space: A Research Journal on Peace, Conflict and Community Relations in Northern Ireland* 2 (2006): 47–48.

33. Northern Ireland Housing Executive, "Northern Ireland House Condition Survey 2006. Main Report," http://www.nihe.gov.uk/housing_conditions_survey_2006.pdf (accessed 30 June 2010).

34. Sara McDowell, "Selling Conflict Heritage through Tourism in Peacetime Northern Ireland: Transforming Conflict or Exacerbating Difference?" *International Journal of Heritage Studies* 14, no. 5 (2008): 405–21.

35. Max Weber, *The City* [1921] (New York, 1958), and Lewis Mumford, *The City in History: Its Origins, Its Transformations and Its Prospects* (London, 1961).

36. Peter Marcuse, "'Dual City': A Muddy Metaphor for a Quartered City," *International Journal of Urban and Regional Research* 13, no. 4 (1989): 697–708.

37. Balibar, "Europe as Borderland," 202, emphasis in original.

38. Georg Simmel, "Bridge and Door" [1909], in *Simmel on Culture*, ed. David Frisby and Mike Featherstone (London, 1997), 171.

39. William E. Connolly, *Identity/Difference: Democratic Negotiations of Political Paradox* (Minneapolis, 1991), 163.

40. Peter Marcuse, "Not Chaos, But Walls: Postmodernism and the Partitioned City," in *Postmodern Cities and Spaces*, ed. Sophie Watson and Katherine Gibson (Cambridge, MA, 1994), 251.

II

Border Zones

CHAPTER 5

~:~

Border Guarding as Social Practice

A Case Study of Czech Communist Governance and Hidden Transcripts

MURIEL BLAIVE AND THOMAS LINDENBERGER

České Velenice, a little Czech town on the border with Austria that used to be the industrial suburb of the Lower Austrian town of Gmünd, appears to have been the ideal of a communist border community. Arising from the ashes of the Austrian empire in 1918 after a generous redrawing of the borders between Austria and Bohemia, the town served for over forty years as a small fortress for the Czechoslovak (Socialist) Republic, finding itself after 1948 at the foot of the Iron Curtain and at the hinge between the antagonistic world systems of capitalism and communism. After the communist coup in February of that year, the country became an integral part of the Soviet sphere of hegemony and propaganda and answered to the same basic ideological values: proletarian internationalism, freedom from capitalist exploitation, and the utopia of a modern, egalitarian society to be constructed under working-class leadership as embodied by its political vanguard, the Communist Party.

To all appearances the Soviet technology for governing border zones, including villages such as České Velenice, was imported into the Czechoslovak segment of the Iron Curtain in a swift and uncontested manner. The fortified communist border remained unchallenged for decades. Except during the Prague Spring in 1968, when it was briefly open, this specific feature of communist statehood, dating back to the first decades of Bolshevik dictatorship in the USSR, featured as an element of continuity in what Czechs nowadays call in shorthand the "totality"—the totalitarian rule of the communist regime. Not until 4 December 1989 were the Czechoslovak checkpoints along the Iron Curtain to West Germany and Austria finally opened for all to pass. The way border regions were managed in these countries shows the consequences the border had for their political culture and further economic and social development. Indeed, in terms of territorial administration, militarization of everyday life, and homogenization of the residential population, our case study of České Velenice presents a Soviet-style border community par excellence. It shows that communist governance (practice of rule) was predicated not only on controlling physical borders but also on social and political limits imposed on average citizens in their daily lives. This implementation of the border guarding technique and its ultimate success were intimately linked to how a "hidden transcript" of noncommunist national (anti-Austrian) values was translated into a "public transcript" of communist legitimization (guarding the border).[1] But before examining this local adaptation of Soviet-style border guarding, let us first recall the latter's basic features as they were established in the prewar USSR.

Soviet-Style Border Governance: A Short Retrospective

What did the communist governance of border regions represent? The way Soviet power brokers guarded state borders stands out as a historically unique variant in the history of modern European statehood. It was developed as an innate feature of the young Bolshevik state during its first stabilization phase in the wake of civil war. As long as they had been on the offensive, the communist authorities had practiced a policy of rather porous borders that allowed cross-border communication and exchange. This policy, also meant to further the proletarian revolution in neighboring states, often instrumentalized ethnic and national issues concerning the communities living on both sides of the border, as in the cases of Karelia and Finland or Ukraine and Poland.

When the world revolution failed to topple the West and the Soviet Union remained the only country under communist rule, at least for the time being, border regions were turned into areas of intensified police surveillance, and the political police started to administer them. With the dogma of "socialism in one country," which was established as the guiding principle for the country's development, the borderline acquired a new meaning: it was no longer a transition zone from which the revolution could be disseminated across the rest of Europe, but a *front* where hostile interventions from the capitalist world had to be stopped. Everywhere in the Soviet Union this front and its immediate hinterland became an area in a permanent state of emergency, cleansed in several waves of its "unreliable elements."[2] A special Politburo commission, established in 1925 to devise direct control of the Soviet border regions, redefined the periphery zone with a set of specific features:

+ a "restricted zone" 7.5 km wide (at times even wider) was drawn, and its residents were required to obtain a resident's permit or to resettle further inside the country, while special permits were issued to allow temporary access to the zone;

+ border guards were permanently deployed and became part of the local population; simultaneously the political police dominated all public affairs on-site;

+ after several waves of deportation and forced resettlement, border populations were ethnically, socially, and politically homogenized, and the remaining residents were forced to participate in guarding the border by assisting the border guards and other armed organs, in particular the (political) police.

When forced collectivization reached the rural regions of Ukraine and Belorussia, several waves of what we would today call ethnic cleansing affected zones with strong non-Russian minorities. In 1937 the border regions were also scoured for unreliable elements and "enemies of the people" on a massive scale. At the same time, the border-guard soldier came to epitomize Soviet heroism, representing the safety and eternity of the holy land of the communist future.[3]

World War II brought about a shift of the Soviet Union's western borders and a different, historically new kind of neighbor: the "people's republics." Nonetheless, Soviet leaders reinstalled the old border regime in the newly acquired regions, subjecting them to the same cleansing measures. The Red Army exported Soviet techniques and knowledge of border governance to these countries along with the communist dictatorship. All over Eastern and Central Europe, border regions between the new allies but mainly along the Iron Curtain were thoroughly sovietized. Reversing century-old traditions and practices in this part of Europe, a "good" border increasingly became an impenetrable one, a frontier that no one could or was supposed to cross under normal conditions.[4] As this sketch of border guarding in the Soviet system shows, border regions present a good case to study the consistent and sustaining sovietization of the new satellite states.

České Velenice's Hidden Charms

The Soviet methods of governance that formed the local institutions and infrastructure in České Velenice were not simply imposed from above, and the script for living at the border to capitalism was accepted not just out of servility and opportunism prompted by the party-state's terror and by sheer angst. People *chose* to live there for their own reasons, and they devised ways to get ahead and care for their own needs. The results of field research undertaken in 2008, eighteen years after the fall of communist rule, depict stability, albeit with an underside of internal strife and local antagonisms that betray claims to social harmony and a saturated idyll. The findings of the oral history study presented below derive from a total of thirty-nine interviews conducted in České Velenice by Muriel Blaive (M.B.), chosen in an effort to represent both sexes, multiple generations, and a variety of social milieus. Interviewees were chosen in a "snowball" process in which each one recommended others and usually served as a go-between to arrange the interviews. The interviews lasted an average of one hour and took place at the interviewee's workplace or home. The semi-open questionnaire evoked such topics as the contingencies of life at the border to a capitalist country; political, social, and economic aspects of this life; the experience of guarding the border; suffering under but also participating in repressive policies; staying and escaping; denouncing and protecting.[5]

That this town was allowed to continue to exist after the war, even though it literally touched the western border, was not at all inevitable. After the expulsion of the Sudeten Germans in 1945–47, most of these settlements remained devastated; the new inhabitants of the border regions took up residence at some physical distance from the barbed-wire fence. České Velenice was different because it was an industrial town with a proletarian past—it was home to an important railway factory—and had been given to the first Czechoslovak Republic in 1918, even though it did not historically belong to the lands of the Bohemian Crown. Hence it was emblematic of the Czech national victory over the Austrian Empire, a victory reconfirmed by the defeat of the German/Austrian Reich in 1945. In exchange for being allowed to live and work there at all, the town's population was strongly expected, if not outright compelled, to participate in guarding the border. Residents were either officially enrolled in the Auxiliary Border Guard or simply invited to practice the "civic duty" (of denunciation) to an even higher degree than anyone else in the country. Through the opportunistic usage of the angst of the "Other," specifically of the dangerous "foreigner" (the "Austrian" from Gmünd) who was characterized as an immediate threat, the regime justified the need to control not only "dissenters" but also "opponents," anybody who disagreed with its basic tenets, and the population in general. The "external threat" found its counterpart in the "internal threat" posed by candidates for emigration, who traveled to the town from all over the country looking for a way to break through the Iron Curtain. Guarding the borders against these trespassers was presented to the locals as a patriotic, necessary, just, and dangerous task. In the name of fighting against these internal and external threats, the regime largely convinced the local population to monitor itself and to entertain voluntarily a climate of terror turned against its own body. Indeed, any local who failed to denounce such an internal enemy (that is, a potential escapee), thus endangering the efficiency of the border guard, would have to be denounced by another local.

These three enemies—foreigners, dissenters and opponents, and other internal enemies—contributed to molding social and power relations and to re-creating a specific kind of political community after 1945. Even if fear of the first enemy rapidly became obsolete (Austria was a democratic state, not a revanchist one), the policy that sustained the general fear addressed existing sensitivities, soothed them with questionable historical references and well-anchored prejudices, and combined the whole with other factors such as envy or jealousy. The climate of mutual denunciations rapidly emerged. Josefa Kramárová, now a 38-year-old railway station employee, articulated her views of the state as follows:

M.B. Why was the regime so tough here and not elsewhere?

J.K. Because people created this among themselves. They made it worse.

M.B. Because they collaborated with the border guards, the militia, the secret police?

J.K. Yeah, they simply went too far. The people themselves denounced each other. They simply made it worse. Not the regime but the people made it tougher for themselves in this regime. People created this themselves!

Olga Rájová, a 58-year-old industrial photographer, held a similar view:

O.R. Here every other person was an "auxiliary," either with the border guards or with the police. They denounced each other, they hid things from one another, they envied each other.

M.B. What would they denounce, for instance?

O.R. Small crap things, I would say. Nobody had any relationships, there was nothing here, actually everything was monitored.... And people have still remained the same [now].

When asked if she thought there was a high percentage of communists in her town, Josefa Kramárová responded:

J.K. There was. There *was*.

M.B. For instance in your workplace?

J.K. Yes. There were many, but half of them were *fake*. They were communists only because they really wanted this flat, for instance, you see, or they wanted their child to study in a good school. Like 90 percent of the communists in this country. Because they wanted their child to study, because they wanted a flat, to get a plot of land to build a house, to get something somewhere, yeah, they had to sign up. You see? It was a condition. It was just like that: you want something? Then do this for us. Yeah, just a tit for a tat, you see?

While discussing the locals' participation and/or collaboration in guarding the border, Blaive asked Jakub Obědval, a 39-year-old director of the train repair factory, if a majority of the people approved of the regime:

J.O. No, on the contrary, I would say a majority disapproved.... Of course some things were good and other things were bad. Even today, some things are good and other things are bad. But of course the regime was founded on something [an ideological basis] which wasn't good. Clearly. So that I don't believe that a majority of the people would defend it much. But of course one has to be reasonable about the fact that something was good and something ... I'm saying it was a negligible number. Some people did it [denounced escapees] to help protect public property and their own.

M.B. Which is not necessarily political...

J.O. Exactly, which may not necessarily be understood as something political, something linked to political beliefs.

Jakub Obědval emphasized that not all escapees were freedom-craving, decent people; they could also have been petty or major criminals, swindlers, or assassins who then passed themselves off as political refugees in the West:

M.B. So the border between good and bad is not always clear?

J.O. It isn't. Why should it be? Nothing is like this in life. What is the border between good and bad? Can we draw a thick line? It's not possible.

In hindsight it seems that the border-guarding system was predicated on the actual blurring of lines between these categories. "Good" and "bad" were so relativized, and compromised so regularly, that it was difficult to maintain a clear view of what should have been proper behavior on the moral level. This moral uncertainty of the "tacit minimal consensus" for guarding the border was linked to at least two additional factors in the case of České Velenice: material advantages and patriotic conviction.[6]

Indeed, not only did České Velenice's inhabitants not use their proximity to the border as a chance to escape, but the town actually attracted new residents because of an appealing housing policy. People in Velenice could get apartments they could not get elsewhere in southern Bohemia. Many inhabitants also enjoyed privileges, and here we encounter one of the crucial bargaining factors in the aforementioned "minimal consensus." A number of locomotive engineers were allowed to take their trains to Gmünd. They thus came into official contact with Austrians and, although it was strictly forbidden and they were threatened with searches, they used the opportunity to pass goods back and forth across the border. Another advantage specific to people in České Velenice was that a large number of the town's employees worked at the railway station and benefited (as they still do) from greatly reduced fares on European railways. They could thus travel around the Eastern Bloc either for recreation or to shop wherever goods were cheaper or more available. This was, for instance, the case of Josef Dortík, the railway station director before and after 1989, who traveled to Poland, Hungary, and East Germany to buy leather shoes and leather jackets and still does so today. The regime also ensured upward social mobility by educating a number of workers' children in the excellent local high school, which specialized in high-voltage electrical engineering for work in the factory. Finally, the fact that the town was secluded and shut off from the rest of the country made it in a way claustrophobic but also exceptionally safe, quiet, and protected—something that has retrospectively come to be highly appreciated.

Yet as the entrepreneur Jakub Obědval stressed, these practices were not guided solely by material privileges or cynicism and petty-mindedness. Some people's convictions, which prompted them to act in a way that might seem morally reprehensible today, were perceived at the time as suggesting noble ideals related to patriotic and civic feelings. In this respect history and the way it was instrumentalized by the regime to boost national feelings and its own national legitimacy were crucially important: let us invoke Alf Lüdtke's claim that socialist regimes found a good basis where their aspirations rejoined the traditional values ("transcripts") of a nation.[7] In the case of Czechoslovakia, the close entanglement of nation-building and egalitarian values during the anti-Austrian fight for autonomy and emancipation in the nineteenth century had fostered the notion of the inherently democratic character of the Czechs as an ethnic group.[8] But democracy as a project was to be achieved *through* the assertion of nationalism, not by overcoming or dodging it. The communist regime instrumentalized this cultural claim to legitimize its leadership in Czechoslovakia.[9] As in numerous other cases in the history of communist dictatorships, the initial seizure of power took place in the name of an anti-imperialist restoration of the nation, cherishing its inalienable values,[10] in this case egalitarianism, democracy, and anti-Germanism. Our close examination of the České Velenice communist dictatorship and of its societal underpinnings reveals the lasting relevance of this specific world of meaning (*Sinnwelt*).[11]

The Silences of Communist Rule in the Czech Borderlands

As a consequence of the Munich Agreement between France, Great Britain, Italy, and post-*Anschluss* Germany in September 1938, which delivered to Hitler the German-speaking borderland of Czechoslovakia, the town of České Velenice was handed over to Nazi Germany on 8 October (in fact to Austria, which had become part of the Reich, although strictly speaking the town historically did not belong to the Sudetenland but rather to Lower Austria).[12] Fearing the occupation forces and the potential draft of men into the German army, 95 percent of the Czech townspeople fled to the hinterland, according to local historians.[13] In total perhaps fifty Czech-speaking families remained in the town during the war.[14] One of the oldest and most irreverent of the 2008 interviewees reflected on this time: "They were all with the Gestapo." After the war the town's population was half of what it had been before the German invasion; many were newcomers. Additionally, the German-speaking minority living in České Velenice before (and during) the war was expelled toward Austria. As several interviewees mentioned, this sudden change in the composition of the population had consequences for the strength of solidarity among the locals: people who did not know each other failed to help each other when in need. Historical ties between České Velenice and its original "mother town" of Gmünd became tenuous because the newcomers knew nothing about the common history of the two towns, and postwar and/or communist propaganda distorted the little they did hear. The common past of the two towns and indeed the common history of the region simply disappeared from history books and public awareness. These local circumstances lent themselves to mobilizing "history" as a means of rule typical of communist regimes.

Terror and the arbitrary exercise of power are classical and intangible elements of domination, but under communist rule history is a distinct mode of domination as well, in particular in the way it thematizes the relationship between the "internal" party history and the history of the nation—and of its enemies. In the case of České Velenice, the politics of history appealed to collective memories of World War II. The 1938 Munich Agreement, the suffering during the war, the liberation by the Red Army, and the expulsion of the so-called Sudeten Germans were fully instrumentalized to justify the local population's participation in guarding the border. Paradoxically, and as we have already hinted, the vague transmission of the historical narrative, according to which the Germans and Austrians were all guilty while the Czechs were all victims, excluded any specific detail about the actual situation in the town. Historical knowledge, both in the schools and more generally in the public sphere, largely took the form of a well-kept silence regarding the region's history during the war and its aftermath, so that the vast majority of České Velenice's inhabitants knew next to nothing about the town's recent history. This was the case even for the youngest generation, who were educated long after 1989.

"The war" in general (World War II) was something interviewees returned to constantly, and it is definitely a constitutive factor in the town's identity. But it was referred to only on an abstract level, as a general threat to which the Czechs responded with a sense of the need to hold the ranks together. Why such vagueness? We shall venture the following hypothesis: the official version of national history would have been dangerously challenged if historians had discovered that the Czechs who remained in Velenice during the war collaborated with the Germans; that no one protested against the deportation of the local Jews (if there were any, which no one was able to tell us with any degree of certainty); and/or that the expulsion of the "Sudeten Germans" concerned not only illegitimate Nazi settlers of wartime vintage but also long-established, relatively or totally "innocent" Austrian families. During the fieldwork the impression arose that words such as "shame," "guilt," or even "unease" were never clearly articulated but seemed to permeate the unspoken part of the narratives.

The testimony of Barbora Tyčková, a 30-year-old medical student, exemplifies both the general historical ignorance of the town's inhabitants and a tangible guilty feeling:

> B.T. I don't really know much about what happened after the war here. My grandmother lived in a small farming village near Třeboň. She remembers the schools closing and German soldiers stealing from their farm. After the war her family bought a bigger farm with large farming and grazing fields. This was a farm that belonged to an Austrian/German (not sure) family whose fate we don't know. Either they left during the war or were expelled afterwards. The Czechoslovak government was selling these border area properties very cheaply. I remember my grandma describing how they found a few belongings of the previous owners in the attic or under the floorboards. They thought the family must have left in a hurry and hidden these things, hoping to find them when they returned. They described feeling bad about it.

When faced with a seemingly obvious question—"What do you know about the expulsion of the Sudeten Germans in this town?"—the interviewees' answers were curt: "They don't write much about it, here" (Jiří Tajemný, 58-year-old locomotive engineer); "I just know that they were expelled…" (Dominika Kolářová, 20-year-old student); "I don't know anything" (Alena Maďárová, 32-year-old cleaning lady); "Nothing at all" (Jakub Obědval, 39-year-old factory director). Zdeněk Lendl, a 48-year-old carpenter, provided a typical response:

> M.B. What do you know about the Second World War in Velenice?
>
> Z.L. Well, I know only what I heard from my dad.
>
> M.B. And what did you hear?
>
> Z.L. Well, that the Americans bombed the town.
>
> M.B. That's all?
>
> Z.L. That's all.
>
> M.B. And the German occupation?
>
> Z.L. Well, I don't know anything.

Josefa Kramárová, a 38-year-old railway station employee, also knew little about this period:

> M.B. What do you know about the liberation of the town by the Red Army?
>
> J.K. The Red Army was ever here?

Nor did František Jasný, a 57-year-old worker:

> M.B. What do you know about the German occupation?
>
> F.J. I don't follow this at all, I'm not interested. That Hitler was an idiot, wasn't he? [laughter]

The selectiveness of communist education thus served to impose a taboo on the question outside of the general perception of a "German threat" and to discourage potential research. Since the town archives are still inaccessible, local historians are left only with the crumbs of information they gather here and there.[15]

There are of course reasons why the communist regime preferred to avoid discussing the historical particulars of Austrian-Czech relations, and not only in České Velenice. Indeed, the so-called "Beneš decrees" have poisoned these relations since the end of World War II. During the 1930s Hitler's Germany ever more urgently demanded the annexation of the portion of Czechoslovak territory that was mostly inhabited by German-speaking people—who all later became simplistically tagged as "Sudeten Germans." In the case of České Velenice, these "Germans" were obviously Austrians who, used to ruling Bohemia, generally had a hard time accepting the authority of the new Czechoslovak state after 1918. As mentioned above, Hitler's troops took Velenice in October 1938. The vast majority of Czechoslovak Germans enthusiastically hailed the Nazi entry first into the German-speaking regions in 1938 and then into the rest of Bohemia-Moravia in 1939.[16] Hitler placed the country under the authority of a "Protectorate of Bohemia and Moravia"; its combination of repression, deportations, and collaboration was shared by all Nazi-occupied European countries. Between the end of 1938 and the fall of 1945, President Beneš, who had fled in October 1938, headed a provisional government, first in exile in London and later in Prague. In the absence of any functioning parliament, he issued 143 ordinances or "decrees." Four of those, dating from spring and summer 1945, proclaimed the expropriation of the Sudeten Germans without compensation (as well as of the Hungarians from Slovakia, of the "collaborators," and of the "traitors"). Almost three million of these "Germans" were expelled toward Germany and Austria—although not by force of the decree but instead in the wake of the Big Three's approval of the decision at the Potsdam Conference in August 1945, provided it would proceed in an "organized and humane manner."[17] Nonetheless, excessive brutality was sometimes used. The expellees were deemed collectively responsible for the ordeal of the Czech nation between 1938 and 1945.[18]

The Czech-German Historical Commission estimated in 1996 that this expulsion resulted in 25,000 to 30,000 dead on the German side.[19] Additionally, on 8 May 1946, just a few days before the first postwar elections, the reconvened Czechoslovak parliament (not yet elected because the political parties had only designated their own provisional MPs) issued Law 115. This amnestied all Czechoslovak citizens from actions committed during their "fight for freedom" between 30 September 1938 and 28 October (not 8 May) 1945—that is, a period long after "freedom" had been restored but during which most of the actions committed against Germans took place.[20] Hence the Czech unease on this question, although the population at the time and still today overwhelmingly approved the principle of expelling the Germans. Consistently from 1995 until today, 50 to 55 percent of people surveyed have considered it "justified" (with a 60 percent peak in 2002), whereas only 1 to 3 percent have considered it "unfair" to the point of rendering it "necessary not only to apologize but also to compensate and/or to restitute property to the victims." For about two-thirds of the population it has been and still would be out of the question to repeal the decrees.[21]

From Anti-Austrian/Anti-German Feelings to Pro-Communist Sentiment

The policy of "silence" in České Velenice concerning the Sudeten German issue is therefore quite typical of the Czech Republic. The benefit the Communist Party of Czechoslovakia extracted from the expulsion and the national legitimacy that this action conferred to its leaders are also typical, although in the beginning it was mainly the democrats and President Beneš who propagated this expulsion. The party masterfully instrumentalized the "national" aspect of the Sudeten Germans' "treason" (that is, their vote of 92 percent for the openly Nazi and irredentist Sudetendeutsche Partei in the last free Czechoslovak elections of May-June 1938) for ideological purposes that went far beyond solely the German issue.[22]

First, the Soviet Union was presented as the guardian angel of Czechoslovakia. The communists exploited the fact that the USSR had not signed the infamous Munich Agreement—mainly because it had not been invited to do so, though this was not part of the propaganda. Second, the Communist Party, which controlled the national committees (that is, the new Soviet-style local administration that replaced the traditional structures in 1945 with the democrats' support), redistributed the property left by the Sudeten Germans (land and houses) with calculated generosity. Between 1945 and 1947, the former Sudetenland was repopulated by almost a million and a half internal migrants, who benefited from numerous advantages. In the free elections held in May 1946, the communist vote in those regions reached 56.7 percent in Ústí nad Labem (Aussig), 52.2 percent in Karlovy Vary (Carlsbad), and 48.5 percent in Liberec (Reichenberg); unfortunately it was impossible to find reliable figures for České Velenice, although it seems the Socialist-Nationals of President Beneš won the elections there.

To "admit" the enemy's existence and to pretend that the enemy is more powerful than it actually is, are tactics that communist and other totalitarian regimes commonly use to justify repression. This "method" as deployed in postwar Czechoslovakia is an avatar of Stalin's famous thesis, according to which the "class struggle intensifies with the construction of socialism." Insofar as communist regimes were predicated on the constant fostering and feeding of "enemies," the "German threat" was an easy propaganda tool for the communists—a practice that did not cease in 1989. It is remarkable, for instance, that President Klaus was elected in 2003 by an electoral alliance of conservative parties and the still existing communists on the basis of the popular belief that his main opponent, former dissident Jan Sokol, favored the abrogation of the Beneš decrees.[23] For us it is interesting that today's government and parliament in the Czech Republic are pursuing a policy that was already determined by President Beneš in 1945 and taken over by the communist regime between 1948 and 1989. That is undoubtedly why the silence that has characterized the Czech side of the border for decades continues today in the specific case of České Velenice: an apparently model Soviet-style guarded border in fact both hid and exploited a very specific local situation.

České Velenice's life was highly politicized because of its proximity to the capitalist border, a phenomenon that we coin here as the "over-determination of the border region." In an extremely ideologized, socially mobilized, and over-policed town it is tempting to attribute the regime's successes and failures to nothing other than the terror policy of a totalitarian state, in the mold of Czech historical literature on the "Iron Curtain."[24] Repression was indeed instrumental in exerting communist domination, but even today there is little reflection in the Czech Republic or in studies of communist dictatorships in this part of Europe on the role of the population itself in the repression. The specific quality of state socialist governance was its conceptual dynamism, which constantly attempted to "integrate the controlled into the activity of controlling."[25] This was a major feature of the regime's presence in České Velenice—namely, the permanent pressure exerted on the town's inhabitants to contribute to the denunciation system. A large part of the town's adult population was not only policed but policing to some degree. Had the police state been so hard to bear, the town residents would have simply moved to the hinterland. And had the town been so "communist," it would not have survived the postcommunist transition so fast and so smoothly. Instead "conjunctures of hope and despair, doubt and relaxation have simultaneously existed, as two parallel realities."[26]

Conclusion

To what extent is České Velenice an exceptional border town when compared to other communities along the Iron Curtain? Some of the interviewees perceived a difference in other Czech communities near the German border with respect to a social climate both less intoxicated by surveillance during communism and more open to exchange and the evolution of communal relations following the removal of the Iron Curtain in 1989.[27] We know from research on GDR border guards that—compared to this Czech case—their social integration into the local population always was a sore point in the ruling party's border control policies.[28] Daphne Berdahl's pioneering study on a little village in East Germany, Kella in the Eichsfelde region, yielded comparable results: in this community of the Catholic diaspora, which was as close to the Iron Curtain as České Velenice was, compliance in assisting the police, indicting suspicious outsiders, and guaranteeing an undisturbed state of "Ordnung und Sicherheit der Grenze" (order and security of the border) went hand in hand with a marked inner distance from the socialist state in general, as far as the majority of the population was concerned.[29] Further comparative work should therefore be based on the assumption that the cohabitation between the Soviet-style border regime and the communities forced to "host" it was compatible with very different, even contrasting, local cultures.

Considering the evident appropriation and adaptation of the Soviet-style border guarding system to local circumstances (although the barbed-wire fence never became popular in the eyes of even the most convinced communists, and the majority of people disapproved of the practice of shooting trespassers), we conclude by once again citing Alf Lüdtke, whose notion of *Eigen-Sinn* or "sense of oneself" is a key term in his analysis of workers' everyday life,

> denoting willfulness, spontaneous self-will, a kind of self-affirmation, an act of (re)appropriating alienated social relations on and off the shop floor by self-assertive prankishness, demarcating a space of one's own. There is a disjunction between formalized politics and the prankish, stylized, misanthropic distancing from all constraints or incentives present in the everyday politics of Eigen-Sinn. In standard parlance, the word has pejorative overtones, referring to "obstreperous, obstinate" behavior, usually of children. The "discompounding" of writing it as Eigen-Sinn stresses its root signification of "one's own sense, own meaning." It is semantically linked to *aneignen* (appropriate, reappropriate, reclaim).[30]

In the context of České Velenice, *Eigen-Sinn* refers to the small, autonomous spaces individuals carved out in their own lives, away from the prying eyes of the regime.[31] Politics could be "privatized" by the individuals, which provided them with strategies of avoidance, withdrawal, and shutting down vis-à-vis the regime.[32] The oral interviews cited here allowed us to deconstruct such strategies. Although the communist regime had a clearly dictatorial nature, the constitution, deployment, and enforcement of the socialist domination system demanded from its subjects a subjective disposition to cooperate. Everybody adapted to the rule at one level or another, which implied, according to the circumstances, both compliance and resistance at the individual level. The notion of modern dictatorship has led us on the one hand to emphasize the communist system's enormous degree of domination, but on the other hand to insist on the relative autonomy of social relations at the ground level of the body politic.[33] This double reality should not, however, conjure the notion of social micro-spaces exempted from the impact of communist domination as evoked in the popular catchphrase of the East German *Nischengesellschaft* (niche society). On the contrary: these realms too were carved out of the daily interaction with the official life of state socialism. Their material and mental existence resulted from the pressure born out of the communist claim to all-pervasive authority (*Durchherrschung*), producing a fragmented form of sociability.[34]

We concur with Lüdtke that in Central Europe the socialist regime found fertile ground where its aspirations could rejoin the traditional values ("transcripts") of a nation—in the case of East Germany, quality of work, cleanliness, and order; in the Czech case, egalitarianism, democracy, and anti-German sentiment. The Czech communist authorities instrumentalized these three pillars of national identity to constitute a large basis for a "tacit minimal consensus" under communism. Or perhaps Czech nationalism instrumentalized Czech communism for its own ends. In any case the regime enjoyed support from the population at a critical minimal level, and in return the regime guaranteed the population minimal benefits, on the border as elsewhere. Like thousands of other border communities in communist dictatorships, České Velenice encapsulates the basic features of communist rule in a particularly condensed way, with regard to both its "public" and "hidden transcripts."

Notes

1. James Scott, *Domination and the Arts of Resistance: Hidden Transcripts* (New Haven, 1992).
2. Sabine Cœuré and Sandrine Dullin, "Introduction," in *Frontières du communisme. Mythologies et réalités de la division de l'Europe de la révolution d'Octobre au mur de Berlin*, ed. Sabine Cœuré and Sandrine Dullin (Paris, 2007), 9–23. On the making of border regimes in Soviet and state socialist dictatorships see other contributions in this pioneering volume, in particular by Nick Baron (on Karelia), Christophe Barthélémy (on the representation of border guards on Soviet posters), Olga Ken (on the border regime as a paradigm for domestic rule), Nicolas Werth (on purges of border regions as part of "mass operations" in the 1930s), and Sandrine Dullin (on border guards at the western borders).
3. Sheila Fitzpatrick, *Everyday Stalinism. Ordinary Life in Extraordinary Times: Soviet Russia in the 1930s* (Oxford, 1999), 71.
4. Sandrine Dullin, "Les protecteurs. Le rôle des gardes-frontières dans la surveillance des frontières occidentales de l'URSS (1917–1939)," in Cœuré and Dullin, *Frontières du communisme*, 381.
5. This oral history study was undertaken under the auspices of the Borders Program of the Ludwig Boltzmann Institute for European History and Public Spheres, originally designed by Berthold Molden (http://ehp.lbg.ac.at/en/research-programme/communist-and-postcommunist-times-central-europe, accessed 22 April 2010). See also

Muriel Blaive and Berthold Molden, *Grenzfälle. Österreichische und tschechische Erfahrungen am Eisernen Vorhang* (Weitra, 2009), also published in Czech under the title *Hranice probíhají vodním tokem. Odrazy historie ve vnímání obyvatel Gmündu a Českých Velenic* (Brno, 2010); Muriel Blaive, "Le 'petit homme tchèque' à la mode socialiste: rupture et continuités depuis 1989," in *Le retour des héros: la reconstitution des mythologies nationales à l'heure du post-communisme*, ed. Korine Amacher and Leonid Heller (Geneva, 2010), 91–115; and idem, "République tchèque. La Révolution de velours vue de České Velenice," in *1989 à l'est de l'Europe. Les fêlures d'un mythe fondateur*, ed. Jérôme Heurtaux and Cédric Pellen (La Tour d'Aigues, 2009), 250–71.

6. Thomas Lindenberger, "Tacit Minimal Consensus: The Always Precarious East German Dictatorship," in *Popular Opinion in Totalitarian Regimes*, ed. Paul Corner (Oxford, 2009), 208–22.

7. Alf Lüdtke, "La République démocratique allemande comme histoire. Réflexions historiographiques," *Annales* (January–February 1998): 3–39.

8. See Muriel Blaive, "La démocratie pour les Tchèques: une légitimité politique et une composante identitaire," *Revue d'études comparatives Est-Ouest* 1 (2003): 59–82.

9. Muriel Blaive, "Internationalism, Patriotism, Dictatorship and Democracy: The Czechoslovak Communist Party and the Exercise of Power, 1945–1968," *Journal of European Integration History* 13 (2007): 2.

10. Gerd Koenen, *Was war der Kommunismus?* (Göttingen, 2010).

11. Pavel Kolář, "Sozialistische Diktatur als Sinnwelt. Repräsentationen gesellschaftlicher Ordnung und Herrschaftswandel in Ostmitteleuropa in der zweiten Hälfte des 20. Jahrhunderts," *Potsdamer Bulletin für Zeithistorische Studien* 40/41 (2007): 24–29.

12. The "Sudetenland" was officially defined by Nazi propaganda as border regions of Bohemia populated by Sudeten Germans since time immemorial; because the "Czech Vitoraz region" had historically belonged to Lower Austria, the Velenice inhabitants entertained the somewhat ludicrous hope that they would not fulfill the "Sudetenland" criteria. On this transaction see Jiří Oesterreicher, Irena Kotrbová, and Harald Winckler, *Společná minulost. Gmünd a České Velenice* (České Velenice, 2005), 48.

13. Jiří Oesterreicher and Lenka Klečatská, *60 let školy 1946–2006 Střední škola České Velenice* (České Velenice, 2004), 12–13.

14. Oesterreicher et al., *Společná minulost*, 50.

15. Located in Jindřichův Hradec, they are allegedly not yet indexed, that is, still in their boxes without an inventory, and the public is therefore not allowed to consult them—at least, that is what we were told in these archives.

16. On this issue see Muriel Blaive, "De la démocratie tchèque et des 'décrets Beneš,'" in *L'Europe et ses passés douloureux*, ed. Georges Mink and Laure Neumayer (Paris, 2007), 118–27; Muriel Blaive and Georges Mink, eds., *Benešovy dekrety. Budoucnost Evropy a vyrovnávání se s minulostí* (Prague, 2003).

17. Radomír Luža, *The Transfer of the Sudeten Germans: A Study of Czech-German Relations, 1933–1962* (New York, 1964), 279–80.

18. On the moral conflict between democracy and the expulsion see Blaive, "La démocratie pour les Tchèques."

19. Anne Bazin, "Produire un récit commun: les commissions d'historiens, acteurs de la réconcilation," in Mink and Neumayer, eds., *L'Europe et ses passés douloureux*, 113.

20. Anne Bazin, *Le retour de la question allemande dans la vie politique tchèque* (Paris, 1994).

21. See the numerous opinion polls on this topic on: www.cvvm.cz.

22. For a more thorough review of this policy see Muriel Blaive, *Une déstalinisation manquée. Tchécoslovaquie 1956* (Brussels, 2005).

23. See his commentary on this issue in Josef Beránek, *Jan Sokol: nebát se a nekrást* (Prague, 2003).

24. Alena Jílková and Tomáš Jílek, eds., *Železná opona. Československá státní hranice od Jáchymova po Bratislavu 1948–1989* (Prague, 2006); and Pavel Vaněk, *Pohraniční stráž a pokusy o přechod státní hranice* (Prague, 2009).

25. Thomas Lindenberger, "Creating State Socialist Governance: The Case of the Deutsche Volkspolizei," in *Dictatorship as Experience: Towards a Socio-Cultural History of the GDR*, ed. Konrad Jarausch (New York, 1999), 130.

26. Lüdtke, "La République démocratique allemande comme histoire," 8.

27. Muriel Blaive, "Ceské Velenice, eine Stadt an der Grenze zu Österreich," in Blaive and Molden, *Grenzfälle*, 168–69.

28. Gerhard Sälter, *Grenzpolizisten. Konformität, Verweigerung und Repression in der Grenzpolizei und den Grenztruppen der DDR 1952 bis 1965* (Berlin, 2009).

29. Daphne Berdahl, *Where the World Ended: Re-Unification and Identity in the German Borderland* (Berkeley, 1999), 44–71.

30. See the glossary in Alf Lüdtke, ed., *The History of Everyday Life: Reconstructing Historical Experiences and Ways of Life* (Princeton, 1995), 313–14.

31. Thomas Lindenberger, "Die Diktatur der Grenzen. Zur Einleitung," in *Herrschaft und Eigen-Sinn in der Diktatur. Studien zur Gesellschaftsgeschichte der DDR*, ed. Thomas Lindenberger (Cologne, 1999), 13–44.

32. Lüdtke, "La République démocratique allemande comme histoire," 35.

33. On dictatorship see Jürgen Kocka, "The GDR: A Special Kind of Modern Dictatorship," in Jarausch, *Dictatorship as Experience*, 17.

34. On *Durchherrschung* see Alf Lüdtke, "'Helden der Arbeit' – Mühen beim Arbeiten. Zur mißmutigen Loyalität von Industriearbeitern in der DDR," in *Sozialgeschichte der DDR*, ed. Hartmut Kaelble, Jürgen Kocka, and Hartmut Zwahr (Stuttgart, 1994), 188; Thomas Lindenberger, "The Fragmented Society: 'Societal Activism' and Authority in GDR State Socialism," *Zeitgeschichte* 37, no. 1 (2010): 3–20; and Lüdtke, "La République démocratique allemande comme histoire," 32–33.

CHAPTER 6

A "Complicated Contrivance"
West Berlin behind the Wall, 1971–1989

DAVID E. BARCLAY

> The age of heroes is said to be over.
> —Eleanor Lansing Dulles, "Berlin after the Four Power Talks," 1971[1]

Writing in the 1960s, the novelist and essayist Wallace Stegner insisted that the postwar history of Berlin cried out for epic literary treatment: "The *great* book on Berlin is going to be a sort of Iliad, a story that dramatizes a power struggle in terms of the men who waged it."[2] Indeed, the experience of Germany's once and future capital after 1945 is full of high drama and powerful personalities, from Stalin and Truman to Ernest Bevin, Lucius Clay, Ernst Reuter, Willy Brandt, Walter Ulbricht, John F. Kennedy, and the "daring young men" who flew the Airlift in 1948–49. Berlin seemed to be the epicenter of the Cold War, the site of superpower confrontation, of "wars of nerves," of America's "finest hour," the place where two competing political, economic, and cultural systems collided and competed spectacularly.[3] After August 1961 it was the site of the Wall, that grisly and constant reminder of the abnormal division of the world and of a great city.

But the period of West Berlin's history after the mid 1960s, and especially after 1971–72, was decidedly unheroic and in many ways anticlimactic; it certainly did not lend itself to epic mythmaking. The historian Andreas Daum has written tellingly of the evolution of "America's Berlin" after 1948, while Dominik Geppert has investigated the "mythology" of Berlin as the "frontline" or *Frontstadt* in the Cold War.[4] Yet after 1965 or 1966, the mythology of "America's Berlin" lost much of its cultural salience and its evocative power, in the United States and in West Berlin itself. Symbolic of this development is what happened to the West Berlin Congress Hall (Kongresshalle). Built in 1956–57 at the height of West Berlin's "heroic" phase, designed by the American architect Hugh A. Stubbins, and strongly promoted by the indefatigable US diplomat and Berlin friend Eleanor Lansing Dulles, the Congress Hall was intended to be an ideological statement about the American relationship to Berlin, a showcase for American design and American values. In 1980, however, its roof partially collapsed, killing one person and injuring several others.[5]

When one US official was asked if the Americans wanted to help rebuild it, he replied "that there had been no great public interest and to my knowledge no serious suggestion that US money might be available for its reconstruction."[6] The halcyon days of "America's Berlin" were long gone, even though the building was eventually rebuilt according to Stubbins's original plans.

Key to the post-1960s transformation of West Berlin were global shifts in the Cold War that in turn contributed to a mutual desire to deescalate the situation around Berlin and, with that, the potential for a future Berlin crisis to spiral out of control. Thus, the real turning point in West Berlin's history, and one that signaled the end of its "heroic" phase, was the negotiation and implementation of the Quadripartite Agreement of 1971–72 among the four postwar occupying powers. Supplemented by intra-German arrangements on the regularization of transit between West Berlin and the Federal Republic, the Quadripartite Agreement represented an attempt to create a semblance of normality in an abnormal situation. A "magnificent piece of pragmatic diplomatic obfuscation," it was designed to make the Wall and the division it had cemented into something that, if not permanent, at least seemed to be an enduring part of the German and European political map.[7] Crucial to that endeavor was not only the "normalization" of West Berlin's relationship with the Federal Republic, the German Democratic Republic, and the Soviet Union but also the careful maintenance of a structural status quo in West Berlin, based in turn on continued Allied occupation rights and a steady flow of subsidies from the Federal Republic. In the words of the British diplomat Sir Christopher Mallaby, West Berlin's post-1971 situation depended on "a very complicated contrivance ... which tremendously and triumphantly succeeded." It was, he concludes, "one of the wonders of the modern world."[8]

This contrived normality persisted for almost two decades and helped to sustain a curious—indeed, unique—social and political culture in West Berlin itself, one in which the Wall was at once omnipresent and barely noticed. To understand how the Wall affected post-1972 West Berlin, it is thus necessary to consider in some detail the reciprocal and complex relationship between the Allies in West Berlin and the culture of the truncated city itself. Among other things, so "normal" had the contrived reality of West Berlin become in the 1970s and the 1980s that the Allies themselves sometimes needed to be reminded why they were there in the first place. And though West Berlin's disparate cultures—political activists, artists, immigrants, students, adherents of alternative life styles including squatters and anarchists, and an aging "native" population—increasingly came to ignore or criticize the Allies, the unique "island" *Biotop* that made these cultures possible depended almost wholly on the Allied presence and on the maintenance of the status quo that the Quadripartite Agreement had enshrined. Until 1989–90 the Allies ensured that the island stayed secure, while the Wall itself increasingly became a kind of "absent presence" to West Berliners—always visible, always there, always apprehended, often resented, but somehow not as important a part of lived daily experience as outsiders might have thought. People get used to boundaries, and in West Berlin they also had long been used to the presence of the soldiers who made the boundaries seem permanent and stable. This chapter examines the role of the soldiers and of the Wall alike and how the quadripartite settlement of 1971–72 affected them both.

The Quadripartite Agreement and the Allies in West Berlin

It is surprising that, with a couple of notable exceptions, the Quadripartite Agreement of 1971–72 has attracted relatively little attention from historians in recent years, despite the complexity and significance of the discussions that took place in Berlin, Bonn, Moscow, and Washington.[9] Yet there can be little doubt that the agreement profoundly affected the nature and quality of life behind the Wall in West Berlin and that in many respects those effects were as much psychological and cultural as political or strategic. Moreover, the agreement itself is an almost classic example of the reciprocal interactions during the Cold War among the global calculations of the competing superpowers, the interests of the two German states, and the realities of life on the ground in Berlin itself.

Those realities, of course, had been profoundly altered by the construction of the Wall after August 1961. Ordinary West Berliners were now cut off from access to and communication with East Berlin and the German Democratic Republic (GDR). Telephone services were interrupted. Transit travel across the GDR, never easy under the best of circumstances, became even more fraught with time-consuming difficulties and uncertainties. Between 1963 and 1966, East German authorities did permit West Berliners briefly to visit relatives in East Berlin during certain designated holiday seasons, such as Easter or Christmas, but after 1966 even those possibilities were closed down, except for "urgent family cases."[10] And although the first decade after the building of the Wall was marked by dramatic visits from Allied leaders who vigorously reasserted the Western commitment to the beleaguered city—such as John F. Kennedy in 1963, Queen Elizabeth II in 1965, or Richard M. Nixon in 1969—the years of walled-in isolation contributed significantly to West Berlin's various demographic, psychological, economic, and financial problems. These problems in turn were complicated by the emergence of a radical student left in West Berlin and by the bitter conflict between the student movement and the dominant Springer press in the city. Moreover, the remote possibility persisted, even after Nikita Khrushchev's fall from power in 1964, that a new crisis over Berlin could still escalate into a major superpower confrontation, and both sides in the Cold War maintained active military contingency plans in the event of such a confrontation.[11] Indeed, Western defense plans for Berlin, based on an Allied organization called "Live Oak," continued into the détente and post-détente era after the 1960s "as a signal to the Soviet bloc of the continued Allied determination to defend Berlin and Allied rights of access"—a determination that had been at the heart of Allied-Soviet disputes since the 1940s.[12]

By the late 1960s a number of well-informed observers were reflecting rather glumly that West Berlin was in the grip of a "malaise" from which it would be difficult to escape. To be sure, they noted, West Berlin remained a vibrant place that could still draw on its "heroic" post-1948 tradition and its older traditions of cultural openness and innovativeness. Still, as one British diplomat astutely pointed out in 1967, West Berlin's vibrancy and energy were "superficial." The walled-in rump city had already lost much of its "heroic" allure, as the Soviet threat had been ratcheted down during the Brezhnev era, and though West Berliners were feeling more secure, he continued, "a certain confusion, and even neurotic introspection" was the logical result: "the malaise affecting Berlin is essentially the consequence of an unnatural situation which is unlikely to change in the foreseeable future."[13]

Serious Allied negotiations with the Soviet Union on Berlin began in 1970—less out of a concern for the city's political and psychological doldrums than out of a desire, in the context of détente and *Ostpolitik*, to defuse the situation in and around Berlin while continuing to guarantee Allied occupation and access rights. The negotiations, like the ultimate Quadripartite Agreement itself, were complex by any diplomatic standard, driven by such factors as Soviet interest in ensuring West German ratification of the Moscow Treaty of 1970, the Soviet desire for a European security conference, the reality of Richard Nixon's overtures to China, Henry Kissinger's complex tactics of "linkages" and "back-channel" diplomacy, and the *Ostpolitik* initiatives of Willy Brandt and Egon Bahr. They included formal discussions among the four ambassadors at the Allied Control Council building in West Berlin, expert discussions in Bonn, German-German negotiations involving Egon Bahr and his East German counterpart, Michael Kohl, and, as just noted, "back-channel" discussions in Washington and elsewhere.[14] One measure of the Agreement's complexity and ambiguity was its opening paragraph, which referred not to Berlin or West Berlin but to the "relevant area." Moreover, because East and West German translations of the Agreement differed, it was decided that only the English, French, and Russian versions would be official.[15] Described by one State Department observer as "a cliff-hanger to the last," the document was finally signed on 3 September 1971, a day later than planned, because US Ambassador Kenneth Rush was suffering from high blood pressure.[16] But even then the Agreement (it was not a "treaty" in the traditional sense) did not go into effect. It had to wait until the two German states had agreed on a transit accord, which took further weeks of negotiation and, of course, ratification by the West German parliament.[17] But by June 1972 everything was in place, and for the next seventeen years West Berlin's place in the world was largely determined by the 1971–72 accords.

The Quadripartite Agreement not only included the basic agreement itself but also several appendices and notes; it was kept purposefully vague and ambiguous in many of its particulars. The cumulative effect of the 1971–72 accords, however, was to underscore joint Allied responsibility for and continued occupation rights in Berlin. In the words of the American diplomat Martin Hillenbrand, the Soviets agreed to repudiate their frequent claims between 1958 and 1963 "that Allied rights in West Berlin were somehow capable of being abrogated or exhausted."[18] The four powers agreed that all future disputes would be settled peacefully, thus defusing Berlin as a potential site of armed superpower confrontation. For their part, the Soviets received a consulate general in West Berlin, which had long been one of their goals. With their willingness to sign the Quadripartite Agreement, they also were able to ensure West German ratification of Chancellor Willy Brandt's *Ostpolitik* treaties.

Among the most ambiguous points in the Quadripartite Agreement were those that concerned West Berlin's relationship to the Federal Republic, which thus remained a matter of endless controversy and frequent protest on the part of the Soviets.[19] But for ordinary West Berliners living behind the Wall, the accords finally offered an opportunity to travel to East Berlin and the surrounding GDR, though of course under a variety of bureaucratic restrictions; and the Agreement also meant that vehicular traffic between West Berlin and the Federal Republic was more or less normalized. Moreover, the 1971-72 accords led to territorial exchanges between the GDR and West Berlin that ended some bizarre administrative anomalies, the most famous being the West Berlin exclave of Steinstücken, a tiny village of around two hundred people located about a kilometer from the main body of West Berlin. Steinstücken was completely surrounded by its own version of the Wall, with an American helicopter landing spot in the middle of the village.[20] After 1972, as a result of the territorial exchanges, West Berlin officials were able to link Steinstücken to the rest of West Berlin; the road itself was hemmed in on both sides by an expanded Wall, creating a bizarre tunnel effect.

For West Berlin the effects of the Quadripartite Agreement were immediate and obvious. As the journalist Peter Bender put it, "The Quadripartite Agreement of 1971 concluded the demythologizing of Berlin. It was a victory of practical reason over Eastern as well as Western missionary zeal, and the island city became a recognized part of the status quo. Never before had its existence been so thoroughly assured, but the purpose of that existence became questionable."[21] From the Allies' perspective, the Quadripartite Agreement served several useful functions. Sir Christopher Mallaby says that it was "a demonstration daily that the German question was still open" and that, despite the apparent stabilization of Europe during the détente era, not all outstanding questions of Europe's postwar order had been resolved.[22] According to the American diplomat John Kornblum, it meant further that the Soviets had accepted the idea that the Allies had certain "originary rights" in Berlin dating to 1944–45, and that, pending some larger settlement of the kind that finally happened in 1990, the Allies' presence in Berlin was recognized by the Soviets, which in turn worked to the Allies' strategic advantage.[23]

Not surprisingly, those parts of the Quadripartite Agreement that were the most vague—such as the extent to which agencies of the Federal Republic could meet or be represented in West Berlin—continued to be a source of almost ritualized rancor and dispute between the Soviets and the Western Allies.[24] Moreover, during an especially rocky phase of the later Cold War in the early 1980s, the Soviets could still threaten to hold West Berlin and the Quadripartite Agreement hostage to the dispute over Soviet and NATO medium-range missile deployment in Europe.[25] Regular problems and disputes concerning the transit routes also persisted throughout the 1970s and 1980s, especially in 1974, when the Soviets and East Germans began to disrupt transit traffic to protest the presence of a West German government agency in West Berlin. This sort of harassment could sometimes lead to long delays and traffic jams at the border crossings. But these were the exception rather than the rule. For the most part, traffic between West Berlin and the Federal Republic flowed relatively smoothly throughout the eighteen years in which the Quadripartite Agreement was in force.[26]

Forgetting the Commitment? The Allies and West Berlin after 1972

Indeed, the Agreement was so effective that it seemed to increase the possibility that the Allies—and especially the Americans—might forget their obligation to Berlin, or that they might assume that this commitment had been overtaken by events. West Berlin's political leaders had long been worried that this might happen, and as early as 1972 it seemed to some Americans that the Allied role in West Berlin had now been "relegated to minor importance."[27] By 1973, according to John Kornblum, "the understanding of the strategic importance of Berlin in the United States government reached almost zero.... There was a false, totally false understanding of what the intra-German treaties meant, and there was a strong predilection in the US government to assume that was the end of the German question."[28] By 1975, Kornblum contends, American understanding of the continued importance of West Berlin had reached such a low level that he felt it necessary to organize a special, high-powered State Department seminar for the new US ambassador to the GDR, the former

Kentucky senator John Sherman Cooper. A clever and insightful man, Cooper listened to the assembled luminaries and then exclaimed, "This is all very interesting. But the war was thirty years ago. Why are we still in West Berlin?" Nobody could provide a clear or convincing answer.

In response, Kornblum—then an official with the State Department's policy planning staff—prepared a special report in which he argued that the continued American presence in the walled city could be justified for four reasons: (1) West Berlin remained the fulcrum of the East-West conflict, especially in Europe; (2) the US could maintain its originary rights in the heart of Europe at a relatively low cost; (3) the US thereby found itself in a strategically advantageous position for further negotiations with the Soviets; and (4) the US still had an obligation to protect Europe from possible Soviet aggression.[29] Five years later, in 1980, Kornblum—now political adviser to the US Mission in Berlin—still felt obliged to remind American policymakers that Berlin remained the one place "on earth where we have been more consistent" than any other. In yet another memorandum to his colleagues, Kornblum insisted that

> our major strength in Berlin is the continuity of our commitment stretching back to the early postwar days. This commitment includes our promise to defend West Berlin militarily, if necessary. It also includes continued political support for the overall status of the city and an engagement to maintain the practical improvements made possible by detente and in particular by the Quadripartite Agreement. "Continuity" therefore means continued defense of the "island" of West Berlin.[30]

Kornblum's vigorous support for a continued Allied presence resulted directly from his continued concern that US—and to an extent British and French—interest in the city had become attenuated now that the divided city was out of the headlines.

As we know, the Western Allies did indeed remain in Berlin until 1994, and until 1990 their structures, organizations, and practices remained largely unchanged.[31] The French remained concentrated in the city's north and northwest, focused on the Quartier Napoléon in Wedding and at Tegel airport; the British were mainly in Tiergarten and Spandau; and the Americans could be found in the city's southern districts, especially in Zehlendorf, at Tempelhof airport, and in Lichterfelde-West. They continued their patrols into East Berlin and their military missions in Potsdam. The Allied Kommandatura, the Allied governing body for the entirety of Berlin, had met since 1945 (but without the Soviets since 1948) and continued to meet in West Berlin's leafy Dahlem suburb. The Western commandants and their civilian counterparts regularly met with the governing mayor and with members and officials from the West Berlin *Senat*.

Allied forces continued their regular maneuvers, and certain events, such as the British Tattoo or the German-American and Franco-German Festivals, continued to follow their regular annual course. Allied dignitaries, including US and French Presidents or British royalty, regularly visited the city, most famously Ronald Reagan in 1987. For their part, mayors of West Berlin regularly visited all three Allied capitals, especially right after their elections: the last such trip before the events of November 1989 was Walter Momper's visit to Washington, DC, in the spring of 1989. But these events tended to be increasingly ritualized and even pro forma observances, without the charged political and symbolic significance of earlier affairs. The Allied presence in West Berlin, although integral to the contrived normality of the years after 1971–72, had become "normal." It defined West Berlin behind the Wall but had become a nondramatic backdrop to daily life. Thus it is hardly surprising that West Berliners at all levels increasingly tended to take the Allied presence for granted. Moreover, the numbers involved were not exactly overwhelming in a city of two million: in 1988 the US garrison, the largest of the three Allied groups, numbered about 6,500 soldiers, accompanied by about 7,500 civilian dependents.[32]

As often as not, ordinary West Berliners accepted the Allies as part of the landscape of their walled-in city. Indeed, for the most part West Berliners largely ignored them, even if they listened to Allied forces radio stations such as the American Forces Network or the British Forces Broadcasting Service. For their part Allied soldiers and their families were extremely isolated and rarely had anything to do with Germans. Kerstin Schilling, a native West Berliner born in 1962, observed:

> In fact the Allied soldiers were hardly noticeable. Of course it could happen that the unexpected noise of tanks could disrupt the quiet of our streets. This meant that they were going on maneuvers. And this took place not only in more remote areas but also in the middle of the city. It could sometimes happen that we would be shopping in Wedding's Müllerstraße and run into young French soldiers next to our parked cars.

For younger West Berliners, she noted that the American, British, and French residential areas, shopping centers, and barracks had no meaning "other than as mere orientation points in West Berlin."[33]

As West Berlin became more "normal" after 1972, West Berliners themselves were increasingly inclined to complain about certain aspects of the Allied presence. To be sure, anti-American demonstrations in the city had taken place with great frequency after 1966. Despite an uptick during the early 1980s, though, they were probably less numerous after the end of the Vietnam War in 1975, and violence directed against the Allies remained limited. More frequent were complaints about the noise and destructiveness of Allied maneuvers or about the environmental consequences of Allied actions.[34] Sometimes these were simply matters of mutual cultural misunderstanding, as when the prominent Christian Democratic politician Franz Amrehn complained vehemently to US authorities about his American neighbors' predilection for letting their dogs bark and their children play noisily on Sunday, thereby disrupting the German tradition of *Sonntagsruhe*.[35] On other occasions, grassroots environmental activists organized campaigns against American and British plans to build new housing for military personnel or to cut down trees. On one occasion in 1978, the Community for the Protection of Berlin Trees filed a much ballyhooed civil suit against the commander in chief of US forces in Europe, the secretary of the Navy, and the US commandant in Berlin in a vain attempt to stop construction of a 250-unit, thirteen-acre housing project for US military families in the environmentally sensitive Düppeler Feld close to the Berlin Wall. Construction was finally permitted on the basis of Allied occupation law, which took precedence over Berlin or German statutes.[36] On another occasion, the British decision to fell 33,000 trees near their airbase at Gatow resulted in large public protests, leading one American diplomat to conclude that the "younger generation does not share the experience of the older generation that without the presence of the Allies in Berlin during the crises of the postwar era, Berlin would have been a lost outpost."[37]

At critical or controversial moments like these, West Berliners were often reminded that their lives were shaped both by the Wall and by the realities of the Allied presence within the walled-in city. To cite yet another important example: in the late 1970s and early 1980s several Polish airplanes were hijacked and flown to Tempelhof airport. Occupation and US law superseded Berlin and German justice in each case, and a 1979 hijacking trial took place under the auspices of a special US court that was based in New York but conducted its hearings in Berlin.[38]

Not surprisingly, a succession of West Berlin mayors chafed under many of the restrictions that were imposed upon them by the requirements of the Allied occupation. This was not new. Back in the late 1940s and early 1950s Ernst Reuter himself had long sought to expand the purview of his office, reduce the Allies' role in matters of local governance, and broaden the autonomy of West Berlin's various local authorities. After 1972, however, while insisting on their determination to work with the Allies, West Berlin's mayors often tried to circumvent Allied occupation rules and expand their own room for autonomous decision making, especially in the context of relations with the GDR. According to Allied diplomats in Berlin at the time, the two Christian Democratic mayors in the 1980s, Richard von Weizsäcker and Eberhard Diepgen, were known for occasionally "playing fast and loose" with Berlin's four-power status, especially in connection with plans for the city's 750th anniversary celebrations in 1987.[39]

In light of all these developments, John Kornblum is convinced that the combination of growing Allied—and especially American—indifference to West Berlin and West German eagerness to reach an accommodation with the GDR in the late 1980s might well have made it impossible for the West to maintain the post-1972 status quo in West Berlin: "Had the Russians not collapsed in '89 as they did, I personally don't think we could have held our position in Berlin politically for ten years, maybe not five years."[40] We shall never know, of course, because the events of 1989–90 did indeed permanently alter the physical, political, and cultural landscape of Berlin. But in looking back at the last two decades of West Berlin's history, it is clear that without the Allies and the Quadripartite Agreement, West Berlin would not have been able to develop and maintain its strange and unique culture in the shadow of the Wall. A brief look at some aspects of that culture will shed additional light on the reciprocal influences of the Allies, the Wall, and the citizenry of the island city in an unheroic age.

"A Sunny Affair"? West Berlin and the Wall after 1972

The former West Berlin mayor Klaus Schütz has argued that, as a consequence of the changes the truncated city experienced after 1971–72, the experience of those West Berliners who were born after 1961 differed sharply from the experiences of those who remembered the "heroic" times.[41] His observations are repeatedly confirmed in the memoir literature and by numerous personal conversations and interviews. Even non-native newcomers to West Berlin, such as the journalist Claus Christian Malzahn, born in 1963, could observe that life "in the shadow of the Wall was a sunny affair."[42] And Malzahn actually lived in a flat directly adjacent to the Wall in the district of Neukölln. In most respects, though, his experiences with the Wall resembled those of the natives: "The world was beautiful. We never thought a single second about the Wall, mines, and barbed wire, although all that was right in front of our noses. For us West Berliners the 'Protective Wall' had become transformed over the course of time into a piece of furniture, like an old fashioned chest of drawers, an unloved heirloom.... At any rate the Wall was a part of Berlin, like the Ku'damm or the Funkturm. Most residents hardly even noticed it." On its western side, in other words, it had become a tourist attraction.[43] Other younger West Berliners, new arrivals and native-born alike, tend to echo Malzahn's perceptions. For example, Kaya Tiglioglu, who arrived in West Berlin from Turkey in 1969, asserted that "The Wall never bothered me," while the journalist Olaf Leitner wrote: "And at some point the West Berliners no longer noticed the Wall. Just imagine, there's a Wall and nobody goes there. And that's the way they acted."[44]

But was West Berlin in fact, as another journalist described, a "paradise between the fronts" in the Cold War?[45] Not everyone was enamored of the divided city's "scene," or the uniqueness and supposed excitement of its various lifestyles in the shadow of the Wall. Demographically, post-1972 West Berlin with its artificially aged population managed to hang on into the late 1980s with a population of about 2.1 million, thanks to, among other things, an infusion of immigrants from countries such as Turkey. But economically, West Berlin was on constant life support from the Federal Republic. It had been a subsidized city since the 1950s, and that remained the case throughout the unheroic era after 1972. For contemporaries such as Henryk Broder, "West Berlin was hysterical, petty, shitty, full of dog crap—a city where you constantly were running your nose into something, because it really was a totally enclosed little enclave. With hysterical people and with such a demonstrative survival symbolism."[46] Even sympathetic writers such as Peter Schneider—whose *Mauerspringer* (*Wall Jumper*, 1982) is perhaps the most famous literary evocation of the Wall and its effects—could observe that West Berlin managed to maintain a vital and cosmopolitan culture despite its "unhealthy isolation" in a "luxurious Alcatraz." But it was also "a society without a future" and a place, according to Schneider, where one always encountered the same people and the same faces.[47] One British official noted insightfully that post-1972 West Berlin was a strange combination of "agreeable backwater" and metropolis: "Having no hinterland to speak of, the Western part of the city is relatively free from traffic jams and the rush hour. Lying on no through routes in any direction, it has the tranquillity of a cul-de-sac."[48]

West Berlin was always an artificial entity, an artificial place, and after 1972 it was a place that no longer quite seemed to fulfill a central or clear role in the Cold War, despite Allied assertions of its continued importance and their determination to stay and to assert their occupation rights. Thus it tended to breed an artificial, hothouse culture, or rather several hothouse cultures. The GDR that surrounded West Berlin has frequently been described as a *Nischengesellschaft*, a society in which individuals tried to find a private niche for themselves as a refuge from the oppressiveness and stuffiness of the larger political system. But in its own democratic and very different way, West Berlin was also a *Nischengesellschaft*, full of people in very different kinds of neighborhoods, living very different kinds of lives and looking for very different sorts of things. The "heroic" and consensual culture of anti-communist defiance that had bound the *Insulaner*—the "islanders"—together had already begun to dissolve by the mid 1960s with generational shifts and the coming of the student movement.[49]

These changes accelerated after 1972. Having lost much of its traditional working-class base, West Berlin continued to be a city full of aging natives for whom the more recent arrivals might as well have come from another planet. West Berlin had become a place where various kinds of people sought refuge, from young men seeking to avoid the West German draft to young people searching for places, such as the Berlin district of Kreuzberg, that were open to alternative—and inexpensive—forms of social experimentation.[50] Those experiments could range from "ecoshops" to anti-authoritarian childrens' centers (*Kinderläden*) to nontraditional living arrangements to out-and-out squatting and the renovation of unoccupied buildings: in other words, expressions of a society within a society that helped to give rise after the mid 1970s to modern forms of feminism and environmental activism, embodied in the "Alternative List" (Alternative Liste), West Berlin's variation on the Greens. The city's curious combination of cosmopolitanism and provincialism was also attractive to non-Germans, including overseas rock stars such as David Bowie, Iggy Pop, and Brian Eno, who lived in the city in the mid and late 1970s and produced some of their most famous work at the Hansa-Studio there. Bowie's complex song "Heroes," about lovers in the shadow of the Wall, has been described as a kind of anthem for young West Berliners born in the early to mid 1960s.[51]

In short, behind the Wall and under the aegis of the somewhat inattentive Allies, West Berlin after the 1960s—but especially after 1972—sustained several interrelated kinds of cultures: a subvention culture, an alternative culture, a niche culture, and, not to be overlooked, a culture of violence that assumed almost ritualized forms.[52] That culture, which had begun to emerge about 1966, could occasionally assume terrorist forms connected to other terrorist actions in the Federal Republic, such as the assassination of Judge Günter von Drenkmann in late 1974 or the kidnapping of the Berlin Christian Democratic leader Peter Lorenz in 1975. But by the early 1980s a rather different, Berlin-focused culture of violence had emerged, one that, at least initially, mainly involved confrontations with the police over issues of housing and squatting. Of course, there was nothing uniquely "West Berlin" about alternative or squatter cultures or even a culture of violence during these years. Hamburg and Frankfurt, for example, also had significant alternative "scenes." But it can be argued that the scope and extent of these cultures was greater and more enduring in West Berlin, not least because of the unique situation of that city.

By the early 1980s squatters had seized a number of empty buildings in West Berlin, and the city government responded with a mixture of conciliation, negotiation, and toughness. Violence often erupted when police attempted to empty occupied buildings.[53] On one such occasion in September 1981, an eighteen-year-old man named Klaus Jürgen Rattay was killed when he was accidentally hit by a bus during a melee; his death in turn led to further violence in which ninety-three police officers were injured and numerous buildings and automobiles were attacked and set alight.[54] Other forms of violence, usually directed against buildings, automobiles, and the police, also developed in the 1970s and especially in the 1980s. These often took the predictable form of violence on the margins of otherwise peaceful demonstrations, or they could assume ritualized forms, like the frequent disruptions on May Day that continued well after unification in 1990.

One might mention a few more cultures in post-1971 West Berlin: a culture of immigrants, embodied mainly in the large population of Turkish origin; a very visible "official" culture, symbolized by the Berlin Philharmonic Orchestra and West Berlin's stunning museums, theaters, and musical life and closely connected to the "subvention culture"; and a "culture of mediocrity," symbolized by the generalized decline in the quality of West Berlin's political class after the early 1970s, despite such exceptions as mayors Hans-Jochen Vogel or Richard von Weizsäcker. Symbolic of that political culture of mediocrity—and grist for the mills of the radical oppositional cultures—was a succession of sleazy scandals in the 1970s and 1980s involving assorted construction projects and dubious property speculators.[55] In its last years, then, West Berlin hardly offered an edifying or inspiring spectacle. Its heroic days were long gone.

Conclusion: An Oddly Dialectical Relationship

West Berlin after the Quadripartite Agreement was a walled-in city in search of a mission or a function, but apart from offering a cultural *Biotop* unique in Europe, it never really succeeded in finding one.[56] It never really managed to become a kind of international meeting place or a site of mediation between East and West, despite the construction of the massive International Congress Center in the late 1970s (ICC Berlin, now itself a candidate for demolition). Its last great public attempt to develop a new kind of identity for itself, at least architecturally, came with the city's 750th anniversary in 1987, when West Berlin hosted the International Building Exhibition (*Internationale Bauausstellung* or IBA) and sponsored significant architectural innovations and renovations in many parts of the city. For most West Berliners, though, IBA did not change much. Neither did elections in early 1989, which resulted in the formation of a new-style coalition government headed by Walter Momper that included the Social Democrats and the Alternative List.

Then the Wall came down. And with it West Berlin disappeared. Always artificial, a quintessential and historically unique creation of the Cold War, West Berlin had survived for almost two decades after 1972 based on the maintenance of an internationally agreed status quo, an arrangement that encouraged an oddly dialectical and generally unnoticed relationship between the Allies and the various cultures of West Berlin, the existence of which was only possible if the Allies were also present. The Allies were there to ensure the maintenance of their own occupation rights but also to guarantee a "normal" life behind the Wall, and the different cultures that arose there depended—in ways that many of them would never have consciously or overtly accepted—on a continued

Allied presence. That largely unconscious relationship between the Allies and the cultures of West Berlin was mediated by the reality of the Wall itself. It was quite unheroic, but, as Christopher Mallaby asserts, in its own strange way it worked brilliantly, and for a rather long time.

Notes

1. Eleanor Lansing Dulles's "Berlin after the Four Power Talks," an unpublished memorandum dated 4 February 1971, is held in the National Archives and Records Administration, College Park, Maryland (hereafter: NARA), RG 59, Lot 80 D225, Bureau of European and Canadian Affairs, Office of Central European Affairs, Berlin Desk, Political Subject Files 1970–1972, Berlin Negotiations: German Eastern Policy to Texts: Inner German Agreements, Box 2.
2. Wallace Stegner, "On the Writing of History," in *The Sound of Mountain Water* (New York, 1997), 203. I am grateful to my colleague James Lewis for calling this essay to my attention.
3. Richard Reeves, *Daring Young Men: The Heroism and Triumph of the Berlin Airlift, June 1948–May 1949* (New York, 2010); Andrei Cherny, *The Candy Bombers: The Untold Story of the Berlin Airlift and America's Finest Hour* (New York, 2008). Notably less "epic" and heroic in its treatment is Paul Steege, *Black Market, Cold War: Everyday Life in Berlin, 1946–1949* (New York, 2007).
4. Andreas W. Daum, "America's Berlin, 1945–2000: Between Myths and Visions," in *Berlin: The New Capital in the East. A Transatlantic Appraisal*, ed. Frank Trommler (Washington, DC, 2000), 49–73; idem, *Kennedy in Berlin*, trans. Dona Geyer (New York, 2008); Dominik Geppert, "'Proclaim Liberty throughout All the Land': Berlin and the Symbolism of the Cold War," in *The Postwar Challenge: Cultural, Social, and Political Change in Western Europe, 1945–1958*, ed. Dominik Geppert (Oxford, 2003), 339–63.
5. Klaus Grimberg, "The Cold War in Architecture," *The Atlantic Times* (September 2007). See also Axel Besteher-Hegenbarth, Dina Koschorreck, and Bernd M. Scherer, eds., *Das Haus. Die Kulturen. Die Welt. 50 Jahre: Von der Kongresshalle zum Haus der Kulturen der Welt* (Berlin, 2007), esp. the articles by Steffen de Rudder, Michael S. Cullen, Harald Jähner, and Claus Leggewie.
6. J. Richard Bock, memorandum of conversation with Eberhard Diepgen, 28 October 1980, NARA, RG 84, US Mission Berlin, Subject Files 1945–1990, Senat Liaison Officer, Sent Chrons August–December 1979 to Sent Chrons November–December 1981, Box 1.
7. Peter Millar, *1989 The Berlin Wall: My Part in Its Downfall* (London, 2009), 37–38.
8. Sir Christopher Mallaby, comments in panel discussion on "The Fall of the Berlin Wall: London – Bonn – Berlin (East and West)," in Allied Museum Berlin, *The Windsor Park Seminar. Berlin: The British Perspective 1945–1990. 1–2 September 2009, Cumberland Lodge, Windsor Park, London* (transcript on CD-ROM, Berlin, 2011), 47. http://www.alliiertenmuseum.de/download/windsor_park_seminar.pdf (accessed 11 January 2012).

9. An otherwise excellent documentary collection on the British in Berlin only mentions the Quadripartite Agreement briefly: Keith Hamilton, Patrick Salmon, and Stephen Twigge, eds., *Documents on British Policy Overseas*, Series III, vol. 6, *Berlin in the Cold War, 1948–1990* (London, 2009), 81, similar to Frederick Taylor, *The Berlin Wall 13 August 1961–9 November 1989* (London, 2006), 367–68, and more recently Edgar Wolfrum, *Die Mauer. Geschichte einer Teilung* (Munich, 2009). Thorough treatments are to be found in M. E. Sarotte, *Dealing with the Devil: East Germany, Détente, and Ostpolitik, 1969–1973* (Chapel Hill, NC, 2001), chaps. 4–5, esp. 113–34; David C. Geyer, "The Missing Link: Henry Kissinger and the Back-Channel Negotiations on Berlin," in *American Détente and German Ostpolitik, 1969–1972*, ed. David C. Geyer and Bernd Schaefer, Bulletin of the German Historical Institute, Supplement 1 (Washington, DC, 2004), 80–97; Wolfgang Ribbe, *Berlin 1945–2000. Grundzüge der Stadtgeschichte* (Berlin, 2002), 144–48; Wilfried Rott, *Die Insel. Eine Geschichte West-Berlins 1948–1990* (Munich, 2009), 273–77; older, still useful, but largely superseded studies include Gerhard Wettig, *Die Bindungen West-Berlins seit dem Vier-Mächte-Abkommen* (Cologne, 1978); Honoré M. Catudal Jr., *The Diplomacy of the Quadripartite Agreement on Berlin: A New Era in East-West Politics* (Berlin, 1978); David M. Keithly, *Breakthrough in the Ostpolitik: The 1971 Quadripartite Agreement* (Boulder, CO, 1986).
10. Gerhard Kunze, *Grenzerfahrungen. Kontakte und Verhandlungen zwischen dem Land Berlin und der DDR 1949–1989* (Berlin, 1999), 79–216.
11. Among other things, see Gregory W. Pedlow, "Allied Crisis Management for Berlin: The LIVE OAK Organization, 1959–1963," in *International Cold War Military Records and History: Proceedings of the International Conference on Cold War Military Records and History Held in Washington, D.C. 21–26 March 1994*, ed. William W. Epley (Washington, DC, 1996), 88–116; Sean M. Maloney, "Notfallplanung für Berlin: Vorläufer der Flexible Response 1958–1963," *Militärgeschichte* NF (1997): 3–15; Winfried Heinemann, "Die Doppelfunktion der DDR-Grenztruppen," unpublished paper presented at German Studies Association, 10 October 2009, Washington, DC.
12. S. J. Lambert, "Background Note on Live Oak," 25 June 1975, The National Archives, Kew (hereafter: TNA), DEFE 24/881.
13. R. G. A. Etherington-Smith to Sir Frank Roberts, "The Present Malaise in Berlin," 9 August 1967, TNA, FCO 33/266. Cf. Sir Frank Roberts to George Brown, 22 August 1967, ibid.
14. Sarotte, *Dealing with the Devil*, remains the best analysis of the negotiations. See also David C. Geyer, ed., *Foreign Relations of the United States 1969–1976*, vol. 40, *Germany and Berlin, 1969–1972* (Washington, DC, 2007); David C. Geyer and Douglas E. Selvage, eds., *Soviet-American Relations: The Détente Years, 1969–1972* (Washington, DC, 2007). There is also a substantial memoir literature by many of the main participants; vast amounts of archival materials have yet to be digested, but see especially "Strange Normality: What Was So Special about the Quadripartite Agreement 1971/72?" in Allied Museum Berlin, *Windsor Park Seminar*, 74-91.
15. Official English version of the Quadripartite Agreement in TNA, FO 949/78/1.
16. David Klein (US Mission Berlin) to Department of State, 3 September 1971, in Geyer, ed., *Foreign Relations*, 40: 913.
17. Peter Joachim Lapp, "Die Transitwege von und nach Westberlin," in Friedrich Christian Delius and Peter Joachim Lapp, *Transit Westberlin. Erlebnisse im Zwischenraum*, 2nd ed. (Berlin, 2000), 125–70; Kunze, *Grenzerfahrungen*, 243–80. Official text of the transit accord: NARA, RG 59, Lot 80 D225, Bureau of European and Canadian

Affairs, Office of Central European Affairs, Berlin Desk, Political Subject Files 1970–1972, Berlin Negotiations: German Eastern Policy to Texts: Inner German Agreements, Box 2.

18. Martin J. Hillenbrand, "The Legal Background of the Berlin Situation," in *The Future of Berlin*, ed. Martin J. Hillenbrand (Montclair, NJ, 1980), 62.

19. Ibid., 63–67.

20. Senatskanzlei Berlin, memorandum on "Berlin-Gespräche der Vier Mächte. Hier: Gebietsaustausch," 14 July 1971, NARA, RG 59, Lot 80 D225, Bureau of European and Canadian Affairs, Office of Central European Affairs, Berlin Desk, Political Subject Files 1970–1972, Box 6; Joachim Nawrocki, "Hoffnung für Steinstücken. Gebietsaustausch – ein Thema der Berlin-Verhandlungen," in *war jewesen. West-Berlin 1961–89*, ed. Detlef Holland-Moritz and Gabriela Wachter (Berlin, 2009), 180–84 (originally published in *Die Zeit*, 5 November 1971); Kunze, *Grenzerfahrungen*, 281–85, 394–99. On Steinstücken see Gabriele Leech-Anspach, *Insel vor der Insel. Ein kleiner Ort im kalten Krieg: Berlin-Steinstücken* (Potsdam, 2005).

21. Peter Bender, *Wenn es West-Berlin nicht gäbe* (Berlin, 1987), 28.

22. Sir Christopher Mallaby, comments in panel discussion on "The Fall of the Berlin Wall," Allied Museum Berlin, *The Windsor Park Seminar*, 46-52.

23. John C. Kornblum, interview with author, 22 March 2007, Berlin.

24. R. M. F. Redgrave, "Berlin: How Long Can It Go On?" 11 December 1975 (report to Oliver Wright), TNA, FCO 90/26.

25. Steve Sestanovich and Jeremy Azrael to Thomas Niles, 2 October 1981, NARA, RG 59, Lot 91 D341, Bureau of European and Canadian Affairs, Office of Central European Affairs, Berlin Desk, Records Relating to the Four Power Talks and Quadripartite Agreement, 1961–1987, Box 5, POL 39: Four Power Talks on Berlin 1981.

26. Foreign and Commonwealth Office, Background Brief, "Berlin – 25 Years of the Wall," August 1986, TNA, FO 973/471; Lapp, "Transitwege."

27. Helmut Sonnenfeldt to Henry Kissinger, 7 November 1972, in Geyer, ed., *Foreign Relations*, 40: 1090.

28. John C. Kornblum, interview with author, 22 March 2007, Berlin.

29. Ibid.

30. John C. Kornblum, "Why Are We in Berlin?" unpublished memorandum, 7 November 1980.

31. On the Allies in Berlin after 1972, see Udo Wetzlaugk, *Die Alliierten in Berlin* (Berlin, 1988); Robert P. Grathwol and Donita M. Moorhus, *American Forces in Berlin: Cold War Outpost, 1945–1994* (Washington, DC, 1994); idem, *Berlin and the American Military: A Cold War Chronicle* (New York, 1999); Gabriele Heidenfelder, *From Duppel to Truman Plaza: Die Berlin American Community in den Jahren 1965 bis 1989* (Hamburg, 1998); Friedrich Jeschonnek, Dieter Riedel, and William Durie, *Alliierte in Berlin 1945–1994. Ein Handbuch zur Geschichte der militärischen Präsenz der Westmächte*, 2nd ed. (Berlin, 2007); David E. Barclay, "On the Back Burner – Die USA und West-Berlin 1948–1994," in *Deutschland aus internationaler Sicht*, ed. Tilman Mayer (Berlin, 2009), 25–36; and the publications of the Allied Museum Berlin.

32. Heidenfelder, *Duppel*, 25.

33. Kerstin Schilling, *Insel der Glücklichen. Generation West-Berlin*, 2nd ed. (Berlin, 2005), 119.

34. For example, see J. Richard Bock to John C. Kornblum et al., memorandum on "In-City Training," 11 February 1980, "Senat Contacts between Allies and Berliners," 11 April 1980; idem, "Schoeneberg Debate on U.S. Troop Training," 22 May 1980, NARA, RG 84, US Mission Berlin, Subject Files 1945–1990, Senat Liaison Officer, Sent Chrons August–December 1979 to Sent Chrons November–December 1981, Box 1.

35. J. Richard Bock to Franz Amrehn, 23 June 1980, ibid.

36. See the court documents filed with the US District Court on 29 September 1978 in Washington, DC, in NARA, RG 84, US Mission Berlin, Political Affairs Division, Office of the Legal Adviser, Significant Jurisdiction Cases, 1957–1990, Freedom of Information Act to Miscellaneous Court Papers 4/17, Box 1; also www.berliner-verkehrsseiten.de/wub/Die_Projekte/Tunnel/Die_Burger_und_das_Fenn/die_burger_und_das_fenn.html (accessed 14 February 2010).

37. "Allied Decision on Tree-Felling Action at British Military Airbase in Gatow," 14 November 1979, NARA, RG 84, US Mission Berlin, Subject Files 1945–1990, Senat Liaison Officer, Sent Chrons August–December 1979 to Sent Chrons November–December 1981, Box 1.

38. See the transcripts of the hijacking proceedings, NARA, RG 84, US Mission Berlin, Political Affairs Division, Office of the Legal Adviser, Significant Jurisdiction Cases, 1957–1990, Freedom of Information Act to Miscellaneous Court Papers 4/17, Box 1; cf. Grathwol and Moorhus, *Berlin*, 148–49.

39. Sir Michael Burton and Sir Christopher Mallaby, comments in panel discussion on "The Fall of the Berlin Wall," in Allied Museum Berlin, *Windsor Park Seminar*, 41-52.

40. John C. Kornblum, interview with author, 22 March 2007, Berlin.

41. Klaus Schütz, interview with author, 27 February 2007, Berlin.

42. Claus Christian Malzahn, *Über Mauern. Warum das Leben im Schatten des Schutzwalls eine sonnige Sache war* (Berlin, 2009), 8.

43. Ibid., 22.

44. Jürgen Scheunemann and Gabriela Seidel, *Was war los in West-Berlin 1950–2000* (Erfurt, 2002), 83; Olaf Leitner, ed., *West-Berlin! Westberlin! Berlin (West)! Die Kultur – die Szene – die Politik. Erinnerungen an eine Teilstadt der 70er und 80er Jahre* (Berlin, 2002), 16.

45. Rudolf Lorenzen, *Paradies zwischen den Fronten. Reportagen und Glossen aus Berlin (West)* (Berlin, 2009).

46. Henryk M. Broder, "Hysterisch, klein und zugeschissen," interview in Leitner, *West-Berlin!*, 390.

47. Peter Schneider, "Eine Vereinigung wie bei Daimler und Chrysler," interview in Leitner, *West-Berlin!*, 39.

48. R. M. F. Redgrave, "The Future of Berlin," memorandum (31 December 1975), TNA, FCO 90/26.

49. John Borneman, *Belonging in the Two Berlins: Kin, State, Nation* (Cambridge, UK, 1992), chap. 8.

50. Horst Bosetzky, *West-Berlin. Erinnerungen eines Inselkindes* (Berlin, 2006), 97–102.

51. Author's interviews with West Berliners; Nicholas Pegg, *The Complete David Bowie*, 4th ed. (London, 2006), 90–93; Thomas Jerome Seabrook, *Bowie in Berlin: A New Career in a New Town* (London, 2008), 159–87.

52. David E. Barclay, "Benno Ohnesorg, Rudi Dutschke, and the Student Movement in West Berlin: Critical Reflections after Forty Years," in *Berlin: Divided City, 1945–1989*, ed. Philip Broadbent and Sabine Hake (New York, 2010), 125–34.

53. Borneman, *Belonging*, 260–62; Rott, *Insel*, 328–36.
54. Klaus Hübner, *Einsatz. Erinnerungen des Berliner Polizeipräsidenten 1969–1987* (Berlin, 1997), 335–74; Rott, *Insel*, 345–47.
55. Rott, *Insel*, 313–21, 338–41, 377–84.
56. Though note the somewhat more positive assessment by Hermann Rudolph, "Das Glitzerding. Abschied von der geteilten Stadt (1): West-Berlin, ein Lebensgefühl, das (vielleicht) weiterlebt," *Tagesspiegel* (Berlin), 30 August 1999.

CHAPTER 7

Moving Borders and Competing Civilizing Missions

Germany, Poland, and Ukraine in the Context of the EU's Eastern Enlargement

STEFFI MARUNG

What happens when a frontier moves, especially if that border is the cultural and, for many, civilizational frontier of a supranational entity such as the European Union? How do people and states make sense of political orders when boundaries shift, affiliations change, and new memberships become possible? After the Berlin Wall fell and the Cold War ended, the EU integrated a number of states that had long been hidden behind the effective political and psychological border of the Iron Curtain. As a consequence of this eastern enlargement, the citizens of the East Central European states gained access to the European Union and its transnational pledge of welfare and security, freedom of mobility, and nascent common foreign policy. EU enlargement not only resulted in the redefinition of membership and affiliation for the new EU citizens; it also initiated the transfer of Western values, norms, and social models to the East and introduced categories of backwardness and progress, as well as notions of modernization and imagined power relations among the EU and candidate countries. The new openness put both the EU and future member countries under pressure to develop coherent interpretations for defining Europe.

Looking at the EU's new eastern borders raises questions about how political spaces and the political and economic opportunities linked to them were renegotiated. The moving frontier was associated with changes in understandings of the political relationships between Western and Eastern Europe. The Polish case offers a revealing example of how official efforts were made to validate changing citizenship affiliations and at the same time to develop coping strategies for cultural and social changes before and after EU enlargement. This chapter focuses on the distinct spatial representations evoked by Polish politicians, on the one hand to transcend the nation-state as the political point of reference and on the other to help stabilize it. These representations I tentatively describe as a "civilizing mission à la polonaise," since here historical interpretations (stemming from a pre-national Polish past) were adapted to define the new place of Poland in a changing Europe.[1] The distinctiveness of this civilizing mission has three dimensions. First, it implies recourse to a notion of former "greatness" that simultaneously bolsters an argument for the current claim to leadership in the region. Second, it emphasizes Poland's special bridging position between "East" and "West," asserting that it plays an important role in transferring Western values to its eastern neighbors. Third, this claim is simultaneously based on and substantiates Poland's "Europeanness." The civilizing mission envisions a political space beyond Polish national boundaries—in Europe, East Central Europe, and its eastern borderland. Polish political actors used regional affiliations in the East together with an idealized understanding of Western Europe to strengthen the national position in the EU. Traditional Polish discourse on European and eastern-oriented policy represented important sources in the quest for a new positioning toward the West following the Cold War confrontation, and the shared history of Poland and its eastern neighbors was of vital importance to this goal. In this respect the eastern Polish borderlands served as the key symbolic space for imagining a new eastern frontier that reflected Polish visions of a changing European geography.

The Polish effort to legitimate its "return to Europe" did not begin with the signing of the Europe agreement in 1991 or with negotiations for accession in 1994; rather it arose before the fall of the Berlin Wall as a hotly debated issue among Polish expatriates and dissidents. Upon its conversion from EU outsider to insider in 2004, the new Polish political elite developed a novel perspective on its eastern neighbors, especially Ukraine, Belarus, and Russia. Polish foreign policy officials started to articulate a vision of how to shape relations with them in the context of an enlarged European Union, actively participating in the development of both the European Neighbourhood Policy (ENP) in 2003 and the EU's more recent "Eastern Partnership" in 2008.[2] The ENP, developed from a 2002 British initiative, became an EU foreign policy instrument to handle the new relationship with the EU's would-be eastern and southern neighbors by adapting methods used already in the pre-accession assistance of the enlargement process.[3] It sought to strengthen the integration of economic spaces across the EU external border, to encourage a more flexible border regime operation, and to restructure regional policy.[4] However, it offered "everything but institutions" and thus served as a substitute to full membership.[5] The newly developed "Eastern Dimension" within this policy framework intensified cooperation with those eastern neighbors critical of the ENP's substitute character. Cooperation with the EU's southern neighbors, especially Morocco, Algeria, and Tunisia, focused meanwhile on migration management and security-related issues. These states have not articulated particular ambitions to join the EU.

The definition of cultural—or civilizational, to employ a term often applied in Polish statements—differences between the two adjacent spaces of Western and Eastern Europe played a critical role in the process of renegotiating the new political order on the European continent. The EU's eastern enlargement can be interpreted as a readjustment of the relation between Europe and Non-Europe, as the redefinition of the EU's cultural boundaries and the quest for a new mode of coping with the Other, and as a mode of what historically and pointedly can be described as the European civilizing mission.[6] The notion of the civilizing mission "has two prerequisites: on the one hand the idea that the superiority of specific legal norms with regard to competing notions can be discursively justified.... Secondly the term implies ... that under certain conditions it would be necessary and legitimate to impose these civilizational categories through intervention into 'the affairs of the other.'"[7] A European civilizing mission as used in postcolonial studies and the historiography of empires refers to a conceptualization of global relations that scholars have criticized as a "diffusionist" world model: Europe was seen as the origin and the promoter of global modernization processes that other world regions also needed to adopt.[8]

At the core of these interpretations is the translation of cultural and political difference into a spatial hierarchy between center and periphery.[9] The concept of the "civilizing mission" in this respect became a critical term and often linked analyses of imperial projects of expansion and colonial practices; such an approach is well established in the historiography of eighteenth- and nineteenth-European expansion in Britain, France, Germany, and occasionally Russia.[10] Yet it is less commonly found when referring to the East Central European historical context.[11] I argue, nonetheless, that recent Polish political discussions about its place in Europe and its position toward its eastern neighbors should be interpreted historiographically to include the historical Polish mission in the East and the long tradition of describing Poland's place in Europe and its relation to its eastern neighbors.[12] This does not mean that I attribute imperial aspirations or a colonial mindset to present-day Polish politicians and intellectuals. Rather, by introducing the notion of a "civilizing mission," I draw attention to interpretative strategies of political actors who seek to establish a connection between different cultural and political spaces through the use of hierarchies, claims of modernization, and unidirectional transfers. This civilizational and spatial strategy, in other words, appears not only in Western narratives but also in Polish ones.[13]

In this chapter I adopt the concept of "civilizing mission" to analyze political arguments that attempt to make plausible shifting borders, expanding political communities, and the opening up of adjacent spaces. I investigate how Polish politicians—prime ministers, foreign ministers, presidents, and other high-ranking officials in the field of Polish foreign policy—have translated historical traditions into the current political language that describes the Polish place in Europe after the end of the Cold War, in the course of the enlargement process, and after accession to the EU. After investigating the Polish-German partnership before the accession of Poland to the EU, I turn to the concept of a Polish mission in the East, first pointing to the historical sources for these spatial representations and then indicating how they were integrated into a new language in the course of accession and afterward. I focus mainly on official political discourse, drawn from sources of the Polish Foreign Ministry over the past ten years, that demonstrates how the concept of dealing with the European Other has shifted due to the redefinition of the EU.

German-Polish Neighborhood: From Euphoria to Hangover

The Polish publicist Adam Krzemiński recently described the German-Polish partnership as a "test case for Europe."[14] Comparable to the German-French partnership, he argued, the German-Polish relationship is a cornerstone of the European Union's political order. This specific alliance has changed considerably over the last twenty years, with regard to both the interpretation and the structure of cooperation.[15] After the fall of the Berlin Wall, a unique process of reconciliation was instituted that served as a model for Polish representatives who worked on settlements between Poland and its eastern neighbors, in particular Ukraine. Bilateral treaties established the territorial integrity of both partners, principles of good neighborliness, and mechanisms of close cooperation.[16] The noticeable euphoria that fueled this process of reconciliation—at least in some circles of the political elites and the committed public—has, I would argue, cooled since the late 1990s. In recent academic discussions, pessimism about the success of the German-Polish partnership has grown.[17] Taking the EU enlargement into account, the alleged failure (or at least crisis) in creating truly neighborly relations should be considered against the backdrop of frictions between German and Polish ambitions for an eastern policy. In this context Dieter Bingen deplored the lack of a strategy for seeking a common German-Polish position in the enlarged EU, and Anna Wolff-Powęska criticized the lack of a vision for the EU's future eastern neighborhood. Wolff-Powęska also noted Germany's weak concept for eastern political relations, a concept and vision that is not actually "lacking" but from a Polish perspective focuses too exclusively on Russia, disregards immediate Polish neighbors in the east (such as Ukraine), and underestimates Polish expertise and interests in developing a novel EU eastern policy.[18]

Polish politicians tried to benefit from the alliance with Germany by drafting a new common EU eastern policy.[19] Yet the United States and Scandinavian countries such as Sweden turned out to be more willing partners in this en-deavor.[20] Two examples illustrate these special relations. The United States and Poland together founded the Polish-American Ukraine Cooperation Initiative (PAUCI) in 1998, which remains active today and has given rise to a lively net-work of US-American, Polish, and Ukrainian NGOs. This project was based on the conviction that, drawing upon the successful Polish experience of mak-ing comprehensive political, economic, and social transformations after 1989, similar democratic reforms could be promoted in Ukraine. Here Poland was clearly seen as a model and mediator for integrating Western standards and val-ues in the East: "This mechanism [the trilateral initiative] is designed to share the expertise and experience gained in Poland's free market economic transition in support of Ukrainian economic reform."[21] PAUCI was founded by the US-American development agency USAID and is administered by the US-Ameri-can NGO Freedom House. This led to a peculiar constellation whereby US money financed the creation of an institution to support pro-European values in Ukraine through the transfer of Polish experiences and with the assistance of Polish NGOs. While PAUCI is an example of cooperation between civil societies, at the official political level successful cooperation between Sweden and Poland resulted in a common proposal in 2008 for a new "Eastern Partner-ship" housed within the framework of the European Neighbourhood Policy.[22] Such efforts were followed by the European Council's decision to develop new principles of cooperation with its eastern neighbors in May 2009.[23]

Compared to these activities, the German-Polish cooperation was less pro-ductive, even though it was often referred to as a privileged relationship. Al-though regional cross-border cooperation between Poland and Germany was often celebrated as a core element of this partnership and substantial invest-ments were made to promote it, the results were assessed cautiously.[24] Many observers shared the conviction that actual German-Polish relations had to contend with various sources of potential conflict.[25] The discussion about their painfully entangled history, especially during World War II, and the anticipated fear of masses of job-seeking Poles congesting the German market following EU enlargement, were only two of the most vocally debated issues in the media and public discourse.[26] When Polish elections in 2005 brought the twins Lech and Jarosław Kaczyński into the offices of president and prime minister, rela-tions deteriorated even further, resurrecting old stereotypes.[27]

Beyond this narrow context of bilateral relations, however, the broader pro-cess of European integration more significantly shaped the evolution of mu-tual perceptions of politicians from Germany and Poland. Until Poland joined the EU, official policy interpreted interregional and cross-border cooperation first and foremost as promoting the transfer of "European" standards from the West to the East and thereby leveling regional differences. As declared in the 1991 German-Polish contract on neighborly relations and friendship: "[T]he

Federal Republic of Germany is willing to promote the economic transformation of Poland toward a fully developed market economy both bilaterally and multilaterally. This shall contribute to a considerable reduction of economic and social differences."[28] While this logic—an implicit hierarchical relationship between Germany and Poland, privileging Germany—had become problematic even *before* Poland joined the EU, it was even more tenuous afterward, when not only Poland but also Western European nation-states and the EU as a whole encountered economic and political challenges due to the need for reforms after EU enlargement. This crumbling hierarchy between East and West was also articulated by Polish Prime Minister Marek Belka in 2005:

> Poles are probably the most seasoned of all in weathering change—certainly more than west European societies. Exhausted and frustrated, the Poles are nonetheless more ready for changes and reforms than the French, Germans, or any other stable democracy in western Europe. Compared with west Europe we do everything at the speed of light.... We do everything at a much faster pace than any country in western Europe, and we call this our normal pace. We introduce changes at such a pace that that [sic] I expect our monthly agenda would effectively topple a couple of western governments. We change more in a month than they do in eight years! This of course, is necessary and no cause for exaggerated pride—but it does show our potential.[29]

Polish Foreign Minister Włodziemierz Cimoszewicz had declared already in 2003: "There is no need for us to feel inferior."[30] He added in 2004, shortly before Poland's accession to the EU, that Poland would self-confidently articulate its national interests in the EU while being aware of its duties. Poland would not be a passive but a responsible and active partner: "We will be ourselves."[31] These statements should not be interpreted superficially as some kind of nationalistic boosterism. They must rather be understood as a reaction to repeated claims by Western governments, the Western media, and EU officials that Poland was backward and needed to catch up to "European standards." Both Belka and Cimoszewicz were eager to compromise between a clearly articulated will to adapt to European developments and Polish self-confidence about participating as an equal partner in a common European reform process.

Disagreement about how the future political space of the enlarged EU should be envisioned and what role Poland and Germany would play in it exacerbated these tensions in German-Polish relations. Polish President Aleksander Kwaśniewski explained in 2005:

> [A]fter Poland's EU accession the former model of our bilateral relations, where Poland was the EU candidate and Germany was the candidate's advocate, would become a matter of the past. Today we can say we have achieved the objective we formulated in the early 1990s and should now be looking for a new relation-

ship, one between two EU countries that are aware of their respective potentials, capabilities and ready for cooperation [*sic*].[32]

After Poland joined the EU, the implicitly hierarchical relation between Germany and Poland and between the EU and Poland, respectively, became a bone of contention for Polish statespersons. Poland gained a greater capacity to negotiate a new relationship, and compared with the economically weaker eastern German regions, successful western Polish regions found themselves in a better competitive situation for, among other things, EU funding. In addition, the social and economic divide in the immediate border regions had decreased profoundly after the 1990s. Data illustrate how the economic development on the Polish and German sides of the border gradually equalized. In 1991 a 25 percent growth rate of the GDP in Brandenburg contrasted with a negative rate of -8 percent in Poland. By 2003, however, growth rates were evenly matched at 3 percent. In 1991 the rate of inflation in Poland was 60 percent, whereas in Germany it came close to just 1 percent, but by 2002 the numbers were again almost the same (3 percent in Poland, 1 percent in Germany). A similar trend can be observed for the unemployment rate: in 1990 it was 3 percent in Brandenburg and 11 percent in Poland; by 2002 the rate was even lower in Poland (17 percent) than in Brandenburg (18 percent).[33]

Those who criticized the border opening—especially police and customs officials anticipating more cross-border crime and middle-class entrepreneurs fearing competition from their cheaper Polish counterparts—may even have been disappointed when the rush to the German labor market failed to materialize.[34] Although some of the transitory regulations protecting German labor from the competition of cheaper labor in East Central Europe initially played a role, the increased economic competitiveness of Poland can be traced to three processes. First, migratory flows had been shifting for some time. Recent numbers demonstrate that Poland has turned from a sending to a receiving country, and migrant Polish laborers today prefer the British or Dutch labor market to the German.[35] Second, the border regime at Poland's eastern border was considerably tightened so that migrants from further east were caught in EU detention centers in Ukraine, that is, outside the EU. Third, the socioeconomic situation on both sides of the border had become nearly balanced by 2002; in some regions the relation had even reversed. Especially in the northeastern Brandenburg region, the newly emerging metropolitan area around Szczecin had become attractive for both labor migrants and investors from Poland and Germany.[36] These new economic and social networks defined transnational metropolitan regions and undermined static, hierarchical understandings of the German-Polish neighborhood based upon outdated narratives of a delayed Polish modernization. Polish attention thus shifted eastward: the integration of the eastern policy into the wider context of EU foreign policy became ever more important for Polish political actors by the turn of the millennium.

The Reservoir of History: Defining the Polish Mission in the East

Two prominent observers—one from "the East" and one from "the West"—underlined Poland's new stance toward its eastern neighbors within the context of EU enlargement shortly before the country joined the EU. Russian historian Alexei Miller concluded an article in a special issue of the monthly journal *Transit* (published in 2003 and dedicated to the question of "Poland in the new Europe" with a special emphasis on *Ostpolitik*) with the following remarks:

> The Polish discourse on its eastern policy is not only deeply rooted in history, but even remains its prisoner. It is a mixture between possibly comprehensible phobias and a nostalgic megalomania of being "a regional superpower or being nothing." It is politically counterproductive and it is intellectually and morally by no means superior to corresponding discourses of Poland's eastern neighbors. The Polish discourse on its eastern policy does not contribute to the solution of the problems of Eastern Europe and its relations to the EU, it is rather part of the problem.[37]

Miller argued that all attempts at a Polish eastern policy, even current ones, can be traced back to the fundamental conflict between Poland and Russia about the hegemony over the so-called *kresy wschodnie*, the eastern borderlands of the former Polish-Lithuanian Commonwealth that approximates the western provinces of today's Ukraine, Belarus, and Lithuania.[38] These had been incorporated into the Russian Empire after the partitions of Poland at the end of the eighteenth century. The partitions, which resulted in the eradication of the First Polish Republic, motivated Polish intellectuals to interpret "the fight against Russia as the defense of European civilization against a despotic and barbarian empire. Thus, they called for Europe to come to their rescue."[39]

According to Miller, given the historically unequal conditions, the similarity of claims for leadership and the competing civilizing missions in the same territory nurtured an anti-Russian tendency in Poland's eastern policy that denied potential solutions for future problems. In the same issue of *Transit*, American historian Timothy Snyder came to the opposite conclusion: Polish eastern policy offered a "tradition with a future."[40] He identified the historical experience of the Polish-Lithuanian Commonwealth, founded in 1569 with the so-called Union of Lublin, as the basic source of the Polish approach to its eastern policy, and claimed that the eastern policy drafted in the 1970s and 1980s by exiled members of the Polish opposition living in France and Great Britain led to the development of a new eastern strategy after 1989. But this strategy, he continued, now that it had proven successful, appeared to be outdated.[41] In contrast to Miller, Snyder did not overemphasize Russian-Polish conflicts over the imperial fringe but stressed the "extraordinary significance" of the heritage of the Union of Lublin as a model "in the new world of the European Union."[42]

As these brief statements make clear, many Polish historians and intellectuals have in the past and present interpreted the Polish-Lithuanian Commonwealth as the historical model for legitimating Poland's civilizing mission in the East (although they themselves would not apply this term); that is, they promote a model for the organization of states and societies characterized by the principles of tolerance and diversity.[43] The eastern frontier, the *kresy*, has an important function in this order: they regard it as the space where exemplary strategies of coping with social, political, and cultural diversity were negotiated and translated in the past and where a new beginning for reconciliation today could again be sought. The Polish myth of the eastern fringe of the former Polish-Lithuanian Commonwealth conjures up borderlands between Eastern and Western civilization, the space where the Polish civilizing mission unfolds. The civilizing mission was thus not designed for "the world" as such, but rather aimed at a specifically defined area: the regions east of Poland.

In the public and scholarly debates between journalists, public intellectuals, and politicians in the interwar period (including Roman Dmowski, Józef Piłsudski, Jędrzej Giertych, Feliks Koneczny, and others), the elements inherent in the concept of a Polish civilizing mission in the East were elaborated and partly radicalized, only to reemerge in modified form in the 1970s and 1980s under different conditions. According to German historians Frank Hadler and Mathias Mesenhöller, the former "greatness" of the Polish-Lithuanian Commonwealth is not necessarily an imperial one in Polish historiography. Following this line of argument, it seems convincing to talk of a "civilizing mission without empire," one based on the commonwealth's claimed exemplarity and Poland's embeddedness and entanglement in the history of the West.[44] As argued above, a "civilizing mission" as understood here is not necessarily linked to an imperialist project and colonial practices. In the Polish case the mission's content was historically nuanced and tied to varying strategies, but its central objective understood Poland as bringing Western values and models to the East. These are today framed as "European standards" of democracy, market economy, human rights, and the rule of law—in contrast to a "Russian model" that Polish politicians and the public consider authoritarian and non-Western.

This was the tradition that fed into the unique "Jagiellonian system," a term coined in the 1940s by the influential exiled Polish historian Oscar Halecki to describe the Polish-Lithuanian Commonwealth's structure. It is based on principles of local self-government in multiethnic areas, respect for national rights, and adherence to a defense community against eastern and western imperialisms.[45] Halecki integrated this "Jagiellonian idea" into his concept of East Central Europe in the 1940s.[46] After World War II he described East Central Europe as the region that was pulverized by the expansionism of adjacent empires in the east and west—Russia, or the Stalinist Soviet Union, and Hitler's Germany. Thus, he eliminated any attempt to interpret the history of the Polish-Lithuanian Commonwealth as an imperialist one and emphasized that Poland was a victim.[47] In an interesting parallel development, Czech and Hungarian intellectuals also invoked this conceptualization of East Central Europe in discussions about the region's future in the 1980s by echoing the conflict with Russia that anchored the Polish concept.[48] Milan Kundera, for example, prominently and polemically lamented the "occident kidnappé" in 1983.[49] Expatriates and dissidents who participated in discussions in the 1970s and 1980s could not agree on a common definition of the specific historical region of East Central Europe and where it was located. One can nevertheless discern a number of common features that emerged: a notion of "in-between-ness," a sense of inferiority and backwardness, uncertainty about belonging to Western "civilization" (exacerbated by the region's forced integration into the Eastern Bloc), and the vision of a united European renaissance arising in this space between the two powerful blocs.[50] Notably for the Czech or Hungarian visions of the 1980s, the former Habsburg Empire served as a point of reference, while Halecki's post-World War II Jagiellonian East Central Europe referred to the former Polish-Lithuanian Commonwealth, a different territorial entity that extended farther eastward.[51]

Polish historiographical and public debates suppressed the "Jagiellonian idea" as well as projects for a federalized East Central Europe after World War II. In the People's Republic of Poland, enormous energy was invested in legitimating the country's "Western shift" and justifying the incorporation of former German provinces, known as the "regained territories," into the new Polish state.[52] At the same time Polish expatriates, especially in Paris but also in London and the US, elaborated a critical perspective toward Western realpolitik, which accepted the continent's partition on the basis of supposedly pragmatic reasons, and toward a role for Poland in the Eastern Bloc that relied on a quasi-imperial past before the partitions of Poland. After World War II, especially during the 1970s and 1980s, a group of intellectuals around Jerzy Giedroyc and Juliusz Mieroszewski—authors and editors of the Paris exile journal *Kultura*, which Giedroyc had founded in 1947—called for a new Polish stance toward eastern neighbors. Such calls relinquished dreams of hegemony in the East and were committed instead to reconciliation and responsibility. This agenda, which was highly critical of Polish expansionism and paternalism toward its eastern neighbors, especially during the interwar period, paved the way for the profound reorientation of the Polish eastern policy after 1989.[53] The recent reformulation, however, did not provoke a break with the historical traditions of

Polish eastern policy; one can rather speak of a re-interpretation, in the context of the EU eastern enlargement, of Poland as a bridge rather than a bulwark, as a model for social and political modernization and for democratic transformation in Eastern Europe. This concept, in turn, was rooted in the vision of Poland's specific role in a "Jagiellonian East Central Europe" and in the history of a long-lasting competition between Russia and Poland as two hegemonic states in this region. The nuances and frictions of this translation became visible at the turn of the millennium.[54]

Poland and Its Eastern Neighbors Today: Drafting a New Mission

Two paradigmatic statements by key political leaders reveal basic patterns of Polish efforts to find a new position in post-Cold War Europe even before EU enlargement. In a discussion about the future of the Polish eastern policy in March 2001, Polish Foreign Minister Dariusz Rosati, who served from December 1995 to October 1997, tried to describe the "civilizational border" set in motion by the EU enlargement process and its relation to Polish history in the following way:

> We do not know if this border [the border of Europe] runs through the center or the eastern part of Ukraine; we only can say that this is the borderland of Western civilization. Poland, having been a borderland for a thousand years, also developed a sort of border syndrome: while being a European country from the start, tied to Western Europe by culture, civilization, and religion, we always peered eastward; this was our area for expansion, our sphere of interest, and it was preordained like this for centuries. This was also dictated by the power constellation. It would have been difficult to successfully undertake an expansion toward the West; by contrast the East was easier to access. Poland was a country looking toward the East also because the threats were coming from the East and the South. The wars with Russia and Turkey were always a fight for national survival.[55]

Rosati argued that Europe's civilizational borderland had shifted toward the East as a result of Poland's successful political and social transformation since 1989, which would soon be legalized upon admission to the institutionally founded space of the EU. Rosati furthermore evoked the Polish tradition of being caught between the East and the West, characterizing this in-betweenness on the one hand through the entanglement of Polish history with the West (and hence its social and political models) and on the other hand through the Polish focus toward the East. Finally, the tradition of the *antemurale christianitatis* (bulwark of Christianity) also resonates here: the challenges come from the East and the South. The threatening Other is the Ottoman Empire and the Russian Empire, or, as Rosati translates, Turkey and Russia. The goal of influence in the

East is not necessarily associated with the practice of imperial expansion but is rather a question of "national survival."

In a similar manner, Aleksander Kwaśniewski, president of Poland from December 1995 to December 2005, commented in 2001 on the past before the division of the country in the late eighteenth century to emphasize its ongoing geopolitical and cultural role as a bridge between Western and Eastern Europe. Yet he highlighted reconciliation rather than conflicts, as Rosati did:

> For centuries the Polish tradition was characterized by openness and interest in diversity as well as by tolerance. On Polish soil people of different nationalities met, different cultures and historical experiences merged in this place. We were always neighbors of the East. We were always a bridge between the East and the West, and always will be. This is now especially visible, after the eastern border of Poland has become the eastern border of NATO and in a few years will become also the eastern border of the European Union, the space where it touches Russia, Belarus, and Ukraine. We want to be a link, not a bulwark.[56]

Kwaśniewski refers to the national "tradition" of accepting ethnic and religious diversity as providing a successful model for managing difference. He does not interpret Poland as belonging to the East but argues that Poland is its (European) neighbor, a link between the two imagined spaces of the West and the East. Kwaśniewski's and Rosati's statements reveal the two basic patterns of how the Polish foreign policy elite tried to define a new position for Poland in a novel European political and cultural geography after EU enlargement. Yet a tension remains between Rosati's self-understanding as a bulwark against a civilizationally alien Other and Kwaśniewski's self-image as a bridge between two culturally and politically related spaces. Poland's stance toward its eastern neighbors in an enlarged EU engages the model of the Polish-Lithuanian Commonwealth but also emphasizes the post-1989 Polish success story of political and economic transformation. For example, foreign Minister Radosław Sikorski argued in 2008:

> Having done so, Poland, just as 600 years ago, has become the standard and model of transformation for our Eastern neighbors, in particular for the kindred nation of Ukraine. Then, in the Jagiellonian era, the Republic spread examples of noble liberty and tolerance, become [*sic*] the cohesive force that over subsequent centuries kept together the multiethnic mosaic of elites in our region. It is for this reason that we believe that the mandate of the Lublin Union will be fulfilled only when our Eastern European brothers find themselves within the European Union. This is not an old-new messianism, but a practical observation that strengthening liberty and democracy in our region also serves the interests of our Republic.[57]

Conclusion and Outlook

The main rationale of Polish eastern policy after the end of the Cold War and in the course of its accession to the EU evolved around the goals of promoting the stabilization of democratic and sovereign states east of its national boundaries, preventing new dividing lines in Europe as an effect of EU enlargement, and acting as an advocate for the European ambitions of its neighbors, especially Ukraine. Every Polish government shared these convictions after 1989. Polish eastern policy can be interpreted as a pivotal strategy opposing tightening the new EU eastern border and favoring transforming it into a bridge and transit space for the promotion of "Western standards" in the eastern neighborhood. The goal was to integrate the borderland, to which at least the western part of Ukraine belongs, into the European space, thus shifting the EU's external border somewhat more to the east. This strategy wanted not only to shift mental and symbolic borders but also to assist Ukraine in adapting to European patterns. Poland's Eastern-oriented position had, nevertheless, already developed *before* enlargement. Thus it was not surprising that after accession to the EU, Poland started to play an active and self-confident role in shaping the EU's Eastern Policy, especially in the framework of the ENP. But Western politicians were taken by surprise when they realized Poland's willingness to be treated as an equal. Rather, they perceived the Polish political elite as the "EU's new awkward partner."[58]

In the end Poland succeeded in influencing the new EU Eastern Policy and integrating many of its proposals into a new EU "Eastern Dimension"; the country deserves recognition for its significant innovations in EU foreign policy.[59] However, as the recent shifts in the relations between Poland and Western Europe have demonstrated, it is open to question whether Poland will be acknowledged as a leading partner beyond its eastern borders in the future. A look at regional cross-border cooperation between Poland and Ukraine reveals that the Ukrainian partners not only emphasize intensified competition for scarce resources in the transboundary region but also define themselves increasingly as self-confident players with an extended history of Western and Polish aid programs.[60] At the national level the Ukrainian reaction to the EU's "Eastern Partnership" demonstrates this growing self-image of Ukrainian actors as agents, not as petitioners and receivers. As Ukrainian President Victor Yushchenko commented: "The EU was not brave enough ... Europe will not win the global competition if it is only halfway united.... The integration of Ukraine into the EU is as much an advantage for the European Union as it is for Ukraine."[61]

As I have suggested in this essay, the metaphor of a German-Polish neighborhood as first promoted in 1990 was from the start an asymmetrical relationship, marked by a clear East-West divide defining the direction of transfer of Western norms from West to East. When Poland succeeded in introducing its own concept of a civilizing mission toward the East after EU enlargement in 2004, this narrative was unsettled. As Ukraine becomes increasingly dissatisfied with its unequal partnership vis-à-vis the EU through the new EU Neighbourhood Policy, this pattern will most likely recur. Thus, the players constantly renegotiate the hierarchies in the political spaces of their respective "neighborhoods." The Polish position—first excluded from and later integrated into the EU—is a case that demonstrates how conventional narratives of modernization and "civilization" may be strategically used and called into question when making claims to notions of a tolerant and integrated Europe.

Notes

1. Compare with Norman Davies, *God's Playground: A History of Poland*, 2 vols. (Oxford, 1981).
2. The ENP and the European Neighbourhood Policy Instrument (ENPI, 2004) promote cross-border cooperation and codify strategies to deal with new neighbors in the South and East. See EU Commission, Communication from the Commission, "Wider Europe – Neighbourhood. A Framework for Relations with our Eastern and Southern Neighbours," COM (2003) 104 final, Brussels, 11 March 2003; idem, "European Neighbourhood Policy. Strategy Paper," COM (2004) 373 final, Brussels, 12 May 2004; idem, "Eastern Partnership. Polish-Swedish Non-Paper," May 2008, www.msz.gov.pl/files/PARTNERSTWO%20WSCHODNIE/1en.pdf (accessed 12 July 2010); idem, Communication from the Commission to the European Parliament and Council "Eastern Partnership," SEC (2008) 2974/ COM (2008) 823 final, Brussels, 3 December 2008.
3. This refers especially to the EU assistance programs PHARE, ISPA and SAPARD.
4. See EU Commission, Communication from the Commission, "Wider Europe – Neighbourhood"; idem, Communication from the Commission to the European Parliament and Council, "Eastern Partnership"; idem, Commission Staff Working Document accompanying the Communication from the Commission to the European Parliament and Council, "Eastern Partnership," SEC (2008) 2974, Brussels, 3 December 2008; Council of the European Union, Brussels European Council 19/20 March 2009, "Presidency Conclusions," 7880/09, Brussels, 20 March 2008; European Union, "Joint Declaration of the Prague Eastern Partnership Summit," 7 May 2009, http://www.eu2009.cz/event/1/3555/ (accessed November 2009).
5. Romano Prodi, "A Wider Europe – A Proximity Policy as the Key to Stability," Sixth ECSA World Conference, Jean Monnet Project, Brussels, 5–6 December 2002. http://europa.eu/rapid/pressReleasesAction.do?reference=SPEECH/02/619&format=HTML&aged=0&language=EN&guiLanguage=en (accessed 29 June 2010).
6. On the evolution of the distinction between "Europe" and "Eastern Europe," see Larry Wolff, *Inventing Eastern Europe: The Map of Civilization on the Mind of the Enlighten-*

ment (Stanford, 2000). On the cultural Other see Jürgen Osterhammel, "Kulturelle Grenzen in der Expansion Europas," *Saeculum. Jahrbuch für Universalgeschichte* 46, no. 1 (1995): 101–38.

7. Boris Barth and Jürgen Osterhammel, "Vorwort," in *Zivilisierungsmissionen. Imperiale Weltverbesserung seit dem 18. Jahrhundert*, ed. Boris Barth and Jürgen Osterhammel, (Constance, 2005), 9.

8. Ibid., 7–11; James M. Blaut, *The Colonizer's Model of the World* (New York, 1993); Dipesh Chakrabarty, *Provincializing Europe* (Princeton, 2000); Wolfgang M. Schröder, "Mission Impossible? Begriff, Modelle und Begründungen der 'civilizing mission' aus philosophischer Sicht," in Barth and Osterhammel, eds., *Zivilisierungsmissionen*, 13–32.

9. Jörg Döring and Tristan Thielmann, "Einleitung: Was lesen wir im Raume? Der Spatial Turn und das geheime Wissen der Geographen," in *Spatial Turn. Das Raumparadigma in den Kultur- und Sozialwissenschaften*, ed. Jörg Döring and Tristan Thielmann (Bielefeld, 2008), 23.

10. Osterhammel and Barth, eds., *Zivilisierungsmissionen*. On the German "colonization of the East" see Robert L. Nelson, ed., *Germans, Poland, and Colonial Expansion to the East* (New York, 2009); on Russia see Eva-Maria Stolberg, *Sibirien: Russlands "Wilder Osten". Mythos und soziale Realität im 19. und 20. Jahrhundert* (Stuttgart, 2009); Kerstin Jobst, *Die Perle des Imperiums. Der russische Krim-Diskurs im Zarenreich* (Constance, 2007).

11. Excellent examples of a new perspective closing this gap are Frank Hadler and Mathias Mesenhöller, eds., *Vergangene Größe und Ohnmacht in Ostmitteleuropa: Repräsentationen imperialer Erfahrungen in der Historiographie seit 1918* (Leipzig, 2007); Claudia Kraft and Katrin Steffen, eds., *Europas Platz in Polen. Polnische Europakonzeptionen vom Mittelalter bis zum EU-Beitritt* (Osnabrück, 2007).

12. For the period before the 1792–95 partitions of Poland see Davies, *God's Playground*, especially vol. 1; on the changing modern Polish frontiers see vol. 2, chap. 21 on Granice. On the entangled Polish, Ukrainian, Lithuanian, and Belarusian histories see Timothy Snyder, *The Reconstruction of Nations: Poland, Lithuania, Ukraine, Belarus 1569–1999* (New Haven, 2003).

13. Norman Davies is one of the most prominent European historians who advocates the integration of Polish history into a broader European narrative to avoid an understanding of "Europe" according to its Western traditions only. See Norman Davies, *Europe: A History* (New York, 1996), 15ff.; idem, *God's Playground*, xff.

14. Adam Krzemiński, *Testfall für Europa: Deutsch-polnische Nachbarschaft muss gelingen* (Hamburg, 2008).

15. This history is, of course, much longer; see Klaus Zernack, "Deutschlands Ostgrenze," in *Deutschlands Grenzen in der Geschichte*, ed. Alexander Demandt (Munich, 1990), 140–65.

16. The first was the 1990 "Deutsch-polnischer Grenzvertrag" (German-Polish Border Treaty) published in *Bulletin des Presse- und Informationsamtes der Bundesregierung* 134 (16 November 1990): 1394; see further the 1991 "Deutsch-polnischer Nachbarschaftsvertrag," *Bulletin des Presse- und Informationsamtes der Bundesregierung* 68 (18 June 1991): 541–46.

17. A series of volumes published by more or less the same team of authors started with "the way to a fair partnership" and ended with "the destruction of the dialogue": Dieter Bingen and Krzysztof Malinowski, eds., *Polacy i Niemcy na drodze do partnerskiego sąsiedz-*

twa. Próba bilansu dziesięcioleca 1989–1998 (Poznan, 2000); Anna Wolff-Powęska and Dieter Bingen, eds., *Nachbarn auf Distanz. Polen und Deutsche 1998–2004* (Wiesbaden, 2005); Dieter Bingen, ed., *Die Destruktion des Dialogs. Zur innenpolitischen Instrumentalisierung negativer Fremd- und Feindbilder: Polen, Tschechien, Deutschland und die Niederlande im Vergleich, 1900–2005* (Wiesbaden, 2005). In contrast, efforts to proclaim a common historical transboundary space still persist: Karl Schlögel, ed., *Oder – Odra. Blicke auf einen europäischen Strom* (Frankfurt am Main, 2007).

18. Dieter Bingen, "Vorwort zur deutschen Ausgabe," in Wolff-Powęska and Bingen, *Nachbarn auf Distanz*, viii; and Anna Wolff-Powęska, "Ideelle und politische Voraussetzungen der Entwicklung der deutsch-polnischen Beziehungen," ibid., 17.

19. Włodzimierz Cimoszewicz, "Polska polityka zagraniczna w 2004 r. Informacja rządu przedstawiona przez ministra spraw zagranicznych RP Włodzimierza Cimoszewicza, Sejm RP, 21 stycznia 2004 r" [Polish foreign policy in 2004. Government information presented by Foreign Minister Włodzimierz Cimoszewicz in Parliament on 21 January 2004], *Przegląd Rządowy* 2, no. 152 (2004): 109; Adam Daniel Rotfeld, "Government Report on Poland's Foreign Policy Presented by Foreign Minister of the Republic of Poland Adam Daniel Rotfeld at a Sejm Meeting on 21 January 2005," *Materiały i Dokumenty* 1 (2005), http://www.msz.gov.pl/index.php?page=6661&lang_id=en&bulletin_id=16&document=8448 (accessed 14 July 2010). The English quotations from Polish and German sources are translated by the author, except those from *Materiały i Dokumenty*, as this periodical is also published in English.

20. Bronisław Geremek, "Kierunki polskiej polytiki zagranicznej. Informacja rządu przedstawiona przez ministra sprwa zagranicznych Bronisława Geremeka podczas posiedzenia Sejmu RP, 9 maja 2000 r" [Directions of the Polish foreign policy. Government information presented by Foreign Minister Bronisław Geremek in Parliament on 9 May 2000], *Przegląd Rządowy* 5, no. 107 (2000): 62; Władisław Bartoszewski, "Zadania polskiej polityki zagranicznej w 2001 r., informacja ministra spraw zagranicznych Władisława Bartoszewskiego przedstawiona na forum Sejmu RP 6 czerwca 2001 r" [The tasks for Polish foreign policy. Information of the Foreign Minister Władisław Bartoszewski in Parliament on 6 June 2001], *Przegląd Rządowy* 7, no. 121 (2001): 91; Włodzimierz Cimoszewicz, "Podstawie kierunki polskiej polityki zagranicznej, Informacja ministra spraw zagranicznych Włodzimierza Cimoszewicza przedstawiona na forum Seijmu RP 14 marca 2002 r" [Basic directions of Polish foreign policy. Information of the Foreign Minister Włodzimierz Cimoszewicz in Parliament on 14 March 2002], *Przegląd Rządowy* 5, no. 131 (2002): 130.

21. "Wspólne Oświadczenie w sprawie inicjatywy wsółpracy polsko-amerykańsko-ukraińskiej [Joint statement of the United States-Poland-Ukraine-Cooperation Initiative], Kiev, 29 October 1998, *Zbiór Dokumentów* 3–4 (1998): 7.

22. "Eastern Partnership. Polish-Swedish Non-paper." http://www.msz.gov.pl/files/PARTNERSTWO%20WSCHODNIE/1en.pdf (accessed 14 July 2010).

23. EU Commission, Communication from the Commission to the European Parliament and Council "Eastern Partnership"; European Union, "Joint Declaration of the Prague Eastern Partnership Summit."

24. Steve Wood, "Apprehensive Partners: Germany, Poland and EU enlargement," *German Politics* 11, no. 1 (April 2002): 97–124.

25. Roland Freudenstein, "Poland, Germany and the EU," *International Affairs* 74, no. 1 (1998): 41–54; Klaus Bachmann, "Von der Euphorie zum Misstrauen: Deutsch-Polnische Beziehungen nach der Wende," *Osteuropa* 50, no. 8 (2000): 853–71.
26. On the stereotypes mobilized in these discussions see Beata Ociepka, "Das Bild der Deutschen und Polen in den Medien," in Wolff-Powęska and Bingen, eds., *Nachbarn auf Distanz*, 216–42.
27. Peter Oliver Loew, "Feinde, überall Feinde. Psychogramm eines Problems in Polen," *Osteuropa* 56, no. 11/12 (2006): 33–51.
28. "Deutsch-polnischer Nachbarschaftsvertrag."
29. Marek Belka, "Address by Prime Minister Marek Belka at a debate on the 2007–2013 National Development Plan in Warsaw," 20 January 2005, *Materiały i Dokumenty* 1 (2005), http://www.msz.gov.pl/index.php?page=6661&lang_id=en&bulletin_id=16&document=8448 (accessed 14 July 2010).
30. *Przegląd Rządowy* 2, no. 140 (2003): 90.
31. *Przegląd Rządowy* 2, no. 152 (2004): 109.
32. Aleksander Kwaśniewski, "Address by President of the Republic of Poland Aleksander Kwasniewski during his visit to the Federal Republic of Germany on 26 February 2005," *Materiały i Dokumenty* 2 (2005), http://www.msz.gov.pl/index.php?page=6662&lang_id=en&bulletin_id=16&document=8448 (accessed 14 July 2010).
33. Andrea Blaneck, *Netzwerke und Kooperationen an der deutsch-polnischen Grenze. Untersuchungen zum wirtschaftlichen Milieu in der Grenzregion an der Oder* (Münster, 2005).
34. Two examples from two major German weeklies of this widely discussed topic include Jürgen Rohne, "An der deutsch-polnischen Grenze geht die Angst um," *Der Spiegel*, 1 February 2002, www.spiegel.de/politik/deutschland/0,1518,180137,00.html (accessed 29 June 2010) and Joanna M. Rother, "Am Rande des Reichtums," *Die Zeit* 52, 19 December 2007, www. zeit.de/2007/52/Schengen-Abkommen (accessed 29 June 2010).
35. Heather Grabbe, "The Sharp Edges of Europe: Extending Schengen Eastwards," *International Affairs* 76, no. 3 (2000): 519–36, and the numbers given in Stefan Alscher, "Country Profile 3: Poland," *Polen. focus Migration*, January 2008. www.focus-migration.de/Poland.2810.0.html?&L=1 (accessed on 5 July 2010).
36. Birk Meinhardt, "Stadt, Land, Frust," *Süddeutsche Zeitung*, 21–22 June 2008, 3.
37. Alexei Miller, "In den Fesseln der Geschichte. Der polnische Diskurs über die Ostpolitik," *Transit* 25 (2003): 47.
38. Robert Traba, "'Kresy' oder 'Atlantis des Nordens'? Neue polnische Diskussionen über die Mythologie des Ortes," *Inter Finitimos* 3 (2005): 52–60; Jerzy Kochanowski, "Paradoxien der Erinnerung an die Ostgebiete," *Inter Finitimos* 3 (2005): 61–76.
39. Miller, "In den Fesseln der Geschichte," 43.
40. Timothy Snyder, "Polnische Ostpolitik. Tradition mit Zukunft," *Transit* 25 (2003): 25–39.
41. Ibid., 25–26.
42. Ibid., 39.
43. Stefan Batory Foundation, "Polska Polityka Wschodnia. Pełny zapis dyskusji zorganizowanej prez Fundację im. Stefana Batorego oraz redakcję 'Tygodnika Powszechnego'" [Polish Eastern Policy. Complete transcript of the discussion organized by the Stefan Batory Foundation and the journal *Tygodnik Powszechny*], 1 March 2001. One pro-

tagonist among historians for this perspective on Polish history is Jerzy Kłoczowski, director of the renowned Institute of East-Central Europe in Lublin.

44. Frank Hadler and Mathias Mesenhöller, "Repräsentationen imperialer Erfahrung in Ostmitteleuropa: Einleitende Thesen zu Konzept, Befunden und einer transnationalen Perspektive," in Hadler and Mesenhöller, *Vergangene Größe*, 11–32.

45. Jürgen Bömelburg, "Zwischen imperialer Geschichte und Ostmitteleuropa als Geschichtsregion: Oskar Halecki und die polnische 'jagiellonische Idee,'" in Hadler and Mesenhöller, *Vergangene Größe*, 119f.

46. Ibid., 110f.

47. Ibid., 121.

48. See Rafał Stobiecki, "Comparing Polish Historiography on the Petersburg Empire: Second Republic – People's Republic – Exile," in Hadler and Mesenhöller, *Vergangene Größe*, 281–300.

49. Milan Kundera, "Un occident kidnappé ou la tragédie de l'Europe centrale," *Le débat* (November 1983); English translation published in two versions: "A Kidnapped West or a Culture Bows Out," *Granta* 11 (1984) and "The Tragedy of Central Europe," *New York Review of Books*, 26 April 1984.

50. Exemplary contributions include those by Timothy Garton Ash, Tony Judt, and George Schöpflin in the special issue "Eastern Europe – Central Europe – Europe," *Daedalus* 119, no. 1 (1990). See also Alexei Miller, "Tema zentral'noij Evropy: Istorija, sovremennyje diskursy i mesto v nich Rossij," *Novoe Literanurnoe Obozrenie* 52 (2001): 75–96.

51. Maciej Janowski, "Pitfalls and Opportunities: The Concept of East Central Europe as a Tool of Historical Analysis," *European Review of History* 6, no. 1 (1999): 91–100.

52. This resulted in a renaissance of the so-called "Piast" traditions in the "regained territories." See Markus Krzoska, *Für ein Polen an Oder und Ostsee. Zygmunt Wojciechowski (1900–1955) als Historiker und Publizist* (Osnabrück, 2003); idem, "Die Renaissance der piastischen Idee. Der polnische Raumdiskurs in der ersten Hälfte des 20. Jahrhunderts," in *Amicus Poloniae. Teksty ofiarowane Profesorowi Heinrichowi Kunstmannowi w osiemdziesiątą piątą rocznicę urodzin*, ed., Krzysztof Ruchniewicz and Marek Zybura (Wrocław, 2009), 235–48.

53. For an overview see Sebastian Gerhardt, *Polska Polityka Wschodnia. Die Außenpolitik der polnischen Regierung von 1989 bis 2004 gegenüber den östlichen Nachbarstaaten Polens (Russland, Litauen, Weißrussland, Ukraine)* (Marburg, 2007); Renata Makarska and Basil Kerski, eds., *Die Ukraine, Polen und Europa. Europäische Identität an der neuen Ostgrenze* (Osnabrück, 2004).

54. The death in 2000 of Jerzy Giedroyc, who had been the mentor of the new Polish eastern policy after 1989, coincided with the countdown to EU enlargement and the onset of negotiations for the Treaty of Nice. This created extraordinary pressure to redefine conventional positions and adapt to a changing environment.

55. Dariusz Rosati, "Statement," in Stefan Batory Foundation, "Polska Polityka Wschodnia, 16f. www.batory.org.pl/ftp/program/forum/ppw.pdf (accessed 30 November 2009).

56. Aleksander Kwaśniewski, "Wykład prezydenta Polski Aleksandra Kwaśniewskiego 'Ewolucja środowiska międzynarodowego – szanse i zagrożenia' podczas spotkania zorganizowanego prez Genewski Klub Dyplomatyczny" [Lecture by the Polish President Aleksander Kwaśniewski: "The development of the international environment – chances and threats" during a meeting organized by the Geneva Diplomatic Club],

Geneva, 22 May 2001], excerpts published in *Zbiór dokumentów* 57, no. 2 (2001): 14–22, here 19f.

57. Radosław Sikorski, "Address by Foreign Minister of the Republic of Poland Radosław Sikorski at the Sejm, 7 May 2008," *Materiały i Dokumenty* 5 (2008), http://www.msz.gov.pl/index.php?page=12964&lang_id=en&bulletin_id=16&document=8448 (accessed January 2010).

58. Heather Grabbe, "Poland: The EU's New Awkward Partner," *Bulletin of the Centre of European Reform*, February/March 2004, www.cer.org.uk/articles/34_grabbe.html (accessed February 2009).

59. Polish Ministry of Foreign Affairs, *EU Eastern Policy in the Context of EU Eastern Enlargement and Central Europe Enlargement: The Polish Perspective* (Warsaw, 2001); idem, "Non-Paper with Polish Proposals Concerning Policy toward the New Eastern Neighbours after EU Enlargement," www.mfa.gov.pl/?document=2041 (accessed 14 July 2010); "Eastern Partnership. Polish-Swedish Non-Paper."

60. This is part of a larger forthcoming study of mine, to be published in 2012.

61. Claudia von Salzen et al., "Die EU hatte nicht genug Mut," interview with Victor Yushchenko, *Tagesspiegel*, 4 May 2009, www.tagesspiegel.de/politik/international/Ukraine-Gasstreit-Europa-Juschtschenko;art123,2788497 (accessed 4 May 2009).

III

❦

Migrating
Boundaries

CHAPTER 8

Migrants, Mosques, and Minarets
Reworking the Boundaries of Liberal Democracy in
Switzerland and Germany

PATRICIA EHRKAMP

On 29 November 2009, Switzerland's citizens shocked many of their European neighbors by voting in a referendum to ban the construction of minarets on Swiss mosques. A clear majority of Swiss citizens voted "yes" in the referendum, which the Volksinitiative gegen den Bau von Minaretten (Popular Initiative against the Construction of Minarets, hereafter Volksinitiative) initiated in 2008. The ban on minarets neither ends the construction of mosques or (Muslim) places of worship themselves, nor applies to existing minarets and mosques, but bans the future construction of minarets as a symbol of what some groups deem Islamist or fundamentalist expression. Numerous rightwing parties and extremist groups on the political right in Europe welcomed the ban, but it also prompted strong criticism from politicians in Western Europe and elsewhere. Most comments from centrist and leftist segments of the political spectrum attributed the vote to fear and xenophobia, and commentators highlighted that the Swiss vote needed to be understood as an "expression of intolerance" toward Muslims.[1]

By contrast, only three weeks earlier a hotly contested mosque construction project finally had gotten underway in the Cologne neighborhood of Ehrenfeld with the ceremonial laying of the foundation stone. The Cologne mosque, initiated as a "Zentralmoschee" (central mosque) for the city by the Germany-wide organization Diyanet İşleri Türk Islam Birliği (DITIB or Diyanet Turkish Islamic Union), had been debated for years and continues to be contested. Representatives of the municipal government originally envisioned it as providing a centralized place of worship for many different Muslim groups in the region. The DITIB mosque, once finished, will be one of numerous new mosques that have been built in German cities in recent years. Despite debates about Islam and opposition to mosque construction, a new landscape of prestigious mosques—most with minarets, although the architecture varies from traditional Ottoman to modernist designs—has emerged in German cities. Yet 44 percent of Germans would vote *for* banning minarets in Germany, according to a representative poll about the minaret ban in Switzerland conducted by TNS-Infratest on behalf of the news magazine *Der Spiegel*. In the same poll, 45 percent stated they would vote *against* banning minarets.[2] This nearly even split highlights Islamophobia's prevalence in Germany as well, which becomes even more evident in the answers to other questions in the same poll: for instance, 78 percent answered "yes" to the question of whether they feared further struggles with radical forces of the Islamic world in the future. Building permits for mosques thus are not indicators of the absence of Islamophobia or the acceptance of Islam in Germany.

Building new prestigious mosques and banning minarets are but two expressions of the ways that Islam has occupied the imagination and public debate of Western European societies in recent decades. Since the late 1990s Islam has been at the center of debates about the integration of immigrants in Germany and Western Europe more generally. Some of these debates have explicitly focused on the ways that migrant groups' transnational ties to Islamic organizations undermine liberal democratic values and threaten the security of Western European nation-states. Whether centered on headscarves (the so-called "Kopftuchstreit"), calls for prayers in the late 1990s, or more recently on forced marriages, honor killings, and the construction of prestigious mosques in German cities, a central question of public discourse with regard to immigration has been whether Islam is commensurate with the values of liberal democracy.[3] The attacks of 11 September 2001 in the United States and later attacks (and failed attempts) by violent Islamist groups in London and Madrid, as well as the murder of Dutch filmmaker Theo van Gogh in 2004 at the hand of an Islamist extremist, have led to heightened scrutiny of Muslims residing in Europe. Muslim groups have become the target of surveillance measures aimed at making states more secure while doubly marginalizing Muslims as a religious minority and as potential terrorists.[4] These debates demonize Islam and are indicative of a wider "war on Muslims" that cannot deny racist elements and motivations.[5]

Examining the treatment of Muslims and immigrants in Western European societies highlights the ways that racism and Islamophobia permeate political decisions and legislation about immigration, citizenship, and membership. Debates about citizenship, belonging, and liberal democracy as they are waged over the inclusion and exclusion of Islam in European societies and cities provide important insights into the construction of political subjectivities among members of society and the polity. I argue that rather than simply taking for granted the notion of Western racism as the basis for the exclusion of Muslims in contemporary Europe, these debates provide insights into what the "war on

Muslims" means for the shape and future of liberal democracy in immigrant receiving societies.

Immigration and the Boundaries of Liberal Democratic Citizenship

Questions of immigrants' social, economic, cultural, and political incorporation have occupied scholarship across the social sciences and philosophy since the early twentieth century. Initially immigration research considered the incorporation of migrants a societal process of adaptation that would increase similarity between longer-term residents and newcomers.[6] Assimilation theories suppose that immigrants adapt to receiving societies both socioeconomically and culturally.[7] Processes of globalization have increased the cultural diversity of migrants as women and men move from increasingly different places of origin to a larger number of destinations, necessitating new approaches toward understanding immigrant integration. Migrants' increased ability to maintain ties across borders and to create transnational spaces has further led scholars to examine the consequences of migrant transnationalism for immigrant integration, nation-building processes, and loyalties toward sending and receiving societies.[8] Together these changing processes have brought about a rethinking of the concepts of integration and assimilation. Such works increasingly challenge assumptions of an already formed "host society" and of linear processes of assimilation.[9] Recent changes to immigration, integration, and citizenship laws further suggest an increasing need to consider societal, political, and legal processes in relation to one another to account for the increasing complexity of contemporary immigration.

Migrants' greater ability to maintain political, social, and religious ties across borders has subjected them to greater scrutiny by receiving states. Public discourses depict the transnational ties and religious practices of Muslim migrants as undermining notions of secularism and the authority of the liberal democratic state. The rhetoric of the supposed anti-democratic tendencies of Islamic groups, in which violent practices such as honor killings are ascribed to Islam, has very real material effects. States have increased the surveillance of Islamic associations and Muslim migrants in the interest of governance.[10] Muslims are increasingly scrutinized in the contemporary period, as the definition and redefinition of rights and of liberal democratic systems and values are at stake. The securitization of migration provides a mechanism to reduce the risk that liberal democracy faces when allowing for cultural, religious, and political differences in the space of the polity.[11] Katharyne Mitchell suggests that Western European countries have moved away from notions of multiculturalism and instead exert more assimilation pressures on migrants.[12] The French government's efforts at banning headscarves in schools to promote assimilation of Muslims into the French nation is a recent example of how wholesale ascriptions of culture have led to attempts at disciplining visible difference.[13] Yet to uphold the French ideal of "egalité," the government also had to ban religious symbols of Christians and Jews. The assimilation of Muslim immigrants and their political incorporation into the receiving polity thus have tangible consequences for non-Muslims and restrict the freedom of religious expression for *all* members of French society.

These recent developments suggest that the boundaries of belonging and the values and ideas of liberal democracy are being renegotiated in Europe. Liberal democratic citizenship entails the guarantee of rights in exchange for certain duties and responsibilities to the state.[14] More important, it also defines a moral community that frequently highlights citizens' obligations toward the political community.[15] Such obligations include the affirmation of secularism, which can in turn be considered a form of governance aimed at immigrants.[16] Debates about the cultural "fit" of Muslim migrants, for example, certainly display traits of nationalism and racism aimed at the exclusion of so-called Others.[17] Media and public discourses have instrumentalized Muslim migrant women (and their ascribed oppression) in particular to justify heightened scrutiny, restrictive legislation, and demands for more integration and commitments to liberal democracy.[18] Feminist scholars have shown that public discourses about forced marriages portray Muslim women as the victims of their culture. In such discourses, that culture in turn appears to be static and to determine Muslim women's practices, providing no room for independent thinking or acting.[19] Ascribing at the same time the potential for violence to Muslim men, these discourses demonize Muslims and Islam more broadly.[20]

In this current climate, Muslim migrants (especially Muslim women) are faced with demands that they act as if they were citizens and assert their gender equality in particular. This active practice of citizenship increasingly becomes a condition for formal citizenship for Muslim migrants, rather than being afforded to them as a benefit of such membership. While migrants do need to show their commitment (and willingness to assimilate) to liberal democracy, nonmigrant Germans are not asked to affirm democratic values by practicing them. Such differentiated expectations of enacting and affirming the values of liberal democracy undermine ideals of citizenship such as equality because not *all* citizens are expected to practice active citizenship.[21] Negotiations over legal restrictions and the conditions under which receiving states will accept newcomers thus also affect longer-term residents when citizenship rights and responsibilities become subject to debate. Although debates currently question whether Muslim immigrants and their beliefs are commensurable with the ideals of liberal democratic citizenship, such questions clearly have consequences for non-Muslims and non-immigrants as states redraw the legal and cultural boundaries of belonging.

In the following I examine three recent instances that rework democratic rights and responsibilities in relation to religious expression. I begin with a brief analysis of prolonged debates about a so-called "Deutsche Leitkultur" in Germany. Translated as the "German guiding culture" and understood as rooted in Judeo-Christian traditions and liberal democracy, politicians mobilize the term to demand immigrant assimilation without a notion of force (hence the ostensibly benign pedagogical idea of "guiding"). The 2009 minaret ban in Switzerland and conflicts over the building of the Cologne-Ehrenfeld mosque provide two further instances. Together these cases shed light on the ways that the boundaries of liberal democracy are being redrawn in contemporary Western Europe. They highlight how discussions of the right of religious expression aimed at Muslim migrants (and legal changes that ensue as a result) also have consequences for the broader understandings and practices of liberal democracy in Germany and Switzerland. But these debates further show how migrants themselves participate in liberal democracy as they engage in debates and pursue their ideas of citizenship and integration.

Leitkultur, Democracy, and Islam in Germany

Since the late 1990s, the landscape of Germany's citizenship and immigration laws has changed dramatically. Germany enacted a new citizenship law in 2000 and added entirely new, comprehensive immigration legislation coupled with an integration law in 2005. These were enacted at the same time to set criteria for the admission of new immigrants to Germany and to improve the integration of immigrants already residing in Germany. These legal changes were important steps in redefining Germany's overall attitudes, as the government finally began distancing itself from the statement "Germany is not a country of immigration." But they also brought new expectations and regulations for immigrant assimilation, including mandatory participation in "Integrationskurse" (integration courses) upon arrival in Germany. The new citizenship law in particular met with obstacles and objections, even after careful deliberations that involved scaling back more generous provisions for dual citizenship.

The new citizenship law added elements of jus soli (territorial birthright citizenship) to the previously valid jus sanguinis, an ethnic definition of citizenship that had prevailed since 1913. Along with this added territorial notion, the new law created provisions for dual citizenship that allow children born to noncitizen parents to hold German as well as their parents' citizenship until the age of twenty-three, when they must decide to retain either German citizenship or their parents' nationality. The requirement of having to choose a nationality emerged as a compromise after the Christian Democratic Union (CDU), which had rejected earlier proposals of the new law on the basis that it undermined loyalty to the state and integration into German society, collected about five million signatures in a campaign against dual citizenship.[22] This provision, while still upholding the idea that citizenship is singular and entails membership in only one nation-state, also sought to accommodate the reality of migrants living for long periods of time outside the country of their formal membership by opening up new spaces of political membership for resident noncitizens in Germany. Politicians and NGOs hoped that easing access to formal membership would foster immigrant integration.[23]

These newly opening legal-political spaces of membership were quickly reworked and constrained in public debates about the limits and conditions of cultural membership, in particular as directed toward Muslim migrants. Debates about the citizenship law and immigrant integration were accompanied by public discussions about "Deutsche Leitkultur" initiated by Friedrich Merz, a former member of the CDU in the German Bundestag (parliament).[24] Merz formulated expectations for immigrants to adapt and conform to this *Leitkultur*, which he defined as firmly rooted in Christian and occidental values and traditions (i.e., by definition excluding Muslims). His proposal spurred numerous objections from other parts of the political spectrum, even from within his own party, and in 2000 the word *Leitkultur* was declared "Unwort des Jahres" (non-word of the year, chosen annually by an independent jury of linguists at the University of Frankfurt am Main). However, the term remains popular with some segments of German society and polity and has lingered in debates about immigrant integration. Numerous politicians on the left have publicly challenged or rejected notions of a *Leitkultur*, while others have sought to redefine it as within existing liberal-democratic tradition and laws. Yet even this criticism of the term contributes to its circulation and thereby perpetuates, if inadvertently, the notion of *cultural* change as necessary for formal membership and belonging.

CDU members of the Bundestag in particular emphasized that cultural homogeneity increased the possibility of immigrant integration. From such a perspective cultural difference is understood as counterproductive to integration, affirming notions of difference as posing risks for democracy. Moreover, *Leitkultur* becomes the measuring stick for integration, the opposite of which appears to be undesirable ghettoization. For example, CDU Bundestag member Vera Lengsfeld stated that "if cultural value systems are very different and the will to integrate into the *Leitkultur* is missing, then ghettoization is the result, and it is quasi-voluntary ghettoization."[25] The definition of *Leitkultur*, however, remains unclear. Frequently it is contrasted with Turkish identities, modest dress of Muslim women, and Islamic practices. Meanwhile Angela Merkel, freshly reelected as the head of the CDU in December 2004, commented that the *Leitkultur* also included such things as the flag, the national anthem, and *Heimat*, all of which are symbols of national identity. Several scholarly commentators were quick to assume that this "Deutsche Leitkultur" is but another expression of Germany's nationalist or racist tendencies.[26] While these interpretations are important, they primarily look to Germany's past and provide little insight into how understandings of *Leitkultur* are mobilized to shape Germany's future as a country of immigration.

These debates more broadly indicate how the limits and boundaries of liberal democracy in Germany are being negotiated in relation to immigrants and in relation to Muslim migrants in particular. Rather than simply determining a cultural definition of nationhood, *Leitkultur* debates highlight the tensions inherent in values of liberal democracy in Germany such as secularism, freedom of religious expression, and equality. Moreover, the discourse of a guiding or "leading" German culture appears as an important Enlightenment concept mobilized to stabilize identities that may be threatened by globalization and immigration.[27] This is evident in some politicians' declarations. Roland Koch, another prominent CDU politician and minister president of Hesse until his resignation in August 2010, sought to establish normality and naturalize the German majority's identity in face of challenges posed by religious and cultural differences. He called *Leitkultur* a term "that is normal and it is right to articulate it." He was supported by Angela Merkel, who called for "non-negotiable standards and universally valid values by which everyone who wants to live here has to abide."[28] Clearly referencing migrants as "everyone who wants to live here," Merkel delineates *Leitkultur* as the baseline for immigrant integration and membership. Her remarks further highlight the universalizing tendencies of liberal democracy that apply to "everyone." Similar to Vera Lengsfeld's remarks, Koch and Merkel created an apparently homogeneous space of democracy where German values apply to all.

One of the few exceptions in these debates is Rita Süssmuth, former president of the German Bundestag and also a CDU member. Süssmuth led the comprehensive study on immigration and integration that had formed the basis for recommendations upon which Germany's new immigration and integration laws were formulated. She said in an interview with the *Süddeutsche Zeitung*: "We need a *Leitkultur* of living together, of values and norms that are binding for all of us.... You can only achieve integration if there is a reciprocal process of exchange, learning, and expansion. At stake are the dignity of the person, equal rights, and respect for the otherness of the other ["dem Anderssein des Anderen"]."[29] Süssmuth's conception of *Leitkultur* differs greatly from those sketched out above in that she specifically recognizes otherness and argues for respecting rather than assimilating or excluding it. In doing so, she opens a space that does not automatically homogenize and universalize ideas of assimilation and integration.

Even politicians who consider the idea of a *Leitkultur* per se unnecessary or unproductive rarely venture as far as Rita Süssmuth. For example, Otto Schily, former federal minister of the interior (1998–2005) and a member of the SPD (Social Democratic Party), called the concept "moronic" in an interview on Berlin Radio.[30] For Schily, when debating the integration of immigrants, "what matters are the constitutional and democratic principles of the *Grundgesetz* [Basic Law; Germany's constitution]." Still, Schily demands that immigrants in Germany learn German in order to be accepted as members of German society. As Wendy Brown argues, democratic principles are, of course, also cultural values.[31] Schily, in contradistinction to other politicians, insists on democratic principles; the expectation toward immigrants remains a version of assimilation as condition for membership.

These debates tend to reframe questions of immigrant integration as questions of religious or cultural difference. The limits of religious freedom, then, are primarily geared to Muslims, who are deemed more culturally different. Questions of cultural membership in turn reiterate claims for assimilation and the affirmation of democratic values in order to make Muslims acceptable as members of the polity by transforming them into a "new social being."[32] These homogenizing tendencies affirm conservative notions of a bounded and homogeneous political community as the basis for citizenship and democracy rather than accepting immigration as changing the polity. This notion was most firmly brought home in October 2010 when Angela Merkel declared the efforts at establishing a multicultural society in Germany "utterly failed."[33]

Minarets and the Limits of "Tolerance" in Switzerland

Similar logics are at play in the 2009 ban of minarets in Switzerland, which provides insights into the ways that Swiss notions of membership in liberal democracy are both challenged and reaffirmed. The Swiss minaret ban started with a campaign initiated by the so-called Egerkinger Komitee (Egerkingen committee, formed by members of the right-wing Swiss People's Party and the Federal Democratic Union), which collected over 110,000 signatures and submitted them to the Bundeskanzlei (Swiss government) in July 2008. As the Volksinitiative claims, the signature campaign rallied citizens from across Switzerland because the movement's goals and rhetoric resonated with them: to reiterate, on 29 November 2009, 57.5 percent of Swiss voters decided for the ban, which explicitly does not ban Muslim places of worship as such, but the architectural detail characteristic of future mosques.[34] Swiss government attempts in the summer and fall of 2009 to undermine the Volksinitiative's momentum and to motivate citizens to vote "no" on the referendum failed.

Attempting damage control on the international stage after the referendum, Switzerland's Minister of Justice Eveline Widmer-Schlumpf sought to clarify during a trip to the European Union's headquarters in Brussels that "[t]he vote concerned minarets, but of course not the Muslim community. With the minaret ban [Swiss] people obviously wanted to send a signal opposing these fundamentalist developments."[35] She here rescripts the minaret ban as an attempt at containing fundamentalism rather than as geared to excluding Swiss Muslims more broadly. The careful line she seeks to draw between minarets as symbols of "fundamentalist developments" and "the Muslim community" dissolves quickly, however, since religious groups other than Muslims have not expressed interest in building places of worship with minarets. Hence, Widmer-Schlumpf's comments—which make the Swiss citizenry appear less Islamophobic—seem forced and euphemistic, the more so because anti-immigrant sentiment and populism are not uncommon in Switzerland's immigration history, and neither are social movements' attempts at excluding migrants or at promoting expectations for assimilation. As Riaño and Wastl-Walter show, state discourses about "foreigners" have centered on integration or assimilation, highlighted notions of "Überfremdung" (variously understood as loss of Swiss cultural identity, xenophobia, or literally "over-foreignness"), and played on economic or cultural fears more broadly.[36]

The Volksinitiative depicts Islam as expansive, imperialist, and intent on subjecting Swiss citizens to Sharia law. It warns of the imminent Islamicization of Switzerland as a whole. Such right-wing populist arguments have strong racial undertones and play on ideas and ideals of liberal democracy as they "other" Islam. The Volksinitiative's posters and slogans variously depict Islam as the opposite of modernity and the Enlightenment. For example, one of their posters features intolerance as a characteristic of Islam, hinting at the idea of tolerance of difference as part and parcel of democratic societies. "No tolerance for intolerance. Yes to the minaret ban initiative" is but one example of this strategy, which renders Islam "intolerant" and therefore undeserving of Western tolerance.[37] In their other communications, the Volksinitiative creates an even starker contrast between Islam and Swiss democracy by portraying Islam as generally disregarding the rule of law and the state:

> Whoever—and this is a fact in Islam—places religion above the state, and consequently attributes higher meaning to religious directives than to the democratically created rule of law in the (constitutional) state will automatically find themselves in conflict with the constitution. This conflict cannot be evaded. The minaret is the external symbol of a religious-political will to power that questions the constitutional basic rights. The minaret ban demanded by the [Volks-] Initiative will warrant that the societal order and rule of law stipulated in the constitution will continue to be valid without restriction in Switzerland.

> The Initiative does not touch the freedom of religious expression at all, which every person is guaranteed as a basic right by the constitution.[38]

The Volksinitiative went to great lengths to depict all expressions of Islam as antidemocratic and not respecting the rule of law, which of course reveals the Islamophobia and racism at the center of much contemporary opposition to Muslim immigrants.

Insisting on the constitutionality of the anti-minaret campaign, the Volksinitiative affirms its own commitment to liberal democratic principles. Sara Ahmed argues that this affirmation of the nation or of particular values is a strategy of right-wing extremist groups that serves to portray their hate in a positive light.[39] Yet while the Volksinitiative reiterates the putative universality of liberal democracy as applying to "every person," it undermines that very universality since its campaign targets only *some* architectural features of places of worship (i.e., minarets) and not *all* of them (i.e., church steeples). Hence, the campaign and the minaret ban create new boundaries for democracy's universalism because not every person's rights to religious expression are being limited or affirmed. Furthermore, as Swiss citizens interpret the right to religious expression narrowly and out of fear of a few fundamentalist tendencies, they produce legal barriers that affect more than a few, generalizing across a diverse group of people. The way the ascription of fundamentalism to all Muslims becomes a legal ban of minarets disciplines *all* Muslims, not just those suspected of fundamentalist or Islamist sympathies or actions.

These attitudes make clear that attempts to preserve the ideals of liberal democracy may well undermine the very universalism and freedoms that liberal democratic values are supposed to guarantee. They highlight what Jacques Derrida calls the "autoimmune" tendencies inherent in democracy, which always runs the risk of self-destruction, especially when engaging in attempts at self-preservation.[40] But there are different ways of understanding democracy. Rather than conceiving it as a finished and stable construct that subsequently enters into crisis and resorts to extreme measures and emergency politics, the minaret ban may be read as an expression of liberal democracy's constantly emergent and emerging political system.[41] Such a view makes it possible to view the minaret ban as a beginning rather than as an endpoint.

As a consequence of the referendum, Switzerland has seen debate about religious freedom and democratic values more generally, about immigration to Switzerland, and about the integration of immigrants residing there. Numerous commentators faulted the Swiss government for not taking the Volksinitiative seriously because polls had shown that the minaret ban would not obtain a majority vote.[42] The days immediately following the referendum led to court challenges against the minaret ban. One was issued to Switzerland's constitutional court based on arguments that the minaret ban would contradict the democratic rights guaranteed in the constitution. Other challenges—among them one that suggested the Volksinitiative's rhetoric amounted to "seditious propaganda"—were struck down by the federal court as well.[43] However, several court challenges were brought to the European Court of Human Rights in Strasbourg.[44] Swiss legal scholars contended that the minaret ban contradicts Article 14 of the European Human Rights Convention, which guarantees the right to religious freedom. At the time of writing, the Swiss Bundesrat (parliament) had scheduled a new debate on immigrant integration, and the minaret ban was prompting discussion about how Swiss law and international law could be reconciled. Referenda can be revoked when they produce Swiss national laws that infringe on international law.[45] Proposals here include greater scrutiny of petitions before they appear on ballots, so as to avoid having to revoke laws after they are affirmed.

In addition to these discussions and court challenges, prominent legal scholars in Switzerland proposed adding a so-called "Toleranzartikel" (tolerance article) to the Swiss constitution's Article 15 on freedom of conscience and religion.[46] Such proposals show that restrictions of rights primarily geared at Muslims and immigrants may have consequences for the wider Swiss polity. These debates rework the boundaries and limits of democracy and demonstrate that liberal democracies are emergent rather than static, even if the goal of campaigns against minarets is to preserve the fiction of stability and immutability.

Debating Religious Expression: The Cologne Mosque

If secularism and freedom of religious expression are equally important in German debates about immigrant integration, as the *Leitkultur* debates show, the ways that such debates enter into the local lives of migrants and nonmigrants in Germany are spatially differentiated. Since the late 1990s, parliamentary debates and petitions to the German Bundestag have frequently addressed questions of Islam and religious difference in Germany. These debates, as well as election platforms and legislative initiatives, usually assert that freedom of religious expression is a "Grundrecht" (basic right) of German democracy. Some politicians have explicitly welcomed more representative mosque buildings as bringing Islam out into the open and into public space (and by extension into the public sphere and democracy). They deem these positive developments and signs of the integration of Islam, as North Rhine-Westphalia's minister president Jürgen Rüttgers said during his speech at the 2008 ceremonial opening of Germany's largest mosque in Duisburg-Marxloh, in which he welcomed the building of mosques.[47]

Such affirmations of the constitutionally guaranteed right to religious freedom at the national scale and in individual German states, however, do not prevent numerous voices from calling for surveillance of Muslim groups and restrictions on their religious practices. In Cologne, a right-wing populist movement similar to the Swiss Volksinitiative emerged in response to Muslim groups' attempts to secure building permits for mosques. The populist movement pro Köln originally rallied against the construction of the Cologne central mosque in 2004 and has since organized several demonstrations, some of which turned violent. Like the Volksinitiative, pro Köln posits that the mosque is an expression of Islamic imperial ambitions and of Islam's anti-secular and antidemocratic tendencies. Not surprisingly, those right-wing parties and organizations congratulated Swiss voters on banning minarets. In a press release pro Köln celebrated that "Switzerland shows the way" of the future,[48] and the North Rhine-Westphalia-wide party pro NRW's campaign posters for the 2010 statewide election in North Rhine-Westphalia (which pro Köln distributed in Cologne) now picture minarets.

The success of pro Köln has spurred other local organizations, for example, pro München in Munich, a more explicitly right-wing and anti-immigrant movement.[49] Similar to pro Köln, which now is a municipal party with seats in the city government, pro München is organizing as a political entity to gain power at the local level. On the coattails of pro Köln's success, pro NRW emerged on the right of the political spectrum and staged a demonstration in 2010 against minarets in Duisburg-Marxloh, the site of Germany's largest mosque (which has a minaret). There are several other new "pro" groups and parties across Germany, most of them located in cities in North Rhine-Westphalia, as well as a Germany-wide organization, pro Deutschland, formed in Berlin. All share the name, which promises a positive outlook for the cities or spatial entities in which they are located and which they intend to serve. They invariably point to their citizenship practices, their patriotism, and the dangers Islam and immigration pose to German cohesion and peace. In particular, pro München insists that immigration poses a threat for Germany's larger cities and their inhabitants.

In this context of right-wing mobilizations by pro Köln and other local protesters, DITIB is working to garner support and acceptance for the construction of the new mosque to replace its current facilities in Cologne-Ehrenfeld. DITIB is an umbrella organization for approximately 870 local associations in various German municipalities, many of which have begun to build more representative mosques in recent years. It maintains close ties to the Turkish government's Diyanet Ministry for Religious Affairs and coordinates the efforts and services Diyanet provides for Turkish citizens residing in Germany. Among these services are the coordination of sermons for Friday prayers, the training of imams, and the repatriation of Turkish migrants' bodies for funeral services and burials in Turkey. Muslim associations in Germany engaged in building new mosques often assert that more prestigious places of worship better serve their religious needs and practices. Muslim migrants also wish to honor former guest workers' accomplishments and contributions to German society and to provide more dignified spaces for prayer. Similar arguments are found in the debates about the contested DITIB mosque project in Cologne-Ehrenfeld, but the informational flyers about the mosque construction project also emphasize additional aspects of its purpose and design.

Prompted by the objections of pro Köln and other prominent local voices, DITIB has sought to provide detailed information about its mosque construction project and the zoning and planning processes to win support in the city. In publications (informational flyers and their website) DITIB highlights the social and educational aspects of the organization, which range from providing a place of worship to facilitating integration and the acquisition of the German language among its members. DITIB also offers the newly mandated integration courses for immigrants. Its flyer explains that "because the people who live and work in Cologne-Ehrenfeld are meant to identify with the structure, an architectural competition was held in 2005 in collaboration with the Bund Deutscher Architekten [Association of German Architects]." DITIB's stated goal is to establish a community center that is dignified and well integrated into Cologne's urban landscape. Here the flyer emphasizes the relationship to the neighborhood and the wider city of Cologne rather than the importance of adequate spaces of worship for the pious members. As further evidence of the mosque's inconspicuous design, the flyer highlights that the minarets will only be fifty-five meters high, compared to surrounding office towers that are almost twice that height, and it contains a sketch of size and height comparisons with important landmarks such as the famous Catholic Cologne cathedral.[50] Finally, DITIB points out that only a small percentage of the total space of the mosque complex will be used for religious purposes. Together these details suggest that DITIB seeks to counter portrayals (by, among others, pro Köln) of the mosque as reflecting Islamic ambitions to dominate the city and German society.

Citing an unnamed poll, DITIB claims to be speaking for 70 percent of all Muslims living in Germany.[51] The association emphasizes that its activities respect and affirm the values of German liberal democracy. Foremost among its principles, DITIB states, is "the pursuit of goals that are exclusively in accordance with the Basic Law of the Federal Republic of Germany. We commit to the principles of the liberal democratic system."[52] The association also tackles head-on fears and portrayals of Islam as violent, while it emphasizes its focus on "activities that abide by friendship, respect, forbearance, tolerance, and solidarity of humans with one another and in relation to adherents of other faiths. These characteristics correspond to the principles of Islam. And we reject all forms of violence and calls for violence." A more recent flyer adds gender equity to the association's goals and explicitly condemns forced marriages.[53] This condemnation clearly engages the public discourses and politicians that often falsely portray forced marriages as an attribute of Islamic faith.

Obviously, DITIB's informational flyers for the mosque construction seek to dispel fears of Islam and actively create an image of Islam and its organization as contributing to society and being rooted in civic actions such as volunteer work:

> Symbolic demarcations [of boundaries], cultural differences, and the conflicts connected to them have gained new meaning in the contemporary world in which certain traditional societal and political boundaries dissolve. This makes it even more necessary to promote volunteer work [nonprofit work] to overcome symbolic borders and cultural differences. This is a specific goal to which DITIB is committed. The new [mosque] construction is intended to ease communication across group, cultural, and religious boundaries.[54]

Rescripting the mosque as a symbol of its commitment to bridge difference and to promote interreligious dialogue, DITIB shifts discussions of boundaries and borders. Rather than the impermeable cultural borders that some groups inscribe, it highlights boundaries and differences that can be overcome. In one of the informational flyers intended to introduce the mosque project to Cologne's public, DITIB uses the words of Goethe: "Tolerance should really only be a passing disposition. It should lead to acceptance/recognition."[55] This particular quote frequently appears in publications by, and as a motto for, multicultural organizations and pro-immigration advocates. Usually used in its entirety, the quotation has an additional sentence that DITIB omitted, most likely to avoid offending non-Muslims: "to tolerate means to insult" ("dulden heißt beleidigen"). By quoting Germany's foremost classical poet, however, DITIB engages and counters the politics of exclusion pursued by pro Köln and others. It is a direct demand for acceptance of difference rather than toleration. For Wendy Brown, "tolerance" is an exertion of power and creates uneven power relations between those who choose to tolerate and those who have no choice but to be tolerated. Brown suggests that discourses of tolerance do little to advance political engagement because they relegate political, cultural, and gender differences (among others) to spaces outside of the public sphere rather than making them central to negotiations of liberal democratic politics.[56] In other words, the fact that DITIB asserts equality when engaging with German society in the name of difference suggests that it lays claim to the same values of liberal democracy that right-wing groups appropriate to exclude Muslims.

On the one hand, DITIB's publications show that Islamic organizations feel pressured to respond to public discourse and conform to the expectations of liberal democracy—even as these expectations shift and present moving targets. In this vein they may be read as attempts at assimilation and conformity to German society. On the other hand, DITIB's affirmation of the principles of equality also suggests that the organization demands such equality, in particular when it comes to its own right to religious expression. Its demand for acceptance rather than tolerance is a case in point: Germany's predominantly Turkish Muslim population does not want to be tolerated but to claim its place as an equal in the German polity. These claims to belonging find further expression in the urban fabric, as DITIB states "being at home in Ehrenfeld" as the reason for building its mosque in the local neighborhood.[57] It becomes obvious, then, that religious organizations such as DITIB are carefully negotiating the lines of exclusion, acceptance, and inclusion rather than being passive in the process. Instead of accepting what Sherene Razack calls the "eviction of Muslims from Western law and politics," members of DITIB (as much as other Muslim organizations) struggle to be recognized as full members of German society.[58]

Risking Democracy and Difference

Returning to the minaret ban and its implications for democracy in both Switzerland and in Germany, the referendum affected discussions about the values and principles of liberal democracy in Germany in several ways, beyond debates about immigration. In the days immediately following the news of the minaret ban in Switzerland, German media and public intellectuals were eager to discuss the consequences of the decision for Switzerland and its relationship to other countries. German commentators frequently pointed out the decision's short-sightedness and remarked on the racist and nationalist undertones. Swiss journalists, in turn, mocked Germany for insufficiently addressing the problems that religious difference and political expressions in particular were posing for liberal democracies and specifically pointed out that Germans were neglecting problems of integrating Islam.

More important, however, the Swiss referendum and the subsequent minaret ban resulted in debates about the benefits and potential risks of introducing elements of direct democracy in Germany.[59] Several parties, including the Social Democrats, the left-spectrum Bündnis 90/Die Grünen (Green Party) and Die Linke (Left Party, successors to the former Party of Democratic Socialism PDS, itself successor to the former GDR's communist SED party), and the liberal FDP (Free Democrats) had included calls for referenda in their 2007 election platforms.[60] In the wake of the Swiss minaret ban, several German parties' politicians and legal experts suggested that such elements of direct democracy needed to be fine-tuned. Dieter Wiefelspütz, an SPD expert for interior affairs, insisted on the advantages of direct democracy while also conceding that "Democracy is risky. The people may well err."[61] North Rhine-Westphalia's Minister for Integration Armin Laschet suggested excluding questions of religion from ballots because they were too complex. He did not want to see referenda about churches or church bells, or even synagogues, and was worried about what majorities such referenda might produce.[62] Still others, such as the Green Party's legal expert, affirmed the democratic potential of referenda and direct democracy but suggested that basic rights ought to be exempt from referenda, presumably in order to preserve these pillars of democracy.

These conversations about direct democracy in Germany highlight several important aspects of the condition of contemporary liberal democracy. The state (as represented by politicians) doubts its citizens' ability to act democratically and to make the "right" decisions; meanwhile these discussions show that politicians aim to limit democratic liberties in order to preserve democracy. Recent debates about the incorporation of Muslims into the liberal democracies of Germany and Switzerland also reflect the unease with which contemporary immigrant-receiving societies and states address cultural difference and insist on affirmations of liberal democratic values. While the impulse for the minaret ban came from right-wing populist groups in Swiss society (just as protest against mosques comes from the right margins of the German polity), the results of the Swiss referendum and the electoral success of such German parties as pro Köln demonstrate that it is important to engage and counter them. Clearly Islamophobia resonates with the wider citizenry. Attempts at stabilizing what appears to be a finalized liberal democratic system are justified by claims that Islam and anti-secularist tendencies threaten such a democracy. The minaret ban and subsequent debates about it also reveal, however, that democracy is far from stable when it is reimagined by excluding Islamic symbols of religious expression. The German debates about *Leitkultur*, which variably serve the exclusion of Muslims or raise expectations for their assimilation, provide fruitful ground for protests against local mosque-building projects. If politicians at the national scale can question whether Islam is reconcilable with the value system of liberal democracy, then it is not surprising that such questions are raised locally where immigrants and non-immigrants live in close proximity. In both cases democratic values such as tolerance, secularism, and equality are leveraged to justify the exclusion of Muslims who supposedly lack these values or seek to undermine them. Drawing boundaries in terms of the limits of which rights and guarantees may become subject to change (such as exempting basic rights) reveals the risks that liberal democracy is willing to take (or not).

These are questions that Muslim migrants address and use to frame their arguments for building prestigious places of worship. Contrary to accounts that posit the expulsion of Muslims from Western law and politics, DITIB's mosque project in Cologne provides an example of how Muslims "become political," asserting their voice and demanding equality.[63] Muslim migrants are laying claim to membership in the German polity by building prestigious mosques—even in the face of right-wing protests and contestations. A growing landscape of new, representative mosques in Germany shows that Muslims have succeeded in challenging their exclusion. The unintended consequences of such local debates and legislation demonstrate democratic systems' vulnerability to their own practices and procedures. Redrawing the boundaries of liberal democracy in relation to Muslims leads to a reworking of the values and principles of democracy more generally, often at the expense of the universalism and equality that the redrawing of boundaries sought to defend in the first place. Exclusionary politics toward Muslims have consequences that are tangible for members of the polity more broadly. As the examples above show, curtailing liberal democratic rights and freedoms for *some* groups in the name of preserving democracy carries the risk of curtailing democratic freedoms for the entire polity. Moreover, as the ideas and ideals of liberal democratic citizenship are increasingly being reworked and frequently curtailed in the name of preserving democracy, it remains important for scholarship to rethink liberal democracy as both emergent and emerging within the context of immigration and negotiations of cultural difference, to make space for crossing symbolic boundaries.

Notes

1. "Minarettverbot: Ein Ausdruck von Intoleranz. Fotostrecke," *Spiegel Online* (2009), http://www.spiegel.de/fotostrecke/fotostrecke-49289.html (accessed 3 February 2010). *Der Spiegel* here cites French Foreign Minister Bernard Kouchner, who stated: "If one cannot build minarets any longer, then that means that one oppresses a religion. This is an expression of intolerance, and I despise it."
2. "Umfrage: Deutsche gespalten über Minarett-Verbot," *Spiegel Online* (2009) http://www.spiegel.de/politik/deutschland/0,1518,665274,00.html (accessed 21 February 2010).
3. Patricia Ehrkamp, "The Limits of Multicultural Tolerance? Liberal Democracy and Media Portrayals of Muslim Migrant Women in Germany," *Space and Polity* 14, no. 1 (2010): 13–32.
4. Lynn A. Staeheli and Caroline R. Nagel, "Rethinking Security: Perspectives from Arab-American and British Arab Activists," *Antipode* 40, no. 5 (2008): 780–801.
5. Sherene Razack, *Casting Out: The Eviction of Muslims from Western Law and Politics* (Toronto, 2008); Liz Fekete, "Anti-Muslim Racism and the European Security State," *Race and Class* 46, no. 1 (2004): 3–29; and Mehdi Semati, "Islamophobia, Culture and Race in the Age of Empire," *Cultural Studies* 24, no. 2 (2010): 256–75.
6. Milton Myron Gordon, *Assimilation in American Life: The Role of Race, Religion, and National Origins* (New York, 1964).
7. Richard Alba and Victor Nee, "Rethinking Assimilation Theory for a New Era of Immigration," *International Migration Review* 31, no. 4 (1997): 826–75; and Jeffrey G. Reitz, "Host Societies and the Reception of Immigrants: Research Themes, Emerging Theories, and Methodological Issues," in *Host Societies and the Reception of Immigrants*, ed. Jeffrey G. Reitz (La Jolla, CA, 2003), 1–18.
8. Helga Leitner, "The Political Economy of International Labor Migration," in *A Companion to Economic Geography*, ed. E. Sheppard and T. Barnes (Malden, MA, 2000), 450–67; Nina Glick Schiller, Linda Basch, and C. Blanc-Szanton, "Towards a Definition of Transnationalism," in *Toward a Transnational Perspective on Migration*, ed.

Nina Glick Schiller, Linda Basch, and C. Blanc-Szanton (New York, 1992), 1–24; and Nancy Foner, "Immigrant Commitment to America, Then and Now: Myths and Realities," *Citizenship Studies* 5, no. 1 (2001): 27–40.

9. Patricia Ehrkamp, "'We Turks Are No Germans': Assimilation Discourses and the Dialectical Construction of Identities in Germany," *Environment and Planning A* 38, no. 9 (2006): 1673–92; William Jenkins, "Between the Lodge and the Meeting House: Mapping Irish Protestant Identities and Social Worlds in Late Victorian Toronto," *Social and Cultural Geography* 4, no. 1 (2003): 75–98; Caroline Nagel, "Rethinking Geographies of Assimilation," *The Professional Geographer* 61, no. 3 (2009): 400–407; and Roger Waldinger, "The Sociology of Immigration: Second Thoughts and Reconsiderations," in *Host Societies and the Reception of Immigrants*, ed. Jeffrey G. Reitz, 21–43.

10. Razack, *Casting Out*, 175; see also Rupa Reddy, "Gender, Culture and the Law: Approaches to 'Honour' Crimes in the UK," *Feminist Legal Studies* 16, no. 3 (2008): 305–21; Sherene Razack, "Imperilled Muslim Women, Dangerous Muslim Men and Civilised Europeans: Legal and Social Responses to Forced Marriages," *Feminist Legal Studies* 12, no. 2 (2004): 129–74; and Joan Wallach Scott, *The Politics of the Veil* (Princeton and Oxford, 2007).

11. Mathew Coleman, "Immigration Geopolitics Beyond the Mexico-US Border," *Antipode* 38, no. 1 (2007): 54–76; see also Eithne Luibhéid, "Sexual Regimes and Migration Controls: Reproducing the Irish Nation-State in Transnational Contexts," *Feminist Review* 83 (2006): 60–78.

12. Katharyne Mitchell, "Geographies of Identity: Multiculturalism Unplugged," *Progress in Human Geography* 28, no. 5 (2004): 641–51.

13. Banu Gökarıksel and Katharyne Mitchell, "Veiling, Secularism, and the Neoliberal Subject: National Narratives and Supranational Desires in Turkey and France," *Global Networks* 5, no. 2 (2005): 147–65; and Scott, *The Politics of the Veil*.

14. Ehrkamp, "The Limits of Multicultural Tolerance?"

15. Michael Brown, "Sexual Citizenship, Political Obligation and Disease Ecology in Gay Seattle," *Political Geography* 25, no. 8 (2006): 874–98.

16. Razack, *Casting Out*.

17. Semati, "Islamophobia, Culture and Race in the Age of Empire."

18. Werner Schiffauer, "Enemies within the Gates: The Debate about the Citizenship of Muslims in Germany," in *Multiculturalism, Muslims, and Citizenship: A European Approach*, ed. Tariq Modood, A. Triandafyllidou, and R. Zapata-Barrero (London, 2006), 94–116; and Sabine Schiffer, "Der Islam in Deutschen Medien," *Aus Politik und Zeitgeschichte* 20 (2005): 23–30.

19. Anne Phillips, *Multiculturalism without Culture* (Princeton, 2006).

20. Razack, "Imperilled Muslim Women."

21. Ehrkamp, "The Limits of Multicultural Tolerance?"

22. Patricia Ehrkamp and Helga Leitner, "Beyond National Citizenship: Turkish Immigrants and the (Re)Construction of Citizenship in Germany," *Urban Geography* 24, no. 2 (2003): 127–46.

23. Deutscher Bundestag, "Stenographischer Bericht, 40. Sitzung, Bonn, Freitag, den 7. Mai 1999, *Plenarprotokoll* 14/40 (1999).

24. Bassam Tibi, a political scientist, initially conceived Leitkultur as an aspect of multicultural societies and insisted that the concept needed to be at the center of defining Europe's identity; Bassam Tibi, *Europa ohne Identität. Die Krise der multikulturellen Gesellschaft* (Munich 1998). Public debates in Germany about the "Deutsche Leitkultur"

have little to do with his original conception; see Friedrich Merz, "Einwanderung und Identität," *Die Welt*, 25 October 2000.

25. Vera Lengsfeld, "Zuwanderung versus Familienpolitik? Zur Gefahr politischer Glaubensbekenntnisse," in *Vera Lengsfeld, Mitglied des Deutschen Bundestages (CDU). Texte und Reden* (Webarchiv Bundestag, 2002). http://webarchiv.bundestag.de/archive/2005/0204/mdbhome/LengsVe0/reden_lengsfeld.htm (accessed 21 February 2010).

26. Douglas Klusmeyer, "A 'Guiding Culture' for Immigrants? Integration and Diversity in Germany," *Journal of Ethnic and Migration Studies* 27, no. 3 (2001): 519–32; Herwig Pautz, "The Politics of Identity in Germany: The *Leitkultur* Debate," *Race and Class* 46, no. 4 (2005): 39–52; and Semati, "Islamophobia, Culture and Race in the Age of Empire."

27. Stuart S. Hall, "Old and New Identities, Old and New Ethnicities" [1991], in *Culture, Globalization and the World-System: Contemporary Conditions for the Representation of Identity*, ed. Anthony D. King (Minneapolis, 1997), 41–68.

28. Koch and Merkel are both quoted in "K-Frage: Roland Koch gegen vorzeitige Festlegung auf Merkel," *hr-online*, 6 December 2004. http://www.hr-online.de/website/rubriken/nachrichten/index.jsp?rubrik=5710&key=standard_document_3334920 (accessed 22 March 2010).

29. Oliver Das Gupta, "Süssmuth-Interview: 'Wir brauchen eine Leitkultur des Zusammenlebens,'" *Süddeutsche Zeitung*, 13 May 2006.

30. Quoted in "Schily wettert gegen 'Leitkultur' Debatte," *Spiegel Online*, 22 November 2004. http://www.spiegel.de/politik/deutschland/0,1518,329077,00.html (accessed 21 February 2010).

31. Wendy Brown, *Regulating Aversion: Tolerance in the Age of Identity and Empire* (Princeton, 2006).

32. Heidrun Friese, "Spaces of Hospitality," *Angelaki: Journal of the Theoretical Humanities* 9, no. 2 (2004): 71.

33. "Multikulti-Gesellschaft ist 'absolut gescheitert,'" *Focus Online*, 16 October 2010.

34. Marco Antonsich and Phil I. Jones, "Mapping the Swiss Referendum on the Minaret Ban," *Political Geography* 29, no. 2 (2010): 57–62. The authors also present an analysis of the spatial differentiation and voters' characteristics.

35. Eveline Widmer-Schlumpf, Swiss Minister of Justice, 20 November 2009, quoted in "Minarettverbot: Ein Ausdruck von Intoleranz. Fotostrecke," *Spiegel Online*, 2009. http://www.spiegel.de/fotostrecke/fotostrecke-49289.html (accessed 21 February 2010).

36. Yvonne Riaño and Doris Wastl-Walter, "Immigration Policies, State Discourses on Foreigners, and the Politics of Identity in Switzerland," *Environment and Planning A* 38, no. 9 (2006): 1693–713.

37. Volksinitiative gegen den Bau von Minaretten, "Argumente" (2009), http://www.minarette.ch/argumente.html (accessed 21 February 2010).

38. Volksinitiative gegen den Bau von Minaretten, "Darum geht es" (2009), http://www.minarette.ch/darum_geht_es.html (accessed 7 March 2010).

39. Sara Ahmed, *The Cultural Politics of Emotion* (New York, 2004).

40. Jacques Derrida, *Rogues: Two Essays on Reason*, trans. Pascale-Anne Brault and Michael Naas (Stanford, 2005).

41. Bonnie Honig, *Emergency Politics: Paradox, Law, Democracy* (Princeton, 2009).

42. Hans-Jürgen Jakobs, "Wenn der Staat das Volk nicht mehr versteht," *Süddeutsche Zeitung*, 30 November 2009.

43. "Keine 'Staatsgefährdende Propaganda': Bundesgericht hält weitere Minarett-Beschwerde für unzulässig," *Neue Zürcher Zeitung*, 12 February 2010.

44. In mid 2011, however, the European court threw out two of the five challenges to Switzerland's minaret ban.

45. "Die Praxis bewährt sich meistens. Bundesrat sieht keinen unmittelbaren Handlungsbedarf beim Völkerrecht," *Neue Zürcher Zeitung Online*, 9 March 2010, http://www.nzz.ch/nachrichten/schweiz/schweiz_bundesrat_ejpd_voelkerrecht_volksinitiativen_bericht_1.5175807.html (accessed 22 March 2010).

46. Claudia Schoch, "Ruf nach Toleranzartikel," *Neue Zürcher Zeitung*, 1 December 2009.

47. Jürgen Rüttgers, "Rede zur Eröffnung der Moschee in Marxloh" (oral communication, 2008).

48. pro Köln, "Die Schweiz weist den Weg für ganz Europa, "Pressemitteilung" (30 November 2009), http://www.pro-koeln.net/archiv2009.htm (accessed 21 February 2010).

49. See the website of pro München: www.promuenchen.de.

50. DITIB, "Der Moscheebau in Köln-Ehrenfeld. Gemeindezentrum mit Moschee" (Cologne, 2007).

51. DITIB, "Dachverband Türkisch-Islamische Union Der Anstalt für Religion e.V.," (Cologne, n.d.).

52. DITIB, "Der Moscheebau in Köln-Ehrenfeld. Gemeindezentrum mit Moschee" (Cologne, 2007).

53. DITIB, "Der Moscheebau in Köln-Ehrenfeld. Gemeindezentrum mit Moschee" (Cologne, 2008).

54. Ibid.

55. Quoted in DITIB, "Der Moscheebau in Köln-Ehrenfeld. Gemeindezentrum mit Moschee" (Cologne, 2007).

56. Brown, *Regulating Aversion*.

57. Mehmet Yildirim, "Die Kölner Ditib-Moschee – Eine offene Moschee als Integrationsbeitrag," in *Der Moschee-Streit. Eine exemplarische Debatte über Einwanderung und Integration*, ed. Franz Sommerfeld (Cologne, 2008), 66–76.

58. Razack, *Casting Out*.

59. "Direkte Demokratie: Schweizer Minarett-Verbot entfacht Debatte über Volksentscheide," in *Spiegel Online*, 1 December 2009, http://www.spiegel.de/politik/ausland/0,1518,664432,00.html (accessed 10 February 2010); and Steffen Hebestreit, "Direkte Demokratie: Irrtum inbegriffen," *Frankfurter Rundschau*, 1 December 2009.

60. Hebestreit, "Direkte Demokratie: Irrtum inbegriffen."

61. Cited in ibid.

62. Armin Laschet, cited in "Direkte Demokratie," *Spiegel Online*, 1 December 2009, http://www.spiegel.de/politik/ausland/0,1518,664432,00.html (accessed 10 February 2010).

63. Engin F. Isin, *Being Political: Genealogies of Citizenship* (Minneapolis, 2002).

CHAPTER 9

Not Our Kind

Generational Barriers Dividing Postwar Albanian Migrant Communities

ISA BLUMI

Europe's post–World War II history has long been associated with division. The so-called Cold War, pitting the superpowers and their European allies against each other, contributed to Europe's geographical, social, economic, and ideological division. Often lost in this analysis, however, are the secondary divisions that persisted, expanded, and even outlived the dynamics of the Cold War. This chapter will suggest that studying migration patterns from the "East" to the "West" (in this case Germany) over the entire course of the Cold War not only highlights the methodological pitfalls of reducing this period of European history to a reflection of superpower machinations, but also further disaggregates the analytical themes that dominate the study of modern Europe's social, economic, and institutional development.

The presence of large groups of migrants categorically identified by their "country of origin" poses a number of problems to the researcher studying postwar Europe. I will focus in particular on the issue of labeling migrants by association with a postwar state in the Balkans (including Turkey). The careless linkage between label and the subsequent assumed affiliation of an individual migrant often disguises more important sources of division (and tensions that arise from these divides) afflicting European societies. In the case of "source" regions like Yugoslavia (consisting of present-day Serbia, Slovenia, Bosnia, Croatia, Montenegro, Kosovo, and Macedonia), Greece, and Turkey, all major contributors to the reindustrialization of Germany after 1949, important conditions in the respective source countries impacted the circumstances under which some "Turks," "Greeks," or "Yugoslavs" settled in Germany. In particular, the distinctive issues concerning Albanian speakers, all forced to live within the parameters of state bureaucracies that only acknowledged them as Greeks, Yugoslavs, or Turks, directly contributed to the way host societies developed in the postwar era.[1]

The methodological problem thus becomes how scholars can identify and evaluate the reasons why millions of migrants from the Balkans created communities of one kind or another in Germany. Far from constituting an easily defined category of socioeconomic and at times political actor in modern Europe, these peoples may more accurately be understood as amorphous agents whose distinctive experiences in their "host societies" were partially a product of the considerable baggage they brought with them from their homelands. For West Germany in particular, the recruitment of much-needed labor, starting with agreements with Greece in 1960, Turkey in 1961, and later with Yugoslavia in 1968, cannot be separated from the principle factors motivating those countries to ship their subjects off to Western Europe. Over a million "Turkish" guest workers would enter Germany by 1969, as Ankara (along with Belgrade and Athens) developed a set of policies that hoped to address domestic issues through managed migration.[2] In the end, the entire postwar history of migration to Western Europe may be directly linked to these Balkan states' calculated policy of expelling upwards of 1.6 million people who presented long-term challenges to these states' efforts at establishing ethno-national homogeneity. As a consequence of hitherto unacknowledged violence toward "minorities," social pathologies arising from the discrimination experienced in Southeastern Europe by Albanians, Kurds, and others shaped the lived experiences of those who ended up migrating to Germany.

To best monitor how this interpretive angle may contribute to a new way of understanding Europe's divisions, this chapter explores the policies adopted by different German state governments with their social welfare partner organizations over forty years. In city-states like Bremen, Essen, and Berlin, the inflows of largely ignored Albanians (as well as Kurds, Alevis, and Slav Muslims) contributed to postwar German society and government. The experiences of these ignored groups as expelled victims of state persecution at once shaped their settlement decisions and long-term integration strategies, thereby adding a new layer to understanding the boundaries, walls, and borders crisscrossing Cold War-era Europe.

Interviews were originally conducted while analyzing the Kosovar Albanian diaspora in Europe at the height of the "Yugoslav" crisis that culminated in the Dayton Accords of 1995. Discussing the events that led people to settle in countries as diverse as Sweden, West Germany, Switzerland, Holland, Austria, and Belgium, I began to realize the issues that inform this chapter deserved a more structured analysis. Though not formally engaging in "data collection," I did begin to interview members of the various Yugoslav-Albanian, Kurdish, and Alevi communities scattered throughout Europe who had settled before the 1990s. Asking both the elder males of these extended families and their children (many of whom were born in Germany, Switzerland, or Austria) random questions, reflecting the very different, informal contexts of our conversations, I made notes on my impressions and highlighted some of my immediate impressions only after these "interviews." Notes taken from my discussions with male members of the diaspora from the former Yugoslavia and from Turkey in Dusseldorf, Hamburg, Stuttgart, Berlin, Frankfurt, Munich, Graz, Vienna, Zurich, and Bern between 1995 and 2002 make up the content of this chapter.

Disaggregating the Migrant

The first task is to somehow locate these otherwise invisible victims of modern state-building in West Germany's historic record. The failure of Germany's bureaucracies to develop more flexible terms to identify their migrants seems especially crucial to reinterpreting what some argue were the relatively successful integration policies adopted by largely autonomous city-states like Berlin, Nuremberg, Bremen, and Essen.[3] In the context of implementing policies specifically directed at one "dominant" group of migrants, most notably "Turks," "Greeks," and "Yugoslavs," the use of sweeping ethno-national terms proved determinate to the way migrants and the social welfare systems interacted. This meant everyone associated with Turkey, Greece, or Yugoslavia was considered ethnically/culturally a "Turk," "Greek," or "Yugoslav" for much of the postwar era. Those identified as "Turks," therefore, were expected to be directly affected by the state's guest worker management strategies, a fatal flaw in the system that often had devastating consequences for generations of non-Turks. The "Turkish" *Ausländer*, who evolved to become the legitimized *Deutschtürken* by the 1990s, were products of a collaborative process between "ethnic clients" and state and non-state social service providers.[4] This process, far from providing sustenance to migrants, often empowered a few while marginalizing many more who settled in German cities.[5] In other words, in the context of an evolving set of policies laid out in West Germany, who could speak for whom influenced how migrants (and their state/nonprofit counterparts) hoped to navigate the process of settlement.

Unfortunately, despite the fact that migration from Southeastern Europe is now recognized as having contributed to the distinctive evolution of state policies, the experience remains elusive in some important ways. For instance, the fact that many of the "Turks," "Greeks," and "Yugoslavs" identified in the literature were actually as likely to identify themselves as Albanians, Bosnians, Montenegrins, or Macedonians/Bulgarians demands that we disaggregate the generic migrant experience in a divided Europe. One way of doing this is to stress the diversity of factors contributing to individual and group migration. The fact that the "push/pull" factors in the migration of hundreds of thousands of people were not uniform thus contributes to another layer of distinction increasingly recognized in the case of Germany's "Kurds" as well as that of Alevis, a large Muslim community deemed outside the confines of official Turkish state control.[6]

Germany has long balanced servicing the needs of society directly through the state and partnering with nonprofits like the Roman Catholic Caritas, the Protestant Diakonisches Werk and the SPD-founded Arbeiterwohlfahrt, henceforth AWO. Indeed, these nonprofits grew in importance after World War II, when social conservative lawmakers formalized a dual role between large nonprofits and the federal government in 1961. By the time the first train-load of imported laborers from Greece and Turkey arrived in West Germany, these three nonprofits had become dominant players in shaping social policies throughout the federal and state systems and thus were given the primary responsibility of engaging with these migrants.[7] This delegating proved fateful to how Albanians, Kurds, and various Muslim "minorities" were incorporated into Germany's postwar economy.

For reasons I suspect were strategic on the part of the nonprofits, the migrants were organized and then apportioned to each nonprofit according to religious affiliation and then "national background." It needs to be stressed that this took place in the 1960s without any consultation of either the larger public or the migrants themselves. Caritas, for instance, took over social work involving Catholic "Yugoslavs." This group, however, consisted not only of Slavs from Slovenia, Bosnia, or Croatia, but large numbers of Albanian Catholics from Montenegro and Kosovo as well. The fact that these Catholic Albanians were never identified as such during the integration process led to their cultural and economic impoverishment. Similarly, when Diakonisches Werk adopted the same approach in dealing with "Greeks" by 1960, they laid claim to servicing the needs of Orthodox Christians from Yugoslavia and Greece (and any Protestant immigrants) while utterly failing, perhaps in collusion with the source states, to acknowledge that many of these "Greeks" or "Yugoslavs" were Albanian speakers or Macedonians and Bulgarians deserving of cultural and social protection. Lastly, the secular, union-linked AWO took on workers migrating from Turkey by 1962, while also choosing not to consider the conditions in which hundreds of thousands were encouraged to migrate.

In the end, the manner in which these nonprofits proceeded to manage these peoples throughout West Germany would have long-term consequences on how people socialized, politically organized, and ultimately assimilated (or not) within larger German society. These nonprofits, for example, set up job training services for their respective "clients" and then expanded to include social counseling offices that advocated on their "clients'" behalf for start-up funding and community-building initiatives. At times lucrative partnerships were forged between certain "representatives" of these communities and the nonprofits that quickly became the exclusive lifeline between migrants and any state funds.[8] Caritas, Diakonisches Werk, and AWO actively refused to collaborate with associations created at the early stages by communities that did not filter through the formally accepted alliances they had forged with specific "representatives." This constituted a devastating narrowing of representative roles, resulting in the exclusion of Germany's Albanian, Kurdish, and unrepresented Orthodox Christian workers/migrants from much of the social development work done in the 1960–90 period. One consequence of this was those who became the "spokespersons," "partners," and arbiters for Yugoslavs, Greeks, and Turks proved to be diligent guardians of homogenization policies back in the Balkans, respecting an ethnic hierarchy that specifically discriminated against large numbers of non-Slav and non-Turk migrants. In this regard, Germany's evolving migrant management experience became an extension of discrimination, marginalization, and tension within the migrant neighborhoods, often without the knowledge of state governments and their nonprofit partners.

Fortunately, scholars like Jürgen Puskeppeleit and Dietrich Thränhardt have noted, in their study of the fluid postmodern self, that these relations between "client" and the nonprofits reinforced a self-serving, condescending attitude among the nonprofits' leadership toward the "helpless" migrants who seemed incapable of surviving without them.[9] At the same time, the failure to recognize the specific conditions in which large numbers of "Turks" and "Yugoslavs" just never seemed to benefit or develop from the funds allocated to their "community" obscures the fact that so many were Albanians, Kurds, or Alevis who were specifically excluded by "community leaders" who themselves were eager to police the homogeneity of "Turkish" or "Yugoslav" identities. There is a need to theorize, therefore, the sociological impact of this precarious state of being for bureaucratically unacknowledged migrants like the Albanians from Yugoslavia, Greece, or Turkey. In so doing, it is possible to realign the relational factors contributing to the evolution of the postwar German state and the seemingly unassimilated migrants who, by the end of the Cold War, had become a serious problem in Germany.

As much as they modified policies to try to resolve the migrant integration issue, state bureaucracies, police forces, and academic circles monitoring immigration into German-speaking societies simply never had a category for the Albanian immigrants, refugees, or guest workers who populated their cities. Not only would this prove to be a barrier to state authorities' more accurate engagement of a diverse migrant population, crucial when violence in the Balkans erupted in the 1990s, but it also marginalized these same unidentified Albanian speakers within the migrant communities where they lived from the 1960s onward. Indeed, it directly transformed how these peoples evolved as members of communities and accounts for certain kinds of pathologies.[10] It meant that their particular issues festered, as they were never going to be addressed by the "community" representatives who were partners with the big nonprofits, a situation that over time—over generations—created unacknowledged pathologies of alienation, anger, and a sense of powerlessness.

The failure to acknowledge the conditions under which people migrated, which often were equally as brutal as those experienced by migrants in the 1990s, constitutes a generational gap of experience that shapes much of life among immigrants in Europe today. The Albanians from Macedonia, Montenegro, and Kosovo who migrated to Germany in the 1960s and 1970s, either directly from Yugoslavia or via Turkey as part of the "population exchange" agreements between Belgrade and Ankara first signed in the 1930s, never received the "refugee" status many felt they deserved.[11] Their conditions of migration, in other words, were streamlined to disguise their persecution, in turn directly influencing the way housing arrangements, food stipends, help in finding work, special language classes, and most important of all, collective support from the general population were lacking once they reached Western Europe. Instead of being accommodated as persecuted victims of sometimes brutal "ethnic cleansing" policies, almost all the Alevis, Kurds, and Albanians were forced to settle in Western Europe by way of an unwanted association that for generations played heavily on how they formally were processed as a guest workers.

How this translated into interactions with state bureaucracies may prove useful to the larger story. A number of my informants suggested that the first generation of Kosovar Albanians initially attempted to form a distinctive community upon arrival in the 1960s. They did this by opening clubs and mosques that were separate from "Turks." Almost immediately, however, they faced a bureaucratic wall as the AWO refused to engage in community affairs without the mediation of their known "Turkish" partners. In their respective attempts to petition municipal governments for the right to formally set up a religious school/mosque in West Berlin, a cultural, sports, and youth club in Dusseldorf, and a Muslim-orientated newspaper in Nuremberg, they were universally refused permission on grounds that these services were "redundant." In other words, the bureaucracies charged with the care of these guest workers did not recognize the distinctive importance of these sites of culture, identity, and place. In all three cases, it was thought that these proposed institutions "already existed." These projects were "redundancies" in the eyes of local officials because Kosovar Albanians were officially categorized as "Turks" and "Muslims."

Appreciating this factor dramatically changes how postwar European settlement can be studied. As observed from within the Albanian-speaking diaspora in Western Europe during the 1990s, the tendency to lump people together into ethnic identities on the basis of "country of origin" has had consequences for the cultural development and political activism of these Kosovar Albanian communities. In this respect, it may be helpful to think of the identities permitted in bureaucratic and academic publications during the Cold War as precarious sociological moments, vulnerable to a variety of transformative situations contingent on both environmental and ideological factors.[12] Often, the issue was not only one of being physically ignored, but of being seen in a way that Albanian informants claim they did not wish to be seen. This was especially the case in the context of often shifting policies toward enforcing zoning laws for one "category of migrant" or another.

To many of these migrants, the central concern was that they were identified in a context of derogatory sentiment about "Turks," a racist-tinged term that often meant they could be forced to leave settled neighborhoods on account of there being too many "Turks" living in one area. Being associated with "Turks" thus limited Kosovar Albanians' capacity to establish themselves in coherent ways over a period of time in any one city neighborhood. In order to protect the communities they were building—again, largely unacknowledged by the state or the nonprofits, as they operated outside the generic "Turkish," "Greek," and "Yugoslav" institutions—men increasingly flocked to other associations, even if that meant denying the hostilities they faced when doing so. Therefore, ironically, many Albanians whose families, prior to migrating to Turkey, had been persecuted and forced to leave Greece or Yugoslavia actually claimed Yugoslav, Greek, or even Italian heritage to shed their "Turkish" association upon arrival in West Germany. As a consequence, these acts of bureaucratic manipulation also empowered managers of "Yugoslav" or "Greek" or "Turkish" community relations with city-state governments. The result was active suppression of Albanian claims for political and cultural autonomy within the German immigrant management regime.

Individuals' capacity to fit into and modify individual and collective claims within an established administrative context in Western Europe is of primary interest, as it demonstrates the deeper complexities of immigrant communities in general. That Albanians did not want to be identified as Turks does not mean, of course, that they were successful.[13] The individual, caught in the web of association dictated by nonprofits, state bureaucrats, and ethnic entrepreneurs, frequently attempted to communicate "our sense of powerlessness" in often confrontational ways that have been misinterpreted in the larger scholarship as ethnic violence. Among many Albanians I interviewed, the demand for respect from local teenagers caused some interesting manifestations of collective "rage" and frustration at being "without an identity" that translated into "street battles with the Germans." A number of informants who were teenagers in the 1970s and 1980s in Dusseldorf, Stuttgart, and West Berlin spoke of persistent fistfights provoked by catcalls of "Turk" or "Arab," on account of their being Muslim. The anger mostly surfaced at the individual level but would sometimes lead to more permanent pathologies that became legendary among local neighborhood groups of friends.[14]

For the majority of informants, however, violence did not become a daily affair. Although many said it was a secret fantasy to "do battle with those little

Nazis," their parents played a significant role in restricting potentially "damaging" relations between "weak, vulnerable Muslims" (i.e., Turks) and Germans.[15] Most often, informants said they were forced to internalize the anger, and many suggested "self-hatred" became a part of the daily struggle to obey their parents and not respond to the provocations of their German classmates. This sense of internally hemmed in and, perhaps, unrealized "rage" was rationalized in the 1990s as a sign of "moral superiority" and "dignity," a reflection of the self-affirming rhetoric used by the popular political leader Ibrahim Rugova in Kosovo at the time of the Milošević regime. An interesting dynamic of perceived power emerges in these immigrants' lives in Germany following Rugova's demands of passive resistance. The fear that "fighting back" would result in nothing but pain, suffering, and state retribution has been a long and deep tension dividing Kosovar Albanians for generations. But like the "passive" resistance advocated by Rugova and the parents of Kosovar Albanian teenagers growing up in this environment, the unrealized need "to be respected" caused dramatic fissures within individuals and communities.

This experience suggests parallels with how Afro-Americans fragmented into camps that advocated either armed resistance (Black Panthers, Nation of Islam) or passive resistance as preached by Dr. Martin Luther King. But when I pushed the subject, most of my interviewees finally admitted that the problem was more complex. It was not merely that "Germans were Nazis" but that Albanians themselves failed to better organize a campaign to represent themselves as Albanians. Many agreed that much of this was due to their parochial tendencies of settlement in Germany, yet there seemed to be another issue at play as well: as I have suggested elsewhere, many of these unexpressed pathologies are related to the variable "possibilities of identity" available at the time.[16] The fact that informants may have been identified as Turks by their neighbors, while anathema in the mid 1990s, cannot adequately explain how such "imposed identities" were supposed to have been otherwise understood in the context of the 1970s and 1980s.

There were some practical issues to consider. Protecting a cohesive community by living in clusters was, again, a crucial one. Among the most important measures supporting integration into larger German society was the implementation of zoning laws that regulated the dispersal of migrants and their "ethnic group's" proportional distribution within a given area (12 percent of the total population). In short, counting migrants in one way and not another had consequences. That Muslim Albanians came either directly from Yugoslavia or indirectly via Turkey certainly confuses the otherwise well-known policy concerning "overburdening."[17] Albanians said they tried to settle in tight-knit units throughout West Germany during the period in question. Initially these units were comprised of individual men who scattered to find employment, but the eventual consolidation of small niches within larger "immigrant neighborhoods" did happen, according to the first generation of immigrants, once their families joined them. Discussions about these "mahallët Shqiptare" (Albanian neighborhoods or quarters) indicate that asserting a universal Albanian identity was not the central motivating factor for patterns of settlement in these otherwise indistinguishable masses of "immigrant ghettos." Rather, it was the need to work together against being counted as Turks, whose heavy concentration in any neighborhood was likely to lead to a struggle over who would be permitted to reside in these places. Unable to rely on "Serb" community leaders representing Yugoslavs to embrace their cause, large numbers of Albanians forged clusters (*mahalle*) as best they could to collectively deny Turkish identity when issues of rezoning arose.

While it took some prodding, some of the informants finally conceded that these small groupings were created by joining other ethnic groups from the Balkans, as their aggregate numbers rarely reached the 12 percent threshold, whereas being "Turk" could easily result in a bureaucratic barrier to settlement or even in forced relocation. Over time, as a result of these strategies, simply being an Albanian would not necessarily result in joining the *mahalle*. To many, group loyalty did not have any salience in a bureaucratic universe that did not accommodate Albanians, Kurds, or Pomoks (Muslim Bulgarians) as alternative identity claims. For a crucial number of Albanians, being Albanian did not constitute security, strength, or promise for growth in the country that would have to be their family's home.

Fitting In

Any number of testimonials written on the subject have made clear that living the life of an immigrant, be it for economic or political reasons, carries many self-inflicted emotional, not to mention social and cultural, stigmata. Younger generations who must interact with the host society in a more comprehensive way than their parents are under great pressure to avoid such stigma. Attempting not to fit the profile of the stereotypical immigrant or outsider often came at the expense of communal "unity" among the youth. Members of the older generation often complained that their "sincere" efforts to organize local get-togethers were often shunned by their children, who, in their own words, thought the music too "traditional" and "embarrassing."[18] An immigrant community's ability to communicate with its host society through mass culture may be key to its relative success or failure. In particular, the 1990s make this point perfectly clear as older-generation Kosovar Albanians watched their Tamil and Kurdish neighbors mobilize sympathies among Europeans that they had never received. In the 1960s and 1970s, before the explosion of the Internet and cable/satellite television, host countries' collective sympathies were most effectively shaped by the media successes of sports stars from the immigrants' group: if individuals could make associations to that star, a new dynamic was possible. Many noted that Yugoslav sports heroes were well known in their neighborhoods, and conversations around Belgrade Red Star (a famous soccer club) were often the basis for personal exchanges between immigrant and host. Even today, the social spaces where the divides of suspicion, jealousy, and fear are still best traversed are at the local sports bar. Here, sports matches keep patrons affixed to the TV screen and the conversations away from politics or money, two areas of conversation that often led to confrontations between Kosovar Albanians and others.

For Kosovar Albanians, in contrast, there was no way for such a cluster of dispersed communities to find those "new spaces of representation" that Stuart Hall has suggested are key to formulating new, temporary identities.[19] This coreless patch resulted in communal, familial, and existential atomization during the 1970s to 1980s so that even the smaller units the first generation had attempted to form were broken up. It was individuals who actively sought to control the terms in which they interacted with the outside world, since the role of an imagined community-wide structure, even at the level of the loosely formed village-based group, was all but negligible. The majority of those individual spores that sought alternative ways to avoid the stigma of associations with Turks were the children of first-generation migrants. For many among the 1970s generation, in particular, the fact that these small communities could not break out of the stereotype of being Turkish gave little incentive for them to support their parents' efforts to maintain a "dignified" existence as an invisible but "alive and healthy" family. Quite to the contrary, in order to break out of what in the mid 1990s translated into a Turkish identification trap, youngsters often used "adopted" identities that were seen as "cleaner."

As noted in my conversations, "members" of various diasporas in Europe had much to say about the frustrations they felt at the arbitrary associations "locals" made about them, the "outsiders." In the case of the younger Kosovar Albanians who attended school in host societies during the 1970s and 1980s, many sought to escape the label of being a Turk by publicly claiming to be "Yugoslav"—something their parents or more recent immigrants from the Balkans viewed as "treasonous." Informants who in the 1990s reluctantly admitted to presenting themselves as Yugoslav in the past often tried to justify their move by saying in one way or another that nobody was interested in appreciating them as an Albanian. For better or worse, these individuals were considered Turks and dealt with accordingly. Again, by the 1990s, almost all the interviewees articulated this process with resentment, anger, and "pain." These same informants suggested that Germans also ignored their frequent attempts to explain to them the plight of Albanians in Kosovo because of the assumption that Kosovar Albanians or their parents were simply in Western Europe to look for a job and "exploit the system for the benefits, just like the rest of the Turks." Not only did this create a powerful boundary that dictated how "host" and "guest" interacted, but there was also the ever-present reality of feeling unwelcome; together these factors shaped individuals' personae in respect to the "outside world" and how they chose to articulate their identities.[20] In this environment, attempting to force the host society to identify oneself as an "Albanian persecuted by Yugoslavia" seemed impractical and, for many, potentially damaging. In the end, interviewees felt that it was impossible to link their presence in Western Europe to their persecution and their "preferred identity."[21] The proof offered in many cases was the fact that in all the cities where interviews were conducted, there were no publicly funded activist groups until the key post-1981 period.

Caught in this bureaucratic and social limbo, the strategy of choice was to adopt the Yugoslav identity. Many informants who were in their late teens during the 1970s credited an important sense of "certainty" to being associated with a state like Yugoslavia. When asked to elaborate, many felt "proud" of the country at the time. As a well-known, then popular tourist destination, Yugoslavia had a certain cachet that could communicate a sense of immediate positive associations for those who evoked it. Being identified with a recognizable state could be advantageous in the short term for a number of reasons. There were clear psychological gains to be had for those who actively associated themselves with a state that had produced Nobel Prize winning authors and world-class sports heroes. For many the choice was simply between feeling completely marginal due to their ambiguous and unappreciated place in the world, "hated" for being "Turk and Muslim," or being associated with Yugoslavia.

During the period of relative peace in Kosovo and the rising fortunes of Tito-led Yugoslavia in the 1970s, the popular way to introduce oneself in public was as a Yugoslav (but never a Serb or Croat). Apparently, this process of public self-identification operated not only among younger men who had no personal experience of living in Kosovo: informants often accused others of their 1970s generation of doing the same thing. It was common knowledge, I was often assured, that individual X in Frankfurt, for instance, actively claimed to be Yugoslav to his German friends until the mid 1990s, even socializing with Serbs. It must be added, however, that such claims of self-identification took place only in public, away from the scrutiny of the family. Even those who readily admitted to "feeling more Yugoslav" than "a peasant [*katundare*] from Drenica" did not indicate that interactions at home were in any way modified. The language of communication, the food eaten, the music, and the familial politics were all "distinctly Kosovar" throughout this period.[22] It is clear from these conversations with Kosovar Albanians in Western Europe that transcendent factors such as ethnicity or nationality have no solid foundation upon which to rest. While one can accept the significance of individual declarations of being one thing in public and another at home, putting them in specific temporal contexts is of primary importance. As has been suggested here, there are distinctive time lines in the history of this Albanian invisibility.

The pain felt by many referred to a particular sense of "failure," which clarifies much about the mysteries surrounding the invisible Albanian. The pain associated with living as an invisible Kosovar Albanian reflects the stated desire to "retain some link" to a cultural heritage but also to function within society at large. The issue of being "unrecognized" is linked to the reportedly "frustrated" attempts to secure an autonomous space in which to speak their language, listen to their music, and celebrate their heroes while also being able to make friends among Germans and not be excluded from the outside world. As one interviewee stated during a meeting in Zurich, the fact that one's cultural, linguistic, and religious existence had to be carefully sequestered in sparsely attended "cultural clubs" and in meetings that took place just once a week created individuals who perpetually lived a "divided life." This is clearly a central element of most of the testimonials given to me by Kosovar Albanians of the 1960s and 1970s and reflects the parallel streams of consciousness their children experienced while claiming a public Yugoslav identity but living an Albanian one at home.

The whole process of collecting testimonials about the settlement patterns and choices Albanians made to associate themselves as Yugoslav, Greek, or Italian took some prodding. The context in which these questions were asked was decidedly different from the one in which men had navigated the pitfalls of Germany's postwar migration boom. In the 1960s, it was not today's patriotic sentiments that were paramount but rather trust and security, which only a more intimate association with those from the same village or valley could satisfy. It became clear during the course of my discussions how Kosovo's marginal status in the geostrategic world prior to 1989 meant that the admitted parochialism of my older informants had to be qualified with some justifications. The conditions in Kosovo in the mid 1990s may have dictated the sense of "shame" over how, in the 1970s and 1980s, they had failed to create a more universal community that was distinct from their Turkish or Yugoslav affiliations. This suggests that selective forgetting complements their selective remembering during the period of research.

The issue finally seems to be as much a generational as a structural one. Among those who settled in the 1960s and 1970s, the root cause of not being visible earlier was their children's failure to want to preserve their heritage. From the perspective of my second- and third-generation informants, it was not an issue of "betrayal," as their fathers and uncles suggested, but of "social survival." As it was generally framed, while the parents worked two jobs, saved their money, and ultimately opened up small businesses such as Italian restaurants, the children had to grow up in an extremely "competitive" social environment where ethnic labels were often used to keep people in or out of social spaces considered important to teenagers of the time. The children of this first wave of Kosovar Albanians actively sought to distinguish themselves from the arbitrary affixation of secondary ethnic identities, which suggests a powerful gap of perception between parents and their children. But blaming the children does not prove completely accurate, upon exploring the issue further.

One of the most telling expressions of communal identities in the 1990s was people's ability to influence how their host societies saw them. In the eyes of many informants, the "successful" communities in the 1990s held demonstrations, participated in parades, distributed literature, and supported exhibitions and other "outreach" programs. As interviewees stated, Albanian communities never succeeded in such efforts to reach out and be seen. Perhaps sociohistorical factors lie at the root of this inability: it must be remembered that those who were expelled before 1980 had never lived in a political or cultural environment that promoted their Albanian identity. That most of those who arrived in Germany before 1980 were products of a society that brazenly erased non-Slav and Muslim history from the region goes a long way in explaining the organizational incapacity of these dispersed groups of expellees.

The Battle for Albanianness

Contradicting interests and relationships with the "homeland" took an interesting turn in the 1980s. The issue of violence in Kosovo catalyzed an intercommunal rivalry that translated into international intrigue and political violence as well as a reinvigoration of assumed forgotten public identities. The 1981 massacre of Albanian students in Prishtina, which marked the apex of collective Kosovar Albanian consciousness in an organized form, finally transformed Kosovo into an international issue with corresponding political consequences for those who were targeted by the Yugoslav state.[23] Aside from the several thousand Kosovar Albanians in long-term imprisonment, thousands more fled to Western Europe to settle in what little there was of an organized diaspora. Yet there was a dramatic difference between this new, now politically sophisticated generation of expellees and their largely rural and uneducated predecessors. This generation had been politicized in an environment that enabled them to organize as Albanians (the Albanian language was now permitted in schools and used at Prishtina University), yet persecuted them for such mobilization. As a result of wide-scale coverage of Yugoslavia's repression of the student protests, informants told me that at least during this short period of 1981–82, Europeans began to appreciate that Albanians in Yugoslavia were being murdered because of their struggle for cultural and political freedom. This created a new dynamic of community advocacy that produced new opportunities for previously invisible (and perhaps unconsidered) aspirations.

The years that followed saw a consolidation of particularistic Kosovar Albanian identities in Germany. While not the focus of this essay, I note that the economic networks that began to develop in Europe were largely operational only after the creation of this politically active diaspora in the 1980s. Savings accumulated over the postwar years from earnings in restaurants and small businesses helped create strong economic foundations for further investment in a political identity that was now gaining more international attention with the resurfacing of Serbian nationalism after 1986. The impact this had on individual communities is important. The older generation of Albanian speakers, while insisting they were the "leaders" of the newly invigorated community, became noticeably marginal as a new generation of Kosovar Albanian refugees took on the responsibility of defining the hopes and dreams of Kosovar Albanians for the outside world. This new generation adapted as best they could to a new geopolitical context that ultimately created the Democratic League of Kosovo, a belated and unrecognized Republic of Kosovo, and later the various groups that funded the war for liberation in the mid 1990s. In this dynamic of political change in Yugoslavia and Europe as a whole, the conditions for a fundamental change in how Albanian speakers interacted in European host societies helped reshape a desire to be identified as a Kosovar Albanian.

Understanding the channels taken to accomplish this helps explain the relative dispersal of the Albanian experience in German-speaking societies during the last fifty years and suggests that possible parallels were occurring among other communities throughout Europe. This implicitly suggests that a long list of factors merit consideration before personal experiences with self-asserted identities can be assumed to be as "natural" or "primordial" as the scholarship on Balkan nationalism often indicates.[24] To better appreciate this, it is perhaps necessary to reinvigorate a concern for specificity rather than resorting to sweeping generalizations about the immigrant in Europe.

Conclusion

Several suggestions regarding Albanian migration, made throughout this essay, may be helpful to others wishing to study Europe's current attitudes toward foreigners. The combination of socioeconomic and geostrategic factors that changed the way Europeans interacted with the world in the mid 1990s also influenced how male Albanian speakers began to understand their collective identities. As the forces of "globalization" opened doors allowing previously "isolated" or "obscure" identities to flourish, the once generic immigrant communities have subsequently exploded into hundreds of little universes with their own tragic pasts and self-articulated needs. While it has been proven that

Albanians were always there despite Western Europeans' failure to see them, it is clear that Kosovar Albanians also failed to make themselves seen.

I have used this forum to expose an underlying problem with some studies on migration to German-speaking societies: they avoid deconstructing the intellectual and structural limitations of using ethnic and "country-of-origin" criteria to study such migrations. Large numbers of Albanian speakers were among those categorized as Yugoslav, Greek, Italian, and Turkish immigrants settling in Western Europe's cities and towns, their existence all but denied in official records that characterized them as ethnic kin in their countries of immediate origin. This phenomenon compelled individuals to adopt identities in search of a place in the bureaucratic and social spaces provided by host countries. The desire to shed the stigma of being a particular type of foreigner (namely, Turkish) was exaggerated among Albanians who, for a number of reasons, failed to establish their own collective identity in Western Europe prior to 1981. Such failures resulted in the marginalization of individuals, a stigma that translated into manifestations of denial of self and the seeking out of adopted, secondary identities.

It is often assumed in academic circles that we should put the onus on states and their bureaucracies for the substantial personal traumas experienced in the modern world. This is indeed true in the case of the Serb-dominated Yugoslav state, which used a number of legal and extralegal tactics to forcibly evict hundreds of thousands of Albanian speakers from their homes. That said, every one of those interviewed actually placed far more blame for their individual traumas on neighbors, shopkeepers, individual policemen, co-workers, managers, and classmates. This suggests the need for a much more integrated study of how immigrant groups interact with local host populations rather than simply regarding them as closed social units. As noted throughout, the failure to find a space as Albanians in the context of day-to-day life was most traumatic for those involved in this informal study. Simply in order to avoid being invisible, many actively adopted identities that they would otherwise have been reluctant to claim.

The underlying message behind this twentieth-century European mystery, therefore, is not just that institutionalized modifications are needed, but also that efforts to better address, on an individual basis, the largely unarticulated frustrations of many of Europe's people hold great significance. This is still the case in the early twenty-first century. The general feeling among Kosovar Albanians in 2002 was that the Germans are not "getting better but are getting worse." The situation for Albanians from the former Yugoslavia since the end of the wars in the Balkans in 2001 has been particularly difficult, as many have become targets for new forms of institutional harassment. Large numbers of Kosovar Albanians have been forced to return to Kosovo under the pretext that their lives are no longer under threat. Lingering stereotypes about Kosovar links to organized crime, however, remain the biggest source of frustration and fear. Numerous campaigns by right-wing parties in Austria, Switzerland, and Germany specifically target Albanians as universally linked to the drug trade, the trafficking of women, and Islamic fundamentalism. As such, "Albanians" are often identified as "security threats" to host societies, a stigma that has sharpened the divide in some less successfully assimilated groups of Albanians who sense a lingering vulnerability to arbitrary expulsion.[25] In this context there is a persistent fear of such far-right revivalism as has been manifested recently in Italy, Holland, Sweden, Denmark, and Austria, which would result in a second period of forced migration, this time back to Kosovo.[26] A recent backlash in the wake of heightened fears of "Islamic" fundamentalism and persistent representations of Kosovar Albanians in local media as "drug dealers," "gangsters," and "terrorists" only broadens a gap that has clearly been present since the first wave of second-tier migrants arrived in the late 1940s in Switzerland; only temporarily was it ever bridged, during the Kosovo war of 1998–99.

The consequences of not being able to sustain links to a homeland or have one's plight as a persecuted human being recognized are significant for the individual and his/her relationship with the outside world. Lacking control over how the world perceives the individual, the generic migrant's constant struggle to articulate a distinctive identity ultimately contributes to such fragmentation. The exclusivity of being "native" rests on powerful traditions of personal and collective discursive exchanges, implicitly ostracizing individuals tied to such imaginaries. It is hoped these dynamics, traumas, and histories can be reintroduced into narratives in the study of European migration, shedding light on the humanity of the experience and the responsibilities of all of us in the perpetuation of discrimination and the psychological pain that accompanies such journeys. The simple act of recognizing these journeys may help resolve other cases of unimagined European boundaries and perhaps make all that was air solid again.

Notes

1. For the few statistical abstractions that characterize past work on these expulsions, the personal side of the experience was never considered by the only published work that acknowledged an Albanian angle to Yugoslav and Turkish migration. See Hakif Bajrami, *Rrethanat shoqërore dhe politike në Kosovë më 1918–1941* (Prishtina, 1981); and Hivzi Islami, *Rrjedha demografike shqiptare* (Pejë, 1994).
2. See Isa Blumi, "Defining Social Spaces by Way of Deletion: The Untold Story of Albanian Migration in the Post-war Period," *Journal of Ethnic and Migration Studies* 29, no. 6 (November 2003): 949–65.
3. Patrick Ireland, *Becoming Europe: Immigration, Integration, and the Welfare State* (Pittsburgh, 1998), 60–115.

4. Scholars who failed to recognize this dynamic prior to the end of the Cold War include Ilhan Başgöz and Norman Furniss, eds., *Turkish Workers in Europe: An Interdisciplinary Study* (Bloomington, IN, 1985); and Philip L. Martin, *The Unfinished Story: Turkish Labour Migration to Western Europe. With Special Reference to the Federal Republic of Germany* (Geneva, 1991).

5. Brackette F. Williams, "A Class Act: Anthropology and the Race to Nation across Ethnic Terrain," *Annual Review of Anthropology* 18 (1989): 401–44.

6. Martin van Bruinessen, *Kurdish Ethno-Nationalism versus Nation-Building States* (Istanbul, 2000); and Karin Vorhoff, *Zwischen Glaube, Nation und neuer Gemeinschaft: Alevitische Identität in der Türkei der Gegenwart* (Berlin, 1995).

7. Dietrich Thränhardt, "Ausländer im Dickicht der Verbände," special issue, *Neue Praxis* 7 (1983): 62–78; and Klaus-Martin Groth and Johann Müller-Gazurek, *Ausländer-Sozialrecht* (Frankfurt am Main, 1983).

8. Jürgen Puskeppeleit, "Entwicklungslinien und -perspektiven der Sozialdienste," *Informationsdienst zur Ausländerarbeit* 1 (1989): 14–19; and Puskeppeleit and Dietrich Thränhardt, *Vom betreuten Ausländer zum gleichberechtigten Bürger* (Freiburg im Breisgau, 1990).

9. Puskeppeleit and Thränhardt, *Vom betreuten Ausländer*, 125–26.

10. Dieter Filsinger, Franz Hamburger, and Dieter Neubert, "Multikulturelles Nürnberg," *Zeitung des Ausländerbeirates* 6 (October 1983): 3.

11. See Blumi, "Defining Social Spaces," 952–54.

12. This careful inspection of the categorical truisms imposed on such communities follows the interpretive thrust set by, among others, James Clifford, "Travelling Cultures," in *Cultural Studies*, ed. Lawrence Grossberg, Cary Nelson, and Paula Treichler (New York, 1992), 96–112.

13. See the anonymously written article in a Germany-based Albanian diaspora publication: "Shqiptarët e Stambollit," *Ekskluzive* 18 (2001): 61–64.

14. Every one of my informants who had grown up in German cities recalls one or two local "toughs" famous for beating up local Germans who were seen as being "disrespectful" or feigning "superiority."

15. See Blumi, "Defining Social Spaces," 954–56.

16. Isa Blumi, "The Commodification of Otherness and the Ethnic Unit in the Balkans: How to Think about Albanians," *East European Politics and Societies* 12, no. 3 (Fall 1998): 527–69, see especially pages 543–49.

17. Daniel Cohn-Bendit and Thomas Schmid, *Heimat Babylon* (Hamburg, 1993), 111.

18. This is a common complaint among Kosovar Albanians who, in the 1990s, resurrected their patriotic credentials and the love of, for instance, "traditional music." One need only inspect popular culture magazines and websites catering to the Kosovar diaspora in Germany and Switzerland to appreciate the marketability of nostalgia pop among the youth, largely born and raised outside of Kosovo/a. See for instance, http://www.tung.ch/ (accessed 16 January 2011).

19. Stuart Hall, "Cultural Identity and Diaspora," in *Identity: Community, Culture, Difference*, ed. Jonathan Rutherford (London, 1990), 222–37, especially 223–26.

20. Michael J. Shapiro explores the dynamics of the "binding and unbinding" of communities in ways that have informed my understanding of Kosovo/a-Albanian responses. See Shapiro, "National Times and Other Times: Re-Thinking Citizenship," *Cultural Studies* 14, no. 1 (2000): 79–98.

21. Conversations taken up on this theme recently throughout Switzerland and Germany speak of particularly rigid assumptions among local neighbors, many of which persist today in regard to their faith in "Islam." Personal communications in Freiburg, Calw, Munich, St. Gallen and Dusseldorf, 2000 and 2009.

22. Indeed, it is hard to find a family that does not use the Albanian language at home. It is even more interesting that the children of these immigrants have retained the regional accents of their parents, suggesting little integration among Kosovar Albanians until the 1980s.

23. Noel Malcolm, *Kosovo: A Short History* (New York, 1999), 334–37.

24. For an effective critique of this literature, see Maria Todorova, *Imagining the Balkans* (New York, 1997), 116–39.

25. For an example of the working logic of this stereotype see Mary P. Van Hook, Eglan-tina Gjermeni, and Edlira Haxhiymeri, "Sexual Trafficking of Women: Tragic Propor-tions and Attempted Solutions in Albania," *International Social Work* 49, no. 1 (Janu-ary 2006): 29–40; Johann Schmid, "Operationalisierung von Security Sector Reform (SSR) auf dem Westlichen Balkan," Institut für Europäische Politik (Berlin, 2007); and Xavier Raufer, "A Neglected Dimension of Conflict: The Albanian Mafia," in *Po-tentials of Disorder: Explaining Conflict and Stability in the Caucasus and in the Former Yugoslavia*, ed. Jan Koehler and Christoph Zürcher (Manchester, 2003), 62–74.

26. This is a theme often brought up in the commentaries and feature stories of Kosovar Albanian newspapers and magazines published in Europe today: in particular, the monthly *Ekskluzive* and the daily European edition of *Koha Ditore*.

CHAPTER 10

Invisible Migrants
Memory and German Nationhood in the Shadow of the Berlin Wall

JEFFREY JURGENS

Çetin Mert, the five-year-old son of a Turkish guest-worker family, drowned in the Spree River on 11 May 1975. The bank from which he fell belonged to West Berlin, but the river itself was part of the German Democratic Republic, even though it was located outside of the Berlin Wall. As a result of this peculiar jurisdictional arrangement, East German border officials did not allow West Berlin police and fire personnel to search for Mert when the latter arrived on the scene. The incident marked a contentious moment in the diplomatic conflicts surrounding the waters between East and West Berlin. It has not figured prominently in public memories of the Wall, however, for reasons that are closely related to migrants' marginal place in narratives of postwar German history and national belonging.

Over the past three decades, a growing body of interdisciplinary scholarship has sought to reframe conventional understandings of modern Germany through an examination of migration and its social consequences.[1] The strength of this literature lies in its efforts to relate the formation and public perception of large-scale population movements to important geopolitical developments, economic exigencies, and modes of cultural production. This commitment is well illustrated in recent research on the West German recruitment of guest workers from Turkey and other Mediterranean countries as well as the East German employment of contract workers from Vietnam and other socialist states.[2] Nevertheless, one shortcoming of the existing research is that it does not typically address migrants' experiences of local, national, and international boundaries, including the border that divided the two postwar German states. This limitation undermines a more nuanced understanding of the spatial dimensions of division and reunification, particularly the degree to which these events were defined by complex acts of border- and territory-making. But it also inhibits a more sustained engagement with the presence—and absence—of migrants in public and scholarly accounts of the postwar era.

Indeed, as historian Rita Chin has noted, scholarship on labor migration after 1945 remains "peripheral to the master narratives of West German history such as Allied occupation, democratization, and the problem of two states and one nation."[3] In keeping with her observation, I cannot help but note the lack of public and scholarly attention that has been paid to migrants' experiences of division and reunification. On the whole, public appraisals have been more concerned with the so-called "Wall in the head" (*Mauer im Kopf*) that divided "Ossis" and "Wessis" after the Wall itself had opened, and the more discerning treatments have drawn attention to the predominance of West German viewpoints, as East German ones have either been submerged or suffused with nostalgia.[4] To be sure, many accounts have noted that migrants from Turkey and elsewhere became the targets of xenophobic and racist violence after 1989, and a few have employed the metaphor of a "new Wall" to characterize the reluctance among Jews and people of color to venture into the former East Germany, where the hostility against so-called foreigners has been most prevalent. Peter Schneider, a writer well known for his reflections on division and reunification, has given this image a troubling twist: one of his recent essays contends that a "new Berlin Wall" is emerging between the Federal Republic's mainstream populace and its Muslim immigrants, who in his estimation have not adopted the values that define German society.[5] Yet these portrayals merely underscore the uncertain relationship that people of Turkish and other backgrounds maintain with dominant narratives of German nationhood: it is as if they become relevant to the history of division and reunification only after the Wall falls. This blind spot is most noteworthy in Berlin, a city whose postwar history has been defined not only by Allied occupation and the Cold War but also by extensive migration to both its eastern and western halves.

More pointedly, I am struck by the general absence of migrants from Turkey, Vietnam, and other countries not simply in public memories of the Berlin Wall but also in the critical scholarship that addresses them.[6] To the extent that these memories and analyses acknowledge the presence of postwar migrants at all, it is largely to allude to the settlement of guest workers from Turkey and elsewhere in such working-class districts of West Berlin as Kreuzberg, Wedding, and Neukölln. On the whole, though, these accounts fail to note that the arrival of guest workers in West Berlin was closely related to the Wall's construction and that many migrants resided in its immediate vicinity. This omission amounts to a moment of selective forgetting that renders migrants largely invisible within memorials and narratives that cast the Wall as a central figure of national trauma and redemption. Such invisibility is all the more striking, moreover, when viewed in relation to the (hyper)visibility that has greeted Muslims in Germany before and after 11 September 2001 and, in a somewhat different register, the legacy of Jews in the context of the Memorial to the Murdered Jews of Europe and other places of memory in central Berlin.[7] In each of these instances, minority groups are strategically present and absent, remembered and forgotten in ways that assert the Federal Republic's commitment to democratic and humanitarian principles even as they mask disturbing histories of difference, exclusion, and persecution.

This chapter attends both to the social and material circumstances of Mert's death and the representations through which it has been rendered ambiguously (in)visible in German public memory. On the one hand, the circumstances of the drowning highlight the salience of borders as sites where modern states claim and attempt to realize their territorial sovereignty. As a number of scholars in political geography and other fields have noted, one important locus of this sovereignty lies in the practices through which states both monitor and interdict the circulation of people, objects, and currencies into and out of their jurisdictions.[8] In the almost three decades of the Berlin Wall's existence the German Democratic Republic invested heavily in a security apparatus that was designed to police cross-border traffic and to exercise violence over bodies that transgressed its boundaries in unauthorized ways. Hence, Mert's death must be understood in relation to the GDR's efforts to exercise sovereign power and to have that power recognized by its chief ideological opponent, the Federal Republic of Germany. On the other hand, Mert's public invisibility points to the significance of borders as key sites in the production of collective affiliations and narratives of the national past. As anthropologist Daphne Berdahl has argued, the boundary between the two German states provided an important material and metaphorical means for West and East Germans to formulate mutually opposed identity categories and differentially powerful interpretations of historical events, and it retained this significance even after the border became porous and then disappeared altogether.[9]

My analysis runs along analogous lines, although I shall be primarily concerned with the ways that dominant memories of the Berlin Wall inscribe an ethnically uniform nation that encompasses East and West Germans but largely excludes non-German migrants and their descendants. Accordingly I examine not simply the state discourse that emerged on both sides of the Wall immediately after Mert's death, but the texts, images, objects, institutions, and names that subsequently contributed to his shadowy status in German public memory. My use of the term "public memory" rests on the premise that memories are not fixed vessels in which past experiences and impressions are retained, but mutable representations through which the past is actively interpreted and negotiated. Public memory in turn refers not to the recollections of particular individuals, but to shared objects, images, and narratives that circulate widely in the mass media, popular culture, and public memorials. These representations must be analytically distinguished from official historical discourse since they both align with and depart from the authoritative accounts produced by professional historians and other institutions. Nevertheless, they play a vital role in constructing personal and social relations to the past, even as they also reveal the conflicting desires and agendas that guide the formation of national and other group identities. Public memory is thereby implicated in political struggles not only over what defines legitimate knowledge of the past, but also over who and what define the terms of collective membership.[10]

The traces and sites of memory I discuss here have not merely written East and West Germans into narratives of the Wall in particular ways, but have precluded and effaced other group experiences and perspectives, including those of postwar migrants. In the end many of the accounts of the Wall formulated by local and federal state agencies, journalistic and publishing enterprises, and public memorials and museums fortify a conception of the reunified German nation (and its West German predecessor) as a homogeneous collectivity founded on a common ethno-cultural essence. The persistence of this ethno-cultural conception mirrors the retention of jus sanguinis as the primary means of allocating citizenship in the postwar Federal Republic, and it stands in tension with the continuing efforts of Germany's political parties, migrant associations, and other activists to reckon with both the Nazi past and contemporary racism. Public memories of the Berlin Wall thereby constitute one realm where the acknowledgment of migrants' difference and its implications for German liberal democracy have not been fully explored.

The Drowning and Its Aftermath

The very presence of labor migrants in the Federal Republic is closely related to the country's postwar history and the construction of the Wall. During the economic expansion of the 1950s, West Germany relied on ethnic Germans from former Reich territories as well as refugees from the Soviet occupation zone and the later East Germany to remedy its pronounced labor shortage. With the erection of the Wall in August 1961, however, these sources of workers were almost completely cut off, and the Federal Republic responded by increasing its reliance on foreign recruited labor, which it had begun to import from Italy, Spain, and Greece as early as 1955. Among its other effects, this shift resulted in the signing of a bilateral recruitment agreement with Turkey in October 1961, under the terms of which more than 860,000 workers eventually arrived in the Federal Republic.[11]

West Berlin became one of these migrants' primary destinations. The city's wartime damage and uncertain geopolitical status adversely affected its industrial recovery, and it did not experience a sizable demand for foreign labor until the late 1960s.[12] Significantly this was precisely the period when recruitment from Turkey was at its highest: indeed, almost three-quarters of Turkey's guest workers arrived between 1968 and 1973, a period when the country was West Germany's single largest source of foreign labor.[13] At the same time, West Berlin's vulnerable position vis-à-vis the GDR made other labor-exporting states reluctant to send their citizens to the city, given that these workers would be in imminent danger in the event of military conflict. The Turkish government did not share these concerns to the same degree, largely because it was intent on using all available means to reduce the country's high level of poverty. As a result, recruited laborers from Turkey formed the largest contingent of guest workers in West Berlin, and many of them eventually took up residence in working-class neighborhoods in Kreuzberg, Wedding, and Neukölln. Migrant families were particularly attracted to the plentiful low-rent tenement housing in these areas, all of which had experienced a demographic decline and a deterioration of their infrastructure following the construction of the Wall. Çetin Mert's parents Ramis and Münevver, who rented an apartment in eastern Kreuzberg, fit within this broader pattern.[14]

The events surrounding Mert's demise took place on and near the Kreuzberg riverbank known until recently as the Gröbenufer. Only a few minutes walk from the subway at Schlesisches Tor, the Gröbenufer occupies a central location in Berlin's Wall topography. It lies just north of the Oberbaum Bridge, which after 1963 functioned as one of eight regulated border crossings between East and West Berlin (see fig. 10.1). It also stands directly across from the former border strip in the Mühlenstrasse, where the East Side Gallery currently displays the murals of an international cast of artists. And it was the site of multiple escape attempts: Udo Düllick was shot by East German border soldiers in the immediate vicinity on 10 October 1961 when he tried to swim across the Spree. Hans Räwel died there in similar fashion on 1 January 1963. According to West Berlin newspapers, Çetin was playing on the Gröbenufer on Sunday, 11 May 1975, when he fell into the river at 12:20 p.m. A neighbor notified the police at 12:30, and units from the police and fire departments arrived on the scene four minutes later, with a special team of scuba divers following fifteen minutes after that. They were not allowed to search for Çetin immediately on their arrival, however, because this portion of the river fell within East Berlin's jurisdiction, even as the riverbank itself belonged to West Berlin. The divers thus had to seek permission from East German authorities, which they attempted to do first with a passing patrol boat, then with the border post on the Oberbaum Bridge. Border personnel prohibited them from diving in both instances. East German divers eventually arrived at 1:15 p.m. and, as a crowd of several hundred people watched from the Gröbenufer, pulled Çetin's body from the river an hour later.

Figure 10.1. Gröbenufer and Oberbaum Bridge, Berlin (2007). Photograph © Jeffrey Jurgens.

Observers in West Berlin acknowledged that the chances to rescue the boy had been slim, but they nevertheless reacted with an outpouring of righteous indignation. Mayor Klaus Schütz, the Allied authorities, and the major West Berlin newspapers all condemned the GDR for giving geopolitical goals priority over the preservation of human life.[15] The sharply worded critiques accompanied wrenching photos of East German divers pulling Çetin Mert's lifeless body onto a patrol boat. These images were strikingly reminiscent of the iconic photographs of Peter Fechter, the eighteen-year-old who had been killed at the foot of the Wall while attempting to escape East Berlin on 17 August 1962.[16] In both instances the published images were compelling not simply because they depicted the agonizing ends of healthy young people, but because they offered visceral portrayals of the East German regime's readiness to take hold of those bodies that did not conform to its spatial discipline. The photos of Fechter had sparked widespread outrage against the GDR when they first appeared in the West German press, and they established a potent visual vocabulary for subsequent representations of the Wall and its associated security practices. Viewed against these preceding photographs, the images of Mert were difficult for West Germans not to interpret as a denunciation.

Yet the public commentary in West Berlin was not entirely uniform, and it did not single out East Germany alone for criticism. One editorial in the *Berliner Morgenpost* took rescue personnel and other bystanders to task for their lack of initiative: "how many children have to drown," it asked rhetorically, "before a man finds the courage to end this unbearable situation simply by taking off his jacket, jumping in the water, and rescuing the child?"[17] It thereby implied that GDR border personnel would not have prevented a rescue attempt if one had actually been undertaken. The *Tagesspiegel*, meanwhile, ruefully noted that the Gröbenufer, unlike other banks along the river, had not been rendered "child-proof" (*kindersicher*) with a fence.[18] In fact the Gröbenufer ran in a steep incline from the street down to the river's edge and lacked any barrier that might have prevented a person from falling into the water. In the aftermath of the accident, Kreuzberg's local administration planned to hang signs in German and Turkish to warn passersby. It initially refused to erect high fences, however, since these might have hindered "refugees" (*Flüchtlinge*) seeking to escape from East Berlin.[19]

Mert's death and the ensuing accusations drew a heated response from the East German government, which declared that West Berlin bore full responsibility for the incident. According to statements that appeared in *Neues Deutschland* and the *Berliner Zeitung*, the German Democratic Republic had not only demanded that the West Berlin Senate take precautionary steps to prevent "tragic accidents" like this one from occurring but had also proposed an agreement that would allow for rescue efforts from the West.[20] The West Berlin Senate's refusal to entertain this proposal, East German officials contended, only served to underline the fact that it was "not ready to recognize the sovereignty of the GDR in its border waters and the consequences that follow from it."[21] From the perspective of West German officials, however, the agreement had not been completed because the GDR had wrongfully insisted that the Wall and the river marked a "state border" (*Staatsgrenze*) between East and West Germany, while West German and Allied authorities maintained that they only constituted a "sector border" (*Sektorengrenze*) between the Allied and Soviet zones. When the GDR introduced this "state border" language in the context of recent negotiations, West German officials regarded it as an illegitimate effort to undermine Berlin's status as a city under Four Power jurisdiction.

West Berlin public discourse quickly turned to the tragedy's Cold War implications and paid little attention to the local aftermath. The *Tagesspiegel*, however, did report on a protest on 19 May 1975 in which more than one thousand migrants participated.[22] Significantly, the demonstrators who assembled at the Gröbenufer responded to Mert's death in a fashion that not only drew on the icons and idioms of Turkish nationalism but also appropriated prevailing West German interpretations of the GDR. A number of the protesters, for example, carried Turkish flags as well as placards from the National View (Milli Görüş), a migrant organization that has historically aligned itself with Turkey's Islamic political parties. Yet West German flags were also present, as were signs in German and Turkish with slogans such as "Communism – Enemy of Freedom" and "Down with GDR Politics." Another bilingual placard referred to "walls of shame" (*utanç duvarları*) as one of communism's defining features in a turn of phrase that literally translated the German-language *Schandmauer*. The demonstration concluded with the installation of a plaque on the riverbank that stated, "We abhor the communist cruelty that left the boy Çetin Mert to his death." East German patrol boats monitored the gathering, and several protesters threw stones at them, apparently without hitting their mark.

The attention Mert's death received was in its way quite remarkable, for Çetin was actually the fifth boy to drown on the Gröbenufer and another nearby bank after the Wall's construction: he had been preceded by Andreas Senk in 1966, Cengaver Katrancı in 1972, Siegfried Kroboth in 1973, and Giuseppe Savoca in 1974.[23] As the names suggest, three of the boys were from Italian and Turkish migrant families who had come to West Berlin as a result of the government's labor recruitment programs. These prior deaths received less extensive coverage than Mert's, however, and they did not evoke the same moral condemnation.

What was different about this particular incident? Plainly both the East and West German governments had sought to mobilize the tragedy to discredit their respective opponents. Yet this observation cannot explain the dramatic change in migrants' responses. There is no record that protests occurred after the deaths of Cengaver Katrancı and Giuseppe Savoca, and the demonstration following Mert's demise was unusual precisely because it was primarily oriented not to political events in Turkey, as was usually the case for migrant activism in the 1970s, but to the confrontation between the two German states. I am inclined to interpret this change in light of the increasing assertiveness that recruited laborers from Turkey were beginning to display. In the spring of 1973, thousands of Turkish metal workers joined their non-immigrant German counterparts in a series of spontaneous work stoppages, and in August and September of that same year more than five hundred of them participated in a controversial wildcat strike at the Ford auto plant in Cologne.[24] In addition, labor recruitment had officially ended in November 1973, and by the time of Mert's death many workers from Turkey and their families were digging in for a longer stay than they had first anticipated. The protest may thus have signaled migrants' growing awareness that their presence in Berlin would be long-lasting and an increasing readiness to voice their concerns.

Remembering Wall Victims, Forgetting Migrants

Until recently there was little popular recollection of Çetin Mert's death: virtually all of my acquaintances in Berlin, regardless of their age, gender, class location, level of education, and ethnic background, expressed a mixture of ignorance, surprise, and curiosity about the incident's details. This general lack of knowledge should hardly suggest, however, that there is not at all any public memory related to the event. I first became aware of Mert, for example, through writer Dilek Güngör's article "A Wall Victim from the West," which appeared in the *Berliner Zeitung* in the spring of 2000.[25] Güngör's editors had asked her to write about Mert on the twenty-fifth anniversary of his death.[26] They, in turn, had learned about the boy from Peter Pragal, another longtime journalist for the paper, who had briefly discussed Mert in a book he had co-written on the divided Berlin.[27] To my knowledge this book represents one of the first published references to Mert's death and one of the few overall since the newspaper coverage that followed the incident in 1975.

Güngör's article initially caught my eye because it unsettled one of my entrenched assumptions: like many other readers, no doubt, I had simply taken it for granted that the term "Wall victim" referred to residents of East Germany who had died while attempting to cross the border. Yet the story does much more than point out that West Berlin residents were also casualties of the GDR's security regime. It implies that the lives and deaths of postwar migrants were entangled in German division in intimate ways and that they too might have a stake in how officials, scholars, journalists, memorial personnel, and other citizens remember the Wall. On the one hand, Güngör's article draws attention to the degree to which the deaths of Çetin Mert and the other boys have been forgotten within the public memories articulated by state-sanctioned institutions, privately and/or commercially operated memorials, and mainstream publishing and film production organizations. On the other, it points to a troubling shortcoming in the premises that scholars have conventionally adopted in their historical research and writing about the postwar German states. These realms of memory and history converge in the way they downplay if not efface migrants as a central presence in German life, and such occlusion has troubling implications for migrants' ability to lay claim to recognized membership in the nation and its liberal democracy.

Yet for all the attention Mert's death momentarily received, his place in the pantheon of Wall victims today is decidedly ambiguous. Mert and the other boys do appear in an extensive "Chronicle of the Wall" webpage recently launched by the Center for Contemporary Historical Research in Potsdam, among other sponsors.[28] Mert's death in particular is the subject of a detailed account that incorporates photographs and primary documents from the Federal Ministry for Intra-German Relations and the East German Ministry for

State Security. The boys also figure in the timelines of Wall victims on display in the Berlin Wall Documentation Center in Wedding as well as the street-side exhibit on display in the Friedrichstrasse. These latter sites, however, do not provide specific details concerning any of the victims' lives and deaths. As a result, Mert and the other boys tend to be submerged within the longer chronology of Wall casualties and the narrative that conventionally accompanies it. During my visit to the Berlin Wall Documentation Center, for example, one young boy asked his mother about the names and dates that adorned one wall of the exhibition space. She replied: "those are all of the East Germans who died while trying to get into West Berlin." At the same time, two prominent but less scholarly locales effectively exclude Mert and the other boys from their accounts. The well-known memorial between the Brandenburg Gate and the Bundestag, maintained for many years by East German dissident Gustav Rust, deals only with refugees who died while seeking to flee East Berlin. Two crosses commemorate Udo Düllick and Hans Räwel, the two East German men I mentioned earlier who were shot near the Gröbenufer, but there is no reference to Mert or the other boys. The Wall Museum at Checkpoint Charlie, meanwhile, positions East Germans as the Wall's primary if not sole casualties by devoting its exhibit to the cruelties of the socialist regime and some of its citizens' ingenious efforts to escape.

Nevertheless, one display does refer to the situation on the Spree River. This is the so-called "water accident reporter" (*Wasserunfallmelder*), an eye-catching intercom unit with instructions in German, Turkish, and Serbo-Croatian. As the accompanying text relates, twenty of these intercoms were installed along the river as part of the security agreements that were eventually reached between the West Berlin Senate and the East German government, six months after Mert's death. Significantly, one of the images in the display is a photo of the East German divers recovering Çetin's body. I can say this, however, only because I recognize him from the photos that initially appeared in the *Berliner Morgenpost* and the *Tagesspiegel*. No caption explains who the boy is or how he died. The text only notes, "After the construction of the Wall children often drowned where only the bank belonged to West Berlin but the waters to the GDR." Thus, even as Mert is momentarily visible, he does not represent the migrants who, by the mid 1970s, had made a home in West Berlin. He is instead an icon of childhood in general, an evocation of innocence and needless suffering that furthers the museum's larger indictment of the GDR.

An analogous, multilayered erasure recently took place on the Gröbenufer itself (see fig. 10.2). When I first visited the bank in 2007, there was no sign of the plaque left by the demonstrators in May 1975, and the only reference to the Wall was a modest stone marker dedicated "to the unknown refugee" (*dem unbekannten Flüchtling*; see fig. 10.3). To my mind this memorial deflected and encrypted past events at least as much as it commemorated them. It is quite

Figure 10.2. Gröbenufer, Berlin (2009). Photograph © Jeffrey Jurgens.

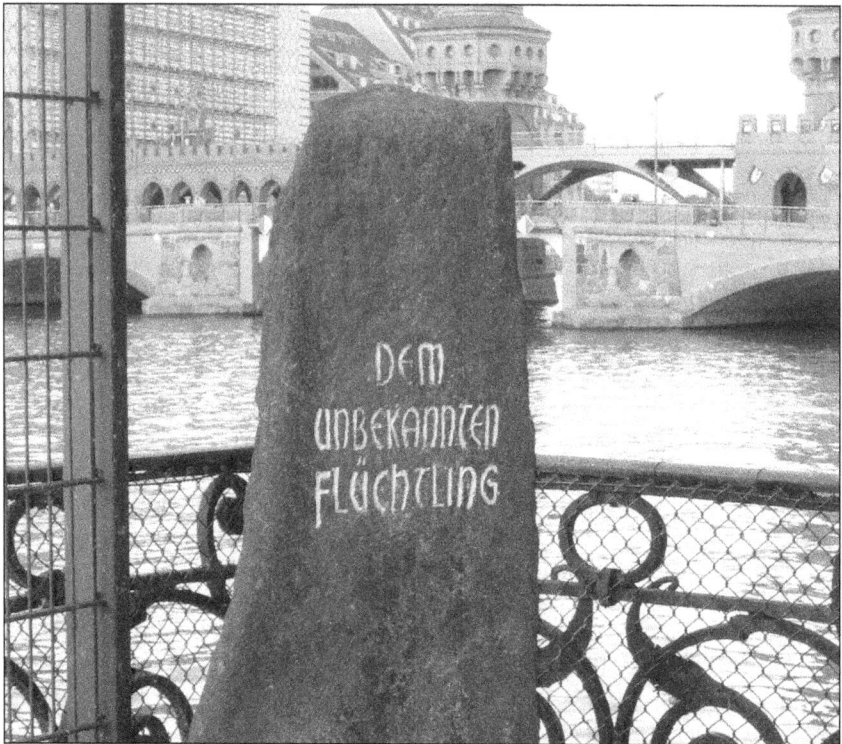

Figure 10.3. To the Unknown Refugee, Berlin (2007). Photograph © Jeffrey Jurgens.

possible, of course, that the marker was meant to offer a generic tribute to the Wall's victims, much as the tomb of an unknown soldier honors the collective sacrifice of a nation's war dead.[29] Nevertheless, the emphasis on an "unknown" victim is curious given the likelihood that most—although perhaps not all—of the people who died near the Gröbenufer are "known" to the extent that their names and some aspects of their lives and deaths are inscribed in accessible records, accounts, and memorials. Meanwhile the use of "refugee" in this context draws attention to those East Germans who attempted to flee the GDR and away from the Wall's other casualties in West Berlin. Once again, Mert and the other boys remain outside the scope of commemoration.

When I returned in the summer of 2009, even this memorial had disappeared. The area had become a construction site, part of a renovation project that has since turned the riverbank into a public promenade with a restaurant, a dock for boat tours, and an exhibition area. According to a sign posted at that time by the Berlin Senate Administration for Urban Development, the significance of the Gröbenufer as a "place for remembering Wall victims" (*Ort des Gedenkens für Maueropfer*) was to be retained through its incorporation into the government-sponsored Berlin Wall historical mile (Geschichtsmeile "Berliner Mauer") and the erection of an informational placard. It was unclear, however, whether this framing would acknowledge Mert and the other boys as Wall casualties with specific connections to the riverbank.

The question of remembering Mert has also emerged in one of Berlin's recurring debates over the politics of local street names. This particular instance, however, differs from the controversies that occupied activists and government officials in the years immediately after reunification.[30] Those conflicts typically concerned the retention and revision of names given to streets and subway stations by the GDR, many of which had commemorated leading figures in the early workers' movement, noted communists and antifascists, and deceased East German politicians. These names in turn had replaced earlier designations dating from the Third Reich, the Weimar Republic, and even the Wilhelmine era, which the GDR had regarded as militarist, fascist, or antidemocratic. By contrast, Çetin Mert's memory was entangled in the renaming of a locale in the western half of the city rather than in the former East, and it was implicated in a debate that addressed both Germany's imperial past and its pluralist present.

The riverbank where Mert died had been known as the Gröbenufer since 1895, when local authorities bestowed the name in honor of Otto Friedrich von der Gröben (1656–1728). As a military officer in the service of the Great Elector Friedrich Wilhelm, von der Gröben had led a naval expedition to the West African coast that secured a foothold for Brandenburg in the transatlantic slave trade. Shortly after landing in what is now Ghana, von der Gröben established a colonial garrison and trading post from which an estimated thirty thousand Africans were shipped into servitude in Europe and the Caribbean. The commemoration of this early German colonial figure had drawn little or no comment for more than a century, but in the spring of 2009 a coalition of Afro-German organizations and other civil society groups successfully petitioned the district council of Kreuzberg-Friedrichshain for a name change.[31] Following the passage of a council resolution in May of that year, the riverbank was rechristened the May-Ayim-Ufer after the Afro-German activist, scholar, and poet also known as May Opitz (1960–96).[32]

Interestingly, the renaming of the Gröbenufer met with opposition not from conservatives or figures on the extreme right but from a left-leaning activist who also sought to represent the perspective of a minority constituency. Frank Segebade, a non-immigrant German man who has lived in Kreuzberg for decades, responded to news of the district council's decision by proposing yet another name for the riverbank: the Çetin-Mert-Ufer. In a letter sent to the city's most prominent Turkish migrant organization, the Turkish Federation of Berlin-Brandenburg, Segebade contended that the May Ayim resolution would "blur the special character" of the place, whereas naming it after Mert would remind residents that the Wall had been located there and that Kreuzberg children, not just East German refugees, were among its victims.[33]

Although a few representatives of the Turkish Federation expressed interest in Segebade's proposal, in the end it gained little traction within the organization or the public at large. No one has accused Segebade of any ill intent, but there are nevertheless several reasons why the notion of a Çetin-Mert-Ufer has not been met more favorably. Above all, Segebade's idea would have pitted minority constituencies against one another in a way that might well have stoked an atmosphere of competitive grievance. Indeed, Berlin witnessed conflicts of precisely this sort in the 1990s, when vociferous debates flared over the disposition of government-sponsored memorials for Jews, Roma, communists, and homosexuals persecuted by the Nazis.[34] Many local activists and government officials were understandably eager to avoid a similar controversy, however sympathetic in principle they might have been to the proposal.

I would also maintain that naming the riverbank after May Ayim was not as problematic as Segebade suggested. Ayim had lived in Berlin for the last twelve years of her life, and as a scholar and activist deeply committed to both antiracism and feminism, she was keenly aware of the exclusions that had informed recent historical events. In her recollection of the interlude between the fall of the Wall and reunification, she wrote:

> Talk in the media was of German-German brothers and sisters, of unified and reunified, of solidarity and togetherness. Yes, even concepts such as homeland, people, and fatherland were—again—on many tongues.... In the first days after November 9, 1989, I noticed that there were hardly any immigrants and

Black Germans visible in the cityscape, at least those with dark skin. I asked myself how many Jews were (not) in the streets.... Like other Black Germans and immigrants, I knew that even a German passport did not constitute an invitation to the East-West festivities. We sensed that an increasing dissociation from the outside world would accompany the imminent German-German unification—an outside that would include us. Our participation at the party was not requested.[35]

In short, the selection of May Ayim as the riverbank's namesake, even if she was not tied to the riverbank as a specific locale, still spoke to those notions of homogeneous German nationhood that have marginalized postwar migrants and other purportedly "foreign" minorities.

Yet even though they were positioned as outsiders in 1989, migrants from Turkey and their descendants often witnessed Berlin's division and reunification firsthand, in a fashion many non-immigrant Germans residing elsewhere in the city and the rest of the country did not. A welter of personal recollections, which I have reconstructed in my field notes since my initial research trip to Berlin in 1997, attest to these experiences of the Wall and its dismantling. One man now in his late thirties, for example, recalled how he could look into East Berlin from the window of his boyhood apartment in Wedding—and how, amid glimpses of everyday life "over there," he once witnessed an unsuccessful escape attempt. A woman who had arrived in West Berlin in the late 1960s, meanwhile, often took walks along a military canal off the Spree that separated Kreuzberg in West Berlin from Treptow in the East. She told me that she used to stick her tongue out at the East German border soldiers whenever they trained their gun-sights on her from the other bank. And one Turkish social worker, who had also arrived in West Berlin in the late 1960s, remembered hugging joyful East Germans in November 1989 as they wandered through Kreuzberg for the first time after the Wall had opened. I learned only later that his nineteen-year-old son had died in 1991 after a confrontation with three young men from Germany's extremist right-wing scene: one of them had beaten him with a baseball bat on the Adenauerplatz, on the western end of the Kurfürstendamm.

One consequence of a lingering ethnocultural understanding of German nationhood is that personal memories like these (however mundane, irreverent, or poignant they might be) have only rarely found their place within public narratives of division. To the degree that they recognize migrants at all, the relevant public memory and historical scholarship has most commonly figured them as an additive rather than an integral component of the nation, a segment of the populace with at most a secondary claim to membership. Of course one cannot discount the impact of the new citizenship policy adopted in 2000, which eased the legal terms of naturalization and introduced an element of jus soli for children of migrant backgrounds born in Germany; nor can one dismiss the immigration law of 2005 which aimed to establish more favorable conditions for migrants' permanent settlement and integration into the Federal Republic. Yet as my analysis of Wall-related commemorative sites and practices indicates, we have yet to witness a comparable transformation of the guiding premises of German nationhood as they pertain to public memory and historical narration. Dominant accounts of the postwar past have simply not kept pace with shifts in the legal and political definition of German citizenship.

Conclusion

By tracing the circumstances of Çetin Mert's drowning and the contours of his ambiguous recollection, I have sought to offer another angle from which Germany's postwar division can be apprehended. My argument underscores the fact that the GDR's violent assertion of sovereignty was not always directed at its own citizens but in a few instances targeted residents of West Berlin as well. More important, though, it throws into relief some of the lingering (in)visibilities that continue to mark Wall-related public memories and broader understandings of German nationhood. For the most part, these memories and understandings still situate postwar migrants at the edges of the nation's postwar history. Nevertheless, a number of indicators pointed to a somewhat more prominent role for Mert in the public commemoration surrounding the twentieth anniversary of the Wall's end. Along with the "Chronicle of the Wall" website, the *Tagesspiegel* profiled Mert's death in August 2009 in two features on the history of the Berlin Wall.[36] The writer Dilek Güngör also received numerous inquiries from journalists who intended to write about Mert's death and hoped—in vain, as it turned out—that she would be able to put them in contact with his family.[37] All of these developments suggest that Germans' present engagements with the lived realities of migration and pluralism are beginning to reconfigure some of the ways that the Wall is being remembered.

Yet we should not underestimate the "cycle of silences" that structure the production of historical narrative in ways that efface Çetin Mert and Kreuzberg's other casualties from many stories of German division.[38] In this regard I am struck not simply by the modest German-language press coverage pertaining to Mert and the other boys at the time of their deaths, but also by the subsequently uneven formation of local archives. The newspaper department of Berlin's Staatsbibliothek, for example, houses the Federal Republic's largest collection of periodicals from Germany and countries throughout Europe, Africa, Asia, and North America, and during my visits there I was able to read the reporting on Mert's death that appeared in East and West Berlin's major newspapers. I was also able to consult the Istanbul edition of *Cumhuriyet*, the one Turkish paper in the department's holdings from that time, which provided a brief initial report on Mert's death (although the boy himself goes unnamed) and, a few days later, a lengthier article on the accusations exchanged by East and West German officials.[39] Significantly, the European editions of Turkey's major dailies, which presumably would have provided more extensive coverage of the incident and its local aftermath, were unavailable: the European edition of *Hürriyet* was archived at the Staatsbibliothek on a consistent basis after June 1977; the archiving of the European edition of *Milliyet* began only in 1982. This dearth of timely Turkish-language press coverage is more than simply inconvenient for those readers who might want to examine migrants' responses to Mert's death. It ultimately reflects the Federal Republic's belated recognition of de facto immigration and the ideal of normative national homogeneity that has decisively informed it.

Such dynamics of remembering and forgetting form one important aspect of the cultural and political struggles that are waged in relation to state borders, including the border that separated East and West Germany. These struggles have not merely concerned the status of the Wall as a "state" or "sector" border in the context of the Cold War, however important a role this issue played in Çetin Mert's death. In the wake of reunification they have also turned on the very definition of the people who constitute the Wall's victims and the social groups with a stake in recollections of division and reunification. Attending to postwar migration should thus prompt us to reexamine the collective affiliations that public memories of the Berlin Wall both articulate and exclude. In the end the master narrative of "two states and one nation" may itself be a limiting rubric, one that a more fully transnational perspective can fruitfully scrutinize and complicate.

Postscript

There is one dimension of Mert's story that is likely to remain lost in even the most inclusive of recent public recollections: the consequences of Çetin's death for his family. As far as I am aware, Dilek Güngör is the only person to have spoken with his immediate relatives and to have written about their recollections in publicly accessible fashion. And so I end by returning to her article, the one that piqued my interest in the first place, in order to etch a few new details into the spare outline of events I have traced thus far.

Both Mother's Day and Çetin's fifth birthday fell on 11 May 1975, and the family had planned a picnic for that afternoon. Mert's mother Münevver had sent him to play with the neighborhood boys after breakfast, and one of them had apparently shoved him into the river as he was trying to retrieve a ball with a stick. When Çetin had not returned home after a few hours, his family began to search for him, only to learn of his fate from police officers who came to their door. After the accident East German authorities retained custody of Çetin's body for several days, relinquishing it only after his parents had paid a sum of 10,000 Marks. The family eventually buried Çetin in Düzce, their hometown in Turkey, and stored his toys, clothes, and photos in their original home before returning to Berlin. They passed his name onto their eldest grandson, who is now approaching thirty years of age. The family home and the mementos of the lost son, however, were destroyed in the earthquake that struck northwestern Turkey in 1999. Traces of Çetin, in short, have been erased not merely in the realm of public recollection, but in the domain of intimate family remembrance as well.

When I asked Dilek Güngör about the process of writing her article, she explained that it had been difficult to locate the Merts, not least because they did not list their address and telephone number in Berlin's directory. She eventually managed to contact the family through other routes and establish a modicum of rapport, but the ensuing conversation was awkward and painful all the same:

> I spoke with Çetin Mert's brother, who was angry about the harassment the family received every year on the anniversary of his death, but who nevertheless talked with me for a bit. I believe things were a bit easier because of the fact that we could both speak Turkish. It is really unpleasant, of course, to call someone out of the blue at home, especially when it has to do with the death of a child. But as a journalist you often don't have another choice.[40]

The brother in question is Yaşar Mert, who was eight on the day of Çetin's death but was not present on the riverbank when his brother drowned. He is, in fact, the only member of the family that Güngör quotes in her article. His parents apparently did not care to talk with her, and their lingering anger and sadness emerge only through Yaşar's words: "the father is full of rage and screams at anyone who asks about the boy, says the brother. The mother cries. Not only now, on the anniversary of his death. 'She always cries,' says Yaşar Mert. 'How can a mother overcome the death of her son, even when she has four other children?'"[41] The sense of "harassment" Yaşar describes may refer to journalists' requests for interviews, infrequent as these seem to have been, at least until recently. Yet I suspect that it may also allude to the efforts of friends, acquaintances, and neighbors to offer condolences. However well-meaning these expressions of sympathy might be, they do not seem particularly welcome.

Some if not all of Çetin's relatives presumably still live in Berlin, but I have not approached the Mert family for the purposes of my research or for that matter even attempted to contact them. Many signs suggest that they do not wish to be sought out. I hope that Çetin's relatives, if and when they learn of this essay, do not regard it as an unwanted trespass on their personal tragedy.

Notes

1. Klaus J. Bade, ed., *Deutsche im Ausland – Fremde in Deutschland: Migration in Geschichte und Gegenwart* (Munich, 1992); idem, *Europa in Bewegung: Migration vom späten 18. Jahrhundert bis zur Gegenwart* (Munich, 2000); Ulrich Herbert, *A History of Foreign Labor in Germany, 1880–1980: Seasonal Workers, Forced Laborers, Guest Workers* (Ann Arbor, 1990); and Jan Motte, Rainer Ohliger, and Anne von Oswald, eds., *50 Jahre Bundesrepublik – 50 Jahre Einwanderung: Nachkriegsgeschichte als Migrationsgeschichte* (Frankfurt am Main, 1999).

2. Jan C. Behrends, Thomas Lindenberger, and Patrice G. Poutrus, eds., *Fremde und Fremd-Sein in der DDR: Zu historischen Ursachen der Fremdenfeindlichkeit in Ostdeutschland* (Berlin, 2003); Rita Chin, *The Guestworker Question in Postwar Germany* (New York, 2007); and Deniz Göktürk, David Gramling, and Anton Kaes, eds., *Germany in Transit: Nation and Migration, 1955–2005* (Berkeley, 2007).

3. Chin, *The Guestworker Question,* 12–13.

4. Daphne Berdahl, *Where the World Ended: Re-Unification and Identity in the German Borderland* (Berkeley, 1999); John Borneman, *After the Wall: East Meets West in the New Berlin* (New York, 1991), idem, *Belonging in the Two Berlins: Kin, State, Nation* (Cambridge, UK, 1992); Svetlana Boym, *The Future of Nostalgia* (New York, 2001), 173–218; and Maren Ullrich, *Geteilte Ansichten: Erinnerungslandschaft Deutsch-Deutsche Grenze* (Berlin, 2006).

5. Caroline Fetscher, "Die neue Mauer," *Tagesspiegel* (Berlin), 30 July 2000; and Peter Schneider, "The New Berlin Wall," *New York Times Magazine,* 5 December 2005, 66–71.

6. Andreas Huyssen, *Present Pasts: Urban Palimpsests and the Politics of Memory* (Stanford, 2003); Brian Ladd, *The Ghosts of Berlin: Confronting German History in the Urban Landscape* (Chicago, 1997); and Karen E. Till, *The New Berlin: Memory, Politics, Place* (Minneapolis, 2005). The absence of migrants' perspectives persists even as researchers have examined memories of the Wall among other groups, including women. See Dinah Dodds and Pam Allen-Thompson, eds., *The Wall in My Backyard: East German Women in Transition* (Amherst, 1994); similarly, Huyssen addresses the general exclusion of migrants' memories from national memories but not of the Berlin Wall specifically in "Diaspora and Nation: Migration into Other Pasts," *New German Critique* 88 (2003): 147–64.

7. Till, *The New Berlin,* 202–4.

8. John Agnew, "Borders on the Mind: Re-Framing Border Thinking," *Ethics and Global Politics* 1, no. 4 (2008): 175–91; and Thomas Blom Hansen and Finn Stepputat, eds., *Sovereign Bodies: Citizens, Migrants, and States in the Postcolonial World* (Princeton, 2005).

9. Berdahl, *Where the World Ended,* especially 3–9.

10. See Marita Sturken, *Tangled Memories: The Vietnam War, the AIDS Epidemic, and the Politics of Remembering* (Berkeley, 1997), and Pierre Nora, ed., *Realms of Memory: Rethinking the French Past,* vol. 1, *Conflicts and Divisions* (New York, 1996).

11. Mathilde Jamin, "Die deutsche Anwerbung: Organisation und Grössenordnung/ Almanya'nın yabancı iş gücü alımı: organizasyonu ve boyutları," in *Fremde Heimat: Eine Geschichte der Einwanderung aus der Türkei/Yaban Sılan Olur: Türkiye'den Almanya'ya Göçün Tarihi,* ed. Aytaç Eryılmaz and Mathilde Jamin (Essen, 1998), 149–70.

12. T. H. Elkins and B. Hofmeister, *Berlin: The Spatial Structure of a Divided City* (New York, 1988), 219–20.

13. Chin, *The Guestworker Question*, 62–63, and Jamin, "Die deutsche Anwerbung."

14. Dilek Güngör, "Ein Maueropfer aus dem Westen," *Berliner Zeitung*, 13 May 2000, 25.

15. "Kind an der Oberbaumbrücke ertrunken: Verhalten der DDR bei den Rettungsversuchen scharf verurteilt," *Tagesspiegel* (Berlin), 13 May 1975, 1 and 2; "Unsere Meinung: Ein Kind," *Tagesspiegel* (Berlin), 13 May 1975, 1; and "Ost-Berlin schiebt die Schuld auf den Westberliner Senat," *Berliner Morgenpost*, 13 May 1975, 3.

16. Fechter had been attempting to scale the Wall near Checkpoint Charlie when East German border personnel shot him and left him bleeding and crying for help just beyond the reach of American soldiers and West Berlin police officers. Fifty minutes later, a team of GDR soldiers gathered Fechter's limp body in their arms and carried him to a nearby hospital, where he died shortly thereafter. Several photojournalists and a television crew documented his final minutes from the western side of the Wall.

17. Walter Brückmann, "Frage des Friedens," *Berliner Morgenpost*, 13 May 1975, 1.

18. "Unsere Meinung: Ein Kind," *Tagesspiegel* (Berlin), 13 May 1975, 1.

19. "Auch nach dem Tod des türkischen Kindes: Grenzgewässer weiter unsicher," *Berliner Morgenpost*, 13 May 1975, 1.

20. "Schuld liegt allein beim Senat von Westberlin," *Neues Deutschland*, 14 May 1975, 1; "Kommentare und Meinungen: Tatsachen widerlegen Hetze gegen die DDR," *Neues Deutschland*, 14 May 1975, 2; and "Tragischer Unfall an der Oberbaumbrücke: Westberliner Haltung verhindert seit langem Vereinbarung," *Berliner Zeitung*, 13 May 1975, 2.

21. "Tragischer Unfall an der Oberbaumbrücke," *Berliner Zeitung*, 13 May 1975, 2.

22. "Türkische Protestdemonstration am Kreuzberger Gröbenufer," *Tagesspiegel* (Berlin), 21 May 1975, 2.

23. Lea Hampel, "Jung, unschuldig, tot," *Tagesspiegel* (Berlin), 13 August 2009.

24. Chin, *The Guestworker Question*, 63–64.

25. Ibid.

26. Dilek Güngör, personal communication, 2009.

27. Peter Pragal and Eckart Stratenschulte, *Der Monolog der Lautsprecher und andere Geschichten aus dem geteilten Berlin* (Berlin, 1999), 58–65.

28. For a detailed account of Mert's death as well as photographs of the demonstration taken by the East German Ministry for State Security, see the entry for Çetin Mert at "Chronicle of the Wall" (www.chronik-der-mauer.de, accessed 30 June 2010), an online project sponsored in part by the Center for Contemporary Historical Research in Potsdam (Zentrum für Zeithistorische Forschung).

29. Benedict Anderson, *Imagined Communities: Reflections on the Origin and Spread of Nationalism* [1983] (London, 1991), 9–10.

30. Ladd, *The Ghosts of Berlin*, 209–15.

31. AfricAvenir International et al., "Pressemitteilung: Weitere Strassenumbennungen nötig," 20 May 2009, http://blog.derbraunemob.info/2009/05/27/berlin-kreuzberg-re-naming-of-street-in-may-ayim-ufer-umbenennung-des-groebenufers-in-may-ayim-ufer (accessed 2 March 2010).

32. Under the name May Opitz, Ayim coedited one of the touchstones of scholarly inquiry into Afro-German experience: May Opitz, Katarina Oguntuye, and Dagmar Schultz, eds., *Farbe bekennen: Afro-Deutsche Frauen auf den Spuren ihrer Geschichte* (Frankfurt am Main, 1986).

33. Eren Ünsal, personal communication, 2009.

34. Ladd, *The Ghosts of Berlin*, 169.

35. I take these passages from Ayim's essay "The Year 1990: Homeland and Unity from an Afro-German Perspective" ("Das Jahr 1990: Heimat und Einheit aus afro-deutscher Perspektive"), trans. Tes Howell, in Göktürk et al., *Germany in Transit*, 126–29.

36. "Sie starben an der Mauer," *Tagesspiegel* (Berlin), 13 August 2009; Hampel, "Jung, unschuldig, tot."

37. Dilek Güngör, personal communication, 2009.

38. Michel-Rolph Trouillot, *Silencing the Past: Power and the Production of History* (Boston, 1995), 26.

39. "Batı Berlin Belediye Başkanı, Doğu Alman makamlarının bir Türk çocuğunun ölümüne neden olduklarını açıkladı," *Cumhuriyet*, 13 May 1975, 1; and "Bonn hükümeti Spree Nehrinde bir Türk çocuğunun boğulması olayını Doğu Almanya nezdinde protesto etti," *Cumhuriyet*, 16 May 1975, 1 and 9.

40. Dilek Güngör, personal communication, 2009.

41. Güngör, "Ein Maueropfer aus dem Westen."

CHAPTER 11

Crossing Boundaries in Cyprus
Landscapes of Memory in the Demilitarized Zone

GÜLGÜN KAYIM

> Know thyself.
> —Inscription on Apollo's Temple at Delphi

The many ethnic groups that have occupied and governed Cyprus, including Greeks, Myceans, Romans, Venetians, Ottomans, Arabs, and, most recently, British, have left their mark on the language and culture of the island. The island's overriding identity and majority population views itself as Greek (80 percent), with the largest minority acknowledging its Turkish heritage (18 percent), and the rest identifying as Latins, Maronites, and Armenians (2 percent). Following the Cypriot Greek-led struggle for independence from British colonial rule, which began in 1931, Cyprus has been in a constant state of violent conflict that culminated in 1974 with the invasion by Turkey and the island's subsequent partition. Two communities currently exist in opposition to each other, separated by a demilitarized buffer zone that physically divides the island. The years of violence and animosity still remembered by its residents and displaced citizens reinscribe this physical boundary across generations and in claims to citizenship and belonging.

I am an artist whose work navigates the pathways of such geopolitical conflict and related movements of people fleeing violence. Based upon personal and cultural memories of division, my site-specific performance pieces invite audiences to cross the social, spatial, temporal, and subjective boundaries that demarcate their lives. As a Turkish Cypriot born into the midst of intercommunal conflict in 1963 in the western port city of Famagusta (the Greek name) or Gazimagusa (the Turkish name), I became part of the Cypriot diaspora when my family migrated to London in 1967. I grew up in the north London borough of Haringey, whose 30,000 immigrants make up the highest concentration of Cypriots in Britain. As an adult I relocated to the United States.

This chapter offers an account of my artistic research and creative process over the past twelve years to consider how performance might offer a strategy of surviving the trauma resulting from living in and leaving a homeland torn asunder by division and violence. The project *Self Portrait ... for now*, initiated in 2007, is a trilogy of biographical performances exploring the themes of conflict, memory, and migration on the island of Cyprus. Although my work for this project is situated within my memories, experiences, and post-memories of Cyprus, the impetus behind the first piece of the *Self Portrait* trilogy was the reportage on the violence taking place in the former Yugoslavia, specifically the massacre at Srebrenica. Quite unexpectedly I began to feel physically affected by the daily news reports on the war, so much so that I created a performance work elicited by images of events in Bosnia, yet rooted and flowing from my tactile memories of the violence and fear I experienced as a child on Cyprus. This first piece was presented in 1998 as *Untitled #1*.

The second work, *The Orange Grove*, presented in 2003, was developed in collaboration with Polish performer and director Ludmilla Ryba, a former member of *Cricot 2* and close collaborator of the late, celebrated Polish theater director and artist Tadeusz Kantor. Known for his work with space and memory, in his performances Kantor separated the corporeal "Self" or the body from the "Other" or non-corporeal reality that lives in the imagination and in memory.[1] In this he signaled an "unavoidable duality" that, according to performance theorist Michal Kobialka, exists in the paradox between the real and imagined, the felt and the thought, perception and memory.[2] My work with Ludka took on the nature of this enquiry between "Self" and "Other" as I explored the possibilities of creating a site-specific "setting" through which the performers' use of objects became the principle mechanism of memory. The play's text and performance vocabulary thus became embodied enactments of the difficulties of narrating personal and familial memory in the context of cultural trauma. The discoveries I made with Ludka allowed me to negotiate, through performance practices, what Yiannis Papadakis calls the struggle with one's own cultural and historical narratives.[3] While my work in both *Untitled #1* and *Orange Grove* addressed childhood experiences and sensations, with the development of *Self Portrait … for now*, the third piece in the trilogy, I moved across temporal boundaries of the "Other," from imagined pasts and presents, to examine the geopolitical division of Cyprus and my identity as a Turkish Cypriot/expatriate/British subject now living in America.

Describing the Division

Cyprus, the largest island in the eastern Mediterranean, is currently divided into two opposing communities, Greek and Turkish, by a United Nations-controlled demilitarized buffer zone (DMZ) that spans and dissects the island. Stretching 180 kilometers from east to west, it is 20 kilometers at its widest (on the west side of the island), where it encompasses the large suburb of Varosha (its Greek name) or Maraş (as it is known in Turkish), and 3.3 kilometers at its thinnest, where the DMZ cuts through the center of the island's capital, Nicosia—one of Europe's only remaining divided cities.[4] The road leading to division began in 1898, when Britain leased Cyprus from the failing Ottoman Empire (which had conquered the island from the Venetians in 1571) to create a strategic base for its efforts to contain Russian ambitions for expansion. The island came under formal British sovereign rule only in 1914, when it was annexed in response to the Ottoman Turks' alliance with the Central Powers. From 1914 on Cyprus, as a British colony, increasingly became the site of violent, ethno-nationalist movements, first visible in 1931 when local Greek protestors burned down the Government House, or the British governor's residence, in Nicosia during a riot. The protestors were calling for independence from Britain and *enosis* (union) with Greece.[5] With the election of Makarios III as archbishop in 1950, violent riots again broke out as Greek protestors demanded freedom from British occupation. By 1955 the nationalist group Ethniki Organosis Kyprion Agoniston (EOKA or National Organization of Cypriot Fighters) had formed an illegal Greek Cypriot military organization established for the sole purpose of achieving *enosis* with Greece. This resulted in further hostilities, which escalated in 1958 following the establishment of the Türk Mukavemet Teşkilatı (TMT or Turkish Resistance Organization), perceived to be a nationalistic, military, and political challenge to EOKA. The TMT was organized around an alternative political strategy: *takism*, or division.

British and Greek tensions reached a peak in 1955 with the establishment of the EOKA insurgency. Because acts of EOKA terrorism pressured British strategic positions on the island, British Governor General Sir John Harding sought to crush the insurgency quickly, using force. To realize this goal he recruited poorly educated and rural men from both ethnic groups on the island for the Cypriot Auxiliary Police Force (CAPF). A disproportionate number of the 1,386 men hastily recruited in 1955 were Turkish Cypriots (37 percent compared with the island's population distribution of 18 percent), even though experienced colonial officials warned against the possible long-term effects of recruiting Turkish police.[6] Moreover, these men were poorly trained, low-paid, and unprepared to carry out their primary purpose: to suppress the rebellion and provide support for the British military's strategic deployments against EOKA insurgents in the rural districts of Cyprus. Facing threats of violence, poor working conditions, and EOKA pressure, Greek recruits soon left the force, so that by 1956 it became an exclusively Turkish Cypriot auxiliary force. By 1958 the CAPF had 1,594 recruits, drawn from the Turkish population and augmented by the Special Mobile Reserve, a marginally better-trained troop of 569 Turkish Cypriots devoted to riot duty only. My father was a member of the CAPF.

According to some scholars, it was British reluctance to grant the Greek Cypriots their demands for *enosis* that lay behind the British implementation of the policy of "divide and rule on the island" (also employed effectively in India and Palestine).[7] The creation of an exclusive ethnic local group to police another ethnic group was instrumental in developing and fermenting the divisions that characterize the tensions on the island today.[8] According to Christopher Hitchens, hostility between Greek and Turkish Cypriots was rare prior to 1955.[9] For James Corum,

> If Harding carefully had planned to alienate the entire Greek population of the island and push the moderate Greeks into full support of EOKA, he could not have done better than by his policy of unleashing a horde of untrained, poorly-led Turkish police on the population. Communal violence, rare in Cyprus before the insurgency, flared up in 1956 and increased throughout the insurgency. When the Turks rose against the Greeks, usually in response to an EOKA killing of a Turkish policeman, the all-Turkish Special Mobile Reserve and Auxiliary Police routinely stood by as Turkish mobs assaulted Greek civilians and ransacked their property.[10]

Division as an instrument of control was effective in two ways: it provided a physical buffer for the British troops to carry out their operations against insurgents; and it manipulated the Turkish and Greek Cypriot populations, providing the British regime with an effective excuse to remain on the island as the sole force of law and order. This colonial policy also had an unintentional impact: it reawakened hitherto dormant mainland Turkish interests in Cyprus.

Following the events of 1955, intercommunal violence continued unabated. Other countries proposed solutions that were not adopted, such as the US "Ball/Acheson Plan" proposed in 1957, which provided for double *enosis*: equal partition of the island and political unification with Greece and Turkey respectively.[11] Between 1959 and 1963, the British finally capitulated to EOKA demands and vacated the island. But rather than grant *enosis* with Greece, the British negotiated an agreement to establish the Republic of Cyprus based on a Greek and Turkish Cypriot power-sharing structure with Greece in the form of a coalition government headed by the Greek President Archbishop Makarios and Turkish Vice President Dr. Fasil Küçük. The Treaty of Guarantee was also created between the new Republic of Cyprus and Britain, Greece, and Turkey, countries that were to act as guarantors of the "independence, territorial integrity, security, and constitutional structure of the Republic."[12] As part of the treaty, Britain retained two sovereign bases at Akrotiri and Dehekelia. Although British occupation formally ended in 1959, this year signaled a critical moment that Hitchens describes as the "Cyprus problem," whereby intercommunal differences continued to be exploited by outside powers.[13] Upon British withdrawal, many of the Turks who had served in the Auxiliary Police and Special Forces, including my father, found themselves in a vacuum as they lost their jobs, became targets for acts of revenge, and were forced to leave the island. Because of historical ties to Britain, many Cypriots fled to London to escape the violent turmoil. Currently an estimated 160,000–170,000 Cypriots live in Britain, about 20 percent more than on the island itself.[14]

With the constitution settled, a brief, if tenuous, peace was established that lasted until 1963, when the fragile constitution collapsed and ethic violence erupted. The British returned to the island in 1964 to mediate the conflict with the help of the United Nations "peace force." British Commander Major-General Peter Young drew a line on a map of Cyprus with a green wax pencil to demark the cease-fire zone between the warring communities, effectively marking out what would become the DMZ. This zone, first known as the "Green Line," was later, in 1974, referred to as the "Atilla Line" on some maps, indicating the Turkish code name for the military intervention undertaken by the mainland Turkish government. In this year the Greek Cypriot nationalist fanatic Nikos Sampson successfully staged a military coup, which was backed by the Greek mainland, and deposed President Archbishop Makarios. Turkey claimed its status as one of the three guarantor countries of Cyprus and intervened to prevent what it viewed as the systematic persecution and slaughter of the Turkish Cypriot minority.[15]

This military operation effectively led to the full partition of the two communities and the physical construction of the current demilitarized buffer zone by the United Nations. The resulting annexation triggered a full-scale population exchange, causing Greeks to flee to the south and Turks to the north for safety, with numerous families from both communities leaving behind their land, homes, and villages. The current partition of the island effectively divides two opposing and distinct ethnic populations and political entities: the southern, Greek side, known as the Republic of Cyprus, which is internationally recognized and is a member of the European Union; and the northern Turkish side, controlled by the Turkish Republic of Northern Cyprus (TRNC), which is not an internationally recognized state and has attempted to make an illegal, unilateral accession. As the only country to have recognized the TRNC, Turkey has jeopardized its possible standing as an EU member; the EU has made clear that Turkey's bid for membership can be considered only if Turkey resolves the Cyprus problem.[16]

From 1974 to 2003, the borders separating the populations in the north and south remained closed. Only a week after the signing of the EU accession treaty, which accepted the Republic of Cyprus as a full member, did Turkey agree to open two border checkpoints in Nicosia. According to news reports, an estimated 5,000 Greeks and 2,000 Turks streamed to the border on the first day to visit the other side.[17] But rather than bringing together estranged communities or broken families, the dispute continued, albeit in different form—even with an open border. Spurred by each side's renewed encounter with its abandoned homes, villages, and memories, persistent acrimony is manifested in a cold war of words and ideas, lawsuits and propaganda, competing versions of histories, traumas, and grievances. Today the DMZ is a hostile and largely uninhabited wilderness, full of land mines and anti-tank ditches. This long territorial "no-man's-land" covers roughly 3 percent of the entire island, encompassing large swaths of land containing abandoned and decaying villages, sealed-off homes, and buildings, including the ghost city of Varosha/Maraş, the suburb located south of the city of Famagusta/Gazimagusa.

An estimated 10,000 people still inhabit parts of the DMZ, including UN and British troops in three bases and three villages. Of these villages only one, Pyla, is still occupied by a very small number of both Turkish and Greek Cypriots. The Varosha/Maraş suburb, once a thriving international tourist destination, was home to a large Greek Cypriot community that abandoned the area during the post-fighting population exchange. The Turks refused to go into what they considered ostensibly Greek territory and sealed off the area. Now it is a shadow city, a haunted place dense with memories, and a powerful symbol of the Cyprus dispute. Under Turkish military control, the local policy for this region remains unchanged, preventing redevelopment or cleanup activities in the suburb for the last thirty-six years. Thus the suburb of Varosha/Maraş has been left to rot, an intentional reminder of the pain and presence of an irresolvable conflict. It languishes, slowly decaying in the sun (fig. 11.1).

These disputed territories have shaped my life and my artistic practice. Trained as a theater artist in experimental performance, I have developed and adapted approaches that combine theater practices with architectural theory to create site-specific performances tailored to specific locations. My preoccupations with place and identity, however, come from being a Turkish Cypriot immigrant. I use the language and sense memory of my artistry to sort through and reexamine historical events, propaganda, stories, and ideas. My earliest site-specific works, *The Orange Grove* and *Untitled #1*, grew out of an insatiable desire to navigate my divided and diasporic histories and find ways to cross both geopolitical and personal boundaries.

Facing Loss: *The Orange Grove* and *Untitled #1*

It began with my father's death in February 1996. My reaction to the loss was to do what I imagine many people do when a loved one dies: record family recollections. I started by informally interviewing family members to collect stories about my father growing up, his exploits on the island of Cyprus, and our migration to London. I then added my own memories and pieced together scenarios from these inconsistent and incomplete stories. This informal effort to keep a record of a life developed into a full-length performance text, *The Orange Grove*, in which my father and I meet again and again. Through these imagined encounters on the island of Cyprus we revisit different versions of my family's traumatic departure from the island and our arrival in London.

This was not a linear effort but an attempt to hold together the pieces of memory, inconsistent as they are, within the pages of a play, an endeavor to grasp through narrative the complexities and contradictions that were my father, all the while knowing this to be an impossible task. The playwriting process organizes and consolidates information so that it can be communicated to, and understood by, a public. Tenuous thoughts, memories, and ideas are called forth, harnessed, controlled, and materialized through the authority of the written word. Recording memory on paper requires that sorted, arranged, and reframed memories conform to the principles of narrative, which of course, in turn, affect the very nature of memory itself. I organized the play to enact the experience of opening a family scrapbook, with stories being told as a means to reanimate and collage the old photographs. As Kobialka writes, there can be "no steady flow of action in a presentation of memories because memories existed only as transparent negatives of old photographs stored somewhere in the mind's scrapbook."[18]

Figure 11.1. Abandoned buildings near the DMZ in Varosha/Maraş District, Famagusta, 2005. Photograph © Gülgün Kayim.

I chose to tell the tales of my father as they had been told to me, communicating them through environmental sounds and the storyteller's language and personality. I did not enact or dramatize the stories but verbally recounted them to the audience through distinct characters. I also created a character representing a five-year-old version of myself: she recites her family history in a child-like mantra, recalling memorized events, dates, names, and places without changing her tone or emotion. Named "Girl 1," she participates in the action, exists in the past moment, and witnesses events while standing apart from them—recounting and relaying her experiences to the audience. Through this character I conflated past and present to evoke what Marianne Hirsch calls "the transgenerational transmission of trauma."[19] In the excerpt below, Girl 1 recalls the trauma and dislocation of migration as described by my mother when she first arrived in London in December 1967:

> *Girl 1*: London ... London ... I remember ... cold ... sleepy. I remember ... tightness ... streets packed with row houses, city crammed with people. I remember ... tight ... claustrophobic ... [*Her words turn to gestures as she tries to communicate. She turns her head sharply to the left as if answering an unheard question.*] The English seemed all red to me, red faced, red cheeked, red and puffy. Pale, translucent skin. Mouths huge with crooked yellowing teeth that emitted mysterious sounds, unfamiliar noises. Eyes clear, lifeless. I was afraid...[20]

I also placed other versions of myself in the work, as a nervous young child waiting to board the ship to England, an older child experiencing the trauma and confusion of migration, and a young woman having arrived at our destination.

The characters representing my father and myself coexisted in the performance space to reexperience and recount his stories. Rather than depict my father's story chronologically in a linear fashion, I wanted to represent all remembered aspects of him at once to evoke the elusive nature of how a family collectively remembers a member in the present. I used the strategy of layering image, sound, and text by, for example, juxtaposing multiple family versions of the past with images taken at different times in the past and sounds that, for me, evoked the island. In the opening scene of *The Orange Grove* I presented my father in three periods: at the end of his life, as a man, and as a young boy.

> Scene 1: A room: an iron bed neatly made up with white bed clothes. Sounds of leaves in the wind, bees, birds, cicadas—sounds of summer.

> A boy emerges from behind the bedstead as though climbing a tree. He reaches the top of the bedpost, sits on it, legs hanging down, back to the audience. He lights a cigarette and hums a tune. Looking down, he laughs, waves to the people down below. Having an idea he pulls down his pants ... settles down to enjoy his cigarette, hum his tune and shit in peace. The outline of a man gradually appears under the bedcovers. His face and torso rise above the covers as though breaking

through the surface of an ocean. He looks out into the audience as he searches for a packet of cigarettes. He takes one, lights it and hums the same tune as the boy behind him.

A chest of drawers slowly opens. From it appears a hand, then an arm, a torso. A man finally emerges and settles on top of the chest of drawers. Dressed in his best suit—old, faded, meticulously pressed, with patches worn at the edges, he reaches into the drawer, pulls out kindling and sets it alight, then uses the fire to light his cigarette.[21]

All three versions of my father were present on stage at once. We saw him at the end of his life dying of cancer, as a young boy escaping a beating by climbing a tree, as a member of the Auxiliary Police who set fire to buildings during the clashes. These multiple ideas of my father were animated in the performance space. Placed in relation to each other, they enacted events recalled by others. Temporal boundaries were embodied and traversed in active relationship and negotiation with the present.

After finishing the work, I put it on a shelf and did nothing more with the project until 2003. The writing process had an effect: I felt compelled to work on *Untitled #1*, another performance script, this time constructed out of my dim memories of early childhood on Cyprus. As a child traumatized by the violence in my homeland and our subsequent migration to Britain, I lost the ability to remember these important events. I have always felt troubled that I had no recall at all of this important period in my life. To remember the earlier period in my life, I have thus relied on my family's stories, attitudes, and hints; on art that deals with war; and on news reports of contemporary global conflicts. Through these various media I feel close to *something*—some trace of recall, the sense memory of childhood that is and isn't there. Using the words and art of others, I attempt to return home, to survive the trauma of displacement, or at least to recapture the atmosphere, feeling, and texture of my early childhood years. As Yi Fu Tuan posits, "the child knows the world more sensuously than the adult. This is one reason why the adult cannot go home again."[22]

Untitled #1 was a broken thing, a collage made out of the words of others, pieces of play text, impressions, memories, and my own words. I borrowed from a variety of historical plays, all of them addressing the subject of war and violence, and how the knowledge of violence is transferred from parent to child, from one generation to the next. From the absurdist Fernando Arrabal's *Picnic in the Battlefield* (1960) I took the opening scene, depicting the soldier Zapo, who, upon encountering his parents on the battlefield, is informed that they have arrived for a visit and family picnic. Zapo is shocked when his father and mother enjoy high tea as spectators of the fighting and coach him in the ways of war. From Antonin Artaud's *A Jet of Blood* (1925), an example of his theater of cruelty, I adopted the energy and dynamism of the two characters Knight and Wetnurse, caught in the violence of destruction, as well as the background atmosphere of confusion and utter chaos. From contemporary Polish poet Tadeusz Rozewicsz's *The Trap* (1982) I borrowed a long monologue spoken by a child while living through the Gestapo's annihilation of his fellow Jews in Poland. The cumulative impact of this speech was especially intriguing, for Rozewicsz does not express Holocaust memories through dramatic events but rather through banal details of everyday events that slowly accumulate to reveal a larger picture of suffering and cruelty. I layered and combined these texts and genres with environmental sounds, such as the flapping wings of pigeons, to enhance the textures of the performance space and communicate the confusion and fear of being a child stranded in a "normal" world of violence. I added my own scenes and words, which grew between the cracks of these borrowed, disparate texts and sounds to create the connective tissue for the larger performance.

I placed *Untitled #1* deliberately inside Drake Marble, an abandoned marble factory situated on the industrial riverfront in St. Paul, Minnesota. I chose this environment for its emotional texture because it "felt right"—it offered an appropriate space for the faded nature of what was in my head. By placing the work in a historic site, I chose to create a performance installation rather than reinscribe the traditional two-dimensional, frontal relationship between performance and spectator. With no backstage, that is, with no place to retreat from the settings, actors, and events, the spectator was surrounded by images and was invited to play a part in experiencing the narrative. The audience was free to fully engage with the space and physical expression of memories about violence, latent hostility, anxiety, pain, suspicion, mistrust.[23] Because I understand my early childhood memories as shattered artifacts of past events, I re-presented them to the audience as fragments. I placed my audience in the middle of this "memoryscape" so that they had to physically walk into and through the constructed scenarios to experience the performance. I wanted to envelope the audience in my memories, broken as they are, and to allow them to develop their own tactile memories of the performance (fig. 11.2).

After completing work on *Untitled #1*, I realized that by animating the material environment through a performance work I could reorganize how audiences view the location and thus the meaning of the work presented. I decided to stage *The Orange Grove* in 2003 at the Thorpe Complex to animate the connections between the war industry and war's effects on populations in conflict. This former World War II-era munitions factory, situated in the industrial area of north Minneapolis, was once part of a larger high-tech weapons manufacturing region. The performance space, an 18,000-square-foot factory floor with the skeletal remains of machinery tracks and assembly bays, was flanked by two watchtowers, signaling to the viewer that high security had once been an important function of this industrial complex. While I could not make a factual

Figure 11.2. *Untitled #1* (1998, © Gülgün Kayim) performed at the abandoned Drake Marble Factory in Saint Paul, Minnesota. Scene 1 with Blayn Lemke and Camilla Little as Mme. and M. Tapan from Fernando Arrabal's *Picnic in the Battlefield*. Photograph © Gülgün Kayim.

Figure 11.3. Jodi Blindauer performing with objects in *The Orange Grove*, Thorpe Munitions Factory, Minneapolis, Minnesota, 2003. Photograph © Tim Heitman.

historical connection for the audience between the weapons systems produced at Thorpe and the missiles that landed on my homeland, I made a symbolic link between the factory's function and my father's lived and felt experiences of war, inviting Minneapolitans to connect the past and present history of their city to my story.

Layering a multidimensional artwork onto a building creates a performance space that resonates with possibility. As the performance becomes complicit with its setting, space is transformed for the viewer into a particular place of remembrance. Material reality is transformed into a symbolic space, inviting the viewer to reconsider the relationship between the manufacturing of war and its relationship to past, present, and future lives. Objects, which in the performance world are more commonly referred to as props, were my principle tools in evoking and layering the past and transitioning temporal boundaries (see fig. 11.3). I selected broken or battered everyday objects that had already lost their mundane functions and could become metaphors: a battered suitcase was not just a suitcase but a pillow, a shelter, a precious container, a treasure chest, an anchor, a sign of despair, a sign of hope. In the opening image of *The Orange Grove*, for example, a lone man enters the cavernous performance space holding an umbrella. He opens the umbrella, and as he walks toward the audience they realize that the umbrella is full of holes and therefore serves no useful function. They now see an object defined by its deficiencies, a metaphor that stands for the figure's helplessness, loss, tragedy, and ridiculousness.

The building itself, moreover, still bore the markings of its former use as an engine of war: the factory floor was soaked with oil and the windows caked with machine grease; overhead machinery hung useless. These indicators of the former owners' diligence and industriousness suggest the role played by the US military in the development and current state of the Cyprus problem. US "national security" interests were and still are connected to the island's geostrategic position.[24] Located close to the Suez Canal and NATO allies Greece, Turkey and Israel, it was considered an important venue to keep the Soviet Union in check; today both the US and the Royal Air Force still use the Akrotiri and Dehekelia British sovereign base areas as staging posts for military aircraft.

Inheriting Memory: *Self Portrait ... for now*

My family fled the island of Cyprus in 1967, when I was five years old. I am told we left in secret because the island was embroiled in a bloody intercommunal conflict, which had by then escalated to dramatic proportions. My family joined my uncle in North London; he had preceded us and secured our lodgings. Growing up in inner-city London amidst an exiled immigrant community of expatriates, my new neighbors were both Turkish and Greek Cypriots.

My bilingual parents relied on those who arrived before us, whether they were Turkish or Greek, to help with the transition into jobs and schools and to negotiate an alien language, culture, and environment. They were bitter, feeling trapped in a hostile foreign environment and unable to return to a home under siege by war; they spoke longingly of the land, villages, and people left behind. Their attitude toward the British "host" society, which they blamed for their predicament, was not forgiving. Many of my earliest memories in London involve watching my parents struggle to earn a living and to transition from their agrarian, premodern lives to the new conditions of the industrialized twentieth century. Typical of many Cypriot women, my mother stayed home to keep house, look after the children, and work in the home rag trade, doing piecework with a sewing machine. Her income was low: she was paid by the load, had no benefits, and paid no taxes. My father worked in a variety of factories along with other Cypriot men, making cabinets.

When I say I *remember* my early childhood, I mean that I have faint images of a few important events. However, I cannot say with any certainty that I was actually present at these events because some of them, I am told, happened before my birth. My memories of life on the island and knowledge of its pivotal historical events derive from personal stories, photographs, and representations mediated through public images and histories.[25] As I have no actual memory of living on the island, I adopted as my own the experiences, memories, photographs, and opinions of my immigrant family members and extended circle of relatives and friends, as mediated by secondary news and public media sources. These were passed on to me with such intensity that there remains a danger, for as Hirsch asks:

> If we thus *adopt* the traumatic experiences of others as experiences that we might ourselves have lived through, if we inscribe them into our own life story, can we do so without imitating or unduly appropriating them? And is this process of identification, imagination, and projection radically different for those who grew up in survivor families and for those less proximate members of their generation or relational network who share a legacy of trauma and thus the curiosity, the urgency, the frustrated *need* to know about a traumatic past?[26]

I so successfully integrated these inconsistent and highly subjective accounts of life on the island that I *felt* as if I had been there, even though I could not possibly have been. For example, when constructing *Untitled #1*, I restaged my mother's memory of straying into a Greek enclave and being almost attacked by the locals. My "memory" of an event such as this feels "real" when I think of it: my body responds, the heart rate increases, palms become sweaty. These are feelings marked by tension and terror. Yet, I am told, I was still in utero at the time this happened. When I think of this and my physical reactions, I am led to ask: can you inherit a memory? And what might be the strategies of surviving the desire for the original experience as well as the persistent presence of post-memories?

> I am told that my family was heavily involved in the fighting on the Turkish side and to escape detection by Greek police my mother stashed guns under my crib. I am told that we were forced by events to migrate in secrecy because it was common for leaders in the Turkish community to harass émigrés who abandoned the struggle against the Greeks. (Journal entry by the author 2007)

Self Portrait ... for now, my current work, expands this personal inquiry by depicting disputed versions of reality through the competing narratives of Turkish and Greek islanders. Again set within the framework of my own family's experiences and stories, the project's personal narrative combines with the narratives of a larger Cypriot community. The project is shaped by research I conducted in 2005 and 2007 when I interviewed Greek and Turkish Cypriots about how they find meaning on an island decimated by war, divided by conflict, and partly invisible to the international community. I asked them to describe specific places on the island to which they still felt attached. These personal stories explore notions of identity and place as framed by two extremely volatile moments in Cypriot history: 21 December 1963 and 15 July 1974. These two dates and the years between them mark the longest, most sustained period of intercommunal fighting in Cypriot history. The first serious violence erupted in Nicosia on 21 December 1963 (four days after my birth), after the departure of the British. The violence that effectively destroyed the tenuous peace between the Greek and Turkish coalition government was ignited by an incident involving a Turkish Cypriot couple killed by a Greek Cypriot police patrol. This set in motion a cascade of events involving reprisal shootings, hostage taking, and murder. December 1963 is notorious because it broke the fragile peace, destroyed the Republic of Cyprus, and eventually caused the UN peacekeepers to create the DMZ in 1974 (fig. 11.4).

The following years were marked by increased political turmoil and violence. Random solitary killings became more common on both sides, along with harassment and arson. The Turkish community, overcome by larger Greek numbers, began to consolidate into ghettos, using the Green Line as a guide for their safety and for strategic reasons. It was more effective to wall themselves off from the Greeks in key villages than to cut off access and supply routes to the island. The siege years, as they are known in the Turkish community, were marked by hardship and shortage. Turkish Cypriots talk of the period of terror and violence when they experienced the greatest losses, either being forced into small urban enclaves or, to escape persecution at the hands of Greeks, fleeing the island. My family's accounts, for example, are framed by the formal start of the intercommunal violence in December 1963 and by July 1974, the start of the Turkish military invasion that ultimately established the DMZ.

Figure 11.4. View of the DMZ from Nicosia, Turkish side, 2005.
Photograph © Gülgün Kayim.

In contrast, the Greek community in general remembers this period as one of political turmoil and controversy with the Greek mainland, culminating in a mainland-sponsored military coup, the installation of a puppet leader, and the attempted assassination of the president.[27]

> Many individuals lost their homes, villages, and connections to place and land during this time. The Cyprus issue defines our lives. The place that I'm living in is unrecognized, it is isolated, no one recognizes my identity. To travel I can use only passports of another country—Turkey. I have no identity. (Alkan Muratoğlu, interview with the author, Famagusta, May 2007)

When I look at my life circumstances, similar questions arise about the location of a "Self" who has no tangible existence because all the places connected to birth, ancestry, or future are either located within the DMZ boundaries or dislocated by migration. I feel no allegiance to any identity or any location. I only long for those places of my origins that no longer exist in real time; they survive only within the "Other," within the boundaries of memory. The Famagusta hospital where I was born is now located in the Varosha/Maraş district, one of the abandoned neighborhoods sealed off behind military barriers on two sides. Deteriorated by bombing and time, my ancestral village is a bullet-ridden, abandoned collection of ruins. Many of my family members in Cyprus live in adopted villages and borrowed homes that they do not consider truly theirs. Others live abroad, yet hold alive the fantasy of those places (the roots of their identity) that no longer exist: "All human beings appear to have personal belongings and perhaps all have need of a personal place."[28]

In developing *Self Portrait*, I felt it was important to explore where the land fit into my personal identity. As part of my research, I decided to visit the Greek side of the DMZ for the first time in a personal search for my place, those places important to my family. Accompanied by my mother, aunt, and uncle, I started by driving to my ancestral village of Paramali, a village vividly painted in stories my mother had told me when I was growing up in London (see fig. 11.5). The reality shattered any illusions of the pastoral setting I had constructed. I discovered a collection of graffiti-covered houses bearing no resemblance to the fertile, verdant valley of my childhood imaginings. The following accounts are from my journal entries of that trip:

> In what was the village square stand the shells of two burnt-out cars. The remains of ruined stone houses in various stages of dilapidation cluster around the desolate square. Like the sockets of a long dead corpse, their sightless windows stare blankly onto the surrounding landscape. The village clings to the barren, craggy hillside covered by ancient olives, overlooking a parched, empty valley, a dried riverbed, a broken bridge. My mother stands in the center of this village, pointing to where her house was, telling her stories of who lives here, who owns this, how she split her lip there. She tells of her wonderful childhood summers, she tells of another world when she was carried as a child to this place on the back of a donkey. In her mind this is still the location of happy memories. I see only a depressing reminder of violence, hatred, and terror. Mocking my mother to the east lie the well-tended green fields of neighboring "Happy Valley," so dubbed by the British army base which is located there. (Journal entry by the author, 23 April 2007)

Cyprus is full of such ghosts: abandoned villages and neighborhoods crumbling in the sun, waiting to be claimed by their absent owners. Like amputated limbs, these spaces are physical reminders of something cut off, absent; they mark the presence of pain.

But also common are the many abandoned homes that over the years have become rehabilitated and occupied by someone else. After our visit to Paramali we went to my Uncle Yalçin's ancestral compound in the nearby village of Tatli Su, built by his great, great-grandfather and now home to a young Greek family. On arrival in the village Yalçin approached the compound, confidently knocked briefly, and when no answer came, walked inside. I held back, feeling in contrast like a trespasser, hesitating before being bustled into the inner courtyard by my mother. We were soon joined by Maria, the present-day owner of the

Figure 11.5. Image of Paramali and the surrounding countryside, 2007. Photograph © Gülgün Kayim.

compound, whose neighbors had presumably alerted her to our arrival (see figs. 11.6 and 11.7). The following journal entry recounts my experience:

> My uncle went through the compound, taking us on a tour with the authority of an owner—describing his environment. As he remembers it, he uses the present tense: "my childhood bed is here, my soccer pictures here, my mother stands here as she washes the clothes..." He is followed by Maria, the young Greek mother whispering her own, competing narrative of this place: "This was a ruin when we found it. We've worked hard to restore this room, the floor is all new. My daughter was born here." My uncle ends this account abruptly. Making what he considers to be a magnanimous gesture, he announces with a smile: "I give you permission to live here." I watch bewildered—this is Cyprus! (Journal entry by the author, Paramali, Cyprus 2007)

Figure 11.6. Uncle Yalçin visits his ancestral home, pictured with the Greek mother who now lives there, 2007. Photograph © Gülgün Kayim.

Figure 11.7. This is Cyprus! Ruined walls covered with graffiti in the village of Paramali, 2007. Photograph © Gülgün Kayim.

Sites of Performance as Zones of Encounter

We are very careful how we locate ourselves, what we call ourselves in Cyprus. There are immigrants who came here from Turkey—they are Turks—there are right-wing Turkish Cypriot people who call themselves "Turkish Cypriots," and there are people willing to have reunification who call themselves "Turkish speaking Cypriots." (Alkan Muratoğlu, interview with author, Famagusta, May 2007)

The former homes, villages, and neighborhoods abandoned by Greek or Turkish Cypriots during the conflict period are disputed sites that appear to be empty but are full of unresolved memories (see figs. 11.8, 11.9). I understand these places as entangled with meaning, shivering with possibility between the material, the evoked, the remembered, the suggested, the recorded, the experienced, the felt, and the thought.[29] Their very persistence indicates the two communities' refusal to come to some sort of compromise, to do the sort of boundary crossings that are needed for future generations to heal. Yet these ruptures in the landscape offer alternative visions of belonging, conflict, and inhabitation.

Through my artistic work I understand performance as a strategy of survival in the search for belonging. Performance spaces are complex, concrete, emotional environments that simultaneously exist within the physical landscape *and* on the borders of memory and experience. For *Self Portrait ... for now*, because the performance site must symbolically and physically represent the unresolved dispute, the intended setting is the demilitarized zone. Not surprisingly, it has been very difficult to gain access to a building to present the work anywhere in the DMZ. With the opening of the borders, there has been some positive movement. Bi-communal organizations, such as the Association for Historical Dialogue and Research, headquartered at the Ledra Palace Hotel inside the buffer zone in Nicosia, aim to foster and promote dialogue around issues regarding the history of Cyprus and historical education more generally. Until the work can be presented inside the DMZ, I see the *Self Portrait* trilogy, much like its author, as a piece that must remain "homeless" or dislocated: to survive, it must be presented in places far from its source.

My second-generation encounters with unresolved sites of conflict in my homeland offer powerful insights and inspirations to those who wish to cross boundaries. By translating them through my artistic practices in other countries, I have tried to locate performance sites for retelling stories, encountering fragments of memory, and working through the subjectivities resulting from the movements across geopolitical space and through generational time. As was the case for *Untitled #1* and *The Orange Grove*, I seek access to appropriate sites in the settings where I currently live that may open up a dialogue

Figure 11.8. An abandoned Turkish mosque in the city of Limmasol, Greek side, 2007. The Arabic inscription on the grave headstone to the right is in old Turkish and includes a Muslim prayer and the dates and details of the deceased. Photograph © Gülgün Kayim.

Figure 11.9. A Greek home decaying in the Karpas region on the Turkish side of the island, 2005. Photograph © Gülgün Kayim.

with the research and content of the *Self Portrait* trilogy. One such possible location exists in what I call Minnesota's DMZ, at the Fort Snelling area located at the confluence of the Mississippi and Minnesota rivers. Established in 1825 as an outpost of American westward expansion, the fort was, according to the Minnesota Historical Society, in part an effort by the United States 5th Regiment of Infantry and the army to mediate tribal disputes among the local native populations.[30] The fort enabled white settlers to gain a foothold and became the center from which the population expanded to establish St. Paul and Minneapolis. Last used by the military during World War II as a training and processing facility for soldiers on their way to Europe, it was eventually decommissioned and designated a historic landmark by the US Department of Interior in 1960. Since then, much of the fort has been preserved by the Minnesota Historical Society; its interpretive center features performers in historic costumes reenacting the early history of settlement, but a large part of the area still remains empty and abandoned.

For me, the abandoned and weathered buildings located at the fort's upper bluff area are similar to those in the Cyprus DMZ, reminders of violent colonization. Yet the view of the white settlers dominates the narrative at Fort Snelling, while the story of racial violence and loss is hidden from view at the interpretive center. Snelling was once the location of the Dakota Indian internment camp (1862–64), where tribes were marched and "housed" in the wake of a congressional order of 1863 that forcibly removed all Sioux Indians from their tribal lands. This order came on the heels of the Dakota Conflict or Sioux Uprising of 1862, which pitted white settlers against the Mdewakanton and Wahpekute Dakota tribes who lived in the region. Many Native American people who were marched to Fort Snelling experienced great hardship or died during the harsh winters of the internment period; later they were removed to South Dakota reservations. These narratives are visible in the haunted and ruined empty hallways of the Bureau of Indian Affairs building and in those barracks where the refurbishment, cleanup, and costumed performers have not yet colonized the space with reinscriptions of romantic heroic narratives about white settlement.

Such a site resonates with the *Self Portrait* project. Like the Cypriot DMZ, the location is protected by codes and regulations and proves difficult to access for political and logistical reasons. The area is also physically sealed off by a high boundary fence and, as an unorganized territory, remains in the control of the federal government, complicating local oversight and jurisdiction of the area. Thus the abandoned, unresolved buildings of the fort's upper bluff signal their history to those with the tenacity to investigate further. It is in and through these places that performance can activate cultural memory and suggest to local communities their promising multidimensional complexity.

Notes

1. Michal Kobialka, "The Quest for the Self/Other: A Critical Study of Tadeusz Kantor's Theatre," in Tadeusz Kantor, *A Journey through Other Spaces: Essays and Manifestos, 1944–1990*, ed. and trans. Michal Kobialka (Berkeley, 1993), 312.
2. Ibid., 313.
3. Yiannis Papadakis, "The Politics of Memory and Forgetting in Cyprus," *Journal of Mediterranean Studies* 3 (1993): 139–54.
4. Anna Grichting, "From Military Buffers to Transboundary Peace Parks: The Case of Korea and Cyprus," paper presented at Parks, Peace and Partnerships Conference, Alberta, Canada (9–12 September 2007), 5. http://peaceparks2007.whsites.net/Papers/Grichting_Korea%20Cyprus.pdf (accessed 13 June 2010).
5. William Mallinson, *Cyprus: A Modern History*, rev. ed. (London, 2008), 6.
6. James Corum, *Training Indigenous Forces in Counter Insurgency: A Tale of Two Insurgencies* (Carlisle, PA, 2006), 26–27.
7. Christopher Hitchens, *Hostage to History: Cyprus from the Ottomans to Kissinger*, 3rd ed. (London, 1997); and Farid Mirbagheri, *Cyprus and International Peacemaking, 1964–1986*, Part 2 (New York, 1998).
8. Corum, *Training Indigenous Forces*; Hitchens, *Hostage to History*; Mallinson, *Cyprus*, xvii, xx.

9. Hitchens, *Hostage to History*, 47.
10. Corum, *Training Indigenous Forces*, 33.
11. Mallinson, *Cyprus*, 97.
12. Mirbagheri, *Cyprus and International Peacemaking*, 12.
13. Hitchens, *Hostage to History*, 51.
14. Kika Orphanides, "The Cypriot Community in Britain," in *Race and Social Work: A Guide to Training*, ed. Vivienne Combe and Alan Little (London, 1986), 81–88. Cypriot immigration to Britain began shortly after World War II, when some 8,000 Cypriots migrated to London for economic reasons. Numbers increased in the 1950s through the early 1960s, corresponding to the increase in ethnic conflicts in Cyprus, dramatically increasing in 1974 when 10,000 refugees arrived in Britain as a direct result of the Turkish invasion.
15. See Mirbagheri's commentary on the 1959 Treaty of Guarantee and the Treaty of Alliance, *Cyprus and International Peacemaking*, 12, and Hitchens, *Hostage to History*.
16. Nathalie Tocci, *EU Accession and Conflict Resolution: Catalysing Peace or Consolidating Partition in Cyprus* (London, 2004), 32.
17. Andrea Talas, "Green Light: Border Opening in Cyprus," *World Press Review* 50, no. 7 (July 2003), www.worldpress.org/Europe/1124.cfm (accessed 19 June 2010).
18. Kobialka, "The Quest for the Self/Other," 326.
19. Marianne Hirsch, "The Generation of Postmemory." *Poetics Today* 29, no. 1 (2008): 103–12.
20. Gülgün Kayim, "The Orange Grove" (unpublished play script, 2003), 9.
21. Ibid., 1.
22. Yi-Fu Tuan, *Space and Place: The Perspective of Experience*, 2nd ed. (Minneapolis, 2007), 185.
23. Kobialka, "The Quest for the Self/Other"; and Richard Schechner, *Environmental Theater* [1969] (New York, 2000).
24. Mallinson, *Cyprus*, 75.
25. Hirsch, "The Generation of Postmemory."
26. Ibid., 114.
27. Yiannis Papadakis, Nicos Peristianis, and Gisela Welz, *Divided Cyprus: Modernity, History, and an Island in Conflict* (Bloomington, IN, 2006), 2 and 6.
28. Tuan, *Space and Place*, 32.
29. Karen E. Till, *The New Berlin: Place, Memory, Politics* (Minneapolis, 2005), 8.
30. Minnesota Historical Society website, http://www.mnhs.org/index.htm (accessed 10 June 2010).

Works Cited

Ackermann, Volker. *Der "echte Flüchtling". Deutsche vertriebene und Flüchtlinge aus der DDR 1945 – 1961.* Osnabrück, 1995.

———. "Homo Barackensis – Westdeutsche Flüchtlingslager in den 1950er Jahren." In *Anknüpfungen. Kulturgeschichte – Landesgeschichte – Zeitgeschichte,* ed. Volker Ackermann, Bernd-A. Rusinek, and Falk Wiesemann, 330–46. Essen, 1995.

Adelman, Jeremy, and Stephen Aron. "From Borderlands to Borders: Empires, Nation-States, and the Peoples in Between in North American History." *American Historical Review* 104, no. 3 (June 1999): 814–41.

AfricAvenir International, et al. "Pressemitteilung: Weitere Strassenumbennungen nötig." 20 May 2009. http://blog.derbraunemob.info/2009/05/27/berlin-kreuzberg-re-naming-of-street-in-may-ayim-ufer-umbenennung-des-groebenufers-in-may-ayim-ufer (accessed 2 March 2010).

Agamben, Giorgio. *Ausnahmezustand (Homo sacer II.I).* Frankfurt am Main, 2004.

———. *Homo sacer. Die souveräne Macht und das nackte Leben.* Frankfurt am Main, 2002.

———. *State of Exception.* Trans. Kevin Attell. Chicago, 2005.

Agnew, John A. "Borders on the Mind: Re-Framing Border Thinking." *Ethics and Global Politics* 1, no. 4 (2008): 175–91.

Agnew, John A., Katharyne Mitchell, and Gearóid Ó Tuathail (aka Gerard Toal), eds. *A Companion to Political Geography.* Malden, MA, 2003.

Ahmed, Sara. *The Cultural Politics of Emotion.* New York, 2004.

Alba, Richard, and Victor Nee. "Rethinking Assimilation Theory for a New Era of Immigration." *International Migration Review* 31, no. 4 (1997): 826–75.

Allied Museum Berlin. *The Windsor Park Seminar. Berlin: The British Perspective 1945–1990. 1–2 September 2009, Cumberland Lodge, Windsor Park, London.* Transcript on CD-ROM. Berlin, 2011. http://www.alliiertenmuseum.de/download/windsor_park_seminar.pdf (accessed 11 January 2012).

Alsayyad, Nezar, and Ananya Roy, "Medieval Modernity: On Citizenship and Urbanism in a Global Era," *Space and Polity* 10, no. 1 (2006): 1–20.

Alscher, Stefan. "Country Profile 3: Poland." *Polen. focus Migration*, January 2008. www.focus-migration.de/Poland.2810.0.html?&L=1 (accessed 5 July 2010).

Anderson, Benedict. *Imagined Communities: Reflections on the Origin and Spread of Nationalism* [1983]. London, 1991.

Anderson, Malcolm, and Eberhard Bort, eds. *The Frontiers of Europe*. London, 1999.

Andreas, Peter. "Introduction: The Wall after the Wall." In Andreas and Snyder, eds., *The Wall around the West*, 1–14. Lanham, MD, 2000.

Andreas, Peter, and Timothy Snyder, eds. *The Wall around the West: State Borders and Immigration Controls in North America and Europe*. Lanham, MD, 2000.

Antonsich, Marco, and Phil I. Jones. "Mapping the Swiss Referendum on the Minaret Ban." *Political Geography* 29, no. 2 (2010): 57–62.

Anzaldúa, Gloria. *Borderlands: The New Mestiza = La Frontera*. San Francisco, 1987.

Articles de la grâce accordée par le Roy au duc de Rohan, et autres ses subjects rebelles, de la Religion prétendue réformée, envoyés par S.M. à M. d'Halincourt. Lyon, 1629.

Autze, Rajan. *Treibgut des Krieges. Flüchtlinge und Vertriebene in Berlin 1945*. Munich, 2001.

Bacha, Julia. *Budrus*. Documentary film, 2010.

Bachmann, Klaus. "Von der Euphorie zum Misstrauen: Deutsch-Polnische Beziehungen nach der Wende." *Osteuropa* 50, no. 8 (2000): 853–71.

Bade, Klaus J. *Europa in Bewegung: Migration vom späten 18. Jahrhundert bis zur Gegenwart*. Munich, 2000.

———, ed. *Deutsche im Ausland – Fremde in Deutschland: Migration in Geschichte und Gegenwart*. Munich, 1992.

Bajrami, Hakif. *Rrethanat shoqërore dhe politike në Kosovë më 1918–1941*. Prishtina, 1981.

Balibar, Etienne. "Europe as Borderland." *Environment and Planning D: Society and Space* 27, no. 2 (2009): 190–215.

———. *We, the People of Europe? Reflections on Transnational Citizenship*. Trans. James Swenson. Princeton, 2004.

Barber, Benjamin K. "Epilogue. An Architecture of Liberty? The City as Democracy's Forge." In *Out of Ground Zero: Case Studies in Urban Reinvention*, ed. Joan Ockman, 184–205. New York, 2002.

Barclay, David E. "Benno Ohnesorg, Rudi Dutschke, and the Student Movement in West Berlin: Critical Reflections after Forty Years." In *Berlin: Divided City, 1945–1989*, ed. Philip Broadbent and Sabine Hake, 125–34. New York, 2010.

———. "On the Back Burner – Die USA und West-Berlin 1948–1994." In *Deutschland aus internationaler Sicht*, ed. Tilman Mayer, 25–36. Berlin, 2009.

Barnstone, Deborah Ascher. *The Transparent State: Architecture and Politics in Postwar Germany*. New York, 2005.

Barth, Boris, and Jürgen Osterhammel, eds. *Zivilisierungsmissionen. Imperiale Weltverbesserung seit dem 18. Jahrhundert*. Constance, 2005.

Barthes, Roland. *Mythologies.* Trans. Annette Lavers. New York, 1998.

Bartoszewski, Władisław. "Zadania polskiej polityki zagranicznej w 2001 r., informacja ministra spraw zagranicznych Władisława Bartoszewskiego przedstawiona na forum Sejmu RP 6 czerwca 2001 r" [The tasks for Polish foreign policy. Information of the Foreign Minister Władisław Bartoszewski in Parliament on 6 June 2001]. *Przegląd Rządowy* 7, no. 121 (2001): 91.

Başgöz, Ilhan, and Norman Furniss, eds. *Turkish Workers in Europe: An Interdisciplinary Study.* Bloomington, IN, 1985.

Bauman, Zygmunt. *Liquid Times: Living in an Age of Uncertainty.* Cambridge, UK, 2007.

Bazin, Anne. *Le retour de la question allemande dans la vie politique tchèque.* Paris, 1994.

———. "Produire un récit commun: les commissions d'historiens, acteurs de la reconciliation." In Mink and Neumayer, eds., *L'Europe et ses passés douloureux*, 104–17. Paris, 2007.

Beck, Ulrich. *The Cosmopolitan Vision.* Trans. Ciaran Cronin. Cambridge, UK, 2006.

Behrends, Jan C., Thomas Lindenberger, and Patrice G. Poutrus, eds. *Fremde und Fremd-Sein in der DDR: Zu historischen Ursachen der Fremdenfeindlichkeit in Ostdeutschland.* Berlin, 2003.

Belka, Marek. "Address by Prime Minister Marek Belka at a debate on the 2007–2013 National Development Plan in Warsaw," 20 January 2005. *Materiały i Dokumenty* 1 (2005). http://www.msz.gov.pl/index.php?page=6661&lang_id=en&bulletin_id=16&document=8448 (accessed 14 July 2010).

Bender, Peter. *Wenn es West-Berlin nicht gäbe.* Berlin, 1987.

Benz, Wolfgang, and Barbara Distel, eds. *Der Ort des Terrors. Geschichte der nationalistischen Konzentrationslager.* 9 vols. Munich, 2005–09.

Benz, Wolfgang, and Angelika Königseder, eds. *Das Konzentrationslager Dachau. Geschichte und Wirkung nationalsozialistischer Repression.* Berlin, 2008.

Beránek, Josef. *Jan Sokol: nebát se a nekrást.* Prague, 2003.

Berdahl, Daphne. *Where the World Ended: Re-Unification and Identity in the German Borderland.* Berkeley, 1999.

Berliner Geschichtswerkstatt. *Zwangsarbeit in Berlin 1940–1945.* Erfurt, 2000.

Bernstein, Hilary J. *Between Crown and Community: Politics and Civic Culture in Sixteenth-Century Poitiers.* Ithaca, 2004.

Besteher-Hegenbarth, Axel, Dina Koschorreck, and Bernd M. Scherer, eds. *Das Haus. Die Kulturen. Die Welt. 50 Jahre: Von der Kongresshalle zum Haus der Kulturen der Welt.* Berlin, 2007.

Béthouart, Antoine. *Le Prince Eugène de Savoie: Soldat, Diplomate et Mécène.* Paris, 1975.

Bingen, Dieter. "Vorwort zur deutschen Ausgabe." In Wolff-Powęska and Bingen, *Nachbarn auf Distanz*, viii–ix. Wiesbaden, 2005.

———, ed. *Die Destruktion des Dialogs. Zur innenpolitischen Instrumentalisierung negativer Fremd- und Feindbilder: Polen, Tschechien, Deutschland und die Niederlande im Vergleich, 1900–2005.* Wiesbaden, 2005.

Bingen, Dieter, and Krzystof Malinowski, eds. *Polacy i Niemcy na drodze do partnier-skiego sąsiedztwa. Próba bilansu dziesięcioleca 1989–1998.* Poznan, 2000.

Blaive, Muriel. "De la démocratie tchèque et des 'décrets Beneš.'" In Mink and Neu-mayer, eds. *L'Europe et ses passés douloureux,* 118–27. Paris, 2007.

———. "La démocratie pour les Tchèques: une légitimité politique et une composante identitaire." *Revue d'études comparatives Est-Ouest* 1 (2003): 59–82.

———. "Le 'petit homme tchèque' à la mode socialiste: rupture et continuités depuis 1989." In *Le retour des héros: la reconstitution des mythologies nationales à l'heure du post-communisme,* ed. Korine Amacher and Leonid Heller, 91–115. Geneva, 2010.

———. "République tchèque. La Révolution de velours vue de České Velenice." In *1989 à l'est de l'Europe. Les fêlures d'un mythe fondateur,* ed. Jérôme Heurtaux and Cédric Pellen, 250–71. La Tour d'Aigues, 2009.

———. *Une déstalinisation manquée. Tchécoslovaquie 1956.* Brussels, 2005.

———. "Internationalism, Patriotism, Dictatorship and Democracy: The Czechoslo-vak Communist Party and the Exercise of Power, 1945–1968." *Journal of European Integration History* 13 (2007): 55–68.

Blaive, Muriel, and Georges Mink, eds. *Benešovy dekrety. Budoucnost Evropy a vy-rovnávání se s minulostí.* Prague, 2003.

Blaive, Muriel, and Berthold Molden. *Grenzfälle. Österreichische und tschechische Er-fahrungen am Eisernen Vorhang.* Weitra, 2009; in Czech *Hranice probíhají vodním tokem. Odrazy historie ve vnímání obyvatel Gmündu a Českých Velenic.* Brno, 2010.

Blaneck, Andrea. *Netzwerke und Kooperationen an der deutsch-polnischen Grenze. Un-tersuchungen zum wirtschaftlichen Milieu in der Grenzregion an der Oder.* Münster, 2005.

Blaut, James M. *The Colonizer's Model of the World.* New York, 1993.

Blumi, Isa. "The Commodification of Otherness and the Ethnic Unit in the Balkans: How to Think about Albanians." *East European Politics and Societies* 12, no. 3 (Fall 1998): 527–569.

———. "Defining Social Spaces by Way of Deletion: The Untold Story of Albanian Migration in the Post-war Period." *Journal of Ethnic and Migration Studies* 29, no. 6 (November 2003): 949–65.

Bömelburg, Hans-Jürgen. "Zwischen imperialer Geschichte und Ostmitteleuropa als Geschichtsregion: Oskar Halecki und die polnische 'jagiellonische Idee.'" In Hadler and Mesenhöller, eds., *Vergangene Größe,* 99–133. Leipzig, 2007.

Borneman, John. *After the Wall: East Meets West in the New Berlin.* New York, 1991.

———. *Belonging in the Two Berlins: Kin, State, Nation.* Cambridge, UK, 1992.

Bosetzky, Horst. *West-Berlin. Erinnerungen eines Inselkindes.* Berlin, 2006.

Boym, Svetlana. *The Future of Nostalgia.* New York, 2001.

Bräutigam, Helmut. "Nationalsozialistische Zwangslager in Berlin IV. Fremdarbeiter-lager 1939 bis 1945." In *Berlin-Forschungen,* ed. Wolfgang Ribbe. Vol. 4, 235–80. Berlin, 1989.

————. "Zwangsarbeit in Berlin 1938–1945." In *Zwangsarbeit in Berlin 1938–1945*, ed. Helmut Bräutigam, Doris Fürstenberg, and Bernt Roder, 17–61. Berlin, 2003.

Bräutigam, Helmut, and Oliver C. Gliech. "Nationalsozialistische Zwangslager in Berlin I. Die 'wilden' Konzentrationslager und Folterkeller 1933/34." In *Berlin-Forschungen*, ed. Wolfgang Ribbe. Vol. 2, 141–78. Berlin, 1987.

Breen, Michael. *Law, City, and King: Legal Culture, Municipal Politics, and State Formation in Early-Modern Dijon*. Rochester, NY, 2007.

Briese, Olaf. *Steinzeit. Mauern in Berlin*. Berlin, 2011.

Broadbent, Philip, and Sabine Hake, eds. *Berlin: Divided City 1945–1989*. New York, 2010.

Brown, Chris. "Borders and Identity in International Political Theory." In *Identities, Borders, Orders: Rethinking International Relations Theory*, ed. Mathias Albert, David Jacobson, and Yosef Lapid, 117–36. Minneapolis, 2001.

Brown, Michael. "Sexual Citizenship, Political Obligation and Disease Ecology in Gay Seattle." *Political Geography* 25, no. 8 (2006): 874–98.

Brown, Wendy. *Regulating Aversion: Tolerance in the Age of Identity and Empire*. Princeton, 2006.

————. *Walled States, Waning Sovereignty*. New York, 2010.

Bruinessen, Martin van. *Kurdish Ethno-Nationalism versus Nation-Building States*. Istanbul, 2000.

Brüns, Elke. *Nach dem Mauerfall. Eine Literaturgeschichte der Entgrenzung*. Munich, 2006.

Bryan, Dominic. *Orange Parades: The Politics of Ritual, Tradition and Control*. London, 2000.

Bundesministerium für Verkehr, Bau und Stadtentwicklung. *Leitfaden: Kunst am Bau*. http://www.bmvbs.de/Bauwesen/Baukultur-,1516/Kunst-am-Bau.htm (accessed 20 May 2010).

Cardenas, Sonia. "The Contested Territories of Ceuta and Melilla." *Mediterranean Quarterly* 7, no. 1 (1996): 118–31.

Casey, Edward S. *The Fate of Place: A Philosophical History*. Berkeley, 1997.

Catudal, Honoré M., Jr. *The Diplomacy of the Quadripartite Agreement on Berlin: A New Era in East-West Politics*. Berlin, 1978.

Cavanna, François. *Das Lied der Baba*. Berlin, 1988.

Chakrabarty, Dipesh. *Provincializing Europe*. Princeton, 2000.

Cheah, Pheng, and Bruce Robbins, eds. *Cosmopolitics: Thinking and Feeling beyond the Nation*. Minneapolis, 1998.

Cherny, Andrei. *The Candy Bombers: The Untold Story of the Berlin Airlift and America's Finest Hour*. New York, 2008.

Chin, Rita. *The Guestworker Question in Postwar Germany*. New York, 2007.

Cimoszewicz, Włodzimierza. "Podstawie kierunki polskiej polityki zagranicznej, Informacja ministra spraw zagranicznych Włodzimierza Cimoszewicza przedstawiona na forum Seijmu RP 14 marca 2002 r" [Basic directions of Polish foreign policy.

Information of the Foreign Minister Włodzimierz Cimoszewicz in Parliament on 14 March 2002]. *Przegląd Rządowy* 5, no. 131 (2002): 130.

———. "Polska polityka zagraniczna w 2004 r. Informacja rządu przedstawiona przez ministra spraw zagranicznych RP Włodzimierza, Sejm RP, 21 stycznia 2004 r" [Polish foreign policy in 2004. Government information presented by Foreign Minister Włodzimierz Cimoszewicz in Parliament on 21 January 2004]. *Przegląd Rządowy* 2, no. 152 (2004): 109.

Clifford, James. "Travelling Cultures." In *Cultural Studies*, ed. Lawrence Grossberg, Cary Nelson, and Paula Treichler, 96–112. New York, 1992.

Cœuré, Sabine, and Sandrine Dullin, eds. *Frontières du communisme. Mythologies et réalités de la division de l'Europe de la révolution d'Octobre au mur de Berlin*. Paris, 2007.

Cohn-Bendit, Daniel, and Thomas Schmid. *Heimat Babylon*. Hamburg, 1993.

Coleman, Mathew. "Immigration Geopolitics beyond the Mexico-US Border." *Antipode* 38, no. 1 (2007): 54–76.

———. "U.S. Statecraft and the U.S.-Mexico Border as Security/Economic Nexus." *Political Geography* 24, no. 2 (2005): 185–209.

Connolly, William E. *Identity/Difference: Democratic Negotiations of Political Paradox*. Minneapolis, 1991.

Corum, James. *Training Indigenous Forces in Counter Insurgency: A Tale of Two Insurgencies*. Carlisle, PA, 2006.

Council of the European Union. Brussels European Council 19/20 March 2009, "Presidency Conclusions," 7880/09. Brussels, 20 March 2008.

———. "Joint Declaration of the Prague Eastern Partnership Summit," 7 May 2009. http://www.eu2009.cz/event/1/3555/ (accessed November 2009).

Daum, Andreas W. "America's Berlin, 1945–2000: Between Myths and Visions." In *Berlin: The New Capital in the East. A Transatlantic Appraisal*, ed. Frank Trommler, 49–73. Washington, DC, 2000.

———. *Kennedy in Berlin*. Trans. Dona Geyer. New York, 2008.

Davies, Norman. *Europe: A History*. New York, 1996.

———. *God's Playground: A History of Poland*. 2 vols. Oxford, 1981.

Davis, Janice. "5 Reasons Theatricality Will Boost Retail Sales." *Display & Design Ideas* 21, no. 11 (2009): 17.

Davis, Mike. *Magical Urbanism: Latinos Reinvent the U.S. City*. New York, 2000.

Debord, Guy. *The Society of the Spectacle*. Trans. Donald Nicholson-Smith. New York, 1995.

de Certeau, Michel. *The Practice of Everyday Life* [1980]. Trans. Stephen Rendall. Berkeley, 1984.

DeJean, Joan E. *Literary Fortifications: Rousseau, Laclos, Sade*. Princeton, 1984.

Delanty, Gerard. "Borders in a Changing Europe: Dynamics of Openness and Closure." *Comparative European Politics* 4, no. 2–3 (2006): 183–202.

Delius, Friedrich Christian, and Peter Joachim Lapp. *Transit Westberlin. Erlebnisse im Zwischenraum*. 2nd ed. Berlin, 2000.

Demps, Laurenz. *Zwangsarbeit und Zwangsarbeiterlager in der faschistischen Reichshauptstadt Berlin 1939–1945*. Berlin, 1986.

Derrida, Jacques. *Rogues: Two Essays on Reason*. Trans. Pascale-Anne Brault and Michael Naas. Stanford, 2005.

Deutscher Bundestag. "Stenographischer Bericht, 40. Sitzung, Bonn, Freitag, den 7. Mai 1999." *Plenarprotokoll 14/40* (1999).

———, ed. *Blickpunkt Bundestag. Sonderthema: Kunst im Bundestag* (2007). https://www.btg-bestellservice.de/pdf/40128800.pdf (accessed 20 May 2010).

"Deutsch-polnischer Grenzvertrag." *Bulletin des Presse- und Informationsamtes der Bundesregierung* 134 (16 November 1990): 1394.

"Deutsch-polnischer Nachbarschaftsvertrag." *Bulletin des Presse- und Informationsamtes der Bundesregierung* 68 (18 June 1991): 541–46.

Diener, Alexander C., and Joshua Hagen, eds. *Borderlines and Borderlands: Political Oddities at the Edge of the Nation-State*. Lanham, MD, 2010.

Die neue europäische Fama. Leipzig, 1735.

DITIB. "Dachverband Türkisch-Islamische Union der Anstalt für Religion e.V." Cologne, n.d.

———. "Der Moscheebau in Köln-Ehrenfeld. Gemeindezentrum mit Moschee." Cologne, 2007, and new edition 2008.

Dodds, Dinah, and Pam Allen-Thompson, eds. *The Wall in My Backyard: East German Women in Transition*. Amherst, 1994.

Döring, Jörg, and Tristan Thielmann. "Einleitung: Was lesen wir im Raume? Der Spatial Turn und das geheime Wissen der Geographen." In *Spatial Turn. Das Raumparadigma in den Kultur- und Sozialwissenschaften*, ed. Jörg Döring and Tristan Thielmann, 7–45. Bielefeld, 2008.

d'Orléans, Charlotte-Elizabeth. *Life and Letters of Charlotte Elizabeth*. London, 1889.

Dörner, Bernward. "Ein KZ in der Mitte der Stadt: Oranienburg." In *Terror ohne System. Die ersten Konzentrationslager im Nationalsozialismus*, ed. Wolfgang Benz and Barbara Distel, 123–38. Berlin, 2001.

Doßmann, Axel. "Barackenlager. Zur Nutzung einer Architektur der Moderne." In *Auszug aus dem Lager. Zur Überwindung des modernen Raumparadigmas in der politischen Philosophie*, ed. Ludger Schwarte, 220–45. Berlin, 2007.

Doßmann, Axel, Jan Wenzel, and Kai Wenzel. *Architektur auf Zeit. Baracken, Pavillons, Container*. Berlin 2006.

Dowler, Lorraine. "In the Shadow of the Berlin Wall: The Peace-Lines of Belfast, Northern Ireland." *Political Geography* 31 (forthcoming 2012).

Driessen, Henk. *On the Spanish-Moroccan Frontier: A Study in Ritual, Power and Ethnicity*. New York, 1992.

Dullin, Sandrine. "Les protecteurs. Le rôle des gardes-frontières dans la surveillance des frontières occidentales de l'URSS (1917–1939)." In Cœuré and Dullin, *Frontières du communisme*, 379–405. Paris, 2007.

"Eastern Europe – Central Europe – Europe." Special issue, *Daedalus* 119, no. 1 (1990).

"Eastern Partnership. Polish-Swedish Non-Paper." May 2008, www.msz.gov.pl/files/ PARTNERSTWO%20WSCHODNIE/1en.pdf (accessed 14 July 2010).

Eckert, Astrid M. "Greetings from the Zonal Border": Tourism to the Iron Curtain in West Germany." *Zeithistorische Forschungen* 1 (2011): 9-36.

Effner, Bettina. "'Eines der größten Wohnungsbauprojekte in Berlin'. Zur Gründungsgeschichte des Notaufnahmelagers Marienfelde." *Mitteilungen des Vereins für die Geschichte Berlins* 102, no. 1 (2006): 290–96.

Ehrkamp, Patricia. "The Limits of Multicultural Tolerance? Liberal Democracy and Media Portrayals of Muslim Migrant Women in Germany." *Space and Polity* 14, no. 1 (2010): 13–32.

———. "'We Turks Are No Germans': Assimilation Discourses and the Dialectical Construction of Identities in Germany." *Environment and Planning A* 38, no. 9 (2006): 1673–92.

Ehrkamp, Patricia, and Helga Leitner. "Beyond National Citizenship: Turkish Immigrants and the (Re)Construction of Citizenship in Germany." *Urban Geography* 24, no. 2 (2003): 127–46.

Ehrlich, Ernst Ludwig. "Ghetto." In *Lexikon für Theologie und Kirche*. Vol. 4. Freiburg, 1960.

Elden, Stuart. *Understanding Henri Lefebvre: Theory and the Possible.* London, 2004.

Elkins, T. H., and B. Hofmeister. *Berlin: The Spatial Structure of a Divided City.* New York, 1988.

Endlich, Stefanie, and Wolf Kaiser. "KZ-Häftlinge in der Reichshauptstadt. Außenlager in Berlin." *Dachauer Hefte* 12 (1996): 230–54.

Erler, Peter, and Thomas Friedrich. *Das sowjetische Speziallager Nr. 3 Berlin-Höhenschönhausen (Mai 1945 bis Oktober 1946).* Berlin, 1995.

Eshelman, Raoul. *Performatism, or the End of Postmodernism.* Aurora, CO, 2008.

EU Commission. Commission Staff Working Document accompanying the Communication from the Commission to the European Parliament and Council, "Eastern Partnership," SEC (2008) 2974. Brussels, 3 December 2008.

———. Communication from the Commission to the European Parliament and Council, "Eastern Partnership," SEC (2008) 2974/ COM (2008) 823 final. Brussels, 3 December 2008.

———. Communication from the Commission, "Wider Europe – Neighbourhood. A Framework for Relations with our Eastern and Southern Neighbours." COM (2003) 104 final. Brussels, 11 March 2003.

———. "European Neighbourhood Policy. Strategy Paper." COM (2004) 373 final. Brussels, 12 May 2004.

———. Mission Report. "Technical Mission to Morocco. Visit to Ceuta and Melilla. On Illegal Immigration." 7–11 October 2005.

Evans, Sterling, ed. *The Borderlands of the American and Canadian Wests: Essays on Regional History of the Forty-Ninth Parallel.* Lincoln, NE, 2006.

Fallois, Joseph de. *L'École de la Fortification ou les éléments de la fortification permanente, régulière et irrégulière.* Dresden, 1768.

Favier, René. *Les Villes du Dauphiné aux XVIIe et XVIIIe Siècles: La Pierre et l'Ecrit.* Grenoble, 1993.

Fekete, Liz. "Anti-Muslim Racism and the European Security State." *Race and Class* 46, no. 1 (2004): 3–29.

Ferrer-Gallardo, Xavier. "The Spanish-Moroccan Border Complex: Processes of Geopolitical, Functional and Symbolic Rebordering." *Political Geography* 27, no. 3 (2008): 301–21.

———. "Territorial (Dis)continuity Dynamics between Ceuta and Morocco: Conflictual Fortification vis-à-vis Cooperative Interaction at the EU Border in Africa." *Tijdschrift voor Economische en Sociale Geografie* 102, no. 1 (2011): 24–38.

Fierro, Annette. *The Glass State: The Technology of the Spectacle, Paris 1981–1998.* Cambridge, MA, 2003.

Filsinger, Dieter, Franz Hamburger, and Dieter Neubert. "Multikulturelles Nürnberg." *Zeitung des Ausländerbeirates* 6 (October 1983): 3.

Fisher, Jaimey, and Barbara Mennel, eds. *Spatial Turns: Space, Place, and Mobility in German Literary and Visual Culture.* Amsterdam, 2010.

Fitzpatrick, Sheila. *Everyday Stalinism. Ordinary Life in Extraordinary Times: Soviet Russia in the 1930s.* Oxford, 1999.

Foner, Nancy. "Immigrant Commitment to America, Then and Now: Myths and Realities." *Citizenship Studies* 5, no. 1 (2001): 27–40.

Foucault, Michel. *Discipline and Punish: The Birth of the Prison* [1975]. Trans. Alan Sheridan. New York, 1977 (1995).

Franck, Julia. *Lagerfeuer.* Cologne, 2003.

Freudenstein, Roland. "Poland, Germany and the EU." *International Affairs* 74, no. 1 (1998): 41–54.

Friedberg, Anne. *Window Shopping: Cinema and the Postmodern.* Berkeley, 1994.

Friese, Heidrun. "Spaces of Hospitality." *Angelaki: Journal of the Theoretical Humanities* 9, no. 2 (2004): 67–79.

Fritz Bauer Institut. *Überlebt und unterwegs. Jüdische Displaced Persons im Nachkriegsdeutschland.* Frankfurt am Main, 1997.

Funder, Anna. *Stasiland.* London, 2003.

Geppert, Dominik. "'Proclaim Liberty throughout All the Land': Berlin and the Symbolism of the Cold War." In *The Postwar Challenge: Cultural, Social, and Political Change in Western Europe, 1945–1958,* ed. Dominik Geppert, 339–63. Oxford, 2003.

Geremek, Bronisława. "Kierunki polskiej polityki zagranicznej. Informacja rządu przedstawiona przez ministra sprwa zagranicznych Bronisława Geremeka podczas posiedzenia Sejmu RP, 9 maja 2000 r" [Directions of the Polish foreign policy. Government information presented by Foreign Minister Bronisław Geremek in Parliament on 9 May 2000]. *Przegląd Rządowy* 5, no. 107 (2000): 62.

Gerhardt, Sebastian. *Polska Polityka Wschodnia. Die Außenpolitik der polnischen Regierung von 1989 bis 2004 gegenüber den östlichen Nachbarstaaten Polens (Russland, Litauen, Weißrussland, Ukraine).* Marburg, 2007.

Gerstenberger, Katharina. *Writing the New Berlin: The German Capital in Post-Wall Literature.* Rochester, NY, 2008.

Geyer, David C. "The Missing Link: Henry Kissinger and the Back-Channel Negotiations on Berlin." In *American Détente and German Ostpolitik, 1969–1972,* ed. David C. Geyer and Bernd Schaefer. Bulletin of the German Historical Institute, Supplement 1, 80–97. Washington, DC, 2004.

———, ed. *Germany and Berlin, 1969–1972.* Vol. 40 of *Foreign Relations of the United States 1969–1976.* Washington, DC, 2007.

Geyer, David C., and Douglas E. Selvage, eds. *Soviet-American Relations: The Détente Years, 1969–1972.* Washington, DC, 2007.

Goethe, Johann Wolfgang von. *Elective Affinities.* Trans. R. J. Hollingdale. Harmondsworth, 1971.

———. *Hermann and Dorothea.* Trans. Daniel Coogan. New York, 1966.

Gökarıksel, Banu, and Katharyne Mitchell. "Veiling, Secularism, and the Neoliberal Subject: National Narratives and Supranational Desires in Turkey and France." *Global Networks* 5, no. 2 (2005): 147–65.

Göktürk, Deniz, David Gramling, and Anton Kaes, eds. *Germany in Transit: Nation and Migration, 1955–2005.* Berkeley, 2007.

Gold, Peter. *Europe or Africa? A Contemporary Study of the Spanish North African Enclaves of Ceuta and Melilla.* Liverpool, 2000.

Gómez-Peña, Guillermo. *Dangerous Border Crossers.* New York, 2000.

———. *Homo Fronterizus.* Cinematographer Gustavo Vazquez. Two-part performance video, 2008.

———. *The New World Border: Prophecies, Poems and Loqueras for the End of the Century.* San Francisco, 1996.

Gordon, Milton Myron. *Assimilation in American Life: The Role of Race, Religion, and National Origins.* New York, 1964.

Grabbe, Heather. "Poland: The EU's New Awkward Partner." *Bulletin of the Centre of European Reform,* February/March 2004. www.cer.org.uk/articles/34_grabbe.html (accessed February 2009).

———. "The Sharp Edges of Europe: Extending Schengen Eastwards." *International Affairs* 76, no. 3 (2000): 519–36.

Grathwol, Robert P., and Donita M. Moorhus. *American Forces in Berlin: Cold War Outpost, 1945–1994.* Washington, DC, 1994.

———. *Berlin and the American Military: A Cold War Chronicle.* New York, 1999.

Gregory, Derek. *The Colonial Present: Afghanistan, Palestine, Iraq.* Cambridge, MA, 2004.

———. "Geography and the Cartographic Anxiety." In *Geographical Imaginations,* 70–205. Cambridge, MA, 1994.

Grichting, Anna. "From Military Buffers to Transboundary Peace Parks: The Case of Korea and Cyprus." Paper presented at Parks, Peace and Partnerships Conference, Alberta, Canada (9–12 September 2007). http://peaceparks2007.whsites.net/Papers/Grichting_Korea%20Cyprus.pdf (accessed 13 June 2010).

Grillon, Pierre. *Les Papiers de Richelieu: Section Politique Intérieure, Correspondance et Papiers d'État* [1629]. Vol. 4. Paris, 1980.

Grimberg, Klaus. "The Cold War in Architecture." *The Atlantic Times*, September 2007.

Groth, Klaus-Martin, and Johann Müller-Gazurek. *Ausländer-Sozialrecht*. Frankfurt am Main, 1983.

Gruner, Wolf. *Judenverfolgung in Berlin 1933–1945. Eine Chronologie der Behördenmaßnahmen in der Reichhauptstadt*. Berlin, 1996.

Hadler, Frank, and Mathias Mesenhöller. "Repräsentationen imperialer Erfahrung in Ostmitteleuropa: Einleitende Thesen zu Konzept, Befunden und einer transnationalen Perspektive." In Hadler and Mesenhöller, eds., *Vergangene Größe*, 11–32. Leipzig, 2007.

———, eds. *Vergangene Größe und Ohnmacht in Ostmitteleuropa: Repräsentationen imperialer Erfahrungen in der Historiographie seit 1918*. Leipzig, 2007.

Halévy, Daniel. *Vauban*. Paris, 1923.

Hall, Stuart S. "Cultural Identity and Diaspora." In *Identity: Community, Culture, Difference*, ed. Jonathan Rutherford, 222–37. London, 1990.

———. "Old and New Identities, Old and New Ethnicities" [1991]. In *Culture, Globalization and the World-System: Contemporary Conditions for the Representation of Identity*, ed. Anthony D. King, 41–68. Minneapolis, 1997.

Hamilton, Keith, Patrick Salmon, and Stephen Twigge, eds. *Documents on British Policy Overseas, Series III, vol. 6: Berlin in the Cold War, 1948–1990*. London, 2009.

Hansen, Thomas Blom, and Finn Stepputat, eds. *Sovereign Bodies: Citizens, Migrants, and States in the Postcolonial World*. Princeton, 2005.

Haraway, Donna. *Simians, Cyborgs and Women: The Reinvention of Nature*. New York, 1991.

———. "Situated Knowledges: The Science Question in Feminism and the Privilege of Partial Perspective." *Feminist Studies* 14, no. 3 (1988): 575–99.

Heffernan, Michael. *The European Geographical Imagination*. Stuttgart, 2007.

Hegel, G. W. F. *Philosophy of Right*. Trans. S. W. Dyde. Kitchener, ON, 2001.

Heidenfelder, Gabriele. *From Duppel to Truman Plaza: Die Berlin American Community in den Jahren 1965 bis 1989*. Hamburg, 1998.

Heinemann, Winfried. "Die Doppelfunktion der DDR-Grenztruppen." Unpublished paper presented at German Studies Association, 10 October 2009, Washington, DC.

Henrikson, Alan K. "Facing Across Borders: The Diplomacy of Bon Voisinage." *International Political Science Review* 21, no. 2 (2000): 121–47.

Herbert, Ulrich. *A History of Foreign Labor in Germany, 1880–1980: Seasonal Workers, Forced Laborers, Guest Workers*. Ann Arbor, 1990.

Heß, Hans-Jürgen. *Unter der Kuppel*. Berlin, 1999.

Hetherington, Kevin. *Capitalism's Eye: Cultural Spaces of the Commodity*. New York, 2007.

Hillenbrand, Martin J., ed. *The Future of Berlin*. Montclair, NJ, 1980.

Hirsch, Marianne. "The Generation of Postmemory." *Poetics Today* 29, no. 1 (2008): 103–28.

Hitchens, Christopher. *Hostage to History: Cyprus from the Ottomans to Kissinger.* 3rd ed. London, 1997.

Hoffmann-Axthelm, Dieter. *Der Große Jüdenhof. Ein Berliner Ort und das Verhältnis von Juden und Christen in der deutschen Stadt des Mittelalters.* Berlin, 2005.

Holland-Moritz, Detlef, and Gabriela Wachter, eds. *war jewesen. West-Berlin 1961–89.* Berlin, 2009.

Honig, Bonnie. *Emergency Politics: Paradox, Law, Democracy.* Princeton, 2009.

Houtum, Henk van, Olivier Kramsch, and Wolfgang Zierhofer, eds. *B/ordering Space.* Aldershot, UK, 2005.

Hrdlicka, Manuela R. *Alltag im KZ. Das Lager Sachsenhausen bei Berlin.* Opladen, 1991.

Hübner, Klaus. *Einsatz. Erinnerungen des Berliner Polizeipräsidenten 1969–1987.* Berlin, 1997.

Hüwe, Josef. "Sechzig Jahre Grundgesetz – und unerledigte Aufträge." *Humane Wirtschaft* (April 2009): 38–40.

Huyssen, Andreas. "Diaspora and Nation: Migration into Other Pasts." *New German Critique* 88 (2003): 147–64.

———. *Present Pasts: Urban Palimpsests and the Politics of Memory.* Stanford, 2003.

Ireland, Patrick. *Becoming Europe: Immigration, Integration, and the Welfare State.* Pittsburgh, 2008.

Isin, Engin F. *Being Political: Genealogies of Citizenship.* Minneapolis, 2002.

Islami, Hivzi. *Rrjedha demografike shqiptare.* Pejë, 1994.

Jackson, John Brinckerhoff. *Discovering the Vernacular Landscape.* New Haven, 1984.

Jameson, Fredric. *Postmodernism, or, The Cultural Logic of Late Capitalism.* Durham, NC, 1991.

Jamin, Mathilde. "Die deutsche Anwerbung: Organisation und Grössenordnung/Almanya'nın yabancı iş gücü alımı: organizasyonu ve boyutları." In *Fremde Heimat: Eine Geschichte der Einwanderung aus der Türkei/Yaban Sılan Olur: Türkiye'den Almanya'ya Göçün Tarihi,* ed. Aytaç Eryılmaz and Mathilde Jamin, 149–70. Essen, 1998.

Janowski, Maciej. "Pitfalls and Opportunities: The Concept of East Central Europe as a Tool of Historical Analysis." *European Review of History* 6, no. 1 (1999): 91–100.

Jarausch, Konrad, ed. *Dictatorship as Experience: Towards a Socio-Cultural History of the GDR.* New York, 1999.

Jarman, Neil. "Diversity, Economy and Policy: New Patterns of Migration to Northern Ireland," *Shared Space: A Research Journal on Peace, Conflict and Community Relations in Northern Ireland* 2 (2006): 45–62.

Jarosinski, Eric. "Building on a Metaphor: Democracy, Transparency, and the Berlin Reichstag." In *Berlin: The Symphony Continues. Orchestrating Architectural, Social, and Artistic Change in Germany's New Capital,* ed. Carol Anne Costabile-Heming, Rachel J. Halverson, and Kristie A. Foell, 59–76. Berlin, 2004.

Jenkins, William. "Between the Lodge and the Meeting House: Mapping Irish Protestant Identities and Social Worlds in Late Victorian Toronto." *Social and Cultural Geography* 4, no. 1 (2003): 75–98.

Jeschonnek, Friedrich, Dieter Riedel, and William Durie. *Alliierte in Berlin 1945–1994. Ein Handbuch zur Geschichte der militärischen Präsenz der Westmächte.* 2nd ed. Berlin, 2007.

Jílková, Alena, and Tomáš Jílek, eds. *Železná opona. Československá státní hranice od Jáchymova po Bratislavu 1948–1989.* Prague, 2006.

Jobst, Kerstin. *Die Perle des Imperiums. Der russische Krim-Diskurs im Zarenreich.* Constance, 2007.

Johnson, Corey, Reece Jones, Anssi Paasi, Louise Amoore, Alison Mountz, Mark Salter, and Chris Rumford. "Interventions on Rethinking 'the Border' in Border Studies." *Political Geography* 30 (2011): 61–69.

Jones, Colin. *Paris: Biography of a City.* London, 2004.

Justi, Johann Heinrich Gottlob von. *Staatswirtschaft.* Leipzig, 1758.

Kaernbach, Andreas. "Dani Karavan: Grundgesetz 49." In *Kunst am Bau. Die Projekte des Bundes in Berlin,* ed. Bundesministerium für Verkehr, Bau- und Wohnungswesen, 34. Berlin, 2002.

———. "Vom Grundgesetz an der Spree zur planetarischen Utopie." *Die Politische Meinung* 416 (July 2004): 85–87.

Kafka, Franz. *The Trial.* Trans. Willa and Edwin Muir. New York, 1968.

Karavan, Dani. "Where Is Dani Karavan?" Artnet Questionnaire (8 May 2008). www.artnet.de/magazine/dani-karavan-artnet-questionnaire-de/ (accessed 15 February 2010).

Kastoryano, Riva. *Negotiating Identities: States and Immigrants in France and Germany.* Trans. Barbara Harshav. Princeton, 2002.

Kayim, Gülgün. *The Orange Grove.* Unpublished play script, 2003.

Keithly, David M. *Breakthrough in the Ostpolitik: The 1971 Quadripartite Agreement.* Boulder, CO, 1986.

Kimmel, Elke. "Das Notaufnahmeverfahren." In *Flucht im geteilten Deutschland. Erinnerungsstätte Notaufnahmelager Marienfelde,* ed. Bettina Effner and Helge Heidemeyer, 115–34. Berlin, 2005.

Klusmeyer, Douglas. "A 'Guiding Culture' for Immigrants? Integration and Diversity in Germany." *Journal of Ethnic and Migration Studies* 27, no. 3 (2001): 519–32.

Kobialka, Michal, "The Quest for the Self/Other: A Critical Study of Tadeusz Kantor's Theatre." In Tadeusz Kantor, *A Journey through Other Spaces: Essays and Manifestos, 1944–1990,* ed. and trans. Michal Kobialka, 267–364. Berkeley, 1993.

Kochanowski, Jerzy. "Paradoxien der Erinnerung an die Ostgebiete." *Inter Finitimos* 3 (2005): 61–76.

Kocka, Jürgen. "The GDR: A Special Kind of Modern Dictatorship." In Jarausch, *Dictatorship as Experience,* 17–27. New York, 1999.

Koenen, Gerd. *Was war der Kommunismus?* Göttingen, 2010.

Koepnick, Lutz. *Framing Attention: Windows on Modern German Culture*. Baltimore, 2007.

Kolář, Pavel. "Sozialistische Diktatur als Sinnwelt. Repräsentationen gesellschaftlicher Ordnung und Herrschaftswandel in Ostmitteleuropa in der zweiten Hälfte des 20. Jahrhunderts." *Potsdamer Bulletin für Zeithistorische Studien* 40/41 (2007): 24–29.

Kolossov, Vladimir. "Theorizing Borders. Border Studies: Changing Perspectives and Theoretical Approaches," *Geopolitics* 10 (2005): 606–32.

Königseder, Angelika. "Das Lager für 'Displaced Persons' in Mariendorf." In *Tempelhofer Ansichten*, ed. Matthias Heisig and Sylvia Walleczek, 39–57. Berlin, 2002.

———. *Flucht nach Berlin. Jüdische Displaced Persons 1945–1948*. Berlin, 1998.

Königseder, Angelika, and Juliane Wetzel, eds. *Lebensmut im Wartesaal. Die jüdischen DPs (Displaced Persons) im Nachkriegsdeutschland*. Frankfurt am Main, 1994.

Kraft, Claudia, and Katrin Steffen, eds. *Europas Platz in Polen. Polnische Europakonzeptionen vom Mittelalter bis zum EU-Beitritt*. Osnabrück, 2007.

Krishna, Sankaran. "Boundaries in Question." In Agnew, Mitchell, and Tuathail, eds., *A Companion to Political Geography*, 302–14. Malden, MA, 2003.

Krzemiński, Adam. *Testfall für Europa: Deutsch-polnische Nachbarschaft muss gelingen*. Hamburg, 2008.

Krzoska, Markus. "Die Renaissance der piastischen Idee. Der polnische Raumdiskurs in der ersten Hälfte des 20. Jahrhunderts." In *Amicus Poloniae. Teksty ofiarowane Profesorowi Heinrichowi Kunstmannowi w osiemdziesiątą piątą rocznicę urodzin*, ed. Krzysztof Ruchniewicz and Marek Zybura, 235–48. Wrocław, 2009.

———. *Für ein Polen an Oder und Ostsee. Zygmunt Wojciechowski (1900–1955) als Historiker und Publizist*. Osnabrück, 2003.

Kundera, Milan. "Un occident kidnappé ou la tragédie de l'Europe centrale." *Le débat* (November 1983). In English: "A Kidnapped West or a Culture Bows Out." *Granta* 11 (1984) and "The Tragedy of Central Europe." *New York Review of Books*, 26 April 1984.

Kunze, Gerhard. *Grenzerfahrungen. Kontakte und Verhandlungen zwischen dem Land Berlin und der DDR 1949–1989*. Berlin, 1999.

Kwaśniewski, Aleksander. "Address by President of the Republic of Poland Aleksander Kwasniewski during his visit to the Federal Republic of Germany on 26 February 2005," *Materiały i Dokumenty* 2 (2005). http://www.msz.gov.pl/index.php?page=6662&lang_id=en&bulletin_id=16&document=8448http:// (accessed 14 July 2010).

———. "Wykład prezydenta Polski Aleksandra Kwaśniewskiego 'Ewolucja środowiska międzynarodowego – szanse i zagrożenia' podczas spotkania zorganizowanego prez Genewski Klub Dyplomatyczny" [Lecture by the Polish President Aleksander Kwaśniewski: "The development of the international environment – chances and threats" during a meeting organized by the Geneva Diplomatic Club], Geneva, 22 May 2001. *Zbiór dokumentów* 57, no. 2 (2001): 14–22 (excerpts).

Ladd, Brian. *The Ghosts of Berlin: Confronting German History in the Urban Landscape*. Chicago, 1997.

La Mare, Nicolas de. *Traité de la Police*. Amsterdam, 1729.

Lavedan, Pierre. *Histoire de l'Urbanisme á Paris, Nouvelle Histoire de Paris*. Paris, 1993.

Leech-Anspach, Gabriele. *Insel vor der Insel. Ein kleiner Ort im kalten Krieg: Berlin-Steinstücken*. Potsdam, 2005.

Lefebvre, Henri. *The Production of Space* [1974]. Trans. Donald Nicolson-Smith. Cambridge, MA, 1991.

———. *The Survival of Capitalism: Reproduction of the Relations of Production*. Trans. Frank Bryant. New York, 1976.

Leitner, Helga. "The Political Economy of International Labor Migration." In *A Companion to Economic Geography*, ed. E. Sheppard and T. Barnes, 450–67. Malden, MA, 2000.

Leitner, Olaf, ed. *West-Berlin! Westberlin! Berlin (West)! Die Kultur – die Szene – die Politik. Erinnerungen an eine Teilstadt der 70er und 80er Jahre*. Berlin, 2002.

Lengsfeld, Vera. "Zuwanderung versus Familienpolitik? Zur Gefahr politischer Glaubensbekenntnisse." In *Vera Lengsfeld, Mitglied des Deutschen Bundestages (CDU). Texte und Reden*. Webarchiv Bundestag, 2002. http://webarchiv.bundestag.de/archive/2005/0204/mdbhome/LengsVe0/reden_lengsfeld.htm (accessed 21 February 2010).

Levi, Primo. *The Drowned and the Saved*. Trans. Raymond Rosenthal. New York, 1988.

Lindenberger, Thomas. "Creating State Socialist Governance: The Case of the Deutsche Volkspolizei." In Jarausch, *Dictatorship as Experience*, 125–41. New York, 1999.

———. "Die Diktatur der Grenzen. Zur Einleitung." In *Herrschaft und Eigen-Sinn in der Diktatur. Studien zur Gesellschaftsgeschichte der DDR*, ed. Thomas Lindenberger, 13–44. Cologne, 1999.

———. "The Fragmented Society: 'Societal Activism' and Authority in GDR State Socialism." *Zeitgeschichte* 37, no. 1 (2010): 3–20.

———. "Tacit Minimal Consensus: The Always Precarious East German Dictatorship." In *Popular Opinion in Totalitarian Regimes*, ed. Paul Corner, 208–22. Oxford, 2009.

Loew, Peter Oliver. "Feinde, überall Feinde. Psychogramm eines Problems in Polen." *Osteuropa* 56, no. 11/12 (2006): 33–51.

Lorenzen, Rudolf. *Paradies zwischen den Fronten. Reportagen und Glossen aus Berlin (West)*. Berlin, 2009.

Lüdtke, Alf. "'Helden der Arbeit' – Mühen beim Arbeiten. Zur mißmutigen Loyalität von Industriearbeitern in der DDR." In *Sozialgeschichte der DDR*, ed. Hartmut Kaelble, Jürgen Kocka, and Hartmut Zwahr, 188–213. Stuttgart, 1994.

———. "La République démocratique allemande comme histoire. Réflexions historiographiques." *Annales* (January–February 1998): 3–39.

———, ed. *The History of Everyday Life: Reconstructing Historical Experiences and Ways of Life*. Princeton, 1995.

Luibhéid, Eithne. "Sexual Regimes and Migration Controls: Reproducing the Irish Nation-State in Transnational Contexts." *Feminist Review* 83 (2006): 60–78.

Luža, Radomír. *The Transfer of the Sudeten Germans: A Study of Czech-German Relations, 1933–1962*. New York, 1964.

Lynn, John A. "A Brutal Necessity? The Devastation of the Palatinate, 1688–1689." In *Civilians in the Path of War*, ed. Mark Grimsley and Clifford J. Rogers, 79–110. Lincoln, NE, 2002.

"Magistratsbeschluß 23. Dezember 1945." In *Die Sitzungsprotokolle des Magistrats der Stadt Berlin 1945/46*, ed. Dieter Hanauske. Vol. 1, 742. Berlin, 1995.

Major, Patrick. *Behind the Berlin Wall: East Germany and the Frontiers of Power*. New York, 2010.

Makarska, Renata, and Basil Kerski, eds. *Die Ukraine, Polen und Europa. Europäische Identität an der neuen Ostgrenze*. Osnabrück, 2004.

Malcolm, Noel. *Kosovo: A Short History*. New York, 1999.

Mallet, Allain Manesson. *Kriegsarbeit oder Neuer Festungsbau*. Trans. Filip von Zesen. Amsterdam, 1672.

Mallinson, William. *Cyprus: A Modern History*. Rev. ed. London, 2008.

Maloney, Sean M. "Notfallplanung für Berlin: Vorläufer der Flexible Response 1958–1963." *Militärgeschichte* NF (1997): 3–15.

Malzahn, Claus Christian. *Über Mauern. Warum das Leben im Schatten des Schutzwalls eine sonnige Sache war*. Berlin, 2009.

Mandel, Ruth. *Cosmopolitan Anxieties: Turkish Challenges to Citizenship and Belonging in Germany*. Durham, NC, 2008.

Marcuse, Harold. *Legacies of Dachau: The Uses and Abuses of a Concentration Camp, 1933–2001*. Cambridge, UK, 2001.

Marcuse, Peter. "'Dual City': A Muddy Metaphor for a Quartered City." *International Journal of Urban and Regional Research* 13, no. 4 (1989): 697–708.

———. "Not Chaos, But Walls: Postmodernism and the Partitioned City." In *Postmodern Cities and Spaces*, ed. Sophie Watson and Katherine Gibson, 243–53. Cambridge, MA, 1994.

Martin, Philip L. *The Unfinished Story: Turkish Labour Migration to Western Europe. With Special Reference to the Federal Republic of Germany*. Geneva, 1991.

Martínez, Oscar J. *Border People: Life and Society in U.S.-Mexico Borderlands*. Tucson, AZ, 1994.

———. "The Dynamics of Border Integration: New Approaches to Border Analysis." In *Global Boundaries*, ed. C. H. Schofield, 1–15. London, 1994.

Marx, Karl, and Friedrich Engels. *The Communist Manifesto*. In *Karl Marx: Selected Writings*, ed. David McLellan. Oxford, 2000.

McCallum, Henry D., and Frances T. McCallum. *The Wire That Fenced the West*. Norman, OK, 1965.

McDowell, Sara. "Selling Conflict Heritage through Tourism in Peacetime Northern Ireland: Transforming Conflict or Exacerbating Difference?" *International Journal of Heritage Studies* 14, no. 5 (2008): 405–21.

Meinhof, Ulrika Hanna, and Anna Triandafyllidou, eds. *Transcultural Europe: Cultural Policy in a Changing Europe*. Basingstoke, UK, 2006.

Meyer, Winfried, and Klaus Neitmann, eds. *Zwangsarbeit während der NS-Zeit in Berlin und Brandenburg. Formen, Funktionen und Rezeption.* Potsdam, 2001.

Millar, Peter. *1989 The Berlin Wall: My Part in Its Downfall.* London, 2009.

Miller, Alexei. "In den Fesseln der Geschichte. Der polnische Diskurs über die Ostpolitik." *Transit* 25 (2003): 40–49.

———. "Tema zentral'noij Evropy: Istorija, sovremennyje diskursy i mesto v nich Rossij." *Novoe Literanurnoe Obozrenie* 52 (2001): 75–96.

Minh-Ha, Trin T. *Woman, Native, Other: Writing Postcoloniality and Feminism.* Bloomington, IN, 1989.

Mink, Georges, and Laure Neumayer, eds. *L'Europe et ses passés douloureux.* Paris, 2007.

Mintzker, Yair. *The Defortification of the German City, 1689–1866.* New York, forthcoming 2012.

Mirbagheri, Farid. *Cyprus and International Peacemaking, 1964–1986.* Part 2. New York, 1998.

Mironenko, Sergej, Lutz Niethammer, and Alexander von Plato. *Sowjetische Speziallager in Deutschland 1945 bis 1950.* 2 vols. Berlin, 1998.

Mitchell, Katharyne. "Geographies of Identity: Multiculturalism Unplugged." *Progress in Human Geography* 28, no. 5 (2004): 641–51.

Morello, Michela, and Rosj Camarda. "Il muro di Padova: un muro di solida paura." *Sociología Urbana e Rurale* 86 (2008): 91–109.

Morré, Jörg, ed. *Speziallager des NKWD. Sowjetische Internierungslager in Brandenburg 1945–1950.* Potsdam, 1997.

Morrissey, Robert, ed. ARTFL Project (University of Chicago). http://artfl-project. uchicago.edu/.

Morsch, Günter. "Oranienburg – Sachsenhausen, Sachsenhausen – Oranienburg." In *Die nationalsozialistischen Konzentrationslager,* ed. Ulrich Herbert, Karin Orth, and Christoph Dieckmann. Vol. 1, 111–34. Frankfurt am Main, 2002.

———, ed. *Konzentrationslager Oranienburg.* Berlin, 1994.

Mosse, George L. *Fallen Soldiers: Reshaping the Memory of the World Wars.* Oxford, 1990.

Motte, Jan, Rainer Ohliger, and Anne von Oswald, eds. *50 Jahre Bundesrepublik – 50 Jahre Einwanderung: Nachkriegsgeschichte als Migrationsgeschichte.* Frankfurt am Main, 1999.

Muir, Richard. *Political Geography: A New Introduction.* New York, 1997.

Mumford, Lewis. *The City in History: Its Origins, Its Transformations and Its Prospects.* London, 1961.

Musiani, Francesca. "Padua Wall: Immigration, Conflict, and Integration," *Peace and Conflict Monitor,* 25 October 2007. http://www.monitor.upeace.org/innerpg. cfm?id_article=448 (accessed 16 June 2010).

Nagel, Caroline. "Rethinking Geographies of Assimilation." *The Professional Geographer* 61, no. 3 (2009): 400–407.

Nagel, Thomas. *The View from Nowhere.* New York, 1989.

Naples, Nancy A. "Borderlands Studies and Border Theory: Linking Activism and Scholarship for Social Justice." *Sociology Compass* 4, no. 7 (July 2010): 505–18.

Nelson, Robert L., ed. *Germans, Poland, and Colonial Expansion to the East*. New York, 2009.

Nevins, Joseph. *Operation Gatekeeper: The Rise of the "Illegal Alien" and the Remaking of the U.S.-Mexico Boundary*. New York, 2002.

Newman, David. "Boundaries." In Agnew, Mitchell, and Tuathail, eds. *A Companion to Political Geography*, 123–37. Malden, MA, 2003.

———. "Boundaries, Territory and Postmodernity: Towards Shared or Separate Spaces?" In *Borderlands under Stress*, ed. Martin Pratt and Janet Allison Brown, 17–34. London, 2000.

———. "The Lines that Continue to Separate Us: Borders in Our 'Borderless' World." *Progress in Human Geography* 30, no. 2 (2006): 143–61.

Nic Craith, Mairead. *Plural Identities, Singular Narrative: The Case of Northern Ireland*. New York, 2002.

Noble, Eustache le. *La Pierre de touché politique*. London, 1691.

Nora, Pierre, ed. *Realms of Memory: Rethinking the French Past*. Vol. 1. *Conflicts and Divisions*. New York, 1996.

Northern Ireland Housing Executive (NIHE). "Northern Ireland House Condition Survey 2006. Main Report." http://www.nihe.gov.uk/housing_conditions_survey_2006.pdf (accessed 16 June 2010).

Nuhoğlu Soysal, Yasemin. *Limits of Citizenship: Migrants and Postnational Membership in Europe*. Chicago, 1995.

Ochs, Eva. *"Heute kann ich das ja sagen". Lagererfahrungen von Insassen sowjetischer Speziallager in der SBZ/DDR*. Cologne, 2006.

Ociepka, Beata. "Das Bild der Deutschen und Polen in den Medien." In Wolff-Powęska and Bingen, eds. *Nachbarn auf Distanz*, 216–42. Wiesbaden, 2005

Oesterreicher, Jiří, Irena Kotrbová, and Harald Winckler. *Společná minulost. Gmünd a České Velenice*. České Velenice, 2005.

Oesterreicher, Jiří, and Lenka Klečatská. *60 let školy 1946–2006 Střední škola České Velenice*. České Velenice, 2004.

Opitz, May, Katarina Oguntuye, and Dagmar Schultz, eds. *Farbe bekennen: Afro-Deutsche Frauen auf den Spuren ihrer Geschichte*. Frankfurt am Main, 1986.

Orphanides, Kika. "The Cypriot Community in Britain." In *Race and Social Work: A Guide to Training*, ed. Vivienne Combe and Alan Little, 81–88. London, 1986.

Osterhammel, Jürgen. "Kulturelle Grenzen in der Expansion Europas." *Saeculum. Jahrbuch für Universalgeschichte* 46, no. 1 (1995): 101–38.

Ó Tuathail, Gearóid (aka Gerard Toal). *Critical Geopolitics: The Politics of Writing Global Space*. New York, 1996.

Paasi, Anssi. "Europe as a Social Process of Discourse: Considerations of Place, Boundaries and Identity." *European Urban and Regional Studies* 8, no. 1 (2001): 7–28.

Pagenstecher, Cord, Bernhard Bremberger, and Gisela Wenzel. *Zwangsarbeit in Berlin. Archivrecherchen, Nachweissuche und Entschädigung*. Berlin, 2008.

Papadakis, Yiannis. "The Politics of Memory and Forgetting in Cyprus." *Journal of Mediterranean Studies* 3 (1993): 139–54.

Papadakis, Yiannis, Nicos Peristianis, and Gisela Welz. *Divided Cyprus: Modernity, History, and an Island in Conflict.* Bloomington, IN, 2006.

Parker, Geoffrey. *The Military Revolution: Military Innovation and the Rise of the West, 1500–1800.* New York, 1988.

Parker, Noel, ed. *The Geopolitics of Europe's Identity: Centers, Boundaries and Margins.* Basingstoke, UK, 2008.

Pautz, Herwig. "The Politics of Identity in Germany: The *Leitkultur* Debate." *Race and Class* 46, no. 4 (2005): 39–52.

Pavlakovich-Kochi, Vera, Barbara J. Morehouse, and Doris Wastl-Walter, eds. *Challenged Borderlands: Transcending Political and Cultural Boundaries.* Aldershot, UK, 2004.

Pedlow, Gregory W. "Allied Crisis Management for Berlin: The LIVE OAK Organization, 1959–1963." In *International Cold War Military Records and History: Proceedings of the International Conference on Cold War Military Records and History Held in Washington, D.C. 21–26 March 1994,* ed. William W. Epley, 88–116. Washington, DC, 1996.

Pegg, Nicholas. *The Complete David Bowie.* 4th ed. London, 2006.

Pflüger, Johann Georg Friedrich. *Geschichte der Stadt Pforzheim.* Pforzheim, 1862.

Phillips, Anne. *Multiculturalism without Culture.* Princeton, 2006.

Picot, George-Marie-René. *Histoire des États généraux considérés au point de vue de leur influence sur le gouvernment de la France de 1355 à 1614.* 4 vols. Paris, 1872.

Pieper, Tobias. *Die Gegenwart der Lager. Zur Mikrophysik der Herrschaft in der deutschen Flüchtlingspolitik.* Münster, 2008.

Planet, Ana. *Melilla y Ceuta: Espacios Frontera Hispano-Marroquíes.* Melilla, 1998.

Plewe, Reinhard, and Jan Thomas Köhler. *Baugeschichte Frauen-Konzentrationslager Ravensbrück.* Berlin, 2001.

Polish Ministry of Foreign Affairs. *EU Eastern Policy in the Context of EU Eastern Enlargement and Central Europe Enlargement: The Polish Perspective.* Warsaw, 2001.

———. "Non-Paper with Polish Proposals Concerning Policy toward the New Eastern Neighbours after EU Enlargement." www.mfa.gov.pl/?document=2041 (accessed July 14 2010).

Pragal, Peter, and Eckart Stratenschulte. *Der Monolog der Lautsprecher und andere Geschichten aus dem geteilten Berlin.* Berlin, 1999.

Prieß, Lutz. "Sachsenhausen – Speziallager Nr. 7 (August 1945 – März 1950)." In Morré, ed., *Speziallager des NKWD,* 63–78. Potsdam, 1997.

Prinz, Joachim. "Jüdische Situation – Heute (1935)." In *Die Verfolgung und Ermordung der europäischen Juden durch das nationalsozialistische Deutschland 1933–1945,* ed. Wolf Gruner. Vol. 1. *Deutsches Reich 1933–1937,* 426–32. Munich, 2008.

Prodi, Romano. "A Wider Europe: A Proximity Policy as the Key to Stability." Sixth ECSA World Conference, Jean Monnet Project, Brussels, 5–6 December 2002. http://europa.eu/rapid/pressReleasesAction.do?reference=SPEECH/02/

619&format=HTML&aged=0&language=EN&guiLanguage=en (accessed 29 June 2010).

pro Köln. "Die Schweiz weist den Weg für ganz Europa." Pressemitteilung 30 November 2009. http://www.pro-koeln.net/archiv2009.htm (accessed 21 February 2010).

Puskeppeleit, Jürgen. "Entwicklungslinien und -perspektiven der Sozialdienste." *Informationsdienst zur Ausländerarbeit* 1 (1989): 14–19.

Puskeppeleit, Jürgen, and Dietrich Thränhardt. *Vom betreuten Ausländer zum gleichberechtigten Bürger*. Freiburg im Breisgau, 1990.

Ranciere, Jacques. *The Politics of Aesthetics*. New York, 2004.

Raufer, Xavier. "A Neglected Dimension of Conflict: The Albanian Mafia." In *Potentials of Disorder: Explaining Conflict and Stability in the Caucasus and in the Former Yugoslavia*, ed. Jan Koehler and Christoph Zürcher, 62–74. Manchester, 2003.

Raumer, Kurt. *Die Zerstörung der Pfalz*. Munich, 1930.

Razac, Olivier. *Politische Geschichte des Stacheldrahts. Prärie, Schützengraben, Lager*. Zurich, 2003.

Razack, Sherene. *Casting Out: The Eviction of Muslims from Western Law and Politics*. Toronto, 2008.

———. "Imperilled Muslim Women, Dangerous Muslim Men and Civilised Europeans: Legal and Social Responses to Forced Marriages." *Feminist Legal Studies* 12, no. 2 (2004): 129–74.

Reddy, Rupa. "Gender, Culture and the Law: Approaches to 'Honour' Crimes in the UK." *Feminist Legal Studies* 16, no. 3 (2008): 305–21.

Reeves, Richard. *Daring Young Men: The Heroism and Triumph of the Berlin Airlift, June 1948–May 1949*. New York, 2010.

Reif-Spirek, Peter, and Bodo Ritscher, eds. *Speziallager in der SBZ. Gedenkstätten mit "doppelter Vergangenheit"*. Berlin, 1999.

Reitz, Jeffrey G. "Host Societies and the Reception of Immigrants: Research Themes, Emerging Theories, and Methodological Issues." In Reitz, ed. *Host Societies and the Reception of Immigrants*, 1–18. La Jolla, CA, 2003.

———, ed. *Host Societies and the Reception of Immigrants*. La Jolla, CA, 2003.

Riaño, Yvonne, and Doris Wastl-Walter. "Immigration Policies, State Discourses on Foreigners, and the Politics of Identity in Switzerland." *Environment and Planning A* 38, no. 9 (2006): 1693–713.

Ribbe, Wolfgang. *Berlin 1945–2000. Grundzüge der Stadtgeschichte*. Berlin, 2002.

Richelieu, Armand Jean du Plessis, Duc de. *Letres d'vn solitaire av Roy, princes, et seigneurs faisans la guerre aux Rebelles*. Poitiers, 1628.

Ricoeur, Paul. *Memory, History, Forgetting*. Trans. Kathleen Blamey and David Pellauer. Chicago, 2004.

Rochas d'Aiglun, Albert de. *Vauban, sa Famille et ses Écrits, ses Oisivetés et sa Correspondance: Analyse et Extraits*. Vol. 2. Geneva, 1972.

Rohne, Jürgen. "An der deutsch-polnischen Grenze geht die Angst um." *Der Spiegel*, 1 February 2002. www.spiegel.de/politik/deutschland/0,1518,180137,00.html (accessed 29 June 2010).

Rokkan, Stein, and Derek W. Urwin. *Economy, Territory, Identity: Politics of West European Peripheries*. London, 1983.

Rosati, Dariusz. "Statement." In Stefan Batory Foundation, "Polska Polityka Wschodnia. Pełny zapis dyskusji zorganizowanej prez Fundację im. Stefana Batorego oraz redakcję 'Tygodnika Powszechnego'" [Polish Eastern Policy. Complete transcript of the discussion organized by the Stefan Batory Foundation and the journal *Tygodnik Powszechny*], 1 March 2001. www.batory.org.pl/ftp/program/forum/ppw.pdfwww.batory.org.pl/ftp/program/forum/ppw.pdf (accessed 30 November 2009).

Rotfeld, Adam Daniel. "Government Report on Poland's Foreign Policy Presented by Foreign Minister of the Republic of Poland Adam Daniel Rotfeld at a Sejm Meeting on 21 January 2005." *Materiały i Dokumenty* 1 (2005). http://www.msz.gov.pl/index.php?page=6661&lang_id=en&bulletin_id=16&document=8448 (accessed 14 July 2010).

Rother, Joanna M. "Am Rande des Reichtums." *Die Zeit* 52 (19 December 2007). www.zeit.de/2007/52/Schengen-Abkommen (accessed 29 June 2010).

Rott, Wilfried. *Die Insel. Eine Geschichte West-Berlins 1948–1990*. Munich, 2009.

Rousseau, Jean-Jacques. *Discours sur les sciences et les arts; discours sur l'origine et le fondement de l'inégalité parmi les hommes* [1754], ed. Jacques Roger. Paris, 1971.

Rousset, Camille. *Histoire de Louvois et de son administration politique et militaire*. 3rd ed. Paris, 1863.

Sahlins, Peter. *Boundaries: The Making of France and Spain in the Pyrenees*. Berkeley, 1989.

Sälter, Gerhard. *Grenzpolizisten. Konformität, Verweigerung und Repression in der Grenzpolizei und den Grenztruppen der DDR 1952 bis 1965*. Berlin, 2009.

Sammartino, Annemarie H. *The Impossible Border: Germany and the East, 1914–1922*. Ithaca, 2010.

Sarotte, M. E. *Dealing with the Devil: East Germany, Détente, and Ostpolitik, 1969–1973*. Chapel Hill, NC, 2001.

Schama, Simon. *Citizens: A Chronicle of the French Revolution*. New York, 1990.

Schechner, Richard. *Environmental Theater* [1969]. New York, 2000.

Scheunemann, Jürgen, and Gabriela Seidel. *Was war los in West-Berlin 1950–2000*. Erfurt, 2002.

Seglow, Jonathan. "The Ethics of Immigration." *Political Studies Review*, 3, no. 3 (2005), 317–34.

Sen, Sankar, Lauren G. Block, and Sucharita Chandran. "Window Displays and Consumer Shopping Decisions." *Journal of Retailing and Consumer Services* 9 (2002): 277–90.

Shields, Rob. *Lefebvre, Love and Struggle: Spatial Dialectics*. New York, 1998.

Schiffauer, Werner. "Enemies within the Gates: The Debate about the Citizenship of Muslims in Germany." In *Multiculturalism, Muslims, and Citizenship: A European Approach*, ed. Tariq Modood, A. Triandafyllidou, and R. Zapata-Barrero, 94–116. London, 2006.

Schiffer, Sabine. "Der Islam in deutschen Medien." *Aus Politik und Zeitgeschichte* 20 (2005): 23–30.

Schiller, Nina Glick, Linda Basch, and C. Blanc-Szanton. "Towards a Definition of Transnationalism." In *Toward a Transnational Perspective on Migration*, ed. Nina Glick Schiller, Linda Basch, and C. Blanc-Szanton, 1–24. New York, 1992.

Schilling, Kerstin. *Insel der Glücklichen. Generation West-Berlin*. 2nd ed. Berlin, 2005.

Schlögel, Karl, ed. *Oder – Odra. Blicke auf einen europäischen Strom*. Frankfurt am Main, 2007.

Schmid, Johann. "Operationalisierung von Security Sector Reform (SSR) auf dem Westlichen Balkan." Institut für Europäische Politik. Berlin, 2007.

Schmitt, Carl. "The Concept of the Political" [1927]. In *The Weimar Republic Sourcebook*, ed. Anton Kaes, Martin Jay, and Ed Dimendberg, 342–45. Berkeley, 1995.

Schmitz, Helmut, ed. *Von der nationalen zur internationalen Literatur: Transkulturelle deutschsprachige Literatur und Kultur im Zeitalter globaler Migration*. Amsterdam, 2009.

Schneider, Peter. *Der Mauerspringer. Erzählung* [1982]. 5th ed. Hamburg, 2006.

———. "The New Berlin Wall." *New York Times Magazine* (5 December 2005): 66–71.

Scholze-Irrlitz, Leonore, and Karoline Noack, eds. *Arbeit für den Feind. Zwangsarbeiter-Alltag in Berlin und Brandenburg 1939–1945*. Berlin, 1998.

Schröder, Wolfgang M. "Mission Impossible? Begriff, Modelle und Begründungen der 'civilizing mission' aus philosophischer Sicht." In Barth and Osterhammel, *Zivilisierungsmissionen*, 13–32. Constance, 2005.

Schwarz, Gudrun. *Die nationalsozialistischen Lager*. Frankfurt am Main, 1990.

Scott, James. *Domination and the Arts of Resistance: Hidden Transcripts*. New Haven, 1992.

Scott, Joan Wallach. *The Politics of the Veil*. Princeton and Oxford, 2007.

Seabrook, Thomas Jerome. *Bowie in Berlin: A New Career in a New Town*. London, 2008.

Segato, Marco. *Via Anelli, la Chiusura del Ghetto*. DVD documentary, 2008.

Semati, Mehdi. "Islamophobia, Culture and Race in the Age of Empire." *Cultural Studies* 24, no. 2 (2010): 256–75.

Sennett, Richard. *The Conscience of the Eye: The Design and Social Life of Cities*. New York, 1990.

Shapiro, Michael J. "National Times and Other Times: Re-Thinking Citizenship." *Cultural Studies* 14, no. 1 (2000): 79–98.

Sheffer, Edith. *Burned Bridge: How East and West Germans Made the Iron Curtain*. Foreword by Peter Schneider. New York, 2011.

Shields, Rob. *Lefebvre, Love and Struggle: Spatial Dialectics* (New York, 1999).

"Shqiptarët e Stambollit." *Ekskluzive* 18 (2001): 61–64.

Sibley, David. *Geographies of Exclusion: Society and Difference in the West.* New York, 1995.

Sikorski, Radosław. "Address by Foreign Minister of the Republic of Poland Radosław Sikorski at the Sejm, 7 May 2008." *Materiały i Dokumenty* 5 (2008). http://www.msz.gov.pl/index.php?page=12964&lang_id=en&bulletin_id=16&document=8448 (accessed January 2010).

Silberman, Marc, ed. *The German Wall: Fallout in Europe.* New York, 2011.

Simmel, Georg. "Bridge and Door" [1909]. In *Simmel on Culture,* ed. David Frisby and Mike Featherstone, 170–73. London, 1997.

Sloterdijk, Peter. "Atmospheric Politics." In *Making Things Public: Atmospheres of Democracy,* ed. Bruno Latour and Peter Weibel, 944–51. Cambridge, MA, 2005.

———. *Im Weltinnenraum des Kapitals.* Frankfurt am Main, 2005.

Snyder, Timothy. "Polnische Ostpolitik. Tradition mit Zukunft." *Transit* 25 (2003): 25–39.

———. *The Reconstruction of Nations: Poland, Lithuania, Ukraine, Belarus 1569–1999.* New Haven, 2003.

Soja, Edward W. *Postmodern Geographies: The Reassertion of Space in Critical Social Theory.* London, 1989.

———. *Thirdspace: Journeys to Los Angeles and Other Real-and-Imagined Places.* New York, 1996.

Sorkin, Michael, ed. *Against the Wall: Israel's Barrier to Peace.* New York, 2005.

———, ed. *The Next Jerusalem: Sharing the Divided City.* New York, 2002.

Sparke, Matthew. "A Neoliberal Nexus: Economy, Security, and the Biopolitics of Citizenship of the Border." *Political Geography* 25, no. 2 (2006): 151–80.

Staeheli, Lynn A., and Caroline R. Nagel. "Rethinking Security: Perspectives from Arab-American and British Arab Activists." *Antipode* 40, no. 5 (2008): 780–801.

Steege, Paul. *Black Market, Cold War: Everyday Life in Berlin, 1946–1949.* New York, 2007.

Stefan Batory Foundation. "Polska Polityka Wschodnia. Pełny zapis dyskusji zorganizowanej prez Fundację im. Stefana Batorego oraz redakcję 'Tygodnika Powszechnego'" [Polish Eastern Policy. Complete transcript of the discussion organized by the Stefan-Batory-Foundation and the journal *Tygodnik Powszechny*], 1 March 2001.

Stegner, Wallace. *The Sound of Mountain Water.* New York, 1997.

Steinman, Susan Leibovitz. "Border Sutures 1990." In *Mapping the Terrain: New Genre Public Art,* ed. Suzanne Lacy, 206–7. Seattle, 1995.

Stobiecki, Rafał. "Comparing Polish Historiography on the Petersburg Empire: Second Republic – People's Republic – Exile." In Hadler and Mesenhöller, *Vergangene Größe,* 281–300. Leipzig, 2007.

Stolberg, Eva-Maria. *Sibirien: Russlands "Wilder Osten". Mythos und soziale Realität im 19. und 20. Jahrhundert.* Stuttgart, 2009.

Strada, Famianus. *Histoire de la guerre de Flandre.* Brussels, 1712.

Sturken, Marita. *Tangled Memories: The Vietnam War, the AIDS Epidemic, and the Politics of Remembering.* Berkeley, 1997.

Takeda, Junko. *Between Crown and Commerce: Marseille and the Early Modern Mediterranean.* Baltimore, 2011.

Talas, Andrea. "Green Light: Border Opening in Cyprus." *World Press Review* 50, no. 7 (July 2003). www.worldpress.org/Europe/1124.cfm (accessed 19 June 2010).

Taras, Ray. *Europe Old and New: Transnationalism, Belonging, Xenophobia.* Lanham, MD, 2009.

Taubman, Alfred. *Threshold Resistance.* New York, 2007.

Taylor, Frederick. *The Berlin Wall: A World Divided, 1961–1989.* London, 2006.

———. *The Berlin Wall 13 August 1961–9 November 1989.* London, 2006.

Temple, Nora. "The Control and Exploitation of French Towns during the Ancien Regime." *History* 51 (1967): 16–34.

Thränhardt, Dietrich. "Ausländer im Dickicht der Verbände." Special issue, *Neue Praxis* 7 (1983): 62–78.

Tibi, Bassam, *Europa ohne Identität. Die Krise der multikulturellen Gesellschaft.* Munich, 1998.

Till, Karen E. *The New Berlin: Memory, Politics, Place.* Minneapolis, 2005.

Tocci, Nathalie. *EU Accession and Conflict Resolution: Catalysing Peace or Consolidating Partition in Cyprus.* London, 2004.

Todorova, Maria. *Imagining the Balkans.* New York, 1997.

Traba, Robert. "'Kresy' oder 'Atlantis des Nordens'? Neue polnische Diskussionen über die Mythologie des Ortes." *Inter Finitimos* 3 (2005): 52–60.

Trebitsch, Michel. "Preface: The Moment of Radical Critique." Trans. Gregory Elliott. In Henri Lefebvre, *Critique of Everyday Life*, vol. 2, *Foundations for a Sociology of the Everyday* [1961], trans. John Moore, xxiv–xxv. New York, 2002.

Trouillot, Michel-Rolf. *Silencing the Past: Power and the Production of History.* Boston, 1995.

Tuan, Yi-Fu. *Space and Place: The Perspective of Experience.* 2nd ed. Minneapolis, 2007.

Turner, Bryan S. "The Enclave Society: Towards a Sociology of Immobility." *European Journal of Social Theory* 10, no. 2 (2007): 287–304.

Ullrich, Maren. *Geteilte Ansichten: Erinnerungslandschaft Deutsch-Deutsche Grenze.* Berlin, 2006.

Van Hook, Mary P., Eglantina Gjermeni, and Edlira Haxhiymeri. "Sexual Trafficking of Women: Tragic Proportions and Attempted Solutions in Albania." *International Social Work*, 49, no. 1 (January 2006): 29–40.

Vaněk, Pavel. *Pohraniční stráž a pokusy o přechod státní hranice.* Prague, 2009.

"Verordnung über die lagermäßige Unterbringung von Arbeitskräften während der Dauer des Krieges (Lagerverordnung, 14. Juli 1943)." *Reichsgesetzblatt, Teil I* (1943): 388–90.

Vetter, Roland. "*Kein Stein soll auf dem andern bleiben.*" *Mannheims Untergang während des Pfälzischen Erbfolgekrieges im Spiegel französischer Kriegsberichte.* Heidelberg, 2002.

Volksinitiative gegen den Bau von Minaretten. "Darum geht es" (2009). http://www.minarette.ch/darum_geht_es.html (accessed 7 March 2010).

———. "Argumente" (2009). http://www.minarette.ch/argumente.html (accessed 21 February 2010).

Vorhoff, Karin. *Zwischen Glaube, Nation und neuer Gemeinschaft: Alevitische Identität in der Türkei der Gegenwart.* Berlin, 1995.

Wagner, Volker. *Regierungsbauten in Berlin: Geschichte, Politik, Architektur.* Berlin, 2001.

Waldinger, Roger. "The Sociology of Immigration: Second Thoughts and Reconsiderations." In Reitz, ed. *Host Societies and the Reception of Immigrants,* 21–43. La Jolla, CA, 2003.

Ward, Janet. *Post-Wall Berlin: Borders, Space and Identity.* Basingstoke, UK, 2011.

———. *Weimar Surfaces: Urban Visual Culture in 1920s Germany.* Berkeley, 2001.

Warmoes, Isabelle, and Victoria Sanger, eds. *Vauban, Bâtisseur du Roi-Soleil.* Paris, 2007.

Weber, Max. *The City* [1921]. New York, 1958.

Wefing, Heinrich. *Kulisse der Macht.* Stuttgart, 2001.

Wege, Astrid. "'Who Decides What Is 'Hauptstadtkultur,' and What Is Not?'" *October* 89 (1999): 127–38.

Weigelt, Andreas. "Jamlitz – Speziallager Nr. 6 (September 1945–April 1947)." In Morré, ed., *Speziallager des NKWD,* 33–42. Potsdam, 1997.

Weizman, Eyal. *Hollow Land: Israel's Architecture of Occupation.* London and New York, 2007.

———. "Strategic Points, Flexible Lines, Tense Surfaces, and Political Volumes: Ariel Sharon and the Geometry of Occupation." In *Cities, War, and Terrorism: Towards an Urban Geopolitics,* ed. Stephen Graham, 172–91. Malden, MA, 2004.

Wettig, Gerhard. *Die Bindungen West-Berlins seit dem Vier-Mächte-Abkommen.* Cologne, 1978.

Wetzlaugk, Udo. *Die Alliierten in Berlin.* Berlin, 1988.

Willems, Susanne. *Der entsiedelte Jude. Albert Speers Wohnungsmarktpolitik für den Berliner Hauptstadtbau.* Berlin, 2002.

Williams, Brackette F. "A Class Act: Anthropology and the Race to Nation across Ethnic Terrain." *Annual Review of Anthropology* 18 (1989): 401–44.

Wise, Michael Z. *Capital Dilemma: Germany's Search for a New Architecture of Democracy.* New York, 1998.

Wolfe, Michael. *Walled Towns and the Shaping of France: From the Medieval to the Early Modern Period.* New York, 2009.

Wolff, Larry. *Inventing Eastern Europe: The Map of Civilization on the Mind of the Enlightenment.* Stanford, 2000.

Wolff-Powęska, Anna. "Ideelle und politische Voraussetzungen der Entwicklung der deutsch-polnischen Beziehungen." In Wolff-Powęska and Bingen, eds. *Nachbarn auf Distanz*, 3–20. Wiesbaden, 2005.

Wolff-Powęska, Anna, and Dieter Bingen, eds. *Nachbarn auf Distanz. Polen und Deutsche 1998–2004.* Wiesbaden, 2005.

Wolfrum, Edgar. *Die Mauer. Geschichte einer Teilung.* Munich, 2009.

Wood, Steve. "Apprehensive Partners: Germany, Poland and EU Enlargement." *German Politics* 11, no. 1 (April 2002): 97–124.

"Wspólne Oświadczenie w sprawie inicjatywy wsółpracy polsko-amerykańsko-ukraińkskiej [Joint statement of the United States-Poland-Ukraine-Cooperation Initiative], Kiev, 29 October 1998. *Zbiór Dokumentów* 3–4 (1998): 7ff.

Yildirim, Mehmet. "Die Kölner Ditib-Moschee – Eine offene Moschee als Integrationsbeitrag." In *Der Moschee-Streit. Eine Exemplarische Debatte über Einwanderung und Integration*, ed. Franz Sommerfeld, 66–76. Cologne, 2008.

Zaiotti, Ruben. *Cultures of Border Control: Schengen and the Evolution of European Frontiers.* Chicago, 2011.

Zámečník, Stanislav. "Dachau-Stammlager." In Benz and Distel, eds., *Der Ort des Terrors.* 2: 246. Munich, 2005–09.

Zernack, Klaus. "Deutschlands Ostgrenze." In *Deutschlands Grenzen in der Geschichte*, ed. Alexander Demandt, 140–65. Munich, 1990.

Zweite, Armin. "Kunst am Bau." In *Kunst am Bau: Die Projekte des Bundes in Berlin*, ed. Bundesministerium für Verkehr, Bau- und Wohnungswesen, 8–9. Berlin, 2002.

Zysberg, André. *Marseille au Temps du Roi-Soleil: La Ville, les Galères, l'Arsenal, 1660 à 1715.* Marseilles, 2007.

❧ INDEX ❧

www.ingramcontent.com/pod-product-compliance
Lightning Source LLC
Chambersburg PA
CBHW060030030426
42334CB00019B/2264